A Genealogist's Guide to

DISCOVERING YOUR
Immigrant
& Ethnic
ANCESTORS

How to find and record your unique heritage

Sharon DeBartolo Carmack, CG

Author of *Organizing Your Family History Search*

BETTERWAY BOOKS
CINCINNATI, OHIO

www.familytreemagazine.com

About the Author

Sharon DeBartolo Carmack is a Certified Genealogist, the editor of Betterway Genealogy Books, and a contributing editor and feature writer for *Family Tree Magazine*. Sharon teaches an online course in personal and family memoir writing for Writer's Digest School, and she serves on the Statue of Liberty-Ellis Island Foundation's History Advisory Committee for the American Family Immigration History Center.

Other Books by Sharon DeBartolo Carmack

- *Organizing Your Family History Search*
- *A Genealogist's Guide to Discovering Your Female Ancestors*
- *The Genealogy Sourcebook*
- *Italian-American Family History: A Guide to Researching and Writing About Your Heritage*
- *Communities at Rest: An Inventory and Field Study of Five Eastern Colorado Cemeteries*
- *The Ebetino and Vallarelli Family History: Italian Immigrants to Westchester County, New York*

A Genealogist's Guide to Discovering Your Immigrant and Ethnic Ancestors. Copyright © 2000 by Sharon DeBartolo Carmack. Manufactured in the United States of America. All rights reserved. No part of this book may be reproduced in any form or by any electronic or mechanical means including information storage and retrieval systems without permission in writing from the publisher, except by a reviewer, who may quote brief passages in a review. Published by Betterway Books, an imprint of F&W Publications, Inc., 1507 Dana Avenue, Cincinnati, Ohio 45207. (800) 289-0963. First edition.

Other fine Betterway Books are available from your local bookstore or on our Web site at www.familytreemagazine.com.

04 03 02 01 00   5 4 3 2 1

Library of Congress Cataloging-in-Publication Data

Carmack, Sharon DeBartolo
    A genealogist's guide to discovering your immigrant and ethnic ancestors / Sharon DeBartolo Carmack.—1st ed.
        p.   cm.
    Includes bibliographical references and index.
    ISBN 1-55870-524-4
        1. United States—Genealogy—Handbooks, manuals, etc. 2. United States—Emigration and immigration. 3. Ethnology—United States. I. Title.
    CS49.C384   2000
    929'.1'072073—dc21

00-033673
CIP

Editor: John Philip Colletta, Ph.D.
Production editor: Christine Doyle
Production coordinator: John Peavler
Interior designer: Sandy Conopeotis Kent
Cover designer: Wendy Dunning
Icon designer: Cindy Beckmeyer

Permissions

Cover photos: Central European family at Ellis Island and immigration ferries at Ellis Island courtesy of National Park Service, U.S. Department of the Interior. Lone Wolf (Guipago), a Kiowa chief, photo no. 75-BAE-1382A-3, and the men of the 369th (15th New York), photo no. 165-WW-127-8, courtesy of the National Archives and Records Administration.

Acknowledgments and Dedication

I am blessed to have friends and colleagues who rarely whine when I ask them to read and comment on yet another manuscript. Mille grazie: To my "best bud" Roger D. Joslyn, who reads and comments on everything I write but doesn't get angry when I ignore many of his comments. To Katherine Scott Sturdevant, who also reads and offers suggestions on everything I write. She is a wonderful friend and mentor, who enjoys four-hour dinners at Carrabba's as much as I do. Kathy also generously composed the Selected Historical Glossary and helped compile the Chronology of American Immigration Policy. To John Philip Colletta for being my content editor and my costar. His comments and overall advice on this book were equally invaluable. To Marcia D. Melnyk for her comments on Part I. To Sherry Walker for her sense of humor and being a reader for Part I. To Marian L. Smith, Senior Historian, U.S. Immigration and Naturalization Service, for her unending patience and comments on chapter six.

Several colleagues came to my rescue at the final hour to read, revise, and in some cases, compose additional material for the sections in Part II relevant to their areas of expertise: Tony Burroughs (African Americans), James W. Warren, Paula Stuart Warren, and Marsha Hoffman Rising (American Indians), Jeanie Chooey Low (Chinese), Duncan Gardiner (Czechs, Slovaks, and Hungarians), Harry Macy (Dutch), Paul Milner (English, Scots, Welsh, and Cornish), John Philip Colletta (French and Italians), Richard Dougherty (Germanic Peoples), Rodger Rosenberg (Japanese), Dwight Radford (Irish and Scotch-Irish), Kyle Betit (Irish), Gary Mokotoff (Jews), Paul Valasek (Poles and Russians), and Ruth Maness (Scandinavians). If errors exist, it is not because my readers did not try to correct me; what remains is my responsibility.

To Bob Fineberg, Clarence Kissler, Lynn Betlock, Warren Cruise, Marcia Wyett, Roger D. Joslyn, John Philip Colletta, Elaine Trigiani, Katherine Scott Sturdevant, and Michael Leclerc for contributing stories of their immigrant/ethnic-ancestor searches. Unfortunately, a few stories had to end up on the cutting room floor, but I appreciate their contributions nonetheless.

Other friends and colleagues to whom I owe a debt of gratitude, which transcends this book: To Marsha Hoffman Rising for her treasured friendship, humor, and guidance. What grade does this book get? To Sandra Hargreaves Luebking and Ann Dallas Budd, who got me started on the right foot. To my husband, Steve, who discovered quite some time ago that I'm high maintenance but stays with me anyway. To my daughter, Laurie, whom I adore and who has not yet discovered that I'm not perfect. To Figaro, the cutest cat in the world, who listened with awed fascination as I read out loud the entire manuscript to him. To Marcia Wyett because we both love Janet Evanovich novels and whom I will trust with my diaries after I'm dead. To Suzanne McVetty for holding my hand in the New York City subways and giving me her penne in vodka sauce recipe. To Anita Lustenberger for always letting me stay in the Gwyn Suite. To Jack Heffron for his patience with my endless E-mails during my cub editorship and for being the "bad" editor whenever necessary. To Kathy Hinckley for her friendship and many hours of late-night gossip while at conferences. To Jim and Paula Warren, the two nicest people I know. To Nancy Reeves and Andrea

(Reeves) Richardson for helping me research my ancestors in Terlizzi, and especially to Nancy for learning Italian well enough so we could get by, even though we ended up on a school bus one morning. To Gordon Remington for great Italian dinners when I visit Salt Lake City. To Jonathan Galli for his contagious enthusiasm. To Shane Sheridan for undertaking the boring task of cataloging my library and who never once complained when I bought more books. To Susan Rust, a great writer and friend. To Ida Burnett and Loretta Hass for cleaning my house. To my mother, Mary Bart, for giving me life. To my father, Sal Bart, who makes me laugh. To my stepmother, Linda Bart, who tries to understand when the Christmas gifts don't get in the mail until July. To Pam Banikowski, who taught me that I can begin a sentence with "and" without my fate being to rot for eternity in English teacher hell. To the administrators at Big Sandy School, who inspired me to quit my day job and pursue a full-time career as a writer and editor. To Elizabeth Shown Mills, who keeps me on my toes. To Olivia Goldsmith for giving me the idea to write acknowledgments this way. To Robert C. Anderson for including me on some of his jaunts to used bookstores. To Ruth Sisson or Annie Brohaugh or whatever her name is for sending me checks when she worked at F&W. To Michael Leclerc, who is just fun to hang out with. To Dave Fryxell for helping me to write fast and not feel guilty about it and for making me "Miss January 2000." To Dr. Gregory Liebshcer, my plastic surgeon. You're the best! To D. Bruce McMahan for encouraging me to get to know my copyright attorney better. To Karen Kreider Gaunt, my copyright attorney, for working the holiday season of 1999. To Stacie Berger, the best publicist I could ask for. To Christine Doyle for her tireless patience and good humor with all the genealogy books we've worked on together. To Tony Burroughs for harassing Jim Warren. To Henry Hoff because he likes to gossip, too. To Brenton Simons, my "East Coast agent." To my oldest and dearest friend, Betty Wiley, for keeping all my secrets (remember, I keep yours, too, Betty). To Marsha, Roger, and Bob for wonderful but overpriced dinners at La Caille and many summer rendezvous memories.

And, finally, this book is dedicated to William Brohaugh, former editorial director at F&W Publications and currently its new media director, known affectionately to some of us genealogists as "Betterway Bill." The acquiring of this book for Betterway's genealogy line was not an easily traveled road, and Bill is the one who made it happen. Within two short years, Bill has gone from being my editor to being a treasured friend. I will forever be in his debt for his continual support and encouragement, and for opening so many doors for me.

—Sharon DeBartolo Carmack

January 2000

Icons Used in This Book

 Brick Wall Buster
How to turn dead ends into opportunities

 Case Study
Examples of this book's advice at work

 Citing Sources
Reminders and methods for documenting information

 CD Source
Databases and other information available on CD-ROM

 \di'fin\ *vb* **Definitions**
Terminology and jargon explained

 For More Info
Where to turn for more in-depth coverage

 Hidden Treasures
Family papers and home sources

 Important
Information and tips you can't overlook

 Internet Source
Where on the Web to find what you need

 Library/Archive Source
Repositories that might have the information you need

 Microfilm Source
Information available on microfilm

 Money Saver
Getting the most out of research dollars

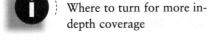 **Oral History**
Techniques for getting family stories

 Printed Source
Directories, books, pamphlets, and other paper archives

 Quotes
Useful words direct from the experts

 Reminder
"Don't-Forget" items to keep in mind

 Research Tip
Ways to make research more efficient

See Also
Where in this book to find related information

Sources
Where to go for information, supplies, etc.

  Step By Step
Walkthroughs of important procedures

Supplies
Advice on day-to-day office tools

Technique
How to conduct research, solve problems, and get answers

Timesaver
Shaving minutes and hours off the clock

Tip
Ways to make research more efficient

Warning
Stop before you make a mistake

Table of Contents
At a Glance

Note to the Reader

Table of Contents

Note to the Reader

- *Whether the ancestor arrived in 1600 or 1900 or was here to greet the newcomers, the start of research is the same. This chapter discusses the importance of oral history interviews and seeking home sources that offer clues to ethnic ancestry and immigrants' arrivals. It will also outline research strategies in tracing ethnic and immigrant ancestors, such as exhausting all American records—"doing your homework," before embarking on foreign research.*

- *Everyone has immigrant ancestors, and each ethnic group has its own migration patterns and traits, arriving at different times in American history. This chapter will introduce genealogists to researching their ethnic heritage, as well as give a general overview of immigration history to America.*

- *After home sources and oral histories have been acquired, it's time to start researching. Genealogists usually begin their search with published finding aids and indexes. Covered are compiled family histories, local and county histories, surname dictionaries, and more.*

- *The next step is to search computer databases, such as those found at the Family History Library in Salt Lake City and its worldwide centers: Ancestral File, International Genealogical Index, Social Security Death Index, and the upcoming Ellis Island Passenger Arrival Lists Database, as well as databases available on the Internet.*

- *After exhausting compiled sources and indexes, it's time to look at original records: cemetery and mortuary records, censuses, church records, city directories, court and probate records, land records, military service records, newspapers, Social Security records, vital records, and voter registrations, to name a few.*

**PART THREE
Leaving a Legacy . . . 233**

Writing Your Ethnic/Immigrant Family History, *234*
- *Gathering materials on your immigrant and ethnic ancestors is fun, but it is only half of the project. Now it's time to take everything you've learned about your ancestors and compile it into a narrative family history.*

Selected Historical Glossary, *240*

Note to the Reader

This guide is intended for those who are just embarking on the journey to discover their immigrant or ethnic ancestors. Like most Americans, you probably have a diverse cultural background, being part this and part that—a "Heinz 57" mixture, if you will. If this is the case, then this guide will be the springboard for your research into the different heritages that you will explore and come to appreciate more fully. Even if you are one of the declining percentage of the population that can claim a background of 100 percent Irish, or Polish, or American Indian, this guide will help you, too.

No single book can be a comprehensive guide to all genealogical research sources and methods dealing with every immigrant or ethnic group in America's history or its corresponding country of origin, and this is certainly not the goal here. My intention is to aid you in identifying and tracing immigrant ancestors back to their time of arrival in America and to suggest American sources that will help you determine origins in the homeland, so you can continue research in another country. While this book deals primarily with groups that have arrived in America in significant numbers from colonial times to World War II, the methods and sources covered in these pages are applicable to other immigrant groups as well. For those with American Indian or African-American ancestry, my goal is to help you get started and to offer you sources that will help you trace these ethnic groups as far back as you possibly can.

This book is divided into three parts and focuses on American sources. Part I, Getting Your Genealogical Research Started, shows you how to begin your immigrant/ethnic search, what kinds of records are available for you to explore, and how certain records relate to tracing immigrant and ethnic origins. The final chapter in this section offers general tips for beginning foreign research.

Part II, Major Ethnic Groups in America: Historical Overviews, is meant to give you an introduction to some of the ethnic groups who settled in America, helping you to see your ancestors as part of a group, as well as when these groups tended to arrive in America and where they tended to settle. Each section includes resources (books, Internet sites, periodicals, organizations) for the group to help you advance your search.

Part III, Leaving a Legacy, offers suggestions for writing about your immigrant/ethnic ancestors. Your search to discover your origins is only half of your journey; writing your family's history creates the legacy you leave for future generations. May you have a pleasant journey.

Important

PART ONE

Getting Your Genealogical Research Started

Enjoying the Journey

Once I thought to write a history of immigrants in America.
Then I discovered that the immigrants were American history.

—Oscar Handlin, *The Uprooted*

Our immigrant and ethnic ancestors made American history. Their names may not appear in the history books, but they were there: the American Indians who solely inhabited the North American continent until the Spanish and English arrived; the African Americans who were brought unwillingly to this country to plant and harvest the fields; the Germans and Irish and Italians and Poles and Chinese who helped build the cities, lay the railroad track, and cultivate the farmlands. Do you know which of these nameless people in American history are your ancestors?

Everyone has *immigrant* ancestors. Whether your ancestors arrived in the 1900s, the 1600s, or were here to greet the rest, all American ancestry leads somewhere else. Some archaeologists have said that the North American continent has been inhabited only recently compared with other continents—when Asian migrants crossed the ancient "land bridge" of the Bering Strait. While descendants of these early "immigrants" have no written contemporary records to aid in tracing their ancestry, their forebears did leave physical evidence in the form of artifacts. For those whose ancestors arrived in America since the 1600s, there is a multitude of sources for researching immigrant origins. And for those who have American Indian ancestry, you will find a surprising amount of information concerning numerous tribes since the "founding" of our nation.

Everyone has *ethnic* ancestors. Maybe you descend from several different ethnic forebears. An ethnic group is one that has a socially distinct cultural heritage. This is what makes Italians Italian, Poles Polish, Chinese Chinese, and Mexicans Mexican. To keep the ethnic identity alive, these cultural features are handed down from one generation to the next. But not everyone cares enough to research the distinct cultural differences that originated with their immigrant ancestors, causing many ethnic groups to no longer be culturally distinct. As sociologists point out, "Ethnic differences are culturally learned, not genetically inherited."

Tracing your ethnic, immigrant heritage is an exciting journey. Many people who begin researching their family history do so to discover who the immigrant ancestors were—the first in their family line to come to America. Many of us feel a need to know who we are and where we came from beyond America's shores. Researching your ethnic ancestors will not only fill that need, but also give you a sense of your ethnic heritage—an invaluable inheritance to pass on to your children and grandchildren.

Though I am one-half Italian, one-quarter Irish, and one-quarter English, I was raised with very little ethnic awareness. My family left the ethnically rich state of New York for southern California when I was four, where I was raised "a white American." Though California is also ethnically diverse, we lived in a white, middle-class, suburban neighborhood in Orange County not far from Disneyland. As a youngster, the only reason I knew I had Italian blood flowing in my veins was because my mother made spaghetti on a regular basis, we had homemade pizza every Sunday night, and we made annual trips "back east" to visit my father's Italian mother. One St. Patrick's Day during my elementary school years, I realized that my mother wasn't Italian, too, when she insisted I wear green to school that day. Not until I became a mother myself and took a serious interest in researching my ancestors did I discover that my mother was not only Irish, but half English, with ancestry dating to the founding of Jamestown.

My search wasn't just to find out the names of dead relatives and how far back in time I could trace my ancestry; it was a search for an ethnic identity. Being a "white American" just seemed so ordinary and unexciting to me. It was fun going to Grandma's house in New York and being Italian. It meant something to wear green on St. Patrick's Day and know that I was Irish.

Though an ethnic identity apparently meant little to my parents, who seemed content to meld into "white" suburban society, as an only child, I shudder to think what would have happened to our ethnic heritage if I had not taken an interest in genealogy. It is because of that interest that I discovered my ethnicity, learned what it means to "be" Italian and Irish, and have chosen to raise my only child, a daughter, with an appreciation for her ethnic heritage, which I hope she will pass on to her children one day.

Why are you interested in tracing your ethnic heritage? Since we are all descendants of immigrants, it is not surprising that many of us want to trace our lineage back to the first arrivals in our ancestry. While you may find that some immigrant lines are easily documented back to a country or even a town of origin, other lines prove to be more difficult in even determining the identity of the immigrant. Keep trying. **Genealogy isn't always easy, but it is always enjoyable.**

Regardless of your reasons for wanting to trace your immigrant or ethnic ancestors, I'm pleased that you are interested enough to pursue them. If it were not for you, your family might also be in danger of losing its ethnic identity. Everyone has an ethnic background, but not everyone cares enough to research it, and, I hope, write about it, so it will not be lost to future generations. You probably didn't realize what a big responsibility it was going to be to discover your ethnic and immigrant ancestors!

Reminder

ONE

Starting Your Ethnic and Immigrant Research

T wo of the most common mistakes researchers make when tracking immigrant origins are focusing research on just one ancestor or family and, once they have identified the immigrant, they anxiously jump the ocean before they have exhausted all the American sources. No one wants to trace the wrong lineage, but it is entirely possible for that to happen if each generation has not been researched thoroughly and documented in American sources—including the immigrant's relatives and acquaintances—before bridging the ocean.

Important

TWO POINTS TO KEEP IN MIND AS YOU BEGIN YOUR SEARCH

Point 1. Do Your Homework

I know you are eager to start researching in Scotland, or wherever, and take your ancestry back to the 1300s, but be patient! You'll get there soon enough. Besides, Scotland is an awfully big place if you don't know the name of the village from whence your ancestor came. That's like saying your ancestor was born in New York or in America. *Where* in New York or America? You need to know the right town in the Old Country. And suppose your ancestor's name, while unique in America, turns out to be the "John Smith" of Scotland. How will you distinguish him in the records once you have determined the village? Know more about the immigrant ancestor than just a name. This is why it is so important to get as much information and details on your ancestor in America first and to thoroughly research each generation back to the immigrant.

Part of doing your homework is also learning what records are available for search in your ancestor's homeland. Learn about the Old Country, its records, and how to access them. Just as you are learning about American sources and how to access them, you also need to do the same for foreign jurisdictions.

That's what the guidebooks listed at the end of each ethnic section in the second part of this book will help you do.

If you have read any other general guidebooks on genealogy, you know that the basic "rule" is to work from the known to the unknown. This rule must be followed when tracing immigrant ancestors if you hope to have any success in another country. Begin with what you know about your ancestors' lives in America (from oral history and home sources), learn the things you didn't know about their lives in America (from original record research), and then you're ready to start retracing your ancestors' footsteps in their homeland (after reading research guidebooks specifically for that ethnic group and foreign country).

Point 2. Broaden Your Search

Throughout history, individuals rarely migrated alone. Friends, relatives, fellow villagers, and/or acquaintances either traveled together or followed one another. Ignoring an immigrant's relatives and other associates will reduce your chances of successfully tracing your immigrant ancestor in America and in foreign sources. Your ancestor may not have left a significant paper trail to help identify the village of origin or further your research in another country, but perhaps a relative, friend, or neighbor did. If you read other researchers' success stories in genealogical magazines and journals, their success is often attributed to also researching the lives of the people who came into contact with their ancestor. It is these auxiliary people who may have created the records that will give you clues to further research on your ancestor. This concept will be discussed more in the next chapter.

RECORDING THE WHO, WHEN, AND WHERE

All genealogical research begins with the who, when, and where: the names of your ancestors; the dates of important events such as births, marriages, deaths, and immigration; and the places these events occurred. **In order to successfully research any immigrant, you need to learn (1) the immigrant's full original name, (2) the approximate date of birth, and (3) the place of birth.** This information may be obtained from research or from talking with relatives.

Research Tip

Just as it is sometimes impossible to determine an exact date of birth or death for some ancestors, it is also a grim reality that you may never find the exact date an ancestor arrived in America. The best you may be able to achieve is to narrow down an approximate time frame of arrival. This makes it all the more important to exhaust every possible record created by, for, or about your immigrant ancestors. By constructing a chronology of your ancestor's life in America based on your search, you will be able to pinpoint, as close as possible, an approximate arrival time.

As you learn the who, when, and where, write down this information. I recommend you use forms such as a pedigree or ancestor chart and a family group sheet. These forms may be downloaded from the Internet at various sites, including <http://www.familytreemagazine.com>. Or you may want to

For More Info

For more information on genealogical software programs, see Marthe Arends's *Genealogy Software Guide.*

Oral History

Warning

purchase a genealogy computer software program, which will create the forms for you. Regardless of where you get the forms, remember to also record the sources of information as you gather facts.

ORAL HISTORY

Even if your ancestor arrived in the 1600s, interviewing relatives for clues is valuable. You probably are not the first one in your family to wonder where your ancestors came from. Often there is a story that has been handed down through the generations about how the family came to America. Keep in mind that the further removed the interviewee is from the time the event occurred, the more likely you are to encounter errors and elaborations of the family lore. So if Aunt Matilda tells you about ancestors who arrived in 1753, she doesn't have personal knowledge about this event, and she's just repeating what some-one told her, someone who wasn't there either. Almost all family stories have some grain of truth, however. Family legends are not usually created out of thin air, and that tiny grain may be the clue that leads you to genealogical success. There are many "myths" that have worked their way into family sto-ries, and perhaps you've already heard some of these. If not, before you begin interviewing relatives, make yourself aware of some of the most common myths, since you may hear variations of one of them during the interview. (Milton Rubincam's *Pitfalls in Genealogical Research* goes into more detail on the vari-ous stumbling blocks researchers may encounter.)

The Cherokee Indian Princess Myth

It's always a *Cherokee* princess, almost never Navajo or Apache or Pueblo or Lumbee. This is an extremely common myth. If there is any story of American Indian ancestry, it always seems to be an Indian princess. The Cherokee, of course, are a large tribe with a diverse culture, divided by the Trail of Tears. They intermarried widely, perhaps increasing the likelihood of Cherokee/white ancestry. One reason this princess myth may have evolved is prejudice. For those who frowned upon a white male ancestor marrying an Indian woman, elevating the woman's status to princess made the truth easier to swallow.

Keep in mind that any story that says you have American Indian ancestry— often Cherokee—may in itself be a myth. My husband's family claims to have some American Indian ancestry. I've researched at least four or five generations on all his lines, and I have yet to find one drop of American Indian blood. Even though it's currently an "in" thing to have American Indian ancestry, just a few decades ago, it might have been the skeleton in your family's closet. As you will see in the next chapter, proving certain ethnic ancestry can be difficult because of prejudice or popularity toward a culture at any given time. Throughout history, some people who were victims of prejudice may have tried to hide their native origins by changing their names or claiming a different ethnicity.

The Three Brothers Myth

It's always *three* brothers who immigrated to America, never two or four or five or six. Sometimes one is lost at sea during the voyage over, or once they got to America, one went north, one went south, and one headed west, never to be heard from again. There are never any sisters involved in the big move across the ocean. Be wary of the brothers myth, and always keep an eye out for additional siblings, both in America and once you start foreign research. You also want to confirm through your research that there were, in fact, three brothers, that the three brothers were indeed brothers and not two brothers and an uncle, for example, or that the three brothers weren't just three men with the same last name.

The Stowaway Myth

For some reason, it is so much more romantic to have an ancestor who came to America as a stowaway on a ship rather than a paying passenger. While there are cases of people who actually did sneak aboard ships, this was not a common practice. If the stowaway was discovered enroute, he will be recorded on the last page of the passenger arrival list. I deliberately use "he" because you almost never hear a story about great-grandma being a stowaway. Even if you have the family story of a stowaway, still check for a passenger arrival list.

The Claim-to-Fame Myth

Everyone who has the surname Bradford or Alden is related to William Bradford and John Alden of *Mayflower* fame, right? And everyone with the last name of Boone is related to Daniel. If you do have American Indian ancestry, then you must be descended from Pocahontas. Is that a red flag I see flying? We all want a famous person to hang on our family tree, but we may not find that person. My interest in genealogy spawned from the family story that we are related to Robert E. Lee. We are. But he's a very distant relation: something like a fortieth cousin, twenty-five times removed. Again, the claim to fame is more likely a myth than a reality.

The Nobility and Coat of Arms Myth

A cousin to the claim-to-fame myth is having royal or noble ancestors who were entitled to display a coat of arms. A good percentage of the people who left their native land for America were not entitled to inherit anything—land, a title, or armory. That's why they left in the first place. Why should a duke or prince give up his due inheritance and leave his homeland for the uncharted frontier of America? Although not a hard-and-fast rule for every foreign county, generally it's the second, third, fourth, and so on son who decided to emigrate because his older brother, the eldest son, would inherit their father's property (a custom known as primogeniture). While it is true that many Americans can trace their ancestry to kings and queens, sometimes they are tracing their ancestry to the *illegitimate* children of the kings and queens. Of course, that in itself holds a special status as well. Royal ancestry is certainly possible, but don't automatically trust the family tradition. Check it out for yourself through research.

Reminder

As far as coats of arms go, keep in mind that **heraldic achievements are granted to a person, not to a family,** and the arms are typically passed from the eldest son to his eldest son and so forth. Younger sons and even daughters may use the main design, but these arms are generally altered to denote a son or daughter and birth order. But what about that beautifully illustrated coat of arms that Uncle Harold has displayed with pride as the Schwartzfedder "family crest"? It may have nothing to do with your ancestors.

The Wrong Ethnic Identity Myth

All Germans are Hessians who fought in the American Revolution. All French are Huguenots. All Hispanics are Mexican. Of course, none of these broad statements is true. As you will read in Part II, we tend to lump certain groups of people incorrectly into one category. "German" is not a distinct enough identifier in genealogy. If family stories indicate that your ancestors were German or from Germany, were they Germans from Imperial Germany, Alsatians, Austrians, Swiss, Luxembourgers, Germans from Russia, or Poles from Germany? Even the records you uncover may not tell you more than "Germany." This is why it is so important to learn the unique cultural traits—customs, traditions, folkways—about the ethnic group. Learning these can point your research in the right direction.

Names, too, may be inaccurate indicators of ethnic identity. Just because the name sounds Italian, is it? The name you are accustomed to may have been changed or inadvertently corrupted over time, obscuring its ethnic origins. The name "Toliver," so common in colonial Virginia, was actually Taliaferro, an Italian name too difficult for most English Virginians to pronounce. Descendants need to check records for both spellings, and they may be surprised to learn they have Italian origins, not English.

The Ellis Island Baptism Myth

This is the myth that an immigrant ancestor's surname was changed by officials during processing at Ellis Island. No evidence whatsoever exists to suggest this ever occurred, and I have challenged countless people who insist their ancestor's name was changed on Ellis Island to provide me with proof. So far, no one has been able to do so. Even the historians at Ellis Island will tell you this is just a colorful family story. During its operation as an immigrant receiving station (1892–1954), Ellis Island was staffed with hundreds of interpreters who spoke more than thirty different languages. Inspectors compared the names the immigrants told them against what was recorded on the passenger lists. These lists were created at the ports of departure. There was no reason to change anyone's surname once they arrived on the island. More likely, immigrants themselves changed their names after they settled in America to avoid prejudice and to blend more easily into American society. Another typical time for forenames, and sometimes surnames, to be changed was when immigrant children entered school and American teachers could not pronounce the foreign names. So they called Francesco "Frank," and Adamczyk became "Adams."

Handling the Myth in Research and Writing

Now that I've shattered your favorite family story, how do you tell Grandpa? Or should you? And how do you handle in print ancient family legends that you've discovered through your research are false? Family legends are part of your family history and should never be ignored or taken lightly. As mentioned earlier, there is usually a kernel of truth to the legend. Rather than bursting Grandpa's bubble with the facts, try to find out how the story originated. When you write your family history, include the family story as it was told to you, noting it as family "tradition," "lore," or "legend." Then explain, if you can, how the story originated, followed by a discussion of your research findings. You may reveal that some elements of a story were true and some were false, or that a story was totally false. Even if you have not been able to prove or disprove the story, acknowledge the lore and say it has yet to be proven.

Technique

Interviewing Tips

When interviewing relatives, here are some details to pursue that will help in your ethnic and immigrant research:

- places where the family settled in America (including ethnic neighbors) and subsequent residences and dates
- name changes and original foreign names
- date of arrival in America
- names of ships
- ports of departure and arrival
- name of the village, province, or country where the immigrant ancestor originated
- whether the ancestor ever returned to the native village, and if so, when
- religious affiliations; special feast or saints' days celebrated
- memberships in ethnic organizations
- occupations
- military service in America and the homeland
- ethnic recipes handed down in the family
- favorite music, dances
- marriage customs
- naming practices
- funeral customs
- attitudes toward education
- attitudes/prejudices toward other ethnic groups
- prejudices felt or experienced from other ethnic groups

Oral History

For More Info

For an excellent guide with hundreds of possible oral history interview questions, see William Fletcher's *Recording Your Family History*.

If you are conducting an interview with an immigrant or the child of an immigrant, do not neglect to ask the "why, how, and what was it like" questions:

- Why did you—or your parents—leave Poland and come to America?
- How did you/they get the money to travel?
- What was the voyage like?
- What was it like for you/them to adjust to life in America?

Case Study

FAMILY LORE YOU CANNOT PROVE OR DISPROVE

My grandmother told me when I was a boy that my great-grandfather Ignazio Colletta came to America from his native Sicily around 1890 to work on the railroads. She said he laid track out West for several years before returning "to the Old Country." When I interviewed elderly cousins, I heard the same story, with the added detail that Ignazio worked on the rails "in Montana." I have yet to discover any documentary evidence to confirm—or disprove—this oral tradition. Nevertheless, it certainly has its place—presented as such, family lore—in the written history of my family. Besides, I believe it is true. Here's why.

Ignazio came to the United States on the *Trinacria,* a British steamship that sailed from Palermo, Sicily, and arrived in New Orleans on 9 June 1890. He was thirty-five years old at the time, and I know that he had a family. But his name does not appear on the passenger list with a wife and children. Rather, Ignazio was enumerated amidst thirteen males, aged sixteen to thirty-five, and it is obvious from their surnames that these thirteen "laborers" were all *paesani* from the same village. All of the surnames appear in the sacramental registers of the village's Catholic parish, and many of them represent families that had intermarried time and again with the Colletta family over many generations.

The list of the *Trinacria* reflects a social phenomenon of the late-nineteenth and early-twentieth centuries that has been explained by scholars, such as Alan Kraut in *The Huddled Masses: The Immigrant in American Society, 1880–1921*: laborers from southern and eastern Europe were recruited in their native towns and transported together to the United States to work in heavy industry, such as mining and construction . . . and laying track. Many of these laborers crossed the Atlantic seasonally, spending the winter months with their families in the mild Mediterranean climate and returning to their jobs in America in the spring. Historians call them "birds of passage." Many others, however—more dogged or perhaps just more desperate—"toughed out" the severe American winters in labor camps, allowing them to pocket the transatlantic fare they saved. Grandmother always said that Ignazio hated the snowy winters out West. Not only was the Sicilian unaccustomed to the cold, but his bushy mustache kept freezing up!

The evidence in the list of passengers, evaluated in light of well-established social history and the dates of birth of Ignazio's ten children, supports the family tradition I heard as a boy. After four years of strenuous toil in America, sending his hard-earned dollars home to support his needy family (and—according to family tradition—losing the hearing in one ear to a particularly brutal winter), Ignazio returned to farming in his native land, content to leave "the immigrant experience" to the next generation of Collettas!

—John Philip Colletta

These are impressions and accounts missing from most genealogical records, firsthand evidence otherwise lost forever.

AN EXAMPLE OF HOW FAMILY STORIES CAN HELP YOUR RESEARCH

Every time I interviewed my mother, she insisted that her mother, Rose (Norris) Gordon, was born in Ireland. The family story she remembered was that Rose had contracted scarlet fever on board the ship. I knew this couldn't be right; I had Rose's birth certificate. She was the youngest of seven children, all born in Greenwich, Connecticut. Even though I knew that there is usually a grain of truth in every family story, I shrugged this one off as the exception to the rule until many years later when I interviewed my mother's older sister. She told me that the family had gone back to Ireland after Rose was born, and on the return trip, Rose had scarlet fever.

On my next trip to the Family History Library in Salt Lake City, I couldn't wait to see if I could verify the story with a passenger arrival list. Sure enough, I found the whole family—all U.S. citizens—returning from Ireland on 31 October 1901 (the day after Rose turned five), although there was no indication on the ship's manifest that Rose had been sick.

In finding the ship's list, I also had another breakthrough on this family. Rose's father, according to his death certificate, was supposedly born in County Tyrone, Ireland, but without a more precise location such as a town or parish, I was unable to pursue research in Ireland. On the passenger list, however, the family's last residence was Cookstown. There are several Cookstowns in Ireland, including one in County Tyrone. Now I have a place in Ireland to look further.

Although my mother didn't have all of the facts straight, her older sister had remembered the story with more accuracy. In all of the documents I have collected on this family, there has been nothing to indicate that they were ever out of the country. So I learned two valuable lessons:

1. Never ignore a family story, no matter how far-fetched it may seem at the time.
2. Never make researching documents a priority over oral history interviewing.

I interviewed my aunt only two years ago. Had I not tried to verify the story with her, I would have never dreamed of looking for the family on a passenger list, and I would have missed a vital clue to my great-grandfather's origins in Ireland.

HOME SOURCES

While you are interviewing your relatives, don't forget to ask to see artifacts, photographs, and documents that will aid in your search. Perhaps Grandma left everything behind in Greece, except she could not part with her mother's silver

candlesticks. Is there a date, craftsman, or place engraved on the bottom? Will that lead you to a village of origin? Thoroughly examine every artifact that may have come from the Old Country or was acquired upon arrival in America. Study family photographs. Were they taken here or in the homeland? You may find in the photograph collection a post card depicting the native village or the ship they arrived on. On family or individual portraits, the photographer may have imprinted his name and locality on the front or back. Analyze all photographs and artifacts for possible clues. (See Maureen Taylor's *Uncovering Your Ancestry Through Family Photographs*.) Ask relatives if they possess any of these documents:

- citizenship papers
- passports
- alien registration cards
- steamship ticket stubs
- journals or diaries
- U.S. Public Health Service inspection cards from the ship
- letters or documents written in a foreign language
- military discharge certificates
- newspaper clippings

Case Study

THE VALUE OF CORRESPONDING WITH RELATIVES YOU'VE NEVER MET

I acquired my first genealogical pen pal in 1981 at the age of fourteen. I had exhausted my grandfather's knowledge about his Danish ancestors, so he gave me the address of his Aunt Ella in California. Born in January 1900, Ella was the last of her generation still living. I wrote to this great-great-aunt of mine, whom I had never met, and asked questions. Taking me and my questions seriously, Aunt Ella laid the foundation for my Danish research.

She sent me a copy of her father's *daabsattest* (baptismal certificate). It showed that Jens Johan Pedersen was baptized in the parish and district of Nim, in the county of Skanderborg, Denmark, on 30 November 1859. His parents were listed as Peder Nielsen and Maren Jensdatter. Many years later, the precise date and place on the *daabsattest* enabled me to go further back. Through my local LDS Family History Center, I borrowed the 1860 Danish census and looked for two-month-old Jens Johan Pedersen. Armed with an English translation of the basic Danish census form, I cranked through pages of incomprehensible Danish. Somehow I found him. Jens was listed with his parents and two brothers, Niels and Stephan, and his grandmother, Cidsel Kirstine Pedersdatter, born in 1789. That census record, in turn, led to a series of discoveries, and over the years I found a number of Danish ancestors.

Although it took me awhile to realize it, Aunt Ella gave me other pieces of

THE VALUE OF CORRESPONDING WITH RELATIVES YOU'VE NEVER MET—Continued

information more important than the *daabsattest*. She shared stories and photographs about her parents, who had emigrated from Denmark to Dodge County, Minnesota, in 1885. She wrote of the hard times they endured in Denmark. Ella recounted that Jens, her father, was indentured to a brick mason, and he always said that "they didn't even dare to pull a carrot out of the garden." Ella sent me a photo of her grandmother, Kjersten Pedersdatter Nielsen, who had immigrated to Hubbard County, Minnesota, in her later years. Kjersten never learned English, and she lived out her days in rural northern Minnesota, caring for an invalid grandson. The photo shows an elderly woman, grim and unsmiling, bundled up in layers of skirts, a long coat, mittens, and a head scarf, standing in a bleak snowy landscape. I know more about Kjersten after seeing that photo.

Ella told me how her favorite sister, Hannah, my great-grandmother who died fifteen years before I was born, met my great-grandfather, Joe. Hannah worked as a waitress at a hotel while attending school in Hayfield, Minnesota. Hayfield was a railroad center and many of the railroad men slept and ate at the hotel. Joe was a railroad man for the Chicago, Milwaukee, and St. Paul line and he and Hannah met at the hotel. So the next time I was in Minnesota, my sister and I found the hotel, now turned into apartments, and gazed on a bit of our family history.

From Ella I learned that Hannah's family—her parents and all seven of her siblings—moved to California in 1910 because Jens got pneumonia every winter. Hannah, newly married, wanted to join her family in California but Joe did not. After learning that, I saw the group photo, taken just before the rest of the family left Minnesota, in a new light. Hannah, captured with her chin held high and a spunky attitude, was about to be left behind.

Aunt Ella gave me a priceless gift in the photos and stories she shared. More precious still was the friendship we developed through our correspondence. Because I lived in the Midwest and on the East Coast, I didn't meet Aunt Ella until February 1997, after fifteen years of correspondence. Six months later, Aunt Ella died at the age of ninety-seven. She left me quite a legacy. My relationship with Aunt Ella taught me that genealogy is about making connections with the present as well as the past.

—Lynn Betlock

LEARNING THE WHY, HOW, AND WHAT

The trend in genealogy has shifted dramatically in the past decade or two. No longer are many genealogists satisfied with just the names, dates, and places (the who, where, and when). They want to go beyond a skeletal pedigree chart to seek the person behind the name—to know *what* it was like to be a colonist, settler, or immigrant; *how* their ancestors came to this country; and *why*. Genealogical records do not ordinarily tell this information. Traditional genealogical documents—censuses, probates, land records, and so forth—tend to leave gaps in the immigrants' stories, no matter when they arrived. In order to supplement information found in records of individuals, we need to study the broader, common experiences, the day-to-day activities, and the folkways of the ethnic group. Naming, inheritance, marriage, religious, and migration patterns are all revealing and important to family historians. As mentioned earlier, learning these details can guide your research in the right direction and help you determine ethnic identity and immigrant origins.

Important

While each group has it own traditions, customs, and immigration experiences, there are two factors common to all immigrants, no matter when they arrived in America or what the ethnic background:

- Upon arrival, free people initially settled with friends and relatives from the homeland, and
- The first generation typically tried to maintain as many of their native customs (folkways) as American society would allow.

Technique

Despite what we may have been taught in history classes, our immigrant ancestors were not always eager to adopt the traits of the dominant culture, nor did they all willingly come to America. **Logically, therefore, in order to identify immigrants and their origins, two research strategies apply:**

- Study the neighborhood and community. Who were the neighbors and where did they come from? Your ancestors may not have left evidence suggesting their origins, but their neighbors and other associates may have.
- Study the social history to learn the folkways and common experiences of the ethnic group. As discussed under family history myths, if all of the genealogical records state only that your ancestor was "German" or came from "Germany," a study of social history in conjunction with the specific genealogical data will be necessary to determine whether the heritage was German, Alsatian, Swiss, Luxembourger, Russian, Austrian, or Prussian. In American records, these groups were generally classified by the language they spoke or their mother tongue: If they spoke German, they were Germans. This dilemma is not exclusive to Germans, of course, although they are one of the most troublesome groups in genealogical research; other groups have similar identity problems in records.

Your research in social histories should be ongoing. As soon as you learn a possible ethnic identity, begin with the overviews provided in Part II of this book. Then look at children's books about the ethnic group to learn more about cultural traits. In particular, Chelsea House Publishers in New York has produced an excellent series called the Peoples of North America, covering forty-nine ethnic groups, and Indians of North America, covering forty-nine tribes. These books are quick to read and provide a concise overview of the ethnic group's culture, migration and settlement patterns, and a bibliography of adult sources.

Continue your social history research while you are conducting interviews and examining original documents. If you have not studied the general, common immigration experiences and folkways of your immigrant ancestor's ethnic group, you may miss some important clues given in genealogical records, or you might overlook records that will yield more information.

JOINING AN ETHNIC GENEALOGICAL SOCIETY

A lot of genealogists are successful at tracing their ethnic ancestors because they network with other genealogists who have the same interest. **Though you may not share a common ancestor, genealogists who have been researching an ethnic group for years can offer you valuable guidance** from their own experience and help you avoid common pitfalls and mistakes. You find genealogists like this by joining an ethnic genealogical society.

Important

Just about every ethnic group has a corresponding genealogical society, and you can find whether a national group exists by consulting Elizabeth Bentley's *The Genealogist's Address Book* and the July/August issue each year of *Everton's Genealogical Helper*, by attending national genealogical conferences, or by surfing the Internet. For those ethnic groups discussed in Part II, I have given names and addresses for one or two genealogical or historical societies. These may not be the only organizations for each group, so consult the resources mentioned. Or you may find groups that have a broader scope, such as the Federation of Eastern European Family History Societies, which covers most countries in eastern Europe.

Ethnic genealogical societies have members from all over the country and sometimes from the foreign country where ancestors originated. Typically, the society produces some kind of periodical, either a newsletter or journal. Members and professional genealogists write articles offering advice on researching the ethnic group in America and in the homeland. You will also find advertisements for those who offer translating services, and professional genealogists who will do research for you, either in America or abroad. Some of these genealogical organizations may also sponsor one- or two-day seminars with programs on conducting ethnic and foreign research.

Sources

Federation of Eastern European Family History Societies, P.O. Box 510898, Salt Lake City, UT 84151-0898. Web site: http://feehs.org. Publishes *FEEFHS Newsletter* and *FEEFHS Address Book and Resource Guide*.

Also check with your local library or genealogical society. Many local genealogical organizations have special-interest groups that focus on an ethnic group, such as Germans from Russia, Palatines to America, African Americans, or Jewish immigrants. These offshoots typically meet apart from the general genealogical society, and members share research tips. Some of these smaller, local groups also publish a newsletter, which includes reports on meetings and provides research tips. Frequently the newsletter will carry lists of Internet sites to aid in researching the group. Meetings typically include a speaker, or there is a discussion topic for the entire group. Almost all of these meetings have food or some kind of refreshment. That alone is reason enough to attend.

Through membership in an American ethnic genealogical society, either local, regional, or national, you may also learn of genealogical organizations you can join in your ancestor's homeland. Keep in mind, however, that some of these foreign genealogical groups are geared toward royal and noble ancestry, not common-folk ancestry.

JOINING AN ETHNIC HERITAGE SOCIETY

Along with joining a genealogical society focusing on your ethnic group, you may also want to join an ethnic heritage society. These groups highlight the cultural aspects of the ethnic group, and often meet monthly, just like genealogical societies. They also typically have a program that centers on the ethnic group, including time for socialization. If there is a significant population of a particular ethnic group in your area, then there is probably a heritage or cultural society. By belonging to one of these groups, you will gain a greater appreciation for what it means to be Irish, or Italian, or Swedish. Check with your local library. For a national group, see Part II of this book or check in the reference section of your library for Lubomyr Wynar's *Encyclopedic Directory of Ethnic Organizations in the United States*. Although dated (it was published in 1975), some of the organizations are still active.

Case Study

JOINING ETHNIC SOCIETIES TO FIND ANCESTORS

The beginning of my genealogy search began when the following meeting notice caught my attention and curiosity:

Germans from Russia Genealogy
Bear Creek Library, 7 P.M.
June 6, 1987
Everyone Welcome

It was this curiosity and the knowledge that "I was one of them" that led me to that initial meeting.

Upon entering a small room at the library, I was greeted with a warm hello and asked if I would sign the guest book and indicate my "village." Village, I thought. I guess they meant the home village of my parents. So I bravely entered Frank, Russia.

Then a Dr. J.R. Lebsack opened the meeting and had everyone introduce themselves and tell "their village." I quickly learned that I was in the right crowd, and that there were others in attendance with ancestry from Frank.

After the meeting, I learned that Dr. Lebsack was also the editor of a Frank, Russia, village newsletter called *Das Frankerer Nachrichtsblatt*. Dr. Lebsack gave me a number of these newsletters. After he died, the newsletter was renamed *The Frank and Brunnental Village Newsletter* and later, *Kolb-Frank Newsletter*. These newsletters contain a wealth of family and historical information for researchers for the Russian villages of Frank, Kolb, and Brunnental.

JOINING ETHNIC SOCIETIES TO FIND ANCESTORS—Continued

At the 1990 convention of the American Historical Society of Germans from Russia, I was introduced to Dr. Igor Pleve from the University of Saratov and learned that he had located early German immigrant and family history documents. In December 1993, I asked Dr. Pleve to make a genealogical investigation of my Kissler family, and in March 1994, I received a detailed Kissler family history chart from him. The chart confirmed that the family came from Germany to the port of Oranenbaum on 15 August 1766 on the ship *Johannes*, and then to the Volga Steppes.

The family history chart Dr. Pleve prepared covered 1766 to 1909, and he found that a number of Kissler families resided in Frank, Russia. The top of the chart revealed that first Kissler to Frank was Johann Peter Kissler from the Independent Province of Rietesel in Germany. The chart contained over three hundred Kissler family names, birth dates, and in some instances, the maiden names of the spouses. Much to my surprise, the chart also provided a notation that a number of Kissler families from Frank immigrated to the United States from about 1880 to 1914, settling in Oklahoma, Washington, Colorado, and Nebraska. This information confirmed that my Kissler family was not the only family from Frank in the United States and led me to new searches.

—Clarence D. Kissler

THE IMPORTANCE OF FURTHERING YOUR GENEALOGICAL KNOWLEDGE

If you are brand new to genealogy, besides reading this and other guidebooks, you may also want to see if there are any beginning genealogy classes offered through your local genealogical society, community college, or adult education programs. By attending classes, you will not only meet other people interested in genealogy, but you will be able to ask questions of the instructor, something you can't do when you rely solely on guidebooks for your education. Check for classes in your area by asking the reference librarian at your library. Considering the recent surge in the popularity of genealogy, no doubt this is a question the librarian has been asked many times before. If you have trouble finding genealogy classes in your area, correspondence courses in genealogy and writing family history, both online and as traditional correspondence courses, are also available (see Appendix B).

Try to also attend as many national genealogical conferences as you can. Two are offered annually: one sponsored by the National Genealogical Society, the other by the Federation of Genealogical Societies (see Appendix B). These three- to four-day conferences are held in different parts of the country each year and always offer lectures on researching different ethnic origins.

GENEALOGICAL MAGAZINES AND JOURNALS

Many of the popular genealogical magazines, such as *Ancestry*, *Heritage Quest*, *Everton's Genealogical Helper*, *Family Tree Magazine*, and *Family Chronicle* publish articles regularly on how to conduct ethnic and foreign research. In the Federation of Genealogical Societies' newsletter, *FORUM*, for example, there is a column devoted to ethnic/international research news (see Appendix B).

As you are gathering information from relatives and home sources, networking with other genealogists, and taking classes, be thinking about your ancestors in a broader historical context. Each and every one of them was a part of American immigration history, and there are some general historical trends that could affect the direction of your research.

TWO

Historical Trends That May Affect Your Research

T here are more than one hundred different ethnic backgrounds among America's population today. Can you name them all without looking at the chart on page 20? Fortunately, not every group came to America at the same time, and while each ethnic group has its own migration, settlement, and assimilation experience that will be discussed in Part II, there are some general historical trends that might affect the direction of your research.

AMERICAN IMMIGRATION HISTORY BY TIME PERIODS

Immigration to America has been constant, but it has ebbed and flowed over the centuries. Historians have conveniently divided American immigration history into these major time periods:

I. Colonial Period (late 1500s–1776)
Main Groups: Spanish, French, English, African, Dutch, German, Welsh, Finnish, Scottish, and Scotch-Irish.

II. 1776–1820
Main Groups: Continuation of the same groups as the colonial period, but in decreasing numbers. Due to international wars and early attempts at immigration restriction, immigration to America grew only slightly during this period.

III. 1820–ca. 1880
Main Groups: Catholic Irish, Norwegian, Swedish, Danish, German, Chinese, Japanese, and French Canadian.

IV. ca. 1880–ca. 1920
Main Groups: Italian, Polish, Austrian, Czech, Slovak, Yugoslav, Romanian, Russian, Hungarian, Armenian, Greek, Arabs, Jews, and Japanese.

ETHNIC GROUPS IN AMERICA

Acadians	Croats	Luxembourgers
Afghans	Cubans	Macedonians
Africans	Czechs	Maltese
Afro-Americans	Danes	Manx
Albanians	Dominicans	Mexicans
Aleuts	Dutch	Muslims
Alsatians	East Indians	Nordic
American Indians	English	North Caucasians
Anglo-American	Eskimos	Norwegians
Anglo-Saxon	Estonians	Oriental
Appalachians	Filipinos	Pacific Islanders
Arabs	Finns	Pakistanis
Armenians	French	Pennsylvania Germans
Aryan	French Canadians	Poles
Asian	Frisians	Portuguese
Assyrians	Georgians	Puerto Ricans
Australians and New	Germans	Romanians
Zealanders	Germans from Russia	Russians
Austrians	Greeks	Scotch-Irish
Azerbaijanis	Gypsies	Scots
Bangladeshi	Haitians	Serbs
Basques	Hawaiians	Slovaks
Belgians	Hispanic	Slovenes
Belorussians	Hungarians	South Africans
Bosnian Muslims	Icelanders	Spanish
Bulgarians	Indochinese	Swedes
Burmese	Indonesians	Swiss
Canadians, British	Iranians	Tatars
Cape Verdeans	Irish	Thai
Carpatho-Rusyns	Italians	Tri-Racial Isolates
Central and South	Japanese	Turkestanis
Americans	Jews	Turks
Chinese	Kalmyks	Ukrainians
Copts	Koreans	Welsh
Cornish	Kurds	Wends
Cossacks	Latvians	West Indians
Creole	Lithuanians	Zoroastrians

Source: Stephan H. Thernstrom, ed., *Harvard Encyclopedia of American Ethnic Groups* (Cambridge, MA: Belknap Press, 1980).

V. ca. 1920–1945

Main Groups: German, Italian, Polish, Czech (especially 1921–1930); British (English, Scottish, Welsh) and Irish; Canadian and Mexican; and refugees from Nazi Germany. Immigration to America declined beginning in 1915 because of U.S. legislation that restricted immigration through quota systems and literacy tests. Migration to and from the homeland was most common during the 1920s. The Great Depression and war limited immigration further.

VI. Post-World War II

Main Groups: Mexican, Central and South American, Caribbean, Korean, Vietnamese, Laotian, Cambodian, Middle Eastern Arab, and Soviet Jewish.

Because of World War II and the cold war, the United States accepted European displaced persons and refugees (for example, German, Italian, and Hungarian) during this period. *Note:* During most periods, immigration from Canada was high and included many British and other European migrants.

If you know your ancestors' ethnic backgrounds, you may find them fitting perfectly into these time frames, having arrived when other members of their group did. If you don't know an ancestor's ethnicity, when did that person arrive? For example, the origins of Cornelius Carmack have stymied family researchers for decades. Some have speculated that he was Irish, others have said Scottish, still others believed he was Scotch-Irish. (The distinctions between these three groups are discussed in Part II.) The first record of him is in Cecil County, Maryland, in 1718, where Cornelius was an appraiser for the estate of a deceased man. Cornelius then moved to Frederick County, Maryland, in the 1730s. Let's see if we can start building a hypothesis of his origins as we explore immigrant history. Notice that the Scots and Scotch-Irish had a more significant presence during the colonial period than the Irish, so my starting hypothesis is that Cornelius may have been Scottish or Scotch-Irish. In the course of my research, I'll be looking for information that will confirm or negate this initial hypothesis. We'll be looking at Cornelius throughout the next few chapters, so you can see how the process works.

MIGRATION FACTORS

While there are many reasons—most rooted in economics—for people to have left one country and resettled in another, British social scientist E.G. Ravenstein identified "The Laws of Migration" in his 1889 essay in the *Journal of the Royal Statistical Society*. These laws include push, pull, and means.

1. **Push Factors:** Elements in the homeland are pushing people to leave, for example, religious persecution, economic hardship, or mandatory military conscription. "Push" migrants tend to be negatively motivated. They may not want to leave but feel forced to because of unfavorable conditions.

2. **Pull Factors:** Life in the homeland is bearable, but people want something better. Elements in the receiving country are pulling them in, such as availability of land, jobs, or freedom from religious persecution. These people are positively motivated.

3. **Means:** One must have the ability, freedom, and physical and monetary means to migrate. Shifts in transportation technology—from sailing to steam ships, for example—or cheap passage inspired great leaps in immigration statistics.

For More Info

For more on immigration history and migration factors, see Roger Daniels, *Coming to America: A History of Immigration and Ethnicity in American Life*; John Bodnar, *The Transplanted: A History of Immigrants in Urban America*; and Thomas Sowell, *Ethnic America: A History*.

CHAIN MIGRATION

There were many notable waves of arrivals: the 1840s–1860s for Irish famine victims, for example, and the 1880s–1920s for eastern and southern Europeans.

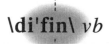

Definitions

Case Study

Immigration naturally declined during wartime and depressions. Whether immigrants arrived as whole family groups or as a few individuals traveling from the homeland together, **historians and genealogists have documented a "chain migration," where earlier arrivals sent letters and money home to friends and family, encouraging them to come to America.** By linking the chain, you may find relatives you didn't know about.

At the time I began researching my Italian "chain," I knew of three relatives who came to America. **When I followed the chain, I discovered four more relatives.** Following the chain is easier when you are dealing with immigrants who came in the early part of the twentieth century, since the passenger arrival lists of this time period record who the immigrant was joining in America. Here's what I found (names are spelled as they were on the passenger list):

- Isabel (Veneto) Vallarelli was listed on a March 1916 passenger list as going to join her son-in-law Salvatore Ebetino of Rye, New York.
- Salvatore Ebetino was listed on an April 1906 passenger list as going to join his brother-in-law Albino DeBartolo of Harrison, New York.
- Albino DeBartolo was listed on a September 1905 passenger list as going to join his cousin Giuseppe Lambarella of Harrison, New York.
- Giuseppe Lamporelli was listed on a March 1905 passenger list as going to join his cousin Francesco Lamparelli in New York City.
- Francesco Lamparello was listed on a December 1904 passenger list as going to join his daughter Giacchina Lamparello in New York City.

Unfortunately, this is where the chain breaks—I haven't yet been able to locate a passenger arrival list for Giacchina—but you get the idea.

RETURN AND SEASONAL MIGRATION

During the age of sailing ships, when crossing the Atlantic was a long and dangerous undertaking, emigrants from Europe never expected (and never did) see their homeland again. The age of steam, however, changed the way people viewed migration to America. Though many of the arrivals in America planned to settle here, many others came temporarily to work and save money, with the goal of returning to the homeland. Travel by steamship, beginning in the 1850s, made seasonal migration possible since travel time was reduced greatly. These migrants would leave America after the fall harvest and return to Europe in time for spring planting. English house painters, for example, came to America in the spring, then traveled to Scotland in the summer, and back to England in the fall and winter. The three groups least likely to return to their homeland were the Jews, Irish, and Germans, mainly because they typically arrived as families. Italians, Poles, and Greeks, however, whose male population migrated first, were more likely to return because their intention was to earn money either to buy land in their native country or to send for their families. **They became known as "birds of passage."**

When you find your ancestor on a passenger list or index, always look for additional entries that may follow or precede by a couple of years, especially if

Definitions

the ancestor was Italian, Polish, or Greek. Albino DeBartolo, an Italian immigrant, was a typical bird of passage. Albino first came to America in 1905; he went back to Italy around 1907–1908; he came back to America in 1909; he went back to Italy about 1911; then he made his final return to America in 1912.

IMMIGRATION EXPERIENCES

Each ethnic group had its own immigration experience: some eighteenth-century Germans traveling from Le Havre came on cargo vessels that had brought cotton from America. The ships were returning to New Orleans, which became the Germans' port of arrival, although they did not settle there. From New Orleans, they traveled on Mississippi River cargo boats headed through the upper Mississippi Valley to settle in places like St. Louis, Cincinnati, and Milwaukee. This is totally different from the Irish experience in the nineteenth century. Many Irish arrived through the port of Boston and settled in enclaves in that city, where their unskilled labor was needed and where relatives and friends from their native towns had already settled. For clues to your ancestor's migration, study the immigration experience and settlement patterns for the time period and ethnic group, as discussed in Part II.

MIGRATIONS FOLLOWED PATTERNS

The people from a particular region, city, or village in the sending country tended to settle in specific regions, cities, or even certain city blocks in the receiving nation. A whole group of villagers may have immigrated together. In 1683, for example, the inhabitants of Krefeld, Germany, left and settled Germantown, Pennsylvania. Two hundred years later in New York City in the 1890s, the area between Houston and Spring streets was occupied by Sicilians, while Italians from Genoa settled on Baxter Street. You may even find social histories of some of these ethnic enclaves. Clues gathered from tracking the origins of neighbors and associates, in conjunction with information found in local histories about the ethnic groups who settled there, may help you determine your ancestor's village of origin.

As immigrants settled in America, they tended to migrate together internally as well. Many Scotch-Irish, for example, typically arrived in America through the Port of Philadelphia. From there, they migrated internally to Pittsburgh and to the back country of southwestern Virginia, moving further south and west along the Cumberland Gap into the Appalachian region.

Immigrants also tended to settle in areas that reminded them of their locality back home. Ever wonder why certain areas in America have a significant population of a particular ethnic group? Look to the geography and climate. **Immigrants had a "geographic affinity" for places in America that resembled their homeland.** If your ancestor came from a mountainous region, he was more likely to settle in a mountainous region in America. The Cominiello family came from Potenza, Italy. The countryside and climate there is strikingly similar to

\di'fin\ *vb*

Definitions

where they ultimately settled in America, the foothills of the Rocky Mountains in Denver.

Now, remember Cornelius Carmack? When we last left him, the theory was he was Scots or Scotch-Irish. If we look at his descendants' internal migration pattern from Maryland to southwest Virginia to Tennessee to Missouri, which was typical of Scotch-Irish, then we have more evidence to suggest he was Scotch-Irish.

FOOD HABITS

While a group of people may appear to be totally assimilated into the dominant culture, food habits were more enduring. Whenever possible, newly arrived peoples would attempt to prepare and eat food that replicated what they consumed in their homeland. Of all the ethnic groups, the Chinese and Italians clung as closely as possible to their native diet, as evidenced by their numerous restaurants throughout America today. But Italians and Chinese were not alone in their attempts to maintain their cultural eating habits and, at the same time, expose "native" Americans to a new menu. Germans who came to America did not give up beer or sauerkraut, Poles made sausages, Hungarians enjoyed goulash, and Jews opened kosher delicatessens. By studying histories on foodways and comparing them with family recipes, you will find that some of these food preferences and methods of preparation were so particular within an ethnic group, that not only a country of origin may be determined, but perhaps even a more precise location in the Old World.

NATIVISM

In learning to understand our ancestors and how to best research them, we also need to learn what motivated them to behave in certain ways. Why did they leave their homeland? Where did they go? And how were they treated once they got there? Some of our ancestors' behavior stems in part from prejudice, or nativism. **The term "nativism" was coined about 1840 and reflected an intense opposition from "native" whites**—Americans of earlier, usually English Protestant, origins—against incoming foreign groups. Terms such as antiforeignism and anti-Catholicism are essentially synonymous with nativism. (See John Higham's *Strangers in the Land: Patterns of American Nativism, 1860–1925.*)

Nativism was sparked by the arrivals of Irish and Germans in the 1840s and 1850s and revived with the influx of southern and eastern Europeans in the 1880s. It is not surprising that hereditary, patriotic, and genealogical societies sprang up during these times, organizations that cultivated status-consciousness and an exclusive sense of nationality.

Realizing that the Yankee stock might eventually be outbred numerically and politically, nativists decided to restrict the number of immigrants, establishing quota laws (see chapter six). This "race suicide" alarm peaked in the early 1900s and was sparked to a great degree by eugenicists—those who believed in genetically improving the qualities of the human race by carefully selecting

For More Info

For more on ethnic cuisine, see Richard Hooker, *A History of Food and Drink in America*; Charles Camp, *American Foodways: What, When, Why, and How We Eat in America*; and Linda Keller Brown and Kay Mussell, *Ethnic and Regional Foodways in the United States: The Performance of Group Identity*.

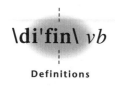

Definitions

\di'fin\ *vb*

For More Info

For further discussion of the immigrant impact on native white society and lobbying by eugenicists, see Margo J. Anderson, *The American Census: A Social History*.

FOUNDING DATES OF GENEALOGICAL AND LINEAGE/PATRIOTIC SOCIETIES DURING PEAK IMMIGRATION DECADES	
Genealogical Society Name	*Date Organized*
New England Historic Genealogical Society	1845
New York Genealogical and Biographical Society	1869
Genealogical Society of Pennsylvania	1892
Genealogical Society of Utah/Family History Library	1894
National Genealogical Society	1903
Genealogical Society of New Jersey	1921
Lineage/Patriotic Society Name	*Date Organized*
Sons of Union Veterans of the Civil War	1881
Daughters of Union Veterans of the Civil War	1885
Holland Society of New York	1885
Sons of the American Revolution	1889
Daughters of the American Revolution	1890
Colonial Dames of America	1890
National Society of the Colonial Dames of America	1891
Daughters of the Republic of Texas	1891
United States Daughters of 1812	1892
Netherlands Society of Philadelphia	1892
General Society of Colonial Wars	1893
Sons of the Republic of Texas	1893
Daughters of the Cincinnati	1894
United Daughters of the Confederacy	1894
National Society of New England Women	1895
Sons of Confederate Veterans	1896
Order of the Founders and Patriots of America	1896
General Society of Mayflower Descendants	1897
Daughters of Founders and Patriots of America	1898
Daughters of Utah Pioneers	1901
Sons and Daughters of the Oregon Pioneers	1901
Welcome Society of Pennsylvania	1906
Sons and Daughters of the Pilgrims	1908
Swedish Colonial Society	1909
Old Plymouth Colony Descendants	1910
Order of the First Families of Virginia	1912
Colonial Dames of the XVII Century	1915
Daughters of the American Colonists	1921
Dames of the Court of Honor	1921

parents, with an emphasis on intelligence. They lobbied for quotas on immigration and encouraged newcomers to limit their family size. While much of this nativism spanned the eastern states, on the West Coast there was prejudice and nativism against Chinese immigrants as well. America's arms have not always outstretched, welcoming "the tired, the poor, or the huddled masses yearning to breathe free."

ETHNIC ENCLAVES AND TENEMENT LIFE

As mentioned, immigrants tended to settle with others from their native land. Many did not venture far beyond the port city and clustered in what social historians call ethnic enclaves. Settling in urban areas was not only a safety net and a way to ease into American society with familiar people who were in the same circumstances, but it was also a result of nativism. Native whites preferred that immigrants be segregated and clustered in one area or part of a neighborhood.

If you want to learn how your urban ancestors may have lived when they came to America in the nineteenth and early twentieth century, **visit the Lower East Side Tenement Museum, 97 Orchard Street in Manhattan, or visit their Web site at <http://www.wnet.org/tenement>**. More than half of the entire population of New York City lived in tenements in the Lower East Side—almost 500,000 people, or about 240,000 people per square mile. If the tenement at 97 Orchard Street is typical, and apparently it is, then many of these dwellings stood five to seven stories high and were designed to house twenty or more families, each living in a three-room apartment. The largest room was the front room (living room or parlor). In the center was a kitchen, with a bedroom in the back. The entire area of an apartment was about 325 square feet. (By comparison, what's the square footage of where you live?) Consider, also, the number of people who occupied this space. Immigrant households typically included seven or more people.

The only room receiving direct light and ventilation from a window was the front living room. Until well into the mid-nineteenth century, these buildings had no toilets, no showers, and no baths. There was heat, however, from a fireplace in the kitchen (the center room). The stairway, running through the center of the building, was unlit. A series of tenement laws beginning in the late 1860s improved plumbing and ventilation conditions, but not substantially, and there were never any laws requiring the installation of electricity.

Internet Source

For More Info

For more on tenement life, see Jacob A. Riis, *How the Other Half Lives* and Oscar Handlin, *The Uprooted: The Epic Story of the Great Migrations That Made the American People.*

HEALTH AND DISEASE

From the arrival of Columbus, diseases and epidemics have plagued the country. When Europeans first invaded the American continent, they brought with them smallpox and other germs that reduced the American Indian population significantly. Not only had the Europeans brought with them childhood diseases for which Indians had no immunities, but historians now think that viruses from the domestic farm animals they brought with them—horses, pigs, cows, sheep, and goats—added to the devastation. Ironically, European colonists and missionaries viewed the rising death toll of American Indians as divine approval that it was the colonists who should inhabit the land. (See Alan Kraut's *Silent Travelers: Germs, Genes, and the "Immigrant Menace."*)

There were also diseases and germs to which the new settlers had no immunity either. Those who settled in the Chesapeake region in the 1600s, for example, fell victim to malaria, resulting in a high mortality rate. As the country became more settled, when a new disease or epidemic hit, nativists tried to place the blame on new arrivals. Philadelphians of the late 1700s experienced a yellow fever epidemic, which they blamed on German immigrants, calling the illness the "Palatine fever." Nativists blamed the cholera epidemics of 1832 and 1849 on Irish immigrants because East Coast cities were struck the hardest, and this is where a large population of Irish had settled.

By the time a cholera epidemic struck the country in 1866, physicians realized there was a connection between disease and unsanitary living conditions. This is also when tenement reform laws were enacted to provide better ventilation and sewage systems in the ethnic enclaves. Also during this time, major cities established boards of public health to monitor health matters and document outbreaks of disease (see chapter five for information on public health records).

When immigrants became ill, they typically turned to folk remedies before consulting a physician, for two reasons: First, physicians were expensive both here and in their homeland, and second, they preferred to turn to their own healthcare providers, who were familiar with their language and culture. When immigrants did require hospitalization, they preferred a hospital catering to their ethnic group, such as these two in Philadelphia: St. Mary's Hospital for Germans and St. Joseph's Hospital for Irish.

Keep in mind that diseases were not selective; when epidemics struck, they struck all nationalities, although some groups may have been hit harder. The Spanish influenza epidemic of 1918, for instance, wreaked just as much havoc on the American Indian population as it did on other groups.

For More Info

For more on this epidemic, see Alfred W. Crosby's *America's Forgotten Pandemic: The Influenza of 1918.*

IMMIGRANT CHILDREN AND CHILDREN OF IMMIGRANTS

As you are researching your immigrant ancestors, consider the effects of immigration upon children. As Selma Cantor Berrol points out on the first page of her book, *Growing Up American: Immigrant Children in America Then and Now*:

> Regardless of the time of arrival or their cultural or geographical background, children who emigrated with their parents in every period of American history suffered trauma from the loss of a familiar place, harsh conditions of travel, difficulties in finding food and shelter, dangerous illnesses, and the possibility of losing one or both parents.

In colonial America, homeless or neglected children may have arrived alone as indentured servants and served until they reached the age of twenty-one. Orphan asylums opened in America in the early 1800s and were run by religious groups such as Catholics and Jews. Ethnicity may have further subdivided these orphanages, for example, by Catholic Irish or German Catholics. Illegitimate children were often placed in orphanages. According to Berrol, American-born white women in the early nineteenth century had more children out of wedlock than any group, but of foreign-born women, it was those from the British Isles and Scandinavia who had the highest rate of illegitimacy. Italians and Jews ranked the lowest for children born out of wedlock.

To relieve some of the burden of homeless children between the 1850s through about 1930, about 200,000 children were sent from the East Coast to the West to be placed in foster homes. Known as orphan trains, the system was initiated by the New York Children's Aid Society in 1853 (see chapter five). According to Marilyn Irvin Holt in *The Orphan Trains: Placing Out in America* (pp. 69–70):

> Within the thirty-year period of 1860–1890, as many as 94 percent of the placements were of American-born or German, English, or Irish immigrant children. The number of placed out Italian children, who were Catholic, and of Jewish children, primarily from Germany or Russia, has been put at less than 1 percent.

Education in America for immigrant children was viewed as a way to assimilate them into society. One way of accomplishing this was to start calling the child by an Anglicized version of the given name: Francesco became Frank, Marguerite became Margaret, and Heinrich became Henry. Naturally, English was spoken and taught in public schools, immersing immigrant children in the language; but when immigrant children returned home, they were expected to speak their native language. As children assimilated and wanted to become more "American," however, their parents had problems communicating with them. As one Italian man later put it, "We were becoming Americans by learning to be ashamed of our parents."

Some immigrant groups, such as Italians, did not put a great emphasis on American education and had high dropout and truancy rates, since they needed the income a child could provide. Some groups may have initially preferred to send their children to parochial schools, such as Irish and German Catholics. Typically, the longer a family had been in America, the longer the children stayed in school. School records, although they may be difficult to obtain, are an important aspect of your research, especially for those children labeled "troublemakers." Write first to the school, if it still exists, which the child attended (find this out from home sources and oral history interviews). Then try the school district or state board of education to see if there is an archive of old school records. Also try local and state historical societies.

Consider also that young children worked in factories and mines in the nineteenth and early twentieth century until child labor laws were enforced. Although you may not find employment records, read social histories of the area, which may discuss child labor. In 1880, for example, more than a million children between the ages of ten and fifteen were employed, so you may find immigrant children on census records with occupations.

As you can see, our immigrant ancestors had many hurdles to overcome once they made the decision to come to America. Whether they came in the 1600s or the 1900s, they were all foreigners at one time in a new land. For those non-English-speaking immigrants who had different customs and traditions from the dominant white culture, it was an especially traumatic experience. For those who came unwillingly as slaves, and for those who were here but treated as if they had no right to be here, life was even more intolerable. With this appreciation for our ancestors' perseverance, let's now look to the records that will help document their lives.

For More Info

For more on immigrant children, see Selma Cantor Berrol, *Growing Up American: Immigrant Children in America Then and Now*; David Nasaw, *Children of the City: At Work and at Play*; and Elliot West, *Growing Up With the Country: Childhood on the Far Western Frontier*.

NAME CHANGES AND IMMIGRANT CHILDREN

Francis Wyrwicki and Johanna Urtnoski were married in 1868 near the city of Bydgoszoz. A blacksmith by trade, Francis served in the German army for three years during the Franco-Prussian War. In 1874, Francis came alone to Buffalo, New York. Johanna followed him a year later, leaving a child buried in the Old Country. From Buffalo, they moved to Duluth, then St. Paul, and finally they settled in Little Falls, Minnesota, where my great-grandfather Henry was born in 1888.

On 1 June 1909, Henry married Susan Moeglein at the Sacred Heart Church of Little Falls, Minnesota. In the newspaper announcement, the couple was presented as Mr. and Mrs. Henry Wyrwicki, but after the wedding, Henry and Susan didn't use the Wyrwicki name. They became Mr. and Mrs. Henry *Smith*. Henry's father, Francis, had been a blacksmith, known as "Smitty," and perhaps "Smith" was a reference to Francis's occupation. Four of Henry's five brothers also took "Smith" as a surname.

The Wyrwickis changed their name for age-old reasons. They didn't want to stand out as different and foreign; they wanted to fit in to mainstream American culture. And Susan may have encouraged the name change. Susan came from a prominent German-American family in Little Falls, and at that time, the Germans were seen as being higher on the social scale than the Poles, the group with the lowest status in town. Instead of Wyrwicki, the couple adopted the most generic of "American" surnames—Smith.

Henry and Susan's five children were given the surname Smith. But from the children's perspective, Smith could be a burden, too. My grandmother, Erna, the fourth of Henry and Susan's children, remembers what a difficult issue it was at report card time. Erna and her siblings all attended St. Aloysius School, where Father Joseph Wessendorf, pastor of Sacred Heart Church, acted as principal. Father Wessendorf knew that the family name should have been Wyrwicki. (There had been no legal name change.) The use of Smith bothered him, and he simply refused to use it. So when he called the students to receive their monthly report cards, he called out "Wyrwicki" and not "Smith." Susan wasn't prepared to give in either, and she instructed her children not to answer to the Wyrwicki name. So month after month and year after year, Erna would sit at her desk and not respond when the Wyrwicki name was called.

Years later, when the banns for Erna's upcoming marriage were read at mass three Sundays in a row, Father Wessendorf still insisted on using the Wyrwicki name. None of the parishioners knew who this Erna Wyrwicki was, and few realized that Erna Smith, whom they did know, was about to be married.

My grandmother, Erna, has had plenty of time to reflect on this issue of names, and today she believes she was cheated out of the name that was her birthright.

NAME CHANGES AND IMMIGRANT CHILDREN—Continued

When she talks about this issue, she says "Smith" as though she has a bad taste in her mouth. Smith is as much as an affront to her as Wyrwicki apparently was to the previous generation. And maybe it is because she feels so strongly about the family name that was denied to her that she imparted such a strong sense of history and family to me. Ironically, the rejection of the Polish name may have prompted me, Henry and Susan's great-granddaughter, to spend an inordinate amount of time in tracking down all those Polish ancestors!

—Lynn Betlock

HISTORICAL CAUSE AND EFFECT

Historical Cause	Possible Effect on Your Ancestors	Impact on Your Research
Migration Factors for the Masses	• Likely reasons to leave one country and come to another	• If you don't know why an ancestor left the homeland and came to America, why did others from that country leave and come to America? The answer will give you possible reasons your ancestors left. • If you don't know how (mode of transportation and means for travel) your ancestors got from one place to another, how did others do it?
Immigration Time Periods	• Likely arrival time frames	• If you don't know when an ancestor arrived in America, when did the vast majority of that ethnic group arrive? Start your search during this time period.
Immigration Experience of the Masses	• Likely entry points	• If you don't know at which port your ancestor arrived, where did the vast majority of that ethnic group arrive? Start your search with this port of arrival.
Chain Migration	• People did not migrate alone	• Look for other relatives or friends from the homeland who arrived before, after, or at the same time as your ancestor.
Return Migration	• May have gone back to the homeland	• If your ancestor disappears in records for an extended period, check for additional passenger arrival lists. Even if you don't note an absence in records, still check previous and subsequent passenger lists or indexes for a bird of passage.
Settlement Patterns	• Likely place where your ancestor settled	• If you don't know where your ancestor settled right after arrival, where did others of that ethnic group settle in America? Start by looking in records and indexes for that locality.
Prejudice/Nativism	• Some ancestors may hide origins (report different ethnic group or change name) • Some cluster in ethnic enclaves • Family birthrates may decline	• If oral history interviews do not reveal ethnic origins and original name, secure every possible record about an ancestor to determine these details. • Look for neighborhoods where others of your ancestors' ethnic group settled. Start your search in that area. • Look for significant gaps between the births of children. If the couple was not separated (war, return migration, etc.), then a possible reason could be reproductive control.

THREE

Published Sources

After gathering information from home sources and relatives, and as you are learning something about ethnic and immigration history, look for your ancestors in published sources. There are many compiled indexes and other reference books that could save you a few steps. For instance, you may find a published family history on one of your ancestral lines that will point you right to the immigrant ancestor and time of arrival. This was the case when I was researching the Donnally family of Gallia County, Ohio. I found a published genealogy that took me right to the name of the immigrant from Ireland.

Published references and indexes will help expedite your research on immigrants, particularly if your ancestors arrived before the twentieth century. These compilations consist not only of name indexes and references to original, contemporary records, but many of the published works will also give you historical background material. Kory Meyerink's *Printed Sources: A Guide to Published Genealogical Records* provides a comprehensive look at the materials discussed below and numerous additional resources. Keep in mind, however, that new sources are published yearly. This chapter will look at general published sources that will help in researching immigrants. **Chapter six will discuss published sources and indexes dealing with passenger lists, immigration, and naturalization records.**

See Also

You first have to find published sources in order to utilize them. Check at your public library to see if there is a genealogy section, and if not, whether another library in the next town or city may have one. Or ask at the local genealogical society meeting. Sometimes they maintain their own library. Most of the works discussed below are standard references that genealogy libraries usually have on their shelves.

Another library you may have in your area is a branch of the Family History Library, operated by the Church of Jesus Christ of Latter-day Saints (the Mormons). Though the main library is in Salt Lake City, Utah, there are branches, known as Family History Centers, throughout the world, and you may find some of the published sources there. Ask at the public library's reference section if a Family History Center is in your area, or look in the Yellow Pages under "Churches—Church of Jesus Christ of Latter-day Saints—Family History Center." If one is not listed, try calling one of the LDS churches listed. They will know if there is one in the area. Or visit the Family History Library's Web site, <http://www.familysearch.org>, for a location near you. Though the library and centers are operated by the LDS church, you do not need to be a member of the church, nor is there a fee for using the library. The only fee is if you rent microfilm or make photocopies (see chapter four).

COMPILED FAMILY HISTORIES AND GENEALOGIES

Library/Archive Source

Before you begin your search in other sources, **check to see if someone has already written and published a family history on your ancestors.** If your immigrant lineage dates back to the colonial and national periods, you will find that quite a few of these lines have already been recorded in compiled genealogies published in books, articles, and lineage society publications. Though published genealogies on recent immigrant families—those who arrived in the late nineteenth and early twentieth centuries—are few in number, you should still check for these. On the other hand, *you* may be the one to write the book you're looking for.

To discover if someone has written a book on your family, check the computer catalog of the Family History Library. At your local Family History Center, you can access the computer catalog of the library's holdings, or you can access it on the Internet at <http://www.familysearch.org/search/searchcatalog. asp>. You can search by surname and quickly see if someone has written something about your family and donated it to the Family History Library. If the book has been microfilmed, you can obtain it through their rental program; if not, then you will have to wait until you can visit the library, hire someone to look at it for you, or check other repositories for a copy.

Another place to check for a published family history is Marion J. Kaminkow's *Genealogies in the Library of Congress: A Bibliography* (two volumes and two supplements) and *A Complement to Genealogies in the Library of Congress: A Bibliography.* Many libraries have these volumes in their collection. Or they might have *Genealogy and Local History Books in Print.* First published in 1985, with supplements in 1990 and 1992, a fourth edition was published in 1995 consisting of three volumes. Now it's in its fifth edition, and contains four volumes: *Family History Volume, General Reference and World Resources Volume,* and two *U.S. Sources and Resources Volumes.*

If you still have not found a published genealogy and family history on your ancestors after checking these sources, that doesn't necessarily mean one hasn't been written. The next step is to write or check online catalogs, if available, for the library or historical society where your ancestors were known to have resided. The author may have donated a copy of the book there and nowhere else.

Analyzing a Published Family History

A word of caution about published genealogies and family histories: not all of them are equally reliable. Some may be well done, thoroughly researched, and well documented. Others may be compiled from little but family stories, contain no documentation, or may have errors in fact or omissions. When in doubt, use published family histories as clues, retrace the researcher's steps, and see if you come to the same conclusions.

Warning

Case Study

I recently found a published family history on the Carmacks titled *The Carmack Family,* by Charles W. Peckham Sr. (1998). Because, as you know from the last chapter, the origins of Cornelius Carmack have baffled family researchers for decades, I was anxious to see if Peckham had uncovered anything new. He had. Peckham postulates that Cornelius was not the immigrant ancestor, as descendants have long surmised. Instead, this author believes that Cornelius was born in Cecil County, Maryland, about 1681. Peckham also listed a possible father for Cornelius—a Christopher *Carmick,* who was born probably in Scotland in 1653 and was transported to Maryland in 1678 aboard the ship *St. George of London.* That's new information, but how accurate is it? Even though the author credits numerous professional genealogists as working on the Carmack family history, I was skeptical, considering many descendants had been working on this line for decades and never uncovered these details.

My next course of action was to analyze the source citations and the author's argument for connecting these Carmacks to one another. In looking at the sources, I noticed that some of the information came from published sources, such as abstracts of records compiled by another researcher. A rule of thumb is to use published sources as a quick and easy starting point, but you should always look at the original source whenever possible, since the abstractor may have made errors in copying the information. Sure enough, this was the case. Peckham cites an entry from V.L. Skinner Jr.'s *Abstracts of the Inventories of the Prerogative Court of Maryland, 1718–1720* (Brookeville, Md.: the author, 1991). In Skinner's work, which Peckham quoted, Skinner recorded an entry for Cornelius with the last name spelled as "*Mac*Carmack." In the original document, however, which I found on microfilm at the Family History Library in Salt Lake City, the name was recorded as Cornelius "*Mc*Carmack." While it may appear as if I'm splitting hairs, how do I know there aren't other, more significant, transcription errors? Additionally, abstractors typically highlight information they deem significant and helpful to family researchers. The original document may contain more clues or information to help you. Think of a published abstract as an index of sorts, then try to locate and view the original document (more on abstracted records on page 41).

I then looked at Peckham's argument for connecting Christopher and Cornelius as father and son. Although the author was careful to note that the identity of Christopher as Cornelius's father was "pure assumption," he apparently based this assumption solely on Christopher coming to America before Cornelius was allegedly born, and that this Christopher was supposedly the right age to be Cornelius's father. The problem was that the document Peckham cites, as will be seen later, did not give Christopher's age, so we have no idea how old he was when he came to America. Peckham admits that beyond the document recording Christopher's arrival, no other records in Maryland or surrounding states have revealed a Christopher Carmack/Carmick. Based on this information alone, I find it hard to accept Peckham's theory that Christopher was Cornelius's father, and that Cornelius was born in America (for which Peckham doesn't provide any evidence). So I'll use Peckham's work as clues, retrace his steps, and draw my own conclusions.

COMPILED GENEALOGIES IN JOURNAL ARTICLES

Another place to check is to see if anyone has written an article about your ancestors. Sometimes there isn't enough material to fill a book, so a researcher will write the information as an article and submit it to a genealogical journal. At the Family History Library or Center, or at a large genealogical library, **ask if they have the *Periodical Source Index* on CD-ROM**, also known as PERSI (pronounced purr-see). This software has the capability of searching by surname, and it will tell you what articles contain that surname. Once you have the title of the article and periodical, ask if the library has that publication. If not, you can order the article on interlibrary loan from your public library or from the Allen County Public Library, which creates PERSI. For the current photocopying fee and an order form, write to the library's Genealogy Department, P.O. Box 2270, Fort Wayne, Indiana 46802.

CD Source

I checked PERSI for Carmack. There was one article that looked promising: "Carmack Family, Frederick County, Maryland," published in the winter 1993 issue of *Maryland's Colonial Families Newsletter*. The Family History Library has a copy of this issue, but when I checked it, the two-page article merely regurgitated what everyone else had written: "Cornelius was born about 1681 in Scotland." There was also a newsletter devoted to Carmack family researchers, *Carmack Cousins*, but I was already aware of it and had been subscribing for years.

Even if you do not find an article about your ancestors, read as many articles as you can about finding immigrant origins. Though the families may not apply, the research strategies will certainly teach you how other researchers have tackled similar problems.

Case Study

STARTING WITH A FAMILY HISTORY

In 1889, seventeen-year-old John Ellert Flak (later Flack) traveled alone to the United States from Norway. He worked in the gold and copper fields of Montana for five years before settling in Little Falls, Minnesota. In 1891, fifteen-year-old Marie Halseth came from Norway with her family to join two older brothers who had already settled in Minnesota. John and Marie met, married in 1897, and eventually became my great-grandparents.

Because John and Marie were the last of my ancestors to immigrate to the

STARTING WITH A FAMILY HISTORY—Continued

United States, I was eager to make connections to Norway. When I was about twelve or thirteen, I discovered a two-page family history Marie dictated in 1937 on file at the Morrison County (Minnesota) Historical Society. As part of a WPA (Works Progress Administration) project, workers in Morrison County had interviewed residents and written brief family histories, now on file at the historical society. Marie's history contained the names and some of the birth dates and places of her parents and two of her grandparents. I wanted to verify this information, and I also wanted to trace further generations in Norway.

From the 1937 family history, I knew that Marie's mother's name was Margaret Hanson; she was born in Overhalla, Nord-Trondelag, on 2 March 1846; and her mother's name was Ingaborg Birgette Hanssen. From the Norwegian-American Historical Association in Northfield, Minnesota, I obtained an address for the *Overhalla historielag* (historical society). I wrote in English to ask for help in finding Margaret Hanson's birth record. Several months later I received a letter from the Overhalla historian. Although the birth date I provided was off by six months, he had found her.

Suddenly, Margaret Hanson became Kjerstina Margarethe Hansdatter Dahl. With that one name change, it was as if she acquired a whole new personality for me. And because of the other information the *Overhalla historielag* provided, she also acquired a father, and paternal and maternal grandparents.

The historian had one more surprise for me. When he examined the chart I sent, he noticed the name of my great-grandfather, John Flak. He wrote, "On the farm Flak, in Namsos there even is today living one John Flak, who is the son of Elias Flak. It is the same family." Although I knew John Flack had a brother and sister who remained in Norway, it simply hadn't occurred to me that any relatives would still be living on the farm that my great-grandfather left in 1889.

I immediately wrote a letter to the address the historian provided and soon received a reply from Edith, a great-granddaughter of John Flack's older brother, Haakon. She sent all kinds of family information. Most striking was a color snapshot of the farm as it looks today. I compared it with my great-grandfather's old black-and-white photo of the farm. Amazingly, all of the buildings matched precisely, as if nothing had changed in the last one hundred years.

Not long after Edith and I began corresponding, I received a letter from a great-grandson of John Flack's younger brother Ole (Fleck), who settled in Washington State. It turns out that he, too, tracked Edith down in Norway, and she gave him my address. Our branches of the family all lost touch long ago, but now, three great-grandchildren of Haakon, John, and Ole Flak have been able to get acquainted and exchange letters and photographs.

—Lynn Betlock

Printed Source

LOCAL AND COUNTY HISTORIES

While many local and county histories have a reputation for inaccurate genealogical data, **these books are excellent sources for events in your immigrant ancestor's new locality.** Besides giving you information on the churches and newspapers in the area, these histories may also provide you with ethnic distribution statistics and the boundaries of ethnic neighborhoods. Local and county histories will also give you an idea of how immigrants were viewed and received by the dominant culture.

In some recently published county histories, especially those published at our nation's bicentennial or for an anniversary of the area, there may be sketches of local people, giving immigrant origins for newcomers to America. In the *History of Elbert County, Colorado,* by Margee Gabehart, published in 1989, there is a sketch of the Ernst Wedemeyer family on page 203, which reads:

> Ernst was born Dec. 23, 1848 in Luthorat Umt Finbeck, Hanover Province, Germany, to Ernst and Johanna Kuhster Wedemeyer. . . . Ernst left Germany to escape conscription into the Prussian Army. He stowed away on a ship bound for America, arriving Feb. 28, 1867 . . . in New York City. Ernst Wedemeyer became a citizen of the United States on Sept. 13, 1870, having reached Central City, Gilpin County, Territory of Colorado.

You can't ask for much better than this. Not only does this sketch give the exact dates of arrival and naturalization, but also places. But, like using published family histories, how much of it is accurate? What troubles me is, "He stowed away on a ship bound for America." Sounds like the "stowaway myth" discussed in the first chapter. Of course, it could be true, but it is a lot more romantic and colorful to think of great-grandpa as a stowaway rather than an ordinary paying passenger. And despite all of the detail, there is no name of the ship. That seems fishy, too. A Wedemeyer descendant supplied the information, but because there are no source citations, I don't know how accurate the details are. In a case like this, it doesn't hurt to try to verify the facts, seeking published sources first, then going to original records whenever possible.

I found a published transcript of the Gilpin County, Colorado, naturalization records for 1863–1910. Sure enough, I found Ernst Wedemeyer, and he became a citizen on 13 September 1870. Since I did not have access to the original records at the time, I moved on to passenger lists. There is a series of books called *Germans to America* (see chapter six), and I checked for Ernst in the volume that covered 1867. When I couldn't find him, I checked a few years before and after. Nothing. There are no National Archives indexes to passenger arrival lists for the Port of New York for 1867, so I searched the actual lists of arrivals, page by page, for the 28th of February and a day before and a day after. Still nothing. Either the story is correct that Ernst was an undiscovered stowaway and didn't get recorded on the passenger list, or he arrived on a different date.

Using County Histories in Immigrant Research

Now let's look for Cornelius Carmack in a county history. His earliest known residence was in Cecil County, Maryland, and there were two county histories at the Family History Library in Salt Lake City: George Johnston's *History of Cecil County* (Baltimore: Regional Publishing Co., 1967), and Alice E. Miller's *Cecil County, Maryland: A Study in Local History* (Port Deposit, Md.: Port Deposit Heritage, Inc., 1949). From Johnston's *History of Cecil County* there was only one reference to Cornelius, on page 192: "The same year [1724] Cornelius McCormack prays to be allowed for eighty-six squirrels' heads and a large number of crows' heads." In other words, Cornelius was asking to be allowed to pay his taxes with these.

In Miller's *Cecil County, Maryland: A Study in Local History*, I did not find any references to Cornelius or other Carmacks in the index, but I learned something about the community in which Cornelius lived: The first permanent settlement in the county was in 1658 and "the line between Cecil and Kent [counties] as it is today was not settled until 1706." This means I may find records about the Carmacks in Kent County, too. Here's another good rule of thumb: If you aren't finding information on your ancestors in the county where they supposedly lived, check the surrounding counties. Even though your ancestors may not have moved, the boundary lines were often in constant flux in the early days of settlement. If your ancestors happened to live closer to the courthouse in the next county over, it was probably more convenient for them to handle their legal business there.

From Miller's county history, I also learned when certain ethnic groups settled in the area. The author had paragraphs on Quaker, Scotch-Irish, and Welsh settlements in Cecil County. As mentioned in chapter two, people tended to cluster with those from their homeland, regardless of when they came to America. In the paragraph on the Scotch-Irish, Miller described how a Scots preacher "rode from house to house in his lonely circuit, which extended as far down [in the county] as the Elk River." Through subsequent research I found out that one of Cornelius's granddaughters was baptized in a church in this Elk River area. So it appears that we're still on the track of someone with Scots or, more likely, Scotch-Irish heritage.

Even when you can't find your ancestors' named in a county or local history, there are still valuable clues you don't want to miss, so don't put the book back on the shelf after checking the index. While you don't have to read the history from cover to cover, look for information on everyday lifestyles, settlement patterns of ethnic groups, and geography. Besides offering you possible leads for research on your immigrant ancestors, you will be gaining background material for writing about them.

SURNAME DICTIONARIES

Surname dictionaries list names alphabetically and tell you not only how the name is pronounced, but also background information of the name, such as its

Case Study

Reminder

Definitions

origins and history. General surname dictionaries will give you clues to a surname's national origin. Foreign surname dictionaries may be more specific, noting regions of the country where the name is prevalent, along with variant spellings. This information, used in combination with the data you have found in genealogical and social history sources, may help pinpoint the origins of your immigrant ancestors. Remember, though, that the name you have may not be the original spelling.

Using Surname Dictionaries

Case Study

Time to go back to Cornelius Carmack and see if a surname dictionary will help with his origins. I began with a general dictionary, such as the *Penguin Dictionary of Surnames*, but it did not list Carmack. So I looked under some spelling variations: Cormack, Karmack, Kormack, and with the prefix Mc and Mac, since some of the records of Cornelius have revealed that spelling. I struck out on the other spellings, but there is a McCormack, and the origins are given as "Irish and Scots Gaelic." Let's see if we can get more information by consulting name dictionaries specifically for Scottish and Irish names. From *The Book of Ulster Surnames*, by Robert Bell (Belfast and St. Paul, Minn.: The Blackstaff Press, 1988), there is still no Carmack or Cormack; the only variant that comes close is MacCormick:

> MacCormick, if taken on its own, constitutes one of the fifty most common names in the province [of Ulster]. MacCormack is much less numerous but is none the less common. Both names can be of Irish or Scottish origin and the difference in the ending is irrelevant in determining which. Both derive from the Gaelic name Cormac. In Ulster the names are most common in counties Antrim and Down.
>
> In Scotland the name derives from one of the Gaelic forms Mac Cormaic, Mac Cormaig or Mac Chormaig. As a generalisation the -ick spelling was more common in the Highlands. . . .
>
> In Ireland the name sprang up independently in a variety of places adopted by individuals whose father was called Cormac. . . .
>
> In counties Down and Derry MacCormack is sometimes originally O'Cormack or O'Cormacan. In mid-nineteenth-century Co. Antrim Mac-Cormick was found almost exclusively in the barony of Carey. At the same time in Down it was almost exclusive to the Ards peninsula.

In Edward MacLysagnt's *The Surnames of Ireland*, sixth edition (Dublin, Ireland: Irish Academic Press, 1991), he lists MacCormack:

> This like MacCormican is formed from the forename Cormac. This name is numerous throughout all the provinces, the spelling MacCormick being more usual in Ulster. For the most part it originated as a simple patronymic. . . . Many of the MacCormac(k) families of Ulster are of Scottish origin, being a branch of the clan Buchanan-MacCormick of MacLaine.

Finally, in Donnchadh Ó Corráin and Fidelma Maquire's *Irish Names* (Dublin, Ireland: The Lilliput Press, 1990):

Cormacc: Cormac (*Kur-mok*) Cormac is perhaps the tenth most popular name in early Ireland. The well-known name Cormac is probably a compound of Corbb and Macc "a son."

What about the name Cornelius? Could its origins be Irish or Scottish? I found two dictionaries of Scottish forenames. Leslie Ann Dunkling's *Scottish Christian Names* (London and Edinburgh, Scotland: Johnston and Bacon, 1978), says:

Cornelius (m) A name more associated with Ireland, where it anglicises Conchobhar, "high will." It also occurs as Connor. Cornelius was [the] 91st most frequently used name in Scotland in 1935. It is now rarely used.

Donald Wythe in *Scottish Forenames* (Toronto: Ontario Genealogical Society, 1986), concurs:

Cornelius. . . . The name has never been prolific in Scotland.

So what does all this mean regarding Cornelius Carmack's possible origins? The name Cornelius is more popular in Ireland, and the surname Carmack (or its variation) was more popular in Ulster, or Northern Ireland, but had its origins in Scotland. As you will see from the discussion on the Scotch-Irish in Part II, these were Scottish people who were forced out of Scotland in the seventeenth century and settled for several generations in Ulster in the north of Ireland. From there, many immigrated to America in the early to mid-1700s. The American term Scotch-Irish distinguishes these people from Catholic Irish and Scots. Four factors, so far, confirm the hypothesis that Cornelius was Scotch-Irish: the origins of his first and last names; his appearance in Cecil County, Maryland, records in 1718, a time when many Scotch-Irish were beginning to arrive in America; a Scotch-Irish settlement in Cecil County, Maryland, during the time Cornelius lived there; and his descendants' migration pattern from Maryland to southwestern Virginia to Tennessee to Missouri.

BIOGRAPHICAL AND GENEALOGICAL COMPENDIA

Biographical and genealogical compendia are works that contain information on several individuals or families. Typically, the individuals or families treated are unrelated; the common bond for inclusion is an ethnic background, time period, or place. *Who's Who* books are good examples of biographical compendia. Look for ones focusing on ethnic backgrounds, such as *Who's Who Among Italian Americans*. Another source is the American Genealogical-Biographical Index, which is an every-name index to about 850 genealogical and biographical sources. An example of a genealogical compendium is Henry Z Jones's *The Palatine Families of New York: A Study of the German Immigrants Who Arrived in Colonial New York in 1710*. In this work, Jones not only identifies the German immigrants who were in colonial New York in 1710, but he also gives genealogies of the families.

Of particular note is a biographical/genealogical compendium known as the

\di'fin\ *vb*

Definitions

Great Migration study (the "Great Migration" usually refers to the arrival of colonial English Puritans). Sponsored by the New England Historic Genealogical Society under the direction of Robert C. Anderson, the Great Migration Study Project produces brief biographical and genealogical sketches of all those people known to have come to New England between 1620 and 1643, the majority of seventeenth-century immigrants to this region of the country. The study accumulated material scattered among several reference works and from original, contemporary records to provide a description of the settlement process in the New England colonies.

Two publications are produced in conjunction with this study. First, there is the *Great Migration Newsletter*. Each issue features news of the project, a bibliography of relevant new articles and books, information on new source material, plus an in-depth article on one of the towns settled during the Great Migration, such as Lynn, Charlestown, Roxbury, Salem, Picataqua, Ipswich, and Hartford. Subscriptions and back issues are available through the New England Historic Genealogical Society (see Appendix B).

The second publication is the meat of the study: *The Great Migration Begins: Immigrants to New England, 1620–1633*. This three-volume set is the most accurate, up-to-date information on more than nine hundred early New England families. It includes information on each individual or family; their port or county of origin, if known; the date and ship on which they arrived in New England, if known; the earliest known record of the individual or family; their first residence and subsequent residence, when known; return trips to their country of origin, whether temporary or permanent; and marriages, births, deaths, and other important family relationships. The volumes are arranged alphabetically by last name, and this is an ongoing project. A continuation of the volumes will cover more years of the Great Migration, starting with arrivals in 1634 and 1635.

LINEAGE SOCIETY APPLICATION PAPERS AND LINEAGE BOOKS

As mentioned in chapter two, many lineage societies were founded to honor and record early American ancestry. Those with an ancestor who came on the *Mayflower* might join the General Society of Mayflower Descendants; or if you have an ancestor who was one of the first colonists in America, you might join the National Society, Daughters of the American Colonists; or if you are a male and can prove descent (following an unbroken male line) from a Dutchman who was a native or resident of New York or the American colonies before 1675, you might join the Holland Society of New York.

When someone wants to become a member of, say, the Jamestowne Society, the applicant must fill out a lineage society application "proving" ancestry to an ancestor who was a stockholder in the Virginia Company of London or was a settler at Jamestown or was on Jamestown Island before 1700. Along with filling out this generation-by-generation application, starting with the applicant and working backward to the qualifying ancestor, the applicant must supply

For More Info

For more on lineage societies and their addresses, see Grahame Thomas Smallwood Jr., "Tracking Through Hereditary and Lineage Organizations," in *The Source: A Guidebook of American Genealogy*, edited by Loretto Dennis Szucs and Sandra Hargreaves Luebking.

proof for all statements of fact—that is, births, marriages, deaths, and the evidence that links one generation to another. Applicants must furnish copies of contemporary documents (see chapter five), such as vital records, wills, and land records, and information from reliable secondary sources, such as documented published family histories. Until about ten to twenty years ago, many of the lineage societies were lax about the type of evidence or proof that was acceptable. Today, qualified genealogists examine each application to ensure accuracy of the lineage.

Tip

Application papers can be invaluable to your research, since they may provide you with clues or references to documents that will uncover your immigrant ancestor. Many of the societies have restrictions on releasing application papers, however. For instance, to obtain papers from the Daughters of the American Revolution, you must be a prospective member.

Some lineage societies also publish rosters or lineage books, listing their members and the ancestors on whom they joined the organization and the lineage. Included in the preface of some of these works is how you may obtain application papers from the society. Some examples of these books are the *National Society of the Colonial Daughters of the Seventeenth Century, Lineage Book* series; *Mayflower Families Through Five Generations* series; *The Order of Founders and Patriots of America Registers*; and *Lineages of Members of the National Society of the Sons and Daughters of the Pilgrims*.

RECORD ABSTRACTS AND TRANSCRIPTIONS

To make records more accessible to more people, genealogical societies or individuals adopt projects to abstract or transcribe a group of records in a given locality or for a specified time period, then publish them. Court records—wills and deeds in particular—are records commonly compiled in this fashion, as are transcriptions of tombstone inscriptions. You can also find abstracts of other records, such as newspapers, that may have an ethnic focus. *The Search for Missing Friends: Irish Immigrant Advertisements Placed in the Boston Pilot* (seven volumes; Boston: New England Historic Genealogical Society, 1989–1999) is one such example. The ads often identify the Irish townland and parish of thousands of immigrants who were seeking relatives already here. The ads below are from Volume IV: 1857–1860, page 315:

\di'fin\ *vb*

Definitions

A transcript is a verbatim copy of a record or tombstone; whereas, an abstract is only the pertinent parts of a document.

20 November 1858 *Information Wanted*

Of Michael Sullivan, of parish Toumplenow [co. Kerry], who sailed from Liverpool on the 15th of April, 1848, landed in Boston May 15th, and worked with Baily and Halden; when last heard from, 4 years ago last June, was in Brooklyn, Indiana. Please address his brother Jeremiah, Xenia, Green County, Ohio.

Of Bridget Carroll, (maiden name Mulvey) of Ballinakill [co. Cork], who landed in Baltimore about 7 years ago; when last heard of she was in Washington, D.C.,—about going to New York. Information received by her sister, Mary Hinds, care of Robert Faulkner, 99 Elliot Street, Boston, Mass.

The Family History Library has an extensive collection of published record abstracts and transcriptions. While on a research trip there, I looked for published abstracts and transcripts of records for Cecil County, Maryland, to check for Cornelius Carmack. There weren't many for the time period when Cornelius was living there. The one I did find, *Land Patents of Cecil County, Maryland*, compiled by the Genealogical Society of Cecil County in 1986, did not list Cornelius in the index. But I won't stop there; I'll still check the index to the actual land records. Keep in mind that I won't just look for the surname to be spelled as Carmack. I'll also check variant spellings: Cormack, Carmick, Cormick, McCarmack/Cormack and -ick, and MacCarmack/Cormack and -ick.

GAZETTEERS AND PLACE-NAME DICTIONARIES

Definitions

\di'fin\ *vb*

Suppose you find among family papers a letter your great-grandmother wrote to her sister, and in it she mentioned how much she misses their mother in Münchenbuchsee. But that's it. Naturally, Great-Grandma didn't say where Münchenbuchsee was located because she and her sister knew where it was. But how can you find out? **One way is to consult a world gazetteer or a place-name dictionary, which are alphabetical listings of places.** The *Columbia Lippincott Gazetteer of the World*, published in 1952, is one you might find in your local library's reference section. You may also find gazetteers or geographical dictionaries for countries, such as *The Imperial Gazetteer of Scotland* and *Cassell's Gazetteer of Great Britain and Ireland*, which will give more detail. In the *Columbia Lippincott Gazetteer of the World*, there is a listing for Münchenbuchsee, which gives the precise location of the town, as well as the industry of the area:

> Münchenbuchsee, residential town (pop. 2,248), Bern canton, NW Switzerland, 5 mi. SW of Gera; woolen and rayon milling, carpet mfg. Has 16th-cent. moated castle.

Warning

There may be several places with the same name, however, so it is important to get as much information about the area where the immigrant came from through oral history interviews and other sources. Also be aware that the native name and the English translation may be significantly different. For example, we know Deutschland as Germany and Eire as the Republic of Ireland. The same is true of town names: Firenze is Florence and Kobenhavn is Copenhagen. Travel guidebooks will likely give both the foreign name and the English spelling.

Another aspect to consider is that some places may be known by more than one name or a nickname. This is true even today in America: the Big Apple (New York City) and the Windy City (Chicago). Usually a town underwent a name change when another country took over and translated the name into its language. For instance, when the Dutch ruled New York, Brooklyn was called Breuckelen. The same is true of towns in foreign countries. By reading histories of the area and talking with people in an ethnic genealogical society, you can determine the names of localities for the time period when your ancestors lived there.

Many books are now being published electronically on CD-ROM and made available on the World Wide Web. In fact, the Internet may have been the place where you picked up the genealogy bug in the first place. I'm afraid Norton doesn't make an antivirus for this computer bug, so you may as well turn the page and learn what else you can explore on the computer.

For More Info

For more tips on identifying foreign place names and using gazetteers and maps, see the Family History Library's 1992 research outline, "Tracing Immigrant Origins," available for a small fee at the Family History Library in Salt Lake City or any of its worldwide centers.

FOUR

Computer Databases

Many genealogists get involved in tracing their ancestry because they have a personal computer. Someone may have given you, or you may have purchased, a genealogical software program to enter your family data into the computer. Or, like so many people, your interest was sparked because of the Internet. With the age of technology comes an endlessly growing number of databases of genealogical information and records.

"Networking" with fellow researchers has always helped genealogists. In the past, it was done using telephone directories and written correspondence—a time-consuming task. Today genealogical networking is greatly facilitated and accelerated thanks to the Internet.

Sources

See Christina K. Schaefer, *Instant Information on the Internet! A Genealogist's No-Frills Guide to the 50 States & the District of Columbia*; Cyndi Howells, *Netting Your Ancestors: Genealogical Research on the Internet*; Thomas Kemp, *Virtual Roots: A Guide to Genealogy and Local History on the World Wide Web.*

THE INTERNET

New genealogy sites hit the World Wide Web daily. From the comfort of your home, you can access thousands of Web sites, giving you information on genealogical organizations, libraries, databases, record abstracts, and images. For new and seasoned genealogists alike, however, this brave new world can be overwhelming. After all, I've heard that there are more than one million Web sites and home pages. So what's on the Internet for genealogists researching their ethnic heritage? How do you gain access to it? How can you communicate with other researchers?

Because Web sites come and go and new ones are added daily, it would be impossible to provide a listing of every Web address that will be of use to you in your search. The best I can do is guide you to some of the more established sites. You may also want to look at some guidebooks on the topic of Internet searches.

One new site is sponsored by the Boston History Collaborative and is known as the Boston Family and Immigrant History Project, <www.BostonFamilyHist ory.org>. This site offers databases of neighborhood information, demographic statistics, ethnic patterns of immigration to Boston over the last four centuries, historical time lines, and a directory of activities and organizations that represent Boston's various ethnic communities today. Phase One includes information on six groups: African Americans, Chinese, Irish, Italians, Jews, and Puerto Ricans. Eventually, every Boston ethnic group will be represented. The collaborative will also help facilitate specific family and immigrant history searches.

There are several Internet sites also geared toward genealogy and family history, such as Family Tree Magazine, Ancestry.com, and Cyndi's List of Genealogy Sites. **Family Tree Magazine's site, <http:www.familytreemagazine.com>, is one of the best starting points because of its SuperSearch feature.** With a single click, you can search some of the most popular genealogical databases. The site offers free E-mail service and links to many genealogy sites. There is also an online bookstore, magazine, electronic newsletter, and courses in writing personal and family memoirs

Internet Source

Ancestry.com, <http://www.ancestry.com> or <http://www.myfamily.com>, has a free E-mail newsletter and several free databases, such as the Social Security Death Index. For a subscriber's fee, you can access hundreds of databases (indexes to records in which you may find your ancestors), with new databases being added daily.

Cyndi Howells maintains Cyndi's List, <www.cyndislist.com>, with links to more than forty-two thousand sites in more than one hundred categories, a quarter of which deal with ethnic and foreign research. Her list is updated daily, so addresses are as current as possible. (See Cyndi Howells, *Cyndi's List: A Comprehensive List of 40,000 Genealogy Sites on the Internet.*) It is well worth your time to explore her site; in fact, her site is one that you could visit a hundred times and there would still be something new to explore.

Another notable site is Immigrant Ships Transcribers Guild, <http://istg.roots web.com/>. This group of volunteers has been transcribing ships' lists from the 1600s to the 1900s, and currently there are three thousand lists available. You can search by the name of the passenger (remember to check variant spellings), the name of the ship, the port of arrival or departure, captain's name, or date. Even though three thousand lists sound like a lot, this is barely a fraction of what is available on microfilm (see chapter six), but the site is still worth checking.

A Word of Caution About the Internet

A serious concern among many established genealogists, who have been in this field long before the computer age, is that there is now a growing group of "computer" genealogists who are Internet-dependent. **They think what they find on the Web is all there is and all they need.** It is true that a number of historical records have been and are being digitized and made available on the Internet. You can even find photographs, newspaper accounts, family Bible records, and *diaries* on the Internet. (Now there's a comforting thought. Someday after you're gone, one of your thoughtful descendants may put *your* diary on the Internet for the whole world to read! Isn't technology *wonderful*?)

Warning

Most of what you will find on the Internet are indexes or databases to the original documents housed in repositories around the country. It is these actual documents you need to examine to research your family history. I don't care how big the Web becomes, it will never have every record available for search. Even the Family History Library cannot boast having every record, and they have more than two million rolls of microfilmed records, equal to more than six million written volumes, and about 700,000 microfiche with even more records, not to mention the thousands of books in their collection, too.

In a 14 July 1999 article in *USA Today* on the use of the Internet and learning about medical conditions, apparently some doctors are just as frustrated about the online explosion as some genealogists. Dr. Adelaide Nardone, a gynecologist in New York, said, "We're not browsing the Internet—we're . . . working. I'm touching people. I'm checking bone density. I'm checking mammograms. I'm not browsing the Internet." A number of genealogists would agree. We're at the libraries and courthouses and archives. We're searching deeds. We're searching probate files. We're searching censuses. We're not browsing the Internet—we're *researching*.

The Internet is a research tool and should be used as such. There is an incredible amount of material available at your fingertips in the virtual world, but there is even more in the real world waiting for you to explore. So please don't stop with your computer.

ONLINE LIBRARY CATALOGS AND BOOKSTORES

Other areas on the Internet that you may find particularly valuable for your research are library catalogs and bookstores. Not only will these save you time before you make a research trip to a particular library, but you can locate books and order them through your library's interlibrary loan service. Or you can purchase used and hard-to-find books. Here are four used bookstore sites:

Advanced Book Exchange	http://www.abebooks.com
Alibris	http://www.alibris.com
Bibliofind	http://www.bibliofind.com
Powell's Used Bookstore	http://www.powells.com

Barnes and Noble, <http://www.barnesandnoble.com>, also has a significant used and out-of-print stock search service. Although Amazon.com has a great selection of new books, as of this writing, it does not carry used and out-of-print books.

Internet Source

Many libraries and archives are now making their catalogs, guides, and indexes available on the Internet. The National Archives in Washington, DC, for example, has made available its microfilm catalog guides for census records, black studies, military records, passenger arrival records, and genealogical and biographical research at <http://www.nara.gov/>. You can also browse the catalog of the Library of Congress at <http://www.loc.gov>. Many state archives have put online indexes to vital records. Millions of people received federal land, and some of those records can be viewed on the Bureau of Land Management's

Web site (see chapter five under Land Records). The Immigration and Naturalization Service also has a Web site for general information, <http://www.ins.usd oj.gov>, as does the Bureau of the Census, <http://www.census.gov>. Also look for Internet catalogs of public and university libraries and state historical societies, which may help you with information on the social history of the ethnic group.

CD-ROMs

CD Source

The use of CD-ROMs to electronically publish genealogical data grows daily, too, since several volumes of books can be contained on one CD-ROM. Most are available for purchase, but the cost may be prohibitive. You can find many CD-ROMs available at public, university, and genealogical libraries. The types of things you'll find on CD-ROM are directories, maps, databases (indexes) to genealogical records, and digitized records such as censuses. These are not limited to American resources; you will also find collections for foreign materials on CD-ROM and passenger lists indexes, such as Family Tree Maker's CD #354, *Family Archives: Passenger and Immigration Lists Index, 1538–1940* (1999 update). By reading genealogical publications and getting on the mailing lists of the genealogical book vendors listed in the appendix, you will learn of items published on CD-ROM. This is another good reason to join an ethnic genealogical society—no doubt new electronic publications will be discussed at their meetings and in their periodicals. (See Marthe Arends's *Genealogy on CD-ROM.*)

THE FAMILY HISTORY LIBRARY

Library/Archive Source

The largest genealogical library in the world is the Family History Library in Salt Lake City, Utah, owned and operated by the Church of Jesus Christ of Latter-day Saints (LDS). It is open to everyone at no cost. If you can't make a trip to Salt Lake City, many of the holdings of the library are available through its worldwide branches, called Family History Centers, and there is probably one near you. To find the location, either check with the Family History Library (see Appendix B), look in your local yellow pages under churches, or check their Internet site at <http://www.familysearch.org>.

Internet Source

Called FamilySearch, there are a number of computer databases available to search either at the main library, at its worldwide centers, or on the Internet at <www.familysearch.org>. Along with the Family History Library Catalog, which lists all of the holdings of the library, those databases of particular value for immigrant research are the Ancestral File, the International Genealogical Index, the Social Security Death Index, and if you have Scots ancestry, Scottish Church Records.

International Genealogical Index

Because of its international scope, the Family History Library's International Genealogical Index (IGI), available on CD-ROM at the library or its centers, on microfiche, and on the Internet, is an important research tool for immigrant origins. The IGI contains birth, christening (baptismal), marriage, and LDS-temple ordinance dates for about 160 million deceased persons, but these people are not linked into family groups or pedigrees as they are in the Ancestral File, discussed below. As with any resource that bridges the ocean, though, you must gather enough information on the immigrant ancestor (original name and approximate birth year) from original records in America in order to confirm you have the right person in foreign sources. Keep in mind, also, that the IGI is an index (hence the name "International Genealogical *Index*"). You should always pursue the source of the entry, which may be an original, contemporary record or a published compilation. To do this, copy all of the information (or make a printout), and then ask the librarian to help you find or order the appropriate microfilm.

Cornelius Carmack was on the IGI for the British Isles; in fact, he had a couple of listings. Most showed him born in 1681 in Scotland; one showed him born in 1671 in Ireland. For all of the entries, I pressed the key that would give me a full record, including a reference to the source of information. Each had the following under Source Information: "Record submitted by LDS Church member. No additional information is available on the [micro]film. Ancestral File may list the same family with the submitter's name and address." So, I'll try that.

Ancestral File

The Family History Library's Ancestral File links individuals into families and pedigrees, offering you clues for immigrant research. LDS members and non-LDS members may submit their genealogical research to be included in this database. But like published genealogies and family histories, researchers need to analyze the information and reference citations, if there are any, for accuracy and completeness.

This database is simple to use: Type in an ancestor's name and birth year. The question is whether or not someone has submitted the information you seek. Though there are a multitude of pedigrees, you may not find your family. Not everyone's ancestry is represented, and it's a good thing; otherwise, genealogy would be no fun at all.

If you do find information, however, you can either make a printout or download the data onto a floppy disk in a GEDCOM file. (A GEDCOM file is one that most genealogical software programs recognize.) It will also give you the name and address of the submitter, so you can contact that person for the sources of the information (that is, assuming the address is still current and the person is still living). Remember, the information is only as good as the researcher who submitted the material. Not all genealogists are created equal!

To submit your ancestral information to Ancestral File, send a copy of your genealogy on a floppy disk using either Personal Ancestral File software or another software compatible with Ancestral File to the Family History Department, Attn: Ancestral File Contributions, 50 East North Temple Street, Salt Lake City, Utah 84150-3400.

I found Cornelius Carmack on the Ancestral File. The only source of information was to the person who submitted the data—a gentleman in Nashville, Tennessee. He had sent copies of his family group sheets to the Family History Library, which then microfilmed them. I checked the microfilm. The family group sheet for Cornelius Carmack didn't give me any new information about him or his family, but the submitter cited as a source another published family history, *Hurley and Glover Genealogies*, by Gwen Newton Ketrenos, published in 1981, which I was unfamiliar with. But in checking it, I did not find any new information.

Social Security Death Index

Social Security was established in 1935. The Family History Library's Social Security Death Index contains files on more than forty-two million deceased people who had Social Security numbers and whose deaths were reported to the Social Security Administration. It covers deaths from 1962 (when the Social Security Administration began computerizing its records) to the present (or whatever date the most recent edition is), although there may be some records from as early as 1937. You may also purchase this index on CD-ROM from several of the genealogical vendors (see Appendix B) or access it via the Internet at <http://www.ancestry.com>.

The information contained in the Social Security Death Index varies slightly, but typically you'll find the person's name, date of birth, date of death, the state of residence when the person applied for a Social Security number, and the place where the death was reported. You may print out or download the information onto a floppy disk in a GEDCOM file.

You do not need to know a person's Social Security number to gain access to the records. Simply type in the person's name. Using the information obtained from the Death Index, you may then send for the original form SS-5, "Application for a Social Security Number" (discussed in chapter five), as well as the person's death certificate, which will not only confirm the identity, but also give you more clues and information for further research.

Scottish Church Records

Another easy-to-use database is the Scottish Church Records, which indexes names extracted from the Old Parochial Registers of Scotland and other records of the Presbyterian Church of Scotland. Most of the records date from the late 1500s to 1854, but there are some from as late as 1900. The index includes birth, christening, and marriage information. Once again, you merely type in a name and date, but it is helpful if you also know parents' names and a parish in Scotland. If you find a match, the database will give you the name of the shire in order to search for church records.

Not surprisingly, I checked for Cornelius in this database under all the variant spellings I had for his last name. Unfortunately, there were no matches. I also looked for a Christopher Carmack, since the published family history had linked him to Cornelius. Still no entries.

ELLIS ISLAND DATABASES

Today, almost half of the country's population can trace its ancestry to the peak years of immigration (1892–1924) through Ellis Island, the major immigrant receiving station. During that time, some twelve million people who entered America were processed at this site. Ellis Island was reopened as an immigration museum in 1990, with more than two million visitors annually. (See Appendix A.) There are three computer databases generated by the Statue of Liberty-Ellis Island Foundation as described below.

American Immigrant Wall of Honor Database

One of the most widely publicized aspects of Ellis Island is the American Immigrant Wall of Honor. More than 500,000 names of ancestors are listed, each placed by a relative or descendant who donated one hundred dollars or more toward the Island's restoration. In order to be included on the Wall of Honor, immigrants did not have to arrive through Ellis Island nor during a specific time. You may find colonial immigrants on the wall, too. These names are also found in a computer database inside the museum, so that visitors can discover who made the donation and subsequently contact that person. Donations are still being accepted, so if you would like to honor you immigrant ancestor or family, see the address in the appendix or visit the Web site. For this particular database, you do not need to go to Ellis Island to access it. You may view it on the island's Web site at <http://www.ellisisland.org>. Keep in mind, however, that the volunteered information is not verified. Surnames have various spellings, dates may be incorrect, and given names may be mistranslated. Like other databases, use it for clues and to contact the submitter.

Oral History Interviews

Another source of information is a collection of taped interviews with immigrants and former employees of the island. These were collected during the restoration years and are still being collected. Ellis Island staff members have been seeking immigrants and former employees who were on the island during its operation to get their experiences on record.

With these interviews, you learn about the Ellis Island experience from someone who lived it and also about the voyage and conditions in the homeland. Through a computer on Ellis Island, you can access the interviews using a person's name, country of origin, time period, or topic. There is also a printed index to the interviews, which is available at the Family History Library. Some interview transcripts are available on microfilm at the FHL or through a Family History Center (Voices from Ellis Island: An Oral History of American Immigration, eight reels, FHL catalog #1689050-57). The interviews are arranged in order of interview number, for example, "No. 010, Santiofer, Rebecca, Ostrow, Poland, July 1920, New York, New York. Interview by Nancy Dallett, 31 January 1985, 38 pp." Even if your ancestor was not interviewed, you can still hear or read about someone else who came to this country during the same time period and from the same country. No doubt that person's experience will be similar to your own ancestor's. Also look for the book *Ellis Island Interviews: In Their Own Words*, by Peter Morton Coan.

The American Family Immigration History Center

The American Family Immigration History Center is still in preparation at this writing. When completed and opened to the public, it will contain valuable genealogical data for discovering Ellis Island ancestry. The research facility, funded by corporate, foundation, and private contributions, will use state-of-the-art technology to house computerized immigration records for the millions of people who came through the Port of New York between 1892 and 1924.

The material is being gathered from ships' passenger arrival lists, then transferred to a giant database. Visitors to Ellis Island will be able to obtain copies of the actual lists, as well as photographs of the ships. This database will also be available at the Family History Library and at its worldwide Family History Centers. Eventually, the American Family Immigration History Center will offer the capability to link, through the Internet, to other genealogical research facilities in this country and abroad.

Beginning your genealogical investigations with published sources, indexes, and computer databases will save you countless hours of research later. Although the information found in these resources could contain transcription or other recording errors, it will provide you with clues and a place to start, and will lead you to the original, contemporary records.

FIVE

Researching in Records

For More Info

For more on how to evaluate records, see Elizabeth Shown Mills, *Evidence! Citation and Analysis for the Family Historian.*

C ontemporary records are documents created at, or close to, the time of an event (for example, censuses, vital records, deeds, passenger arrival lists, city directories, newspapers, and so forth). Just because the record is a contemporary one, however, does not mean that it is completely accurate. All records, whether created by an eyewitness or not, can contain errors. This is one reason genealogists seek as many records as they can about their ancestors. Part of your research is to evaluate the information in documents to determine which information most likely is correct.

You can access records in many ways: through correspondence, on microfilm, in person, or by hiring someone to retrieve them for you. Depending on the repository, you may view historical documents in their original form or on microform (microfilm or microfiche). Many of these sources will reveal data or clues about your immigrant ancestor's village of origin, immigration, or naturalization. Resources of particular value for your immigrant research are highlighted below, but for more in-depth discussions, study general genealogical guidebooks, such as Val Greenwood's *The Researcher's Guide to American Genealogy,* third edition, or Loretto Dennis Szucs and Sandra Hargreaves Leubking's *The Source: A Guidebook of American Genealogy.*

CEMETERY AND MORTUARY RECORDS AND TOMBSTONES

You may find a village or country of origin engraved on an ancestor's tombstone or listed in funeral home/mortuary records. **Many nineteenth- and twentieth-century immigrant groups preferred to engage the services of a funeral home whose owner was of the same nationality or originated from the same region in the homeland.** These morticians retained the funeral practice customs of the Old Country. Most death certificates and often the obituary named the mortuary that handled the funeral arrangements. If not, look at city directories for

Tip

Figure 5-1
Headstone of Catherine Maguire. Native of Co. Monaghan. Ireland. Died Dec. 27, 1889. Aged 68 Years. St. Mary's Cemetery, Greenwich, Connecticut.

names and addresses of undertakers in your ancestors' neighborhoods or of your ancestors' ethnic group. Funeral home or mortuary records are considered private records; generally, you can gain access to them by writing, phoning, or visiting the funeral home. In some cases, the funeral home may not give out information unless you prove that you are a relative. For a funeral home that has gone out of business, check with nearby funeral homes for the records or at libraries and historical societies. Besides trying to identify the funeral home, see if you can determine the monument maker, who may have also retained records. Also, remember to look for published cemetery transcriptions.

A frequently overlooked clue to immigrant origins is the artwork and decoration on the grave memorial. German Americans used figures of women and angels to reflect their overwhelming sense of loss and sadness. Catholic Irish Americans favored the Celtic Cross, the Virgin Mary, or the sacrificial lamb on the altar as sculptures. Jewish Americans utilized the Star of David, perhaps

For More Info

For more on ethnic grave markers, see Kenneth T. Jackson and Camilo Jose Vergara, *Silent Cities: The Evolution of the American Cemetery*, and Richard E. Meyer, *Ethnicity and the American Cemetery*.

Figure 5-2
Headstone of Margial Fuentes. *Fallecio Junio 4, 1930. A 25 años de edad.* Oak Creek Cemetery, Oak Creek, Colorado.

Figure 5-3
Headstone of D. Hongyo. June 16, 1876. June 4, 1937. Oak Creek Cemetery, Oak Creek, Colorado.

Figure 5-4
Headstone of Frank Beni. Born Oct. 23, 1901 in Gigliana Italy. Died Jan. 12, 1942. Oak Creek Cemetery, Oak Creek, Colorado.

accompanied by Hebrew or Yiddish script. Italian Americans displayed crosses and other religious statues (angels, saints, Christ, etc.) as memorials. They also frequently imbedded into the tombstone a specially prepared, tile photograph of the deceased. Spanish-speaking Americans (Spanish, Mexican, Puerto Rican, and Cuban) decorated their gray granite markers by painting them with bright yellows, reds, greens, and blues. Look for separate sections in large cemeteries for ethnic groupings or members of organizations.

CENSUSES

Federal Population Schedules

The U.S. government began taking a count or census of the population in 1790 and has done so every ten years ever since. The schedules between 1790 and 1840 listed by name only the head of the household, with tabulations for family members according to sex and age. Of these early schedules, 1820 and 1830 asked for the total number in the household who were foreign-born but not naturalized, but there is no way to tell which persons this total referred to. Starting in 1850, every member of the household was recorded by name, along with a place of birth for each person, except for slaves and Indians not taxed. While genealogists would like to find a specific origin listed, you will more likely find only the name of the country as the place of birth. Occasionally, however, the census taker provided more information than was required and may have recorded a village of origin.

Information in each federal census varied from decade to decade, with the schedules of the peak immigration years giving the most information. The first census to give clues to immigration was 1870. (See the sections in Part II for information on special American Indian and slave schedules.) Below is a summary, beginning with 1870, of questions in the federal censuses relating to immigration and ethnicity:

1870   race; birthplace of each person and whether the parents were foreign born; male citizens (including naturalized citizens) over twenty-one who could vote

1880   race; birthplace of person and parents; supplemental schedule for American Indians

1900   race; birthplace of person and parents; if foreign-born, year of immigration and whether naturalized; ability to speak English (See Figure 5-5 on page 56)

1910   race; birthplace and mother tongue of person and parents; if foreign-born, year of immigration, whether naturalized, and whether able to speak English, and if not, language spoken

1920   race; if foreign-born, year of immigration to the United States, whether naturalized, and year of naturalization; birthplace of person and parents; mother tongue of foreign born; ability to speak English

1930   race; birthplace of person and parents; if foreign-born, language spoken in home before coming to United States, year of immigration, whether naturalized, and ability to speak English; for American Indians, whether of full or mixed blood and tribal affiliation

1940   race; birthplace; citizenship of foreign-born

1950   race; birthplace; if foreign-born, whether naturalized

1960	race
1970	race
1980	race; Spanish/Hispanic origin or descent
1990	race; birthplace; Spanish/Hispanic origin; citizenship, immigration; ancestry or ethnic origin

Tip

Abbreviations used in the naturalization column included "Na" for naturalized; "Pa" for first papers (declaration of intention) filed; "Al" for alien; or "NR" for not reported.

Federal censuses are governed by privacy laws and are restricted for a period

Note columns 16, 17, and 18 under the heading "Citizenship." These ask of each person enumerated the "Year of immigration to the United States," "Number of years in the United States," and "Naturalization." "Pa" means the first papers or declaration of intention had been filed. "Al" stands for alien. "Na" means the person was a naturalized citizen.

TWELFTH CENSUS OF THE UNITED STATES.

SCHEDULE No. 1.—POPULATION.

Supervisor's District No. Massachusetts

Enumeration District No. 1320

Sheet No. 1 A

Name of Institution,

Ward of city, 11

Precinct 9.

town, or village, within the above-named division, Boston

Enumerated by me on the 4th day of June, 1900, Edward E. Hoxie, Enumerator.

Name	Relation	Color	Sex	Month	Year	Age	Marital	Birthplace	Father's birthplace	Mother's birthplace	Year of immigration	Years in U.S.	Naturalization	Occupation
Cullen, John	Head	W	M	Sept	1844	55	Wd	Ireland	Ireland	Ireland	1871	29	al	Teamster
" Patrick	Son	W	M	June	1877	22	S	Massachusetts	Ireland	Ireland				Wire worker
" John	Son	W	M	Oct	1880	19	S	Massachusetts	Ireland	Ireland				Blacksmith
" James	Son	W	M	May	1881	19	S	Massachusetts	Ireland	Ireland				Blacksmith
" Katherine	Daughter	W	F	Oct	1883	16	S	Massachusetts	Ireland	Ireland				
" Augustine	Son	W	M	Aug	1886	13	S	Massachusetts	Ireland	Ireland				School
Beattie, James	Head	W	M	Aug	1872	27	M	Ireland	Ireland	Ireland	1897	3	al	Laborer (Coal Wharf)
" Mary	Wife	W	F	Apr	1873	27	M	Ireland	Ireland	Ireland	1897	3		
" Francis	Son	W	M	Aug	1899		S	Massachusetts	Ireland	Ireland				
Mackey, Patrick A.	Boarder	W	M	Nov	1861	38	S	Ireland	Ireland	Ireland	1878	12	al	Groom
Salmon, Thomas	Lodger	W	M	July	1857	42	S	Massachusetts	Ireland	Ireland				Stableman
Ward, James	Lodger	W	M	Sept	1870	29	S	Ireland	Ireland	Ireland	1889	10	Na	Coachman
Dillworthy, John J.	Lodger	W	M	Aug	1862	37	S	Massachusetts	England	England				Coachman
O'Neal, Patrick	Lodger	W	M	Mar	1873	27	S	Ireland	Ireland	Ireland	1884	16	al	Stableman
Tully, Arthur	Lodger	W	M	Aug	1869	30	S	Ireland	Ireland	Ireland	1894	5	Pa	Stableman
Finnegan, Barney	Lodger	W	M	Aug	1880	19	S	Ireland	Ireland	Ireland	1899	1	al	Stableman
Nylander, Gottfried	Head	W	F	May	1872	28	Wd	Ireland	Ireland	Ireland	1890	9		Boarding House
" Eleanor F.	Daughter	W	F	Feb	1899		S	Massachusetts	Sweden	Ireland				
" Dorothy	Daughter	W	F	Apr	1899	1	S	Massachusetts	Sweden	Ireland				
" Carl G.	Brother-in-law	W	M	Nov	1865	34	M	Sweden	Sweden	Sweden	1892	8	al	Machinist
"	Sister-in-law	W	F	Aug	1876	23	M	Norway	Norway	Norway	1895	6		
O'Shay, Patrick M.	Lodger	W	M	Mar	1873	27	S	Ireland	Ireland	Ireland	1892	8	na	Choreman
Crane, Bernard	Head	W	M	Feb	1852	48	M	Canada (Eng)	Ireland	Ireland	1882	18	na	Gardner
" Annie	Wife	W	F	Dec	1856	43	M	Canada (Eng)	Ireland	Ireland	1882	18		
" James J.	Son	W	M	Jan	1880	20	S	Canada (Eng)	Canada (Eng)	Canada (Eng)	1882	18		
" Jennie M.	Daughter	W	F	June	1881	18	S	Canada (Eng)	Canada (Eng)	Canada (Eng)				
" Nellie	Daughter	W	F	Aug	1886	13	S	Massachusetts	Canada (Eng)	Canada (Eng)				
" Thomas F.	Son	W	M	Dec	1888	11	S	Massachusetts	Canada (Eng)	Canada (Eng)				
" Annie	Daughter	W	F		1892	7	S	Massachusetts	Canada (Eng)	Canada (Eng)				
Kerr, James	Head	W	M	Mar		34	M	Ireland	Ireland	Ireland	1888	11		
" Jeanne L.	Wife	W	F	Nov	1871	28	M	France	France	France	1890	10		
" Linton	Son	W	M	May	1896	4	S	Massachusetts	Ireland	France				
" Albert J.	Son	W	M	Sept	1897	2	S	Massachusetts	Ireland	France				
Lange, John H.	Head	W	M	June	1842	57	M	New York	Germany	Germany				Choreman
" Frances	Wife	W	F	Jan	1853	47	M	Canada (Eng)	Dist of Columbia	England	1867	33		
" Susie F.	Daughter	W	F	Dec	1872	28	S	Massachusetts	New York	Canada (Eng)				Telephone operator
Flood, Patrick	Head	W	M	July	1837	62	M	Ireland	Ireland	Ireland	1844	55	Na	Prop. Boarding Stable
" Mary E.	Wife	W	F	May	1839	61	M	New York	New York	New York				
" Marguerite O.	Daughter	W	F	Feb	1889	11	S	Massachusetts	Ireland	New York				At School

Under "Nativity," even though only the country of origin is listed, in this enumeration, the census taker recorded the nationality ("Eng.") for those from Canada.

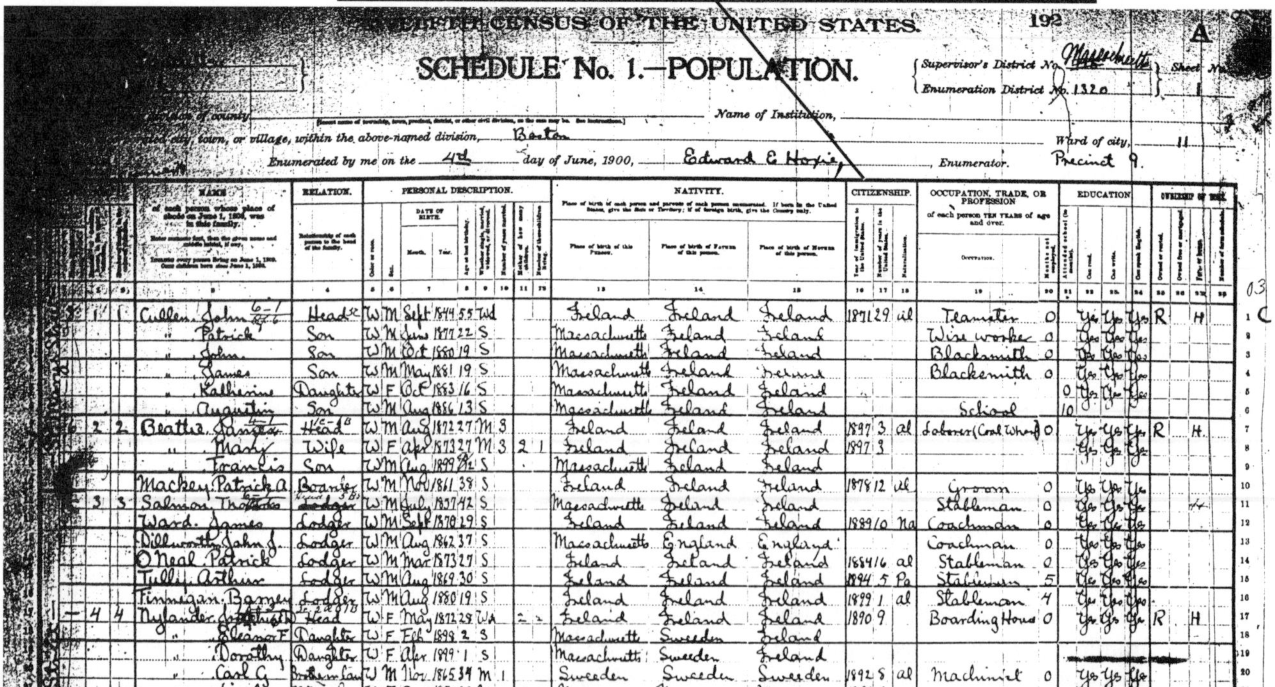

Figure 5-5
1900 federal population schedule, Massachusetts, Suffolk County, Boston, ward 11, enumeration district 1320, sheet 1, NARA microfilm T623, roll 681.

of seventy-two years from the date the census was taken. Schedules for 1790–1920 are open to the public for viewing; the 1930 census will be released in 2002. (Visit the 1930 Census Web page at <http://www.nara.gov/genealogy/1930cen.html> for more information.) There are several repositories around the country that have either all U.S. censuses or a portion thereof: the Family History Library (or you can order them through one of their Family History Centers); the National Archives in Washington, DC, or one of their regional records services facilities (see Appendix B); libraries with major genealogical collections, such as the Dallas Public Library or the Allen County Public Library in Fort Wayne, Indiana; or, if you have access to a microfilm reader at a public library, you can order them through a lending library, such as Heritage Quest or the National Archives microfilm rental program (see Appendix B).

Census Indexes

Most of the censuses are indexed in one manner or another. For 1790–1860, published indexes are available for all states; for 1870, many states are indexed. These are usually available wherever censuses are available for searching, and many are now being put onto CD-ROM. The 1880 through 1920 census indexes are available on microfilm (see below for limitations) in a coded indexing system called the Soundex; in 1910, it was called Miracode, but it worked on the same principle.

The Soundex is based on the way a name sounds rather than how it is spelled, so that names with similar sounds will be coded together. This indexing system is important for you to learn, since other federal records, such as passenger arrival lists, may use the Soundex as well. All surnames are coded using the first letter of the surname, followed by a three-digit number, like this one for Carmack: C652. Before going step by step through how this works, here is how the letters are coded with numbers:

THE NUMBER:	REPRESENTS THE FOLLOWING LETTERS:
1	B P F V
2	C S K G J Q X Z
3	D T
4	L
5	M N
6	R

The letters A, E, I, O, U, W, Y, and H are disregarded. And the first letter of a surname is not coded; it is used as the first part of the code. You only code the first three consonants in a name.

Let's say that I am searching for the surname Gordon. In order to Soundex it, I would start with the first letter of the surname, G, which is not assigned a numeral. Then I would cross out all of the vowels, as well as *w*, *y*, and *h*:

Step By Step

GⵁRDⵁN

Now I am left with the consonants, *r*, *d*, and *n*, which I will convert to numerals. *R* becomes a 6, *d* becomes a 3, and *n* becomes a 5; so the Soundex code for Gordon is G635. Let's try another example: Vallarelli. New rules will apply to this name, but let's begin with the basics. The first letter is not coded, so the Soundex will begin with the letter *V*. Now we cross out all of the vowels, as well as *w*, *y*, and *h*.

VALLARELLI

We're left with *l, l, r, l, l*. Now here's the next new rule: if you have double consonants or two consonants together after crossing out the vowels, then one of them will not be coded. So we are now going to cross out two of the *l*s.

VALLARELLI

Now we're left with just *l, r, l*. So the Soundex code for Vallarelli is V464.

More new rules: If you have more than three consonants left, code only the first three and ignore the rest. If you have less than three consonants, add zeros. For example, Lee would be coded L000, since it only has vowels and no consonants.

If the surname has a prefix, like in DeBartolo, code it both with the prefix (D163) and without it (B634), since the Soundex is not consistent as to whether the indexer coded it with or without the prefix.

At first, this system seems difficult and confusing, but remember that wherever you go to view the census and use the Soundex system, there will be an attendant or volunteer who will help you code your surnames. **Or, you can visit the National Archives Internet site, <http://www.nara.gov/genealogy/soundex/soundex.html>, type in your surname, and it will code it for you.**

Internet Source

After you have coded the surname, go to the microfilmed index for the appropriate census year, state, and code. On the film, you will see index cards arranged by the code numbers, then alphabetically by the *first* name of the head of the household. The reason the cards are arranged like this is because all the surnames have similar sounds and spellings. Copy all of the information from the Soundex card, including county, enumeration district, sheet and line numbers, since this will lead you to the actual census. Do not stop with just the Soundex card; there are lots more data on the census. (See Figure 5-6 on page 59.)

Not all of the censuses for 1880 through 1920 have complete Soundexes, however:

1880   Soundex indexes exist for all states, but indexes only households with children age ten and under
1900   Soundex indexes exist for all states
1910   Soundex (or Miracode) indexes exist for only twenty-one states: Alabama, Arkansas, California, Florida, Georgia, Illinois, Kansas, Kentucky, Louisiana, Michigan, Mississippi, Missouri, North Carolina, Ohio, Oklahoma, Pennsylvania, South Carolina, Tennessee, Texas, Virginia, and West Virginia

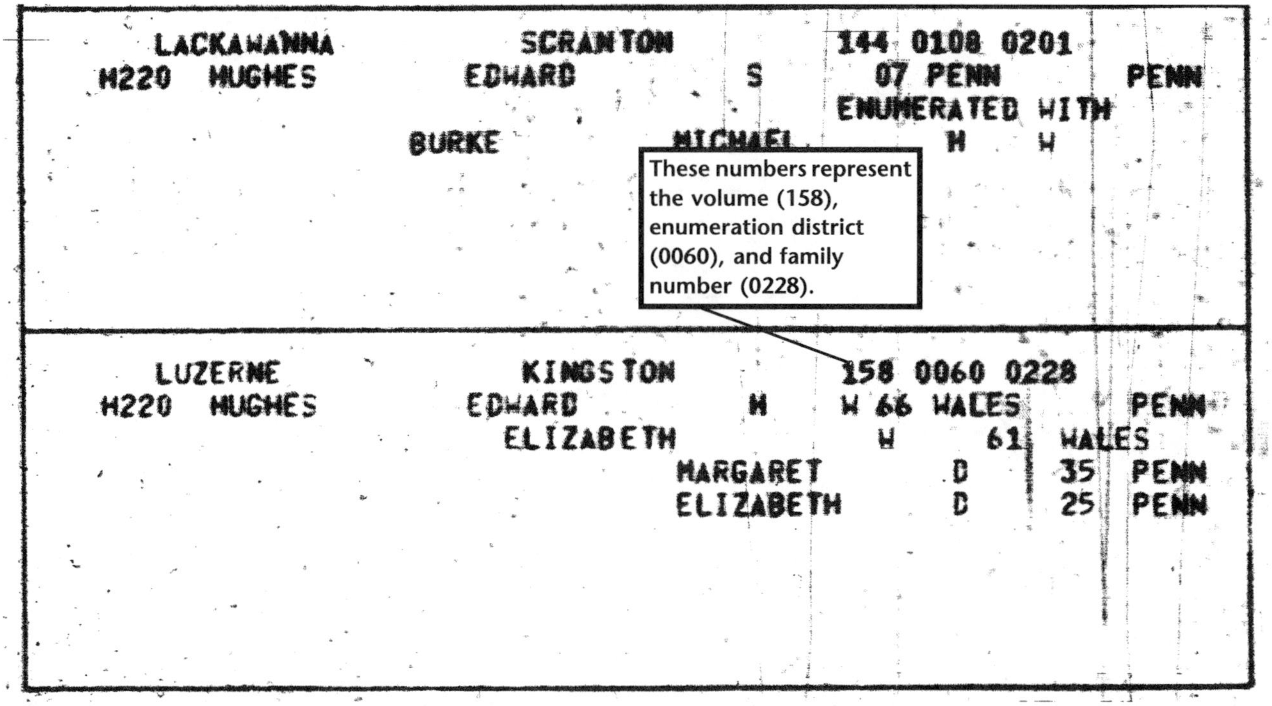

LACKAWANNA   SCRANTON   144 0108 0201
H220 HUGHES   EDWARD   S   07 PENN   PENN
                                                ENUMERATED WITH
              BURKE   MICHAEL   H   H

These numbers represent the volume (158), enumeration district (0060), and family number (0228).

LUZERNE   KINGSTON   158 0060 0228
H220 HUGHES   EDWARD   H   W 66 WALES   PENN
                    ELIZABETH   W   61 WALES
                          MARGARET   D   35 PENN
                          ELIZABETH   D   25 PENN

Figure 5-6
These are index cards (Miracode) for the 1910 census. Use the same coding method for the Soundex as you would for this index. The first line gives the county, then the town or city, then a group of numbers.

1920   Soundex indexes exist for all states (See Figures 5-7 on page 60)

1930   Soundex indexes exist for Alabama, Arkansas, Florida, Georgia, part of Kentucky (the counties of Bell, Floyd, Harlan, Kenton, Muhlenberg, Perry, and Pike), Louisiana, Mississippi, North Carolina, South Carolina, Tennessee, Virginia, and part of West Virginia (the counties of Fayette, Harrison, Kanawha, Logan, McDowell, Mercer, and Raleigh)

Census records are the most commonly used source in genealogy because the schedules reveal so much information. **Start with the most recent census available—1920 as of this writing—then try to locate your ancestors on all censuses, moving backward in time until the point of arrival.**

Keep in mind that the information on each census may or may not be completely accurate. Suppose you find your ancestor on the 1920 census, showing she immigrated in 1895. Then you check the 1910 census, and it lists 1897 as the arrival year. In 1900, the year of immigration is 1895 again. Which do you believe? I would say it's probably 1895, not because two out of three censuses agreed, but because I would be more likely to trust the census that was made closest to the time of arrival. This is not a foolproof method, though. Since the name of the person who supplied the information to the census taker is not included on the census, it could be that the person who reported 1895 was wrong, and the 1897 date is actually correct. One thing is certain, however; you at least have some dates with which to begin searching other records and perhaps you will find a more precise arrival time.

Research Tip

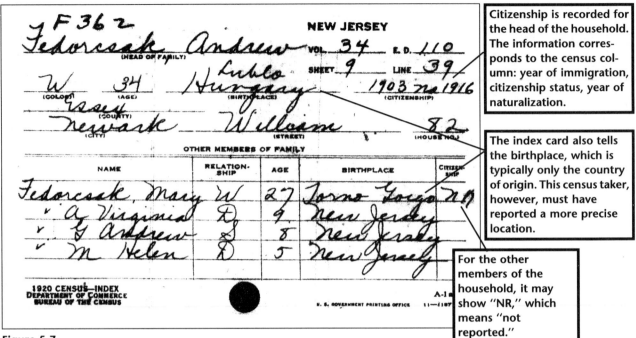

Figure 5-7
This is an index card (Soundex) for the 1920 census. Although the index gives you much information, remember to go to the actual census page for more details about the family.

Mortality Schedules

Mortality schedules list the people who died during the twelve-month period prior to the official census date, or more precisely, for the time span of 1 June through 31 May of 1849–1850, 1859–1860, 1869–1870, and 1879–1880. These federal schedules were taken for the census years 1850, 1860, 1870, and 1880. Some of these schedules have been indexed on microfiche (available through the Family History Library), and some are indexed on CD-ROM. If your immigrant ancestor was considerate enough to die during one of these twelve-month periods for these census years, make sure you check the mortality schedules, even though omissions occurred. These schedules will give you the name of the deceased, sex, age, color, whether free or slave, marital status, place of birth (state, territory, or country), month the death occurred, occupation, disease or cause of death, and the number of days ill. (See Figure 5-8 on page 61.)

Slave and Indian Schedules

See the sections for African Americans and American Indians in Part II.

1880 Defective, Dependent, and Delinquent Schedules

A little-used source is the 1880 Schedule of Defective, Dependent, and Delinquent (DDD) Classes. Ancestors may be found in the DDDs under the headings for insane, idiots, paupers in almshouses, in jails or prisons, as homeless children, or those who were blind, deaf, or mute. These individuals are also enumerated in the population schedules, but without all the information found in this specialized enumeration. If an ancestor was listed as insane and currently an inmate of an

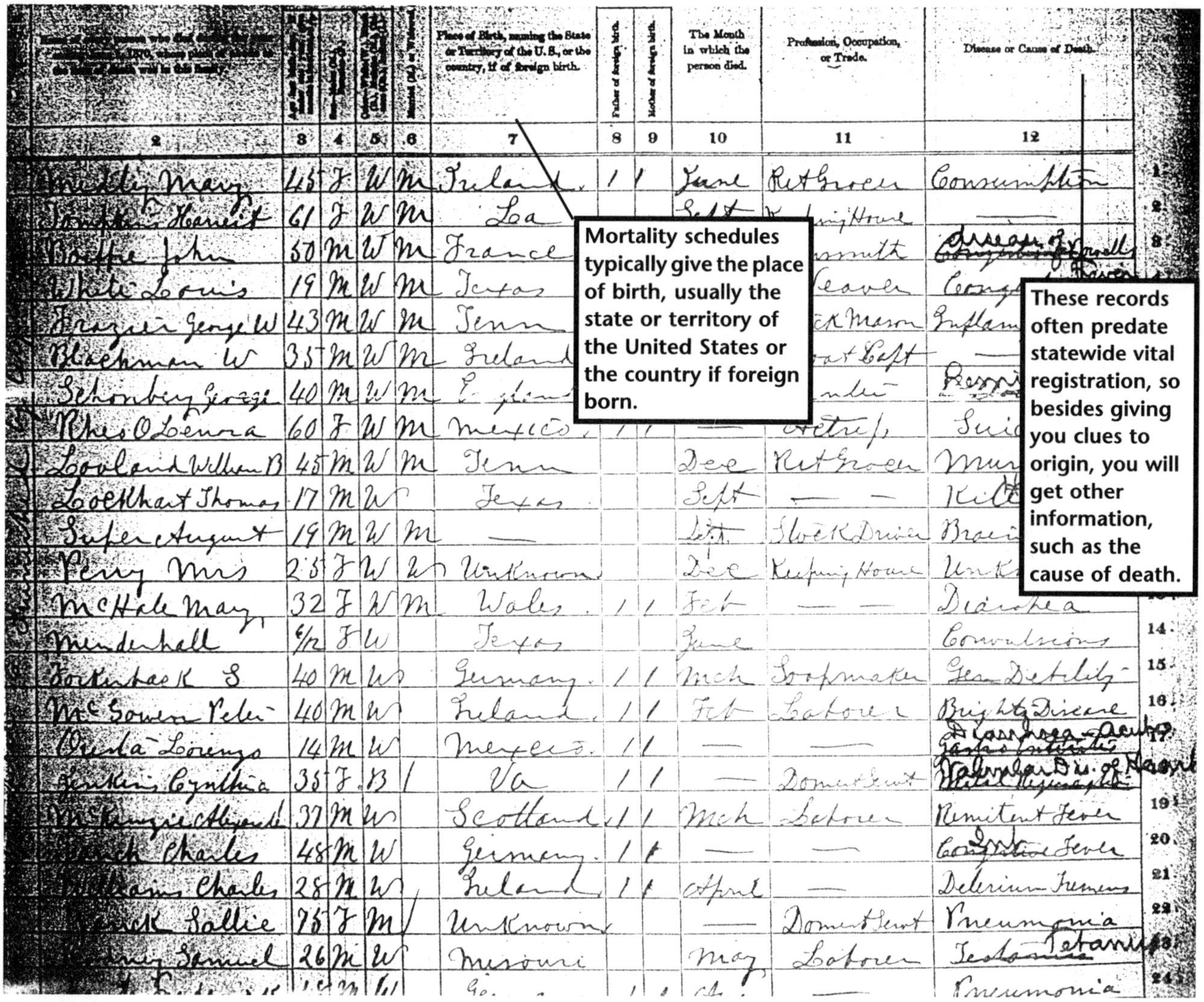

Figure 5-8
1870 federal mortality schedule, Texas, Harris County, Houston, page 5, FHL 1421045.

insane asylum, for example, check the regular population schedules for that institution for more information. See Ruth Land Hatten's "The 'Forgotten' Census of 1880: Defective, Dependent, and Delinquent Classes" in the March 1992 issue of the *National Genealogical Society Quarterly* for availability of these schedules. These schedules do not have an index, but they are easy to search. You must know the county or city in which your ancestors lived, however.

Manufacturing/Industry Schedules

If your immigrant ancestor owned a business, manufacturing/industry schedules are important to your research. And if your ancestor didn't, they're still important. Look at the manufacturing schedules for the area in which your ancestor lived. It will give you a marvelous sense of the time period. No doubt your ancestor patronized some of these businesses. Armed with the names of the businesses in your ancestor's area, you may be able to find some old account books that list your ancestor and purchases.

The type of information you may find on the manufacturing/industry schedules varies depending on the year, but generally you will learn about the manufacturing, mining, fisheries, mercantile, commercial, and trading businesses in the community. The name of the company or owner is given along with the kind of business, capital invested, quantity and value of materials, labor, machinery, and products.

The first manufacturing schedule was taken in 1810, but unfortunately, most of these have been lost. There are a few among the population schedules for this time. The second was taken in 1820. None was compiled in 1830, and for 1840 only statistical information was recorded with nothing but tallies remaining. Between 1850 and 1870, they were referred to as industry schedules, but in 1880 they were called manufacturing schedules again (1880 no longer survives). There were subsequent manufacturing/industry schedules, but these were destroyed by Congressional order.

The 1820 schedule asked for the name of the owner, location of the establishment, number of employees, kind and quantity of machinery, capital invested, articles manufactured, annual production, and general remarks on the business. These schedules are arranged alphabetically by county within each state and are part of the National Archives Record Group 29—twenty-seven rolls of microfilm with an index on each roll. There is also a published index: *Indexes to Manufacturers' Census of 1820: An Edited Printing of the Original Indexes and Information* (Reprint, Knightstown, Ind.: Bookmark, no date).

The information on the schedules of 1850, 1860, and 1870 include data on manufacturing, mining, fisheries, and every mercantile, commercial, and trading business with an annual gross product of five hundred dollars or more. These listed the name of the company or owner, the kind of business, capital invested, quantity and value of materials, labor, machinery, and products.

Important

Agricultural Schedules

Many immigrant ancestors were farmers, so these schedules are extremely important. The agricultural schedules give you a glimpse of your ancestor's farm life, right down to the numbers and kinds of produce and livestock. The enumerations are especially important if you have two men with the same name living in the same community because, after all, no two people would own the same number of acres of land with the exact same livestock.

Though enumerations were taken from 1850 to 1910, only the 1850, 1860, 1870, and 1880 schedules are available to the public. The 1890 schedule went up in smoke with the 1890 population census. The 1900 and 1910 agricultural schedules were destroyed by congressional order.

Farms with an annual produce worth one hundred dollars or more were enumerated in 1850 and 1860. For the 1870 and 1880 schedules, farms with three acres or more or with an annual produce worth five hundred dollars or more were enumerated. The schedules list the name of the owner, agent, or tenant; and the kind and value of acreage, machinery, livestock, and produce.

State Census Records

Just as the federal government took a count of the population every ten years, some states took an enumeration between federal census years. New York, for example, took state censuses in 1825, 1835, 1845, 1855, 1865, 1875, 1892, 1905, 1915, and 1925, and these are all open to the public. In some state census schedules, you will also find information pertaining to immigration, citizenship, and ethnicity. (See Figure 5-9 on page 64.) **These enumerations are important for descendants of birds of passage, who may get missed on the federal censuses.** State census data used in conjunction with federal census information will help you establish the composition and travels of an immigrant family, telling you who was born when and where. See Ann Lainhart's *State Census Records* for a state-by-state listing of these schedules and their availability. Few of these state censuses have indexes, so you will need to narrow your search as much as possible—using an exact address, for instance, learned from city directories—if you are trying to find someone in an urban area.

Important

CHURCH RECORDS

Although each religious denomination is different in the types and availability of records, you may find clues to immigrant origins in church records. New arrivals were likely to attend churches that offered services in their native language and were located within walking distance of their homes. The church marriage record is a likely place to find the town of origin, rather than just the name of the country. This is especially true if the church represented a specific nationality, or if the officiating minister was of the same nationality as the marrying couple. You may also find among church records letters of transfer or letters of introduction. During oral history interviews with family members, try to learn not only your ancestors' religions, but also names and locations of churches they attended in America and in the homeland, if possible. Funeral prayer cards, death notices, and obituaries may give the name of the church to which an ancestor belonged. You may also find the name of a minister on some civil marriage records or in obituaries, which will lead you to a church. City directories can also help locate churches in your immigrant ancestor's neighborhood. Some churches may have a historical archive where records have been deposited, but start with the individual parish. Church records are not public records, so access to them may not always be possible, but you should try.

CITY DIRECTORIES

A city directory is an alphabetical list of inhabitants in a given locality. Though it is an invaluable tool, directories may be frustrating to use since, like many sources, there was no set and universal standard. The information they contained and their availability varied from city to city and from one time period to another. Most directories were issued annually, but some smaller communities published them sporadically.

\di'fin\ *vb*

Definitions

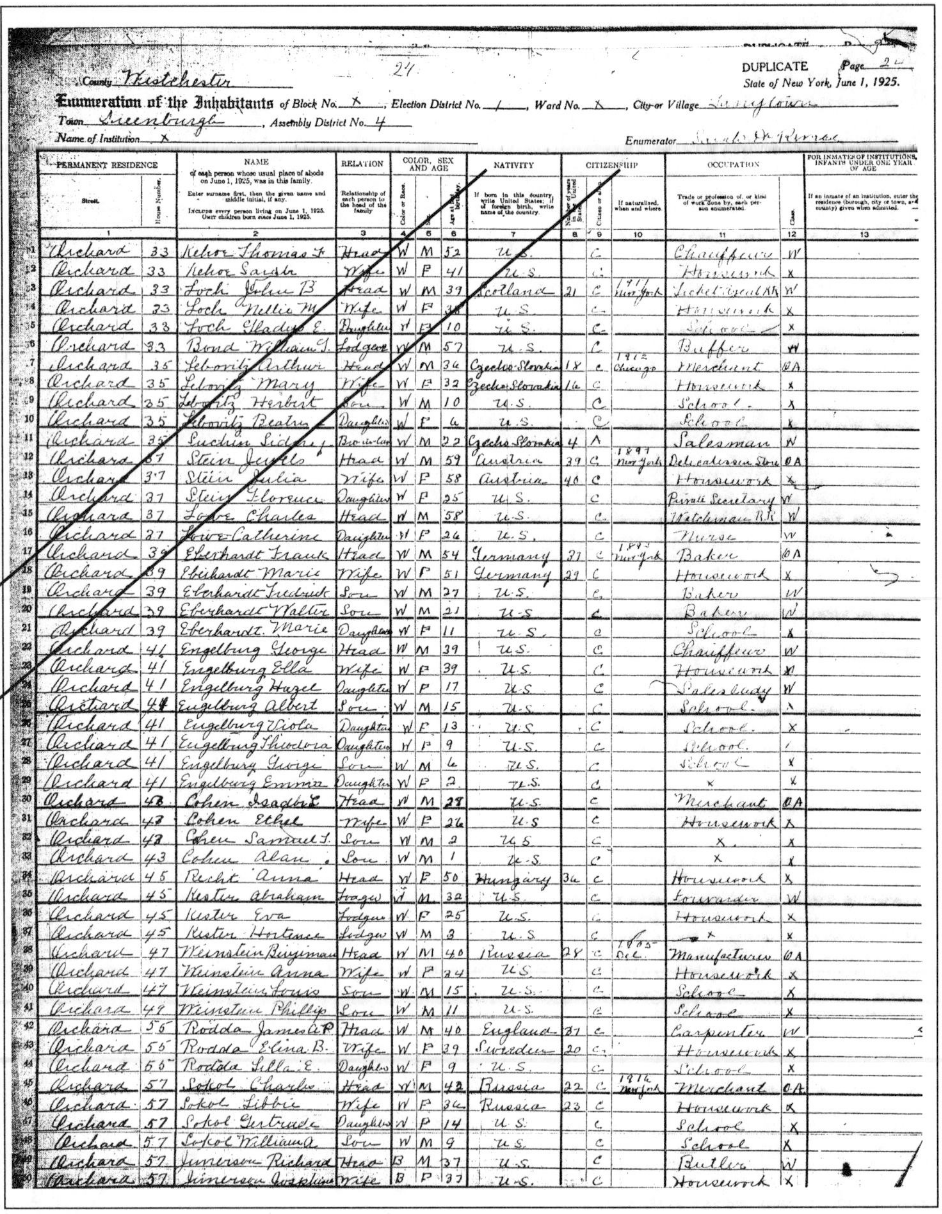

DUPLICATE Page 24
State of New York, June 1, 1925.

County Westchester
Enumeration of the Inhabitants of Block No. X, Election District No. 1, Ward No. X, City or Village Tarrytown
Town Greenburgh, Assembly District No. 4
Name of Institution X
Enumerator

Street	House Number	Name	Relation	Color	Sex	Age	Nativity	Years in U.S.	Citizen or alien	If naturalized, when and where	Occupation	Class	13
Orchard	33	Kehoe Thomas F.	Head	W	M	52	U.S.		C		Chauffeur	W	
Orchard	33	Kehoe Sarah	Wife	W	F	41	U.S.		C		Housework	X	
Orchard	33	Loch John B	Head	W	M	39	Scotland	21	C	1911 New York	Ticket Agent RR	W	
Orchard	33	Loch Nellie M	Wife	W	F	38	U.S.		C		Housework	X	
Orchard	33	Loch Gladys E.	Daughter	W	F	10	U.S.		C		School	X	
Orchard	33	Bond William J.	Lodger	W	M	57	U.S.		C		Buffer	W	
Orchard	35	Lebowitz Arthur	Head	W	M	34	Czecho-Slovakia	18	C	1912 Chicago	Merchant	OA	
Orchard	35	Lebowitz Mary	Wife	W	F	32	Czecho-Slovakia	16	C		Housework	X	
Orchard	35	Lebowitz Herbert	Son	W	M	10	U.S.		C		School	X	
Orchard	35	Lebowitz Beatrice	Daughter	W	F	6	U.S.		C		School	X	
Orchard	35	Suchin Sidney	Brother-in-law	W	M	22	Czecho-Slovakia	4	A		Salesman	W	
Orchard	37	Stein Jewels	Head	W	M	59	Austria	39	C	1891 New York	Delicatessen Store	OA	
Orchard	37	Stein Julia	Wife	W	F	58	Austria	40	C		Housework	X	
Orchard	37	Stein Florence	Daughter	W	F	35	U.S.		C		Private Secretary	W	
Orchard	37	Lowe Charles	Head	W	M	58	U.S.		C		Watchman RR	W	
Orchard	37	Lowe Catherine	Daughter	W	F	26	U.S.		C		Nurse	W	
Orchard	39	Eberhardt Frank	Head	W	M	54	Germany	31	C	1895 New York	Baker	OA	
Orchard	39	Eberhardt Marie	Wife	W	F	51	Germany	29	C		Housework	X	
Orchard	39	Eberhardt Frederick	Son	W	M	27	U.S.		C		Baker	W	
Orchard	39	Eberhardt Walter	Son	W	M	21	U.S.		C		Baker	W	
Orchard	39	Eberhardt Marie	Daughter	W	F	11	U.S.		C		School	X	
Orchard	41	Engelburg George	Head	W	M	39	U.S.		C		Chauffeur	W	
Orchard	41	Engelburg Ella	Wife	W	F	39	U.S.		C		Housework	X	
Orchard	41	Engelburg Hazel	Daughter	W	F	17	U.S.		C		Saleslady	W	
Orchard	41	Engelburg Albert	Son	W	M	15	U.S.		C		School	X	
Orchard	41	Engelburg Viola	Daughter	W	F	13	U.S.		C		School	X	
Orchard	41	Engelburg Theodora	Daughter	W	F	9	U.S.		C		School	X	
Orchard	41	Engelburg George	Son	W	M	6	U.S.		C		School	X	
Orchard	41	Engelburg Emma	Daughter	W	F	2	U.S.		C		X	X	
Orchard	43	Cohen Isador E.	Head	W	M	28	U.S.		C		Merchant	OA	
Orchard	43	Cohen Ethel	Wife	W	F	26	U.S.		C		Housework	X	
Orchard	43	Cohen Samuel J.	Son	W	M	2	U.S.		C		X	X	
Orchard	43	Cohen Alan	Son	W	M	1	U.S.		C		X	X	
Orchard	45	Recht Anna	Head	W	F	50	Hungary	34	C		Housework	X	
Orchard	45	Kester Abraham	Lodger	W	M	32	U.S.		C		Forwarder	W	
Orchard	45	Kester Eva	Lodger	W	F	25	U.S.		C		Housework	X	
Orchard	45	Kester Hortance	Lodger	W	M	3	U.S.		C		X	X	
Orchard	47	Weinstein Benjamin	Head	W	M	40	Russia	28	C	1905 Del.	Manufacturer	OA	
Orchard	47	Weinstein Anna	Wife	W	F	34	U.S.		C		Housework	X	
Orchard	47	Weinstein Louis	Son	W	M	15	U.S.		C		School	X	
Orchard	49	Weinstein Phillip	Son	W	M	11	U.S.		C		School	X	
Orchard	55	Rodda James A.P.	Head	W	M	40	England	31	C		Carpenter	W	
Orchard	55	Rodda Elina B.	Wife	W	F	39	Sweden	20	C		Housework	X	
Orchard	55	Rodda Lilla E.	Daughter	W	F	9	U.S.		C		School	X	
Orchard	57	Sokol Charles	Head	W	M	42	Russia	22	C	1914 New York	Merchant	OA	
Orchard	57	Sokol Libbie	Wife	W	F	36	Russia	23	C		Housework	X	
Orchard	57	Sokol Gertrude	Daughter	W	F	14	U.S.		C		School	X	
Orchard	57	Sokol William	Son	W	M	9	U.S.		C		School	X	
Orchard	57	Jimerson Richard	Head	B	M	37	U.S.		C		Butler	W	
Orchard	57	Jimerson Josephine	Wife	B	F	37	U.S.		C		Housework	X	

Figure 5-9
1925 state census, New York, Westchester County, Tarrytown, town of Greenburgh, enumeration district 1, assembly district 4, page 24, FHL 589899. Some states took their own censuses in between the federal census years. Check Ann Lainhart's *State Census Records* to see if your state of interest took them for time periods when your ancestors were there. Like this 1925 census for New York, state censuses may also ask immigration and naturalization information.

"Nativity" is usually the country of origin.

On this record under the column for "Citizenship," it asks, "Number of years in the United States," "Citizen or alien" with an "A" or a "C" to denote which, and "If naturalized, when and where."

Tracing immigrants backward in city directories may be helpful in pinpointing an approximate year of arrival, but immigrants may not appear in city directories for several years after their arrival, or they may appear sporadically. Historical demographers have noted that most urban immigrant families had a high mobility rate, moving about every ten years once in America, regardless of whether it was across the nation, across town, or across the street. City directories can help track this movement.

A helpful feature of some city directories is the "Householder's Index" or "Criss-Cross Directory," which is more common to twentieth-century editions. This section may be in the back of the book, or it may be a separate directory. Instead of an alphabetical listing of individuals, it was an alphabetical/numerical listing of streets, followed by the house numbers on that street and the names of residents at those addresses. This is useful when researching inhabitants in the neighborhood who may have been related and for determining the general character of the immigrant enclave.

Many of the major city directories are available on microfilm in the Family History Library and may be borrowed through any Family History Center. The Library of Congress in Washington, DC, has the largest collection of city directories, many of which are on microfilm and microfiche, but the Library of Congress is not a lending library. You would have to go there to use them or hire someone to search them. Typically, city directories are kept by the public or state libraries to which the directory pertains, and you can write the librarian and ask for a five- to ten-year search. Be aware that the librarian will probably not check for spelling variations of a surname, whereas, you would. If you were looking for Cory, you would also check under Corry, Corrie, Kory, Korry, Korrie, and so on. Primary Source Media on the Internet, <http://www.citydirec tories.psmedia.com>, has more than two hundred city directories for nearly one hundred cities online. Some of these directories date from 1859, with major cities—where immigrants tended to settle upon arrival—having better coverage. Some directories may be accessed for free, but for full use, you will need to pay a subscriber's fee.

CORONER'S RECORDS

Rich in detail and real-life drama, coroner's records are a wonderful resource. If you have an immigrant ancestor who died from unusual circumstances such as an accidental death (e.g., drowning, burns, drug overdose, mine explosions), alcoholism, suicide, murder, or criminal negligence, then look for a coroner's record. These are typically public records, and family history research is a legitimate reason to gain access to them. Some coroners' reports prior to the twentieth century have been microfilmed and are available through the Family History Library. You may even find that some of these records have been abstracted and published. For New York City, for example, Kenneth Scott abstracted the coroners' reports for 1823–1842 and 1843–1849, and these were published in two volumes by the New York Genealogical and Biographical Society in 1989 and 1991, respectively (*Coroners' Reports, New York City, 1823–1842* and *Coroners' Reports, New York City, 1843–1849*), and more were abstracted in the society's journal, *New York Genealogical and Biographical Record*.

Besides illness as a leading cause of death for children, in previous centuries children were prone to accidental deaths, such as drowning and burns. When you have a child in your ancestry who died young but you don't know the cause of death, it would not hurt to check for a coroner's report. These records often predate vital registration and may be the only record you will find on a particular child or person.

If the coroner determined the death was from criminal negligence or murder, then the coroner held an inquest, and this is where you can get some meaty information. Jurors were appointed and witnesses were called to testify. Some of these witnesses may have been relatives, and typically not only their names and relationship to the deceased were recorded, but also their residences. And for those of you intrigued by medical facts, postmortem findings will be especially fascinating.

Tip

Coroner's records can provide you with some unexpected details about immigrant ancestors. From Scott's abstracts, we learn that thirty-year-old Mary Hogan, born in Ireland, died in New York City from apoplexy in 1847. Catharine Hogan, her sister, told the coroner that they had arrived in the United States about six weeks earlier on the ship *Alexander Stewart*.

Coroners' records may be held at one of three governmental jurisdictions: state, county, or city. First check to see if the records you need have been microfilmed by the Family History Library. If not, you will need to write for the records, visit the coroner's office yourself, or hire someone to check them for you. If the victim died in a metropolitan area, write to the city hall to see how you can access the records. If the death occurred in a small town or county, then it will be the county coroner to whom you will write. If all else fails, try writing to the state medical examiner and ask where the records are kept. The historical documents may have been transferred to an historical society or archive, which has been the case with the New York City coroners' records. They are on microfilm at the city's Municipal Archives as well as at the Family History Library.

Follow up your research into coroners' records with newspaper research. Not only might there be an obituary, but if the death was unusual, such as in a case where a coroner was required, it may have appeared as a feature story. If the death was from criminal negligence or murder, then not only will there be subsequent articles, but you may also find court records when the case went to trial. Be sure to check the newspaper again during the trial to see if there were additional articles.

COURT RECORDS

There are many types of court records: colonial indentures (see Land Records later in this chapter), apprenticeships, orphan/guardianships, land deeds, wills and probate, commitment papers, criminal and civil actions, divorce proceedings, tax records, and more. **While the focus here will be on wills and probate, this is not to imply that you should ignore other court-related records.** For example, in the Ralls County, Missouri, Circuit Court Records, Book A, page 31, dated 21 August 1822, this entry appeared:

Important

> Be it remembered, That Hugh Lackey, a Native of Ireland declared on his
> oath in this Court his intention to become a Citizen of the United States
> and further says that he was born in the Parish of Bangor County of Down
> in Ireland aged 24 Years, Embarked from the port of Belfast in Ireland in
> the month of December 1818 and landed at New Orleans in the month of
> February 1819 and has been in the State of Missouri more than two
> years. . . .

Wills and probate records may reveal the place of origin or they may name relatives in the Old Country. Many immigrants—the Irish in particular—were

HOMELAND FOUND IN BROTHER'S ESTATE SETTLEMENT

The Toolan siblings (the name is also found as Toolen and Toolin) were Irish famine immigrants to Chicago. They soon took up government land in Juneau County, Wisconsin, and here all the brothers and one of the three sisters lived out their lives unmarried and childless. Newspaper obituaries and grave marker inscriptions indicated the siblings were from county Roscommon, Ireland, but I found no specific parish or townland in all the sources I consulted.

Estate settlements (probate records) of unmarried and childless relatives often provide a wealth of information, so I examined those for the Toolan siblings. The earliest revealed a previously unknown brother and sister who remained in Ireland, and the next probate file expanded on the immigrant children of this "new" sister.

Finally, I reached the last probate of the unmarried, childless Toolan siblings. Halfway through the file, a document showed that the probate judge made a partial distribution of the estate, directing the administrator to make a more diligent search to determine if the brother who remained in Ireland had any children.

The very next document was the reply from a priest in Ireland, responding to the law firm in Elroy, Wisconsin, that, at their request, he had checked the parish registers and visited the widow of Edward Toolan in the townland of Lisduff in the parish of Kiltrustan, county of Roscommon. I had found the Irish home of the Toolans.

—Roger D. Joslyn, CG, FASG

likely to leave bequests to relatives back home, naming the hometown. Thomas Major, a merchant in New York, for example, made his will on 18 October 1800. In it, he directed that if he should not have any children by his present wife, then after her death, he gave to "the child or children of my sister Mary Cupples of Killyree, County of Antrim and Kingdom of Ireland the residue of my estate. . . ." (Abstracts of Wills, Liber 43, in *Collections of the New-York Historical Society for the Year 1906* [New York: The society, 1907], 239). This practice of leaving property to those in the Old Country was not unique to the Irish, of course.

Not every ancestor left a will, however, and not every ancestor who died without a will had an estate large enough to be entered into the probate court. Yet you should always check these records. The majority of probate records have indexes.

Begin by checking at a Family History Center to see if the probate indexes and records you need have been microfilmed. If not, you will either have to visit the courthouse in person, write for records, or hire someone to search for them.

IMMIGRANT AID SOCIETIES, SETTLEMENT HOUSES, UNIONS, AND FRATERNAL SOCIETIES

Starting in the 1880s, well-meaning upper- and middle-class women and men opened settlement houses in immigrant neighborhoods to offer a variety of social services. Nativism also sparked the establishment of settlement houses to help educate immigrants in the "spirit of true Americanism." Settlements, such as Jane Addams's Hull House in Chicago, offered courses in the English language, introduced immigrants to American society and culture, and provided a common environment for foreign-born women and their children. Additionally, earlier immigrants established mutual-aid societies and immigrant savings banks for those of their own nationality. More than forty immigrant aid societies were represented at major ports to meet new arrivals and help them assimilate into American society.

Your ancestor may have joined a union or fraternal benefit-life insurance society, such as the Sons of Italy or the Polish Union of the United States of North America, upon settlement in America. Some groups, which may have innocent-enough sounding names, may have actually been politically motivated. The Union of Russian Workers is one such group. Most of the Russian and Ukrainian members joined for socialization with people from their homeland; some may not have realized the society's true mission was anarchy, causing many of its members to be deported.

Hidden Treasures

Ask relatives or check home sources to determine if an ancestor was a member of a union, mutual-aid, or fraternal society. Also ask if any ancestors, particularly women, might have received help from a settlement house. Records of these organizations may include rosters of immigrants who took advantage of the services offered. Extant records were likely transferred to historical societies, archives, or the Immigration History Research Center (see Appendix A), but these may not be on microfilm or have an index, so you will have to visit the repository or hire someone to search the records for you.

Helpful also are Nicholas V. Montalto's *The International Institute Movement: A Guide to Records of Immigrant Society Agencies in the United States*, which gives a state-by-state listing of immigrant women's aid societies, and Erna Risch's article, "Immigrant Aid Societies Before 1820," *Pennsylvania History* 3 (January 1936): 15–32, which covers, among others, societies for Germans, Scots, and Irish. If, from family information, you know the name of an immigrant aid society or a settlement house but are still having trouble locating records, you can also try contacting an ethnic heritage association for the area, or check the *National Union Catalog of Manuscript Collections* (NUCMC), which is available at major public and university libraries. Information about NUCMC may be found online at <http://www.lcweb.loc.gov/coll/nucmc/>. NUCMC contains descriptive listings of where manuscript materials are kept. And for existing records of fraternal organizations, check *The Immigration History Research Center: A Guide to Collections*, by Suzanne Moody and Joel Wurl.

LAND RECORDS

One reason people left their native countries was the opportunity to obtain land inexpensively in America, so land records are important to immigrant research. Land transactions between individuals (deeds) usually give the grantor's (seller) and grantee's (buyer) current town and county of residence no matter what the time period. Finding the first transaction may give the immigrant's origins or at least narrow down the possible date of arrival into an area. During the nineteenth century, most states and territories imposed little or no restrictions on an alien owning property or running a business.

Deeds between individuals are found in county courthouses, or in some New England states like Connecticut, Rhode Island, and Vermont, they are found in town halls. Land records are typically indexed. Many have also been microfilmed by the Family History Library. Unless you have precise information, it may be easier to obtain a microfilmed copy of a record and to check the indexes yourself through a Family History Center rather than writing to a courthouse.

Many arrivals during the colonial period had their passage paid for them in exchange for a period of servitude, averaging seven years, known as an indenture. **The sponsor paying the fare claimed a "headright"—generally fifty acres of uncultivated land for every "head" transported,** including his own and his family's. The headright system was in effect for Virginia from 1619 to 1705. Maryland and the Carolinas abolished their programs shortly thereafter. Here's an example of an abstracted headright claim found in the first volume of Nell Marion Nugent's three-volume work, *Cavaliers and Pioneers: Abstracts of Virginia Land Patents and Grants.* It lists the name of the claimant(s), how many acres, in which county, the date and page number of the record, a land description, the number of people transported, and their names.

\di'fin\ *vb*

> Christopher Robinson & John Sturdevant, 600 acs. Henrico Co., 23 Feby. 1652, p. 172. Upon the heads of the Eastern run of Swift Cr. Known by the name of Mr. Hatchers run &c., towards the Ashen Swamp, etc. Trans. of 12 pers: Wm. Hayward, Elianor his wife, John Kendall, James Hewes, James Sturdey, Robt. Kinge, Edward Bayle, Tho. Edwards, Hester Paulwin. 2 rights by assignmt. From Mihill Masters.

Other helpful sources to identify colonists and servants transported and claimed as a part of the headright system are Gust Skordas's *The Early Settlers of Maryland, an Index to Names of Immigrants Compiled From Records of Land Patents, 1633–1680* (Baltimore: Genealogical Publishing Co., 1968), and A.S. Salley Jr.'s *Warrants for Land in South Carolina, 1672–1711* (Columbia, S.C.: Historical Commission, 1910).

Some people came to America expecting to be auctioned upon their arrival to pay for their passage. Others may have been convicts transported to America who were also placed on the auction block. The many works of Peter Coldham, such as *Emigrants in Chains, 1607–1776,* and *Bonded Passengers to America,* will help you identify an ancestor who came to America under these circumstances. Also look for the actual indenture, which may have been recorded in the land records.

Remember Christopher Carmick who was transported to America in 1678 and who Peckham alleged was the father of Cornelius? Christopher was listed in Gust Skordas's *The Early Settlers of Maryland*, with a reference to the original record—patents series of the Maryland Land Office, liber 15, folio 553—which allowed me to find a microfilm copy of the record to examine. The record only named Christopher, along with 179 other people who were transported and claimed for headrights. It did not give Christopher's age, where he was from, or what became of him. For all I know, Christopher could have been dead upon arrival, since all the claimant was required to do was present a list of the names for whom he paid passage. It didn't matter if one of the transported had died on board ship or after arrival. Maybe this is why researchers found no further record of Christopher in America.

Reminder

Another way immigrant ancestors obtained land was through military service (see Military Records later in this chapter). Bounty land warrants were authorized by Congress in 1776 to entice men to serve in the American Revolution. They entitled the soldier, upon his discharge, to a number of free acres of land. The grant depended upon his rank, and ranged from fifty to one thousand acres, but many men sold their bounty land to speculators and never settled on it. Later legislation granted bounty land for wartime service through 1856. Bounty land application files, and many "surrendered" warrants, have been microfilmed and are available through the National Archives in Washington, D.C. There are also published abstracts of these records: Virgil D. White, *Genealogical Abstracts of Revolutionary War Pension Files* (four volumes) and *Index to War of 1812 Pension Files, 1815–1926* (three volumes). *The Index to War of 1812 Pension Files* contains some bounty land warrants, but does not include the numerous unindexed War of 1812 bounty land files held in the National Archives. Some states also granted land to their veterans. See Lloyd DeWitt Bockstruck, *Revolutionary War Bounty Land Grants Awarded by State Governments.*

Other land attractions for new arrivals were federal land acts, such as the Homestead Act of 1862, with several other land acts following. The Homestead Act gave a settler 160 acres of land for settling on the land for five years and improving it. **Alien residents were eligible to participate in these federal programs as long as they had at least filed a declaration of intention to become a U.S. citizen.** To secure the patent to the homestead at the end of the five-year term, the alien had to have petitioned for and been granted U.S. citizenship. Copies of the declaration and petition should be found in homestead files of foreign-born homesteaders. Keep in mind that even though oral interviews, letters, and diaries may reference a family "homestead," this does not necessarily mean that ancestors acquired their lands under the Homestead Act. Referring to any property as a homestead was common terminology for that time period.

Important

Additionally, many homestead claims were canceled because the applicant did not complete the requirements or did not make all of the deadlines. Of nearly two million homestead entries, more than half were canceled. There should still be a file, however, with the reason the entry was canceled.

Case Study

THE SPIRIT OF THE IMMIGRANT

Ole Gustav Hagstrom's descendants in America had never seen his handwriting, did not know whether he could sign his name. Then they found his homestead file at the National Archives in Washington, DC, and discovered something much more precious than a sample of their immigrant ancestor's literary ability.

Homestead files reveal a great deal about the farms eked out of the North American wilderness by hearty homesteaders: the condition of the land, number of acres broken each year, crops planted, wells dug, cisterns built, description of the house, the barn, chicken coops, livestock. . . . But that's not all. Documents in the file also contain personal information about the homesteader: birthplace and age, whether single or married, the names of wife and children, and, when the homesteader was an immigrant—as so many were!—the facts of his naturalization. But that's not all. Since a homestead file contains any correspondence that transpired between the entryman and the General Land Office, fortunate family historians may sometimes discover—written in his own hand—a portrait of their ancestor's soul.

Buried in Ole Gustav Hagstrom's thick file was a letter he himself penned, in the best Swedish-English he could muster, in 1917. The immigrant had just heard about an amendment to the Homestead Law, and he was seeking further information.

Ole Gustav Hagstrom had left his native village in Sweden, crossed the rough North Sea on a local steamer to England, traversed England by rail to the port

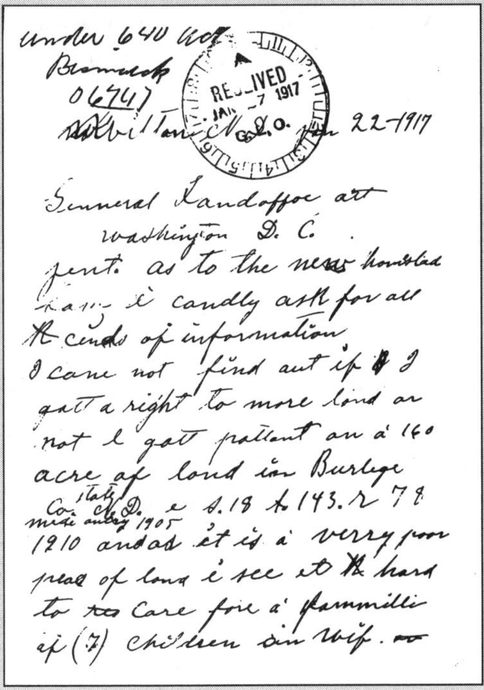

under 640 act
Bismark
06747
Wilton N.D. jan 22-1917
RECEIVED JAN 27 1917

Gennerall Landoffoe att
washington D. C.
jent. as to the new homstead
law i candly ask for all
the cinds of information
I cane not find aut if I
gatt a right to more land ar
not I gatt pattent an a 160
acre af land in Burlege
Co. state N.D. e S.18 T.143.R 78
mede entry 1905
1910 and at it is a verry poor
peas of land i see it the hard
to tae care fore a fammilli
af (7) children an wif.

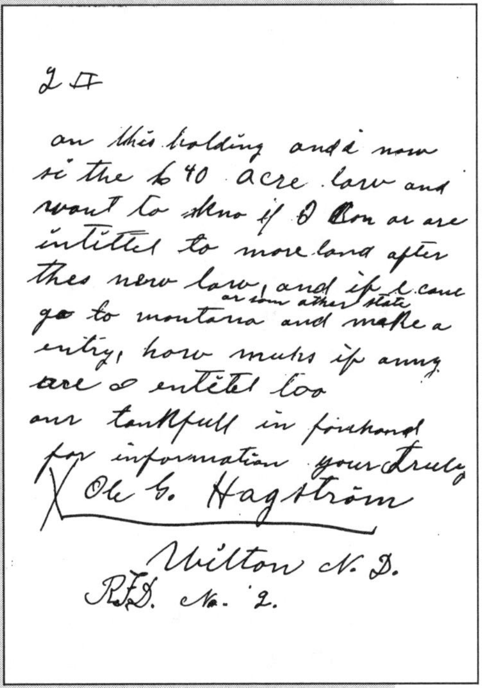

2 II

on this holding and i now
si the 640 acre law and
want to kno if I Bon ar are
intittel to more land after
thes new law, and if i cane
go to montana or som ather state and make a
entry, how muts if anny
are I entitel too
our tankfull in forehand
for information your truly
X Ole G. Hagström

Wilton N. D.
R.F.D. No. 2.

Figure 5-10
Letter written by Ole Gustav Hagstrom, 22 January 1917, to the General Land Office; homestead file of Ole Gustav Hagstrom, Patent No. 248393, filed 15 February 1912, United States Land Office at Bismark, North Dakota; records of the Bureau of Land Management (RG 49), National Archives, Washington, DC. Courtesy of John Philip Colletta.

THE SPIRIT OF THE IMMIGRANT—Continued

of Liverpool, sailed across the Atlantic Ocean in the steerage compartment of the *Cymric* to Boston, traveled 1,800 miles to a virgin wilderness designated on white men's maps as "Burleigh County, North Dakota," wrested by brute strength and determination from the ever-resistant earth a working farm, raised a family of seven children, and now—no longer a young man!—what is this immigrant ready to do if he can get more and better land from the U.S. government?

Chuck it all!

And start all over again, from scratch . . . in Montana!

Could this pioneer have left to his descendants a more precious or more eloquent testimony of his tireless ambition, his optimism, his devotion to his family? Surely, these few scrawled lines portray the spirit of the immigrant!

—John Philip Colletta

Homestead files are found in the custody of the National Archives in Washington, DC, but you should also be able to find the homestead recorded in the county courthouse where the land is located or the state's Bureau of Land Management (BLM) office. In the county record, it should state in which federal land office the claim was made and give a file number. Then you can write to the National Archives for a copy of the complete homestead file or to the appropriate BLM office directly.

Federal land patents, from 1820 to 1908, for the eastern states of Alabama, Arkansas, Florida, Illinois, Indiana, Louisiana, Michigan, Mississippi, Missouri, Minnesota, Ohio, and Wisconsin are available on the Internet, <http://www.glorecords.blm.gov>. Databases for the western federal land conveyances will be added in February 2000, and images of the records will be added over the next three years. You can search the BLM's General Land Office database, which includes homesteads, cash sales, miscellaneous warrants, private land claims, swamp lists, state selections, and railroad lists. The actual case files are not on the Internet, but there are land descriptions and a computerized image of the warrant, which you may print out. By completing a return E-mail, you can request a certified copy of the land patent be sent to you at a nominal fee (posted on the home page). Make sure you request all of the documents in the file.

In California, the Alien Land Act of 1913 prohibited aliens who were ineligible for citizenship—Asians—(see chapter six) from owning agricultural property; however, they could keep any land already owned by this time. The only stipulation was that they could not bequeath or sell the property to an ineligible alien; therefore, many Asians registered deeds under their American-born children's names.

MEDICAL RECORDS
Northwestern Memorial Hospital, Chicago
A group of documents at the Family History Library is from Chicago's Northwestern Memorial Hospital records, 1896–1933 (FHL microfilm numbers

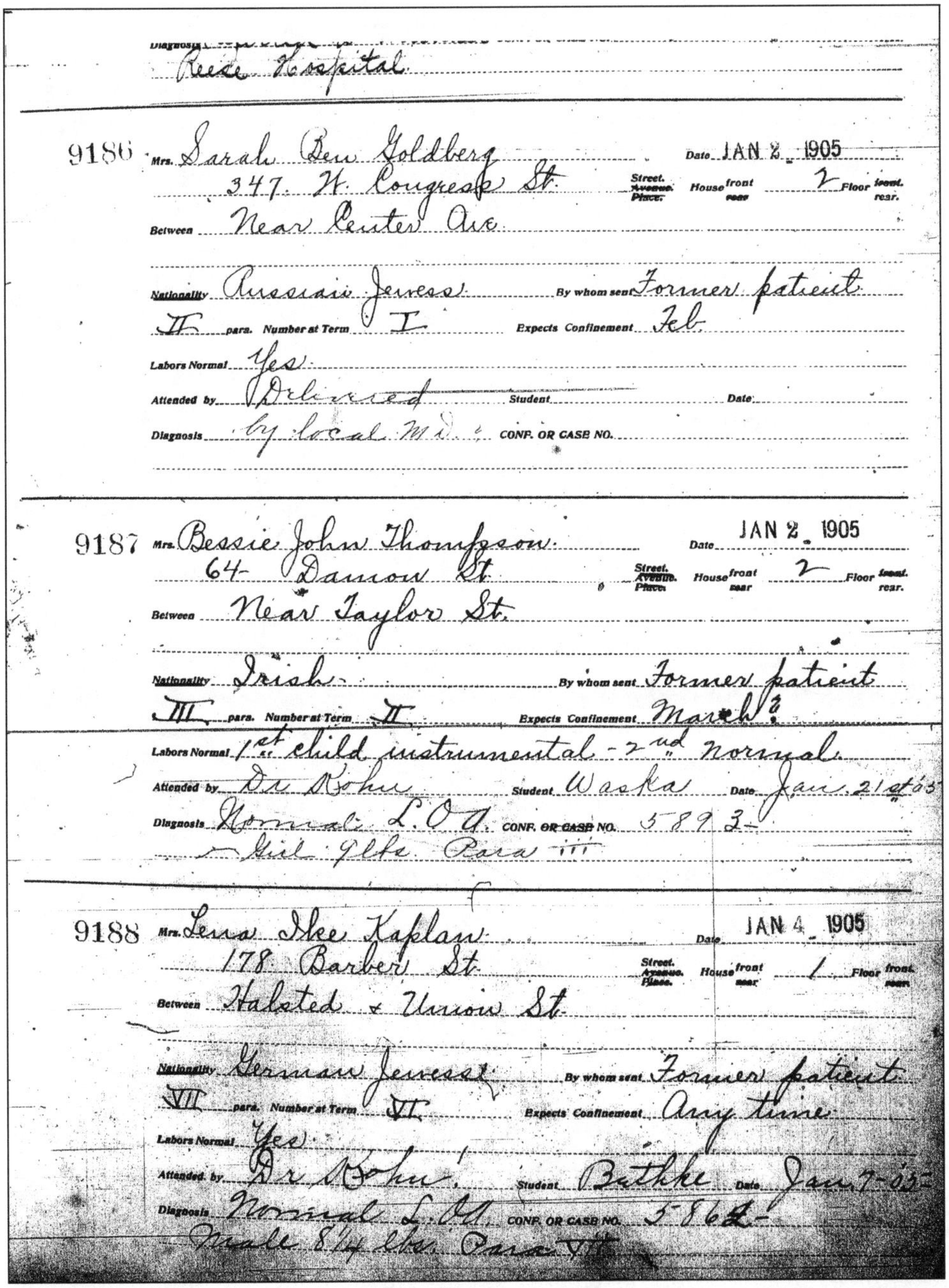
Reese Hospital

9186 Mrs. Sarah Ben Goldberg Date JAN 2 1905
347 W. Congress St Street. House front 2 Floor
Between Near Center Ave
Nationality Russian Jewess By whom sent Former patient
II para. Number at Term I Expects Confinement Feb
Labors Normal Yes
Attended by Delivered Student Date
Diagnosis by local M.D. CONF. OR CASE NO.

9187 Mrs. Bessie John Thompson Date JAN 2 1905
64 Damon St Street. House front 2 Floor
Between Near Taylor St.
Nationality Irish By whom sent Former patient
III para. Number at Term II Expects Confinement March
Labors Normal 1st child instrumental - 2nd normal.
Attended by Dr Kohn Student Waska Date Jan. 21st 05
Diagnosis Normal L.O.A. CONF. OR CASE NO. 5893
Girl Para III

9188 Mrs. Lena Ike Kaplan Date JAN 4 1905
178 Barber St Street. House front 1 Floor
Between Halsted + Union St
Nationality German Jewess By whom sent Former patient
VII para. Number at Term VI Expects Confinement Any time
Labors Normal Yes
Attended by Dr Kohn Student Bethke Date Jan 7-05
Diagnosis Normal L.O.A. CONF. OR CASE NO. 5862
Male 8¼ lbs. Para VII

Figure 5-11
Northwestern Memorial Hospital, Chicago, Illinois, births, 1904–1905, FHL 1315895. Many immigrant women used the services of this hospital.

1315895–05). These records document births, abortions, and miscarriages for thousands of women who lived in the area, primarily immigrant women. Information varies from year to year. The earlier records give the woman's married name, street address, number of living children the woman has delivered, number born at term, ethnicity (many records were for Russian Jews, some Irish Catholics, Polish Catholics, etc.), referral person or agency ("thro former patient," "thro Hull House," etc.), the woman's condition (e.g., "urgent, threatened abortion in 3rd month"), case number, and confinement date. Later records provide the woman's full married name, date, address, nationality, by whom sent, para (live offspring), number at term, when to expect confinement, whether labors were normal, attended by (physician and student), date, diagnosis, case or confinement number (see Figure 5-11 on page 73).

The most recent records also give information commonly found on birth certificates, such as the wife's maiden name, the husband's name, places of birth for husband and wife, the weight of the baby, and the baby's name. The records are grouped by year; unfortunately, they are not indexed. But if you have an ancestor who lived in Chicago between 1896 and 1933 near Northwestern Hospital, and especially if she was a Russian Jew or an immigrant who lived in a nearby tenement, it may be well worth your time to do a page-by-page search.

Midwives' Journals

Another type of medical record to search for is midwives' journals. In New York City alone, five hundred midwives were practicing in 1906, many having immigrant origins and catering to immigrant women. Other urban areas, such as Chicago and Boston, also had large numbers of ethnic midwives. Immigrant women had not only used midwives in their homeland, but they felt more comfortable with a midwife in America who spoke their native language. (See Figure 5-12 on page 75.)

Surviving midwives' journals may be found as a manuscript collection in a library or other repository, such as a historical society, and a few have been microfilmed and are available through the Family History Library. Midwives' records typically contain entries for births, miscarriages, and abortions that the midwife attended. Also check the *National Union Catalog of Manuscript Collections*.

Tuberculin Sanatoriums

Tuberculosis, also known as "consumption," claimed the lives of many immigrants and their children in the late nineteenth and early twentieth centuries. Those who contracted the disease may have spent time in one of the tuberculin sanatoriums around the country. If there is a family story of an ancestor dying from tuberculosis, ask whether that individual was ever treated in a sanatorium. Many immigrants may have been too poor to afford the care of a private tuberculin sanatorium, so they were confined to a state or public institution. To determine the names and the whereabouts of tuberculin sanatoriums, see Philip P. Jacobs's *The Campaign Against Tuberculosis in the United States, Including a Directory of Institutions Dealing With Tuberculosis in the United States and Canada* (New York: Charities Publication Committee, 1908). Though the sanatorium is no longer in existence, the records may have been transferred to a hospital or a historical society or archive. Write to the state historical society, give them the name and location of the tuberculin sanatorium, and ask if they know where the records might be.

Public Health Records

By 1904, sixty cities in America required registration of tubercular patients; four years later, eighty-four had registration laws. Physicians and healthcare

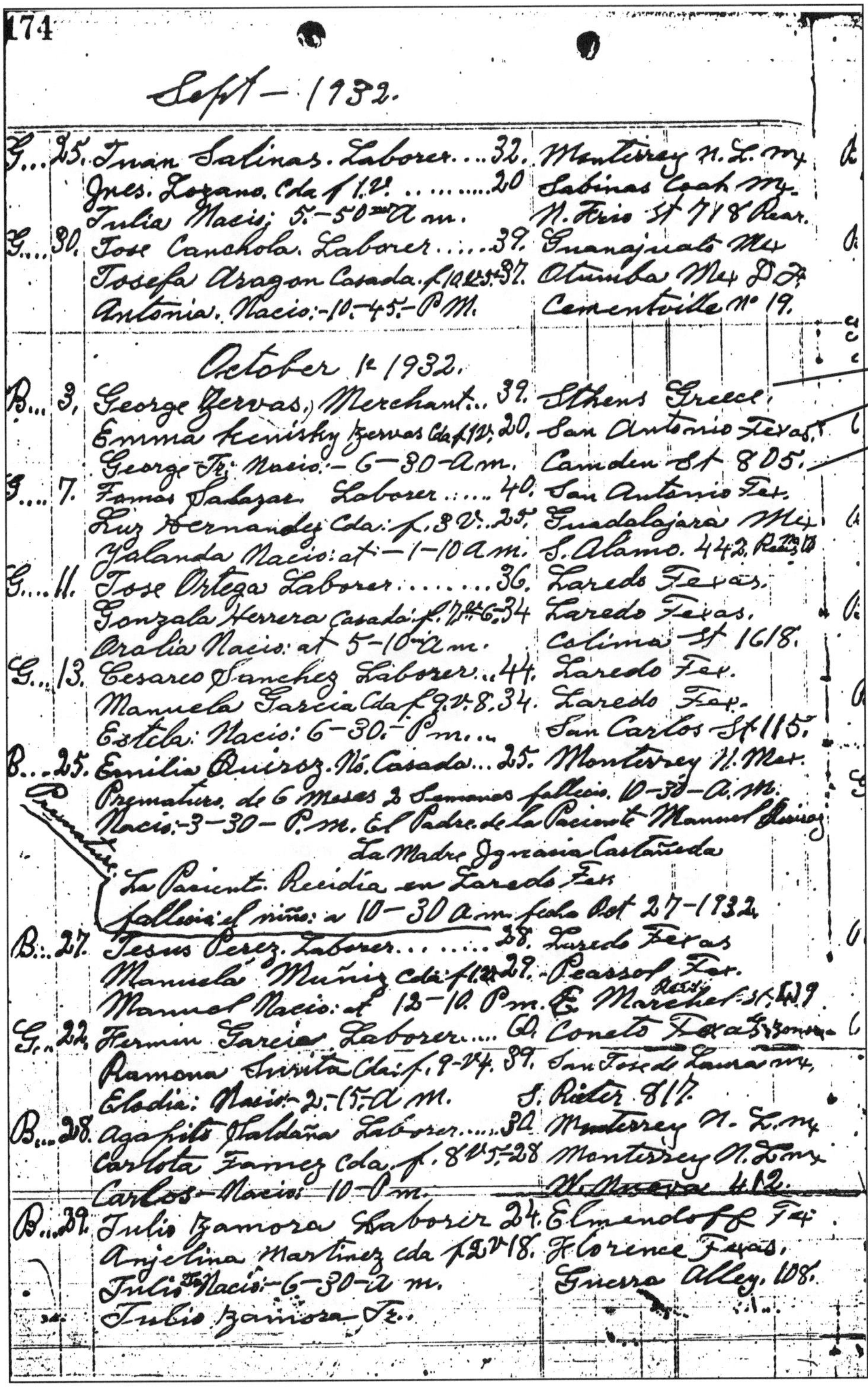

174

Sept – 1932.

G... 25. Juan Salinas. Laborer ....32. Monterrey N. L. Mx
Ines. Lozano. Cda f 1.V. ....20 Sabinas Coah. Mx.
Julia Nacio; 5.–50 A. m. N. Frio St 718 Rear.
G... 30. Jose Canchola. Laborer .....39. Guanajuato Mx
Josefa Aragon Casada. f 10 V 5. 37. Otumba Mx D. F.
Antonia. Nacio:–10.–45.–P.M. Cementville Nº 19.

October 1st 1932.

B... 3, George Zervas, Merchant... 39. Athens Greece,
Emma Kenisky Zervas Cda f 1 V; 20. San Antonio Texas
George Jr. Nacio.–6–30–Am. Camden St 805.
G.... 7. Tomas Salazar Laborer ..... 40. San Antonio Tex.
Luz Hernandez Cda: f. 8 V. 25. Guadalajara Mx
Yolanda Nacio: at –1–10 a.m. S. Alamo. 442
G.... 11. Jose Ortega Laborer ....36. Laredo Texas.
Gonzala Herrera Casada: f. 11 V 6. 34 Laredo Texas.
Oralia Nacio. at 5–10 A m. Calimo St 1618.
G... 13. Cesareo Sanchez Laborer .. 44. Laredo Tex.
Manuela Garcia Cda f. 9 V 8. 34. Laredo Tex.
Estela: Nacio: 6–30.–P m... San Carlos St 115.
B... 25. Emilia Quiroz. Nº Casada ... 25. Monterrey N. Mex.
Prematuro. de 6 Meses 2 Semanas fallecio. 10–30–A. M.
Nacio.–3–30– P. m. El Padre. de La Paciente Manuel Quiroz
La Madre Ignacia Castañeda
La Paciente Recidia en Laredo Tex.
fallecio el niño: a 10–30 a.m. fecha Oct 27–1932.
B.. 27. Jesus Perez. Laborer ....28. Laredo Texas
Manuela Muñiz Cda f 1 V. 29. Pearsall Tex.
Manuel Nacio: at 12–10 P m. E. Marchet St. 419
G.. 22. Fermin Garcia. Laborer ..... 60. Coneto Texas
Ramona Zurita Cda: f. 9–V 4. 39. San Jose de Laura Mx,
Elodia: Nacio–2.–15.–A M. S. Rieter 817.
B... 28. Agapito Saldaña Laborer ..... 32. Monterrey N. L. Mx
Carlota Gomez Cda. f. 8 V 5. 28 Monterrey N. L. Mx
Carlos–Nacio:–10–P m. W. Nueva 412.
B... 29. Julio Zamora Laborer 24. Elmendorf Tx
Anjelina Martinez cda f 2 V 18. Florence Texas.
Julio Jr. Nacio–6–30–A m. Guerra Alley, 108.
Julio Zamora Jr.

In this journal, the father's name is listed first, then his occupation and age, followed by his place of birth. The next line gives information for the mother. The third line is the baby's name, time of birth, and address where the baby was delivered.

Figure 5-12
Midwife's journal of Romona R. Ramos, Bexar County, Texas, 1922–1958, volume 2, FHL 1398716. Many immigrant women felt more comfortable giving birth with the aid of a midwife from their native country. The entries in this journal give the place of birth for the father and mother. Look for surviving midwives' journals among manuscript collections in libraries, archives, and historical societies.

providers were to report to the public health department the names and addresses of everyone diagnosed with TB. If these records are still extant, they would be in the custody of the city's department of public health.

Tuberculosis was not the only disease on which the public health department

For More Info

See Alan Kraut, *Silent Travelers: Germs, Genes, and the "Immigrant Menace"*; Sheila Rothman, *Living in the Shadow of Death: Tuberculosis and the Social Experience of Illness in American History;* and Alfred W. Crosby, *America's Forgotten Pandemic: The Influenza of 1918.*

kept close watch. They recorded cases of other epidemics and plagues, for example, in 1900, the San Francisco Board of Health dealt with an outbreak of the bubonic plague in Chinatown. All Chinese who died and were not under a Caucasian physician's care were given autopsies to determine if the cause of death was indeed the plague. All of Chinatown was placed under quarantine for many weeks.

Boards or departments of public health were established in most major cities during the 1860s. To see if public health records exist for the time period when your ancestors may have been affected by an epidemic, contact the Department of Public Health in the city in question. (See chapter two, Health and Disease.)

Insane Asylums

Thousands of men and women throughout the history of our country have been committed to insane asylums. Some ethnic groups had higher recorded incidences of certain types of mental illnesses. If you discover mental illness recorded in your family history, there are a few records on which you may find your ancestors.

On the federal censuses for 1840, 1850, 1860, 1870, and 1880, there is a column denoting insane persons, but all it will have is a "tick" or "hash" mark, indicating that the person was "insane." If the ancestor survived to 1880, however, you may find more information in the 1880 Schedule for the Defective, Dependent, and Delinquent Classes (see discussion under Censuses earlier in this chapter). Even if the ancestor was discharged from a mental institution before 1880, the person may still be listed on the 1880 DDD.

Also look at court records for commitment papers, which may be in the custody of the probate court. John Norris was the son of Irish immigrants, and according to his commitment file, found in the Greenwich, Connecticut, Probate District records, John was committed by his sister on 23 December 1913. He was initially sent to the Connecticut Hospital for the Insane at Middletown, to be transferred to the Norwich Hospital for the Insane, in Preston, Connecticut. John was declared a pauper and entitled to support from the state for insane paupers. He had "delusions on one particular subject namely that he is being constantly followed by certain Italians whose mission is to kill him at first opportunity. He is indifferent to work and supporting himself and has a suspicious attitude of strangers, especially foreigners. . . . He was arrested for trespassing on property when apparently he was just escaping from his enemies, he himself having no motive of robbery. In some respects he is quiet and peaceful and no evidence that he would commit any rash acts on himself and others."

Records from the mental institution may be difficult to obtain. For the most part, insane asylums no longer exist, so you may have to write to the state historical society or archives and give the name and location of the institution and ask if they know where the records might be. If the records still exist, chances are good that they will be accessible only to next of kin, so you may be asked to prove your relationship to the patient and provide the person's death certificate.

MILITARY RECORDS

While many immigrants left their homeland to avoid mandatory military conscription, they may have enlisted or been drafted once they arrived in America. Depending on the time of arrival, you should determine in which wars your ancestors were likely to have served or registered, then make the appropriate search.

Along with the promise of bounty land, and possibly receiving a pension as well, another enticement for immigrants to serve in the U.S. armed forces was the promise of citizenship on an expedited and simplified basis. Effective 17 July 1862, citizenship was granted to any alien who was age twenty-one or older and who had enlisted in the armies of the United States, either as part of the regular or the volunteer forces, and who had been or was eligible to be honorably discharged. The alien could bypass the first step of filing a declaration of intention and needed to file only a petition for naturalization (see chapter six). This incentive for aliens to perform military service was repeated after the Civil War, such as in the Spanish-American War of 1898, the Philippine Insurrection of 1900–1901, and World War I. A copy of the immigrant's naturalization papers should be among his military service records.

Military service records and veterans benefits records can be obtained by writing to the National Archives in Washington, DC, using Form NATF 80, which can be obtained from one of the regional records services facilities (see Appendix B) or by E-mailing a request to inquire@nara.gov. The minimum information needed for a search is (1) the soldier's full name, (2) the war in which he served or his period of service, and (3) the state from which he served. For the Civil War, you must also indicate whether he served in the Union or Confederate forces. A separate copy of the form must be used for each type of record (e.g., military service, or pension and bounty land warrant applications). For modern military records (World War I and later), write to the National Personnel Records Center (Military Personnel Records), 9700 Page Boulevard, St. Louis, Missouri 63132. Many military service records and pension and bounty land records are also available on microfilm through the Family History Library. For more information on various military records, see James Neagles's *U.S. Military Records.*

World War I

Three draft registrations for World War I were held, two in 1917 and one in 1918, and more than twenty-four million men registered, although not all were inducted into service. **Whether a man was an alien or citizen, if he was between the ages of eighteen and forty-five, he was required to register for the draft.** Besides giving the registrant's name, age, date of birth, address, and occupation, the records also report citizenship status (alien, declarant, naturalized), and whether there was any prior military service (United States or foreign). (See Figure 5-13 on page 78.) This information may lead to domestic or foreign military service records. The WWI draft records are arranged alphabetically by state, then by county or city (the cards for Connecticut, Massachusetts, and

Important

Figure 5-13
World War I draft registration of Rudolf Triepitsch, Wisconsin, Milwaukee Draft Board #5, FHL 1674784. More than twenty-four million men registered for the draft during World War I. Regardless of whether a man was an alien or citizen, he was supposed to register.

Recorded is the citizenship status (a natural-born citizen, a naturalized citizen, an alien, or declared intention).

Also recorded are the town, state, and nation of the person's birth.

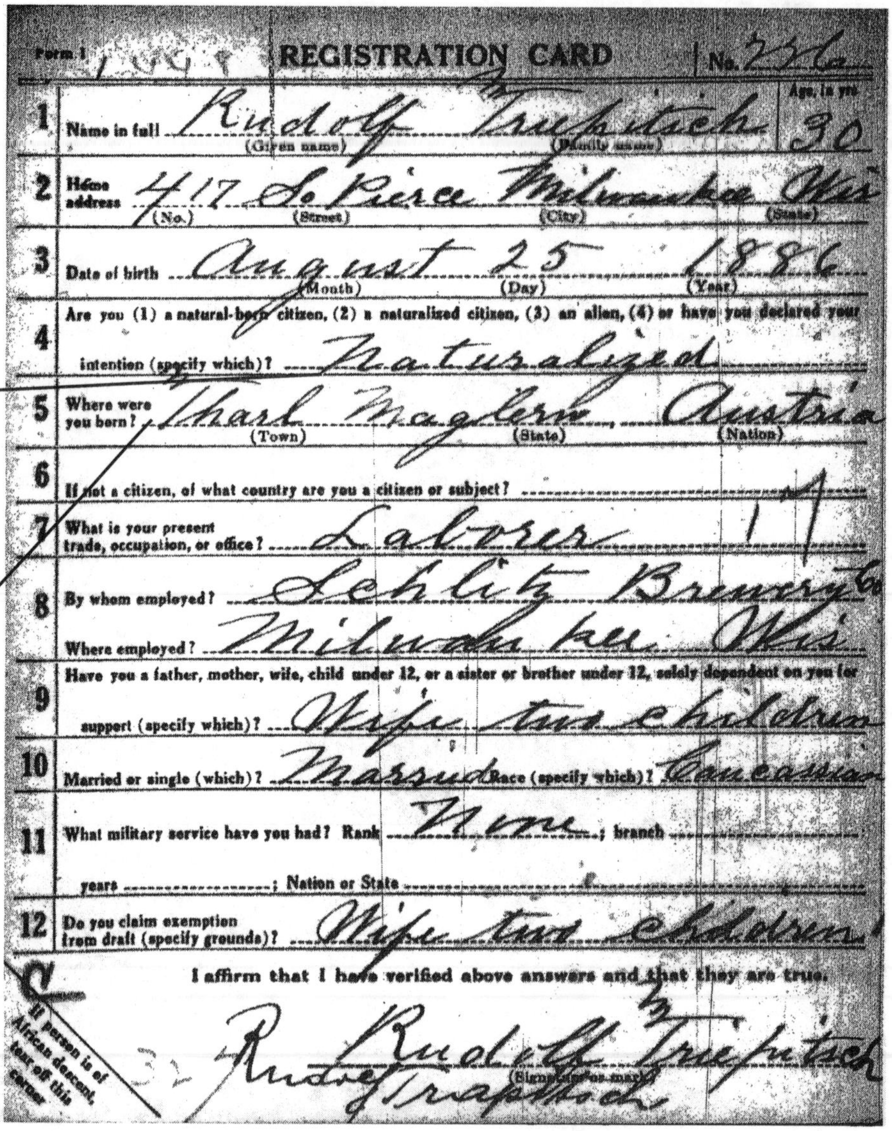
Form 1 ... REGISTRATION CARD No. 226

1 Name in full Rudolf Triepitsch (Given name) (Family name) Age, in yrs. 30

2 Home address 417 So Pierce Milwaukee Wis (No.) (Street) (City) (State)

3 Date of birth August 25 1886 (Month) (Day) (Year)

4 Are you (1) a natural-born citizen, (2) a naturalized citizen, (3) an alien, (4) or have you declared your intention (specify which)? Naturalized

5 Where were you born? Tharl Maglern Austria (Town) (State) (Nation)

6 If not a citizen, of what country are you a citizen or subject?

7 What is your present trade, occupation, or office? Laborer

8 By whom employed? Schlitz Brewery Co
Where employed? Milwaukee Wis

9 Have you a father, mother, wife, child under 12, or a sister or brother under 12, solely dependent on you for support (specify which)? Wife two children

10 Married or single (which)? Married Race (specify which)? Caucasian

11 What military service have you had? Rank None; branch
years ; Nation or State

12 Do you claim exemption from draft (specify grounds)? Wife two children

I affirm that I have verified above answers and that they are true.

Rudolf Triepitsch
(Signature or mark)

If person is of African descent, tear off this corner.

Rhode Island, however, are arranged alphabetically for the entire state by the names of the registrants). To obtain the draft registration record of a man who resided in a major city (where the majority of twentieth-century immigrants settled), you must know the registrant's street address, since there were several draft boards. To locate someone's address, consult city directories. The original World War I draft records are located at the NARA's Southeast Region in East Point, Georgia, but these have been microfilmed and are also available through the Family History Library, or through loan at one of its branch centers. At the Web site, <http://www.ancestry.com>, you will find a database to many of the World War I draft records, but you must be a subscriber to Ancestry.com in order to view this database.

World War II

The records of the fourth draft registration, begun on 17 April 1942, are available through some of the regional records services facilities of the National

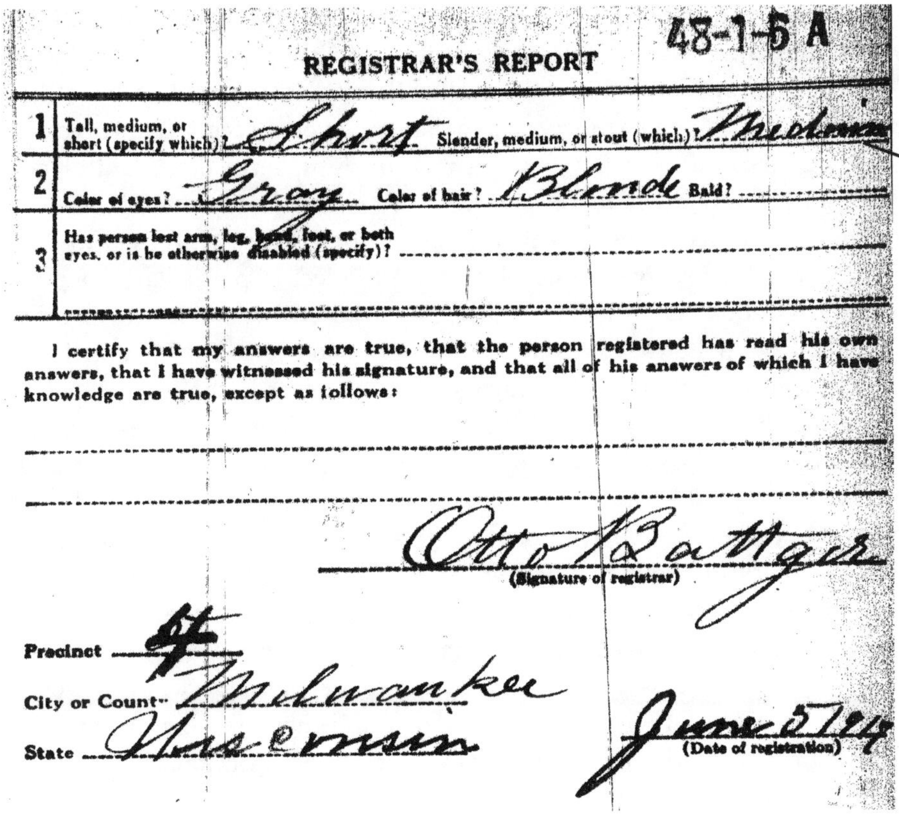

REGISTRAR'S REPORT   48-1-5 A

1 Tall, medium, or short (specify which)? *Short* Slender, medium, or stout (which)? *Medium*

2 Color of eyes? *Gray*   Color of hair? *Blonde*   Bald? ....

3 Has person lost arm, leg, hand, foot, or both eyes, or is he otherwise disabled (specify)? ....

I certify that my answers are true, that the person registered has read his own answers, that I have witnessed his signature, and that all of his answers of which I have knowledge are true, except as follows:

Otto Battgei
(Signature of registrar)

Precinct *4*
City or County *Milwaukee*
State *Wisconsin*

June 5, 1917
(Date of registration)

Figure 5-13A
Second page of World War I draft registration.

The form includes a physical description of the registrant.

Archives for the states in their jurisdiction (see Appendix B). Men born between 28 April 1877 and 16 February 1897, or those between the ages of forty-five and sixty-five, were included in this fourth registration. Though many of these draft cards are restricted by privacy laws, some of the regional records services facilities of the National Archives have acquired the cards for their jurisdiction: Alaska Region (Anchorage), Central Plains Region (Kansas City, Missouri), Great Lakes Region (Chicago), New England Region (Waltham, Massachusetts), Northeast Region (New York City), Pacific Northwest Region (Seattle), Pacific Sierra Region (San Bruno, California), Rocky Mountain Region (Denver), and Southwest Region (Fort Worth, Texas).

Relocation Camps

Besides the standard military records, descendants of Japanese, Italian, and German Americans will find other sources for research. Roughly 120,000 Japanese Americans living on the West Coast were relocated and placed in internment camps between 27 August 1942 and 2 January 1945. Sixty-four percent of them were American citizens with Japanese ancestry. Internees were sent to the following camps: Poston and Gila River, Arizona; Tule Lake and Manzanar, California; Minidoka, Idaho; Heart Mountain, Wyoming; Granada, Colorado; Topaz, Utah; and Rowher and Jerome, Arkansas. Those who passed government investigations were allowed to leave and resettle in nonrestricted areas away from military installations and coastal towns. About thirty-five thousand who were released resettled in the Midwest and East. Adults willing to serve in

For More Info

For information on Japanese-American internment, see Leonard Broom and John I. Kitsuse, *The Managed Casualty: The Japanese Family in World War II*. For information on Italian-American relocation and internment and some German-American internment, see Stephen Fox, *The Unknown Internment: Oral History of the Relocation of Italian-Americans During World War II*.

the U.S. armed forces were also released. The records of Japanese internments may be found at the National Archives in Record Group 85: The Immigration and Naturalization Service, Records of Alien Enemy Internment Camps, 1917–1918 and 1941–1948; some records may have restricted access. These records may provide the full interview, names, relationships, birth dates and places, immigration data, and where the suspects were released or relocated.

Italian and German "enemy" aliens, and in some cases, citizens with "enemy" ancestry, fourteen years and older, who resided, in particular, along the west coast of California from Humboldt Bay to Maricopa, as well as from other areas in the United States, were relocated or interned between 1941 and 1942. These were mostly Italians and Germans who had never become U.S. citizens, even though they may have resided in America for half their lives, nor did they have to have a history of committing overt acts against the United States. Approximately 4,000 Italians and 6,000 Germans were taken into custody and interviewed. Of that number, about 5,700 were actually interned at one of sixteen camps throughout the United States. Fort Lincoln (Bismark), North Dakota, became an exclusively German camp from December 1942 until 1945. As of this writing, Fort Missoula, Montana, records are restricted and are accessible only by an internee, spouse, or upon proof of the internee's death; however, anyone born prior to 1900 is presumed dead, and their files may be viewed. These documents are also part of Record Group 85. See also Italians in Part II, page 199.

NEWSPAPERS

American English-Language Newspapers

Usually located in local libraries for the area they cover, newspapers are often preserved on microfilm and may be accessed through interlibrary loan. They are an excellent source of family and social history, giving accounts from a contemporary viewpoint. Many newspapers were published daily or weekly. Colonial and early national period newspapers included ship arrivals, auctions for passengers who could not afford to pay their passage, announcements of passengers' arrivals, and advertisements for missing friends and relatives (see chapter three, Record Abstracts and Transcriptions). More recent editions, those of the late nineteenth and twentieth centuries, include obituaries, marriage and engagement announcements, reports on fifty-year wedding anniversaries, family reunions, one hundredth birthday celebrations, birth announcements, "local news" or personal columns, and legal notices. Metropolitan newspapers, such as the *New York Times*, have their indexes published; other newspapers may be indexed by the library where the newspaper is published.

Microfilm Source

Foreign-Language/Ethnic Newspapers

New arrivals to America seeking relatives who immigrated before them may have placed an announcement in a foreign-language newspaper, rather than an English-language one. Ethnic newspapers might also contain items typically found in English-language newspapers, such as obituaries, advertisements, club news, names of visitors from the homeland, and letters at the post office. These newspapers will also give you a feel for immigrant social life and concerns. The best way to locate foreign-language or ethnic newspapers is through the Immigration History Research Center (see Suzanne Moody and Joel Wurl, *The Immigration History Research Center: A Guide to Collections*). This repository collects and maintains on microfilm a substantial number of ethnic and foreign-language newspapers, many of which may be obtained through interlibrary loan (see Appendix A).

ORPHAN TRAIN RECORDS

Approximately 200,000 homeless children were sent by train from the east to the west between 1853 and about 1930, to be placed with families (see chapter two). Some of these children were immigrants or children of immigrants. The Orphan Train Heritage Society of America operates a clearinghouse with information on orphan train riders, and it also offers a newsletter and research services. Contact it at 614 East Emma Avenue, Suite 115, Springdale, Arkansas 72764-4634; phone: (501) 756-2780, fax: (501) 756-0769, E-mail: MEJ102333 9@aol.com, Web site: <http://pda.republic.net/othsa>. (For more on orphan trains, see Marilyn Irvin Holt, *The Orphan Trains: Placing Out in America*.)

RAILROAD RETIREMENT BOARD

It is said that our immigrant ancestors of the nineteenth century learned three things when they arrived in America: (1) that the streets were not paved with gold, (2) that the streets weren't paved at all, and (3) that they were expected to pave them. Not only were immigrants a cheap labor force for paving roads, but also for building railroads. For employment records, check with the railway company's archives or museum, or write to the state historical society and ask where the records are kept. Keep in mind, however, that not all records have been retained and are accessible; this will vary from one company to another. If you discover your ancestor's Social Security number from a death certificate or on the Social Security Death Index (see chapter four) and the number begins with 700–728, then you know that person had retirement from the railroad. These 700 numbers were used through 1963. If your ancestor worked for the railroad, especially after 1936, and retired, try writing to the U.S. Railroad Retirement Board, Office of Public Affairs, 844 North Rush Street, Chicago, Illinois 60611-2092. The board will provide information for genealogical purposes on deceased retirees, but you should include with your request a copy of the person's death certificate and state your relationship to the person.

For More Info

See Wendy Elliot, "Railroad Records for Genealogical Research," *National Genealogical Society Quarterly* 75 (December 1987): 271–277 and an addendum, *National Genealogical Society Quarterly* 79 (June 1991): 140.

SOCIAL SECURITY RECORDS

In chapter four, I discussed the Social Security Death Index available on CD-ROM and on the Internet. Once you have your ancestor's Social Security number, you can obtain, for a small fee, a copy of your ancestor's original

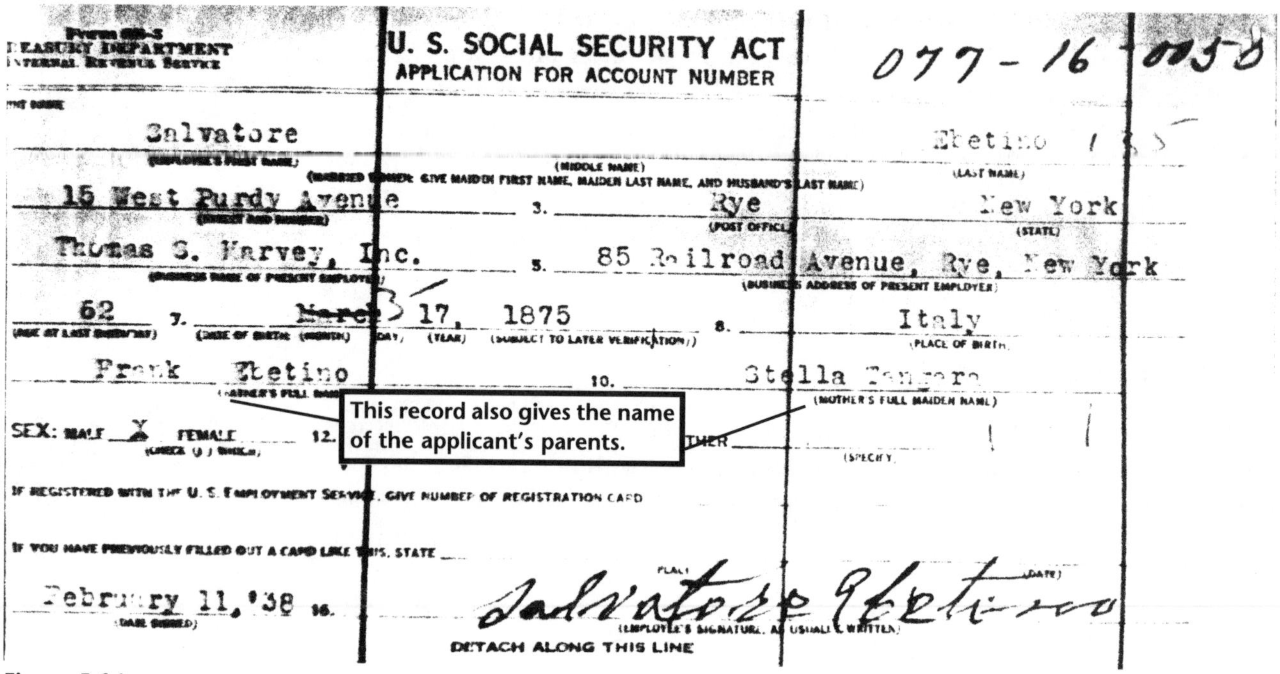
Treasury Department
Internal Revenue Service
U. S. SOCIAL SECURITY ACT
APPLICATION FOR ACCOUNT NUMBER
077 - 16
Salvatore (Employee's first name) (Middle name) Ebetino (Last name)
15 West Purdy Avenue 3. Rye (Post office) New York (State)
Thomas S. Harvey, Inc. (Business name of present employer) 5. 85 Railroad Avenue, Rye, New York (Business address of present employer)
62 (Age at last birthday) 7. March 17, 1875 (Date of birth) 8. Italy (Place of birth)
Frank Ebetino (Father's full name) 10. Stella [illegible] (Mother's full maiden name)
SEX: MALE X FEMALE 12.
If registered with the U. S. Employment Service, give number of registration card
If you have previously filled out a card like this, state
February 11, '38 16. (Employee's signature, as usually written) Salvatore Ebetino
DETACH ALONG THIS LINE

Figure 5-14
Form SS-5, application for a Social Security account for Salvatore Ebetino. Once you have an ancestors' Social Security number, send for the person's form SS-5, which will give you more detailed information than what you will find on the Social Security Death Index. Note here that the place of birth is merely "Italy."

application for a Social Security card, Form SS-5. Write a letter to the Social Security Administration, Freedom of Information Officer, 6401 Security Boulevard, Baltimore, Maryland 21235, or use the form letter provided on Ancestry.com's Social Security Death Index database, <http://www.ancestry.com>. Unlike the Social Security Death Index database, information in the original record will be more detailed, giving the applicant's address, names of the applicant's parents, and the name and address of the employer when the applicant applied (See Figure 5-14 above).

VITAL RECORDS

Marriage and death certificates may give a precise place of origin of an immigrant; more than likely, however, they list only a country of origin. Birth certificates may give specific birth places for foreign-born parents. For some states, death certificates may also reveal how long the deceased lived in the community and/or in the United States, giving clues to the time of arrival. Depending on the knowledge of the person supplying the information, death certificates may also give the names of the immigrant's parents.

Statewide vital registration is fairly recent; many states did not have mandatory reporting of births and deaths until the early twentieth century. Consult Thomas J. Kemp's *International Vital Records Handbook*, which tells when vital registration began in each state, as well as providing forms and listing fees for obtaining records. **Or see the National Center for Health Statistics' *Where to Write for Vital Records*, available on the Internet at <http://www.cdc.gov/**

nchswww/howto/w2w/w2welcom.htm>. Many states now post ordering procedures and fees to obtain vital records on the Internet; some also include indexes. Keep in mind that some states have restrictions on obtaining vital records, or you must prove you are a descendant.

Marriage and sometimes death records found in the county clerk and recorder's office will predate statewide registration, and many of these records and their indexes have been microfilmed by the Family History Library. (See Figure 5-15 below and Figure 5-16 on page 84.) Or, you can write directly to the courthouse, giving full names of both parties and their probable marriage (or death) date.

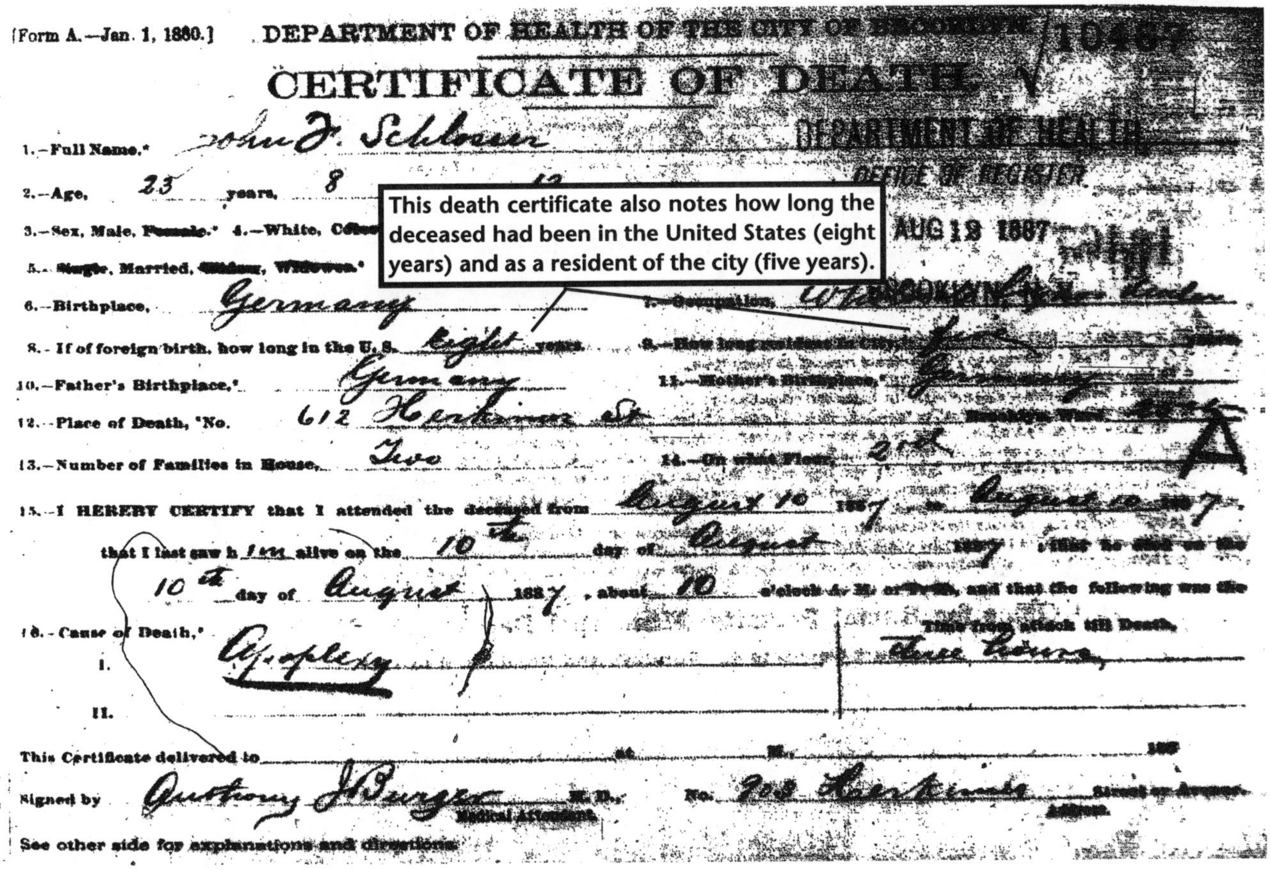
[Form A.—Jan. 1, 1880.] DEPARTMENT OF HEALTH OF THE CITY OF BROOKLYN. 10487

CERTIFICATE OF DEATH.

DEPARTMENT OF HEALTH OFFICE OF REGISTER AUG 19 1887

1.—Full Name. John J. Schlosser

2.—Age, 23 years, 8

3.—Sex, Male, Female. 4.—White, Colored.

5.—Single, Married, Widower, Widowed.

6.—Birthplace, Germany

8.—If of foreign birth, how long in the U. S. eight years.

10.—Father's Birthplace, Germany

12.—Place of Death, No. 612 Herkimer St.

13.—Number of Families in House, Two

15.—I HEREBY CERTIFY that I attended the deceased from August 10 1887 to August 10 1887, that I last saw him alive on the 10th day of August 1887, that he died on the 10th day of August 1887, about 10 o'clock A. M. or P. M., and that the following was the

16.—Cause of Death, I. Apoplexy — Time from attack till Death. three hours

II.

This Certificate delivered to

Signed by Anthony J. Burger M. D. Medical Attendant. No. 902 Herkimer Street or Avenue.

See other side for explanations and directions.

This death certificate also notes how long the deceased had been in the United States (eight years) and as a resident of the city (five years).

Figure 5-15
Death certificate of John J. Schlosser, Brooklyn, New York, FHL 1323827. Often recorded on death certificates is the place of birth, but typically you may only find the country and not a specific place. Some may also record the place of birth for the parents' of the deceased.

VOTER REGISTRATIONS

Prior to 1906, each state had its own residency requirements for aliens and their eligibility to vote. In the early 1880s, at least eighteen states and territories required that an alien need only have filed a declaration of intention to have voting privileges. By 1905, this number was reduced to nine states: Arkansas,

Figure 5-16
Marriage return of Gustav Franz Hederich and Louise Charl. F. Müller, Charleston, South Carolina, marriage records, 1880–1883, volume 2:253, FHL 23411. Information on marriage records varies from state to state and from time period to time period, but some may give you the exact birthplace of immigrant ancestors.

Exact place of birth for the groom and bride.

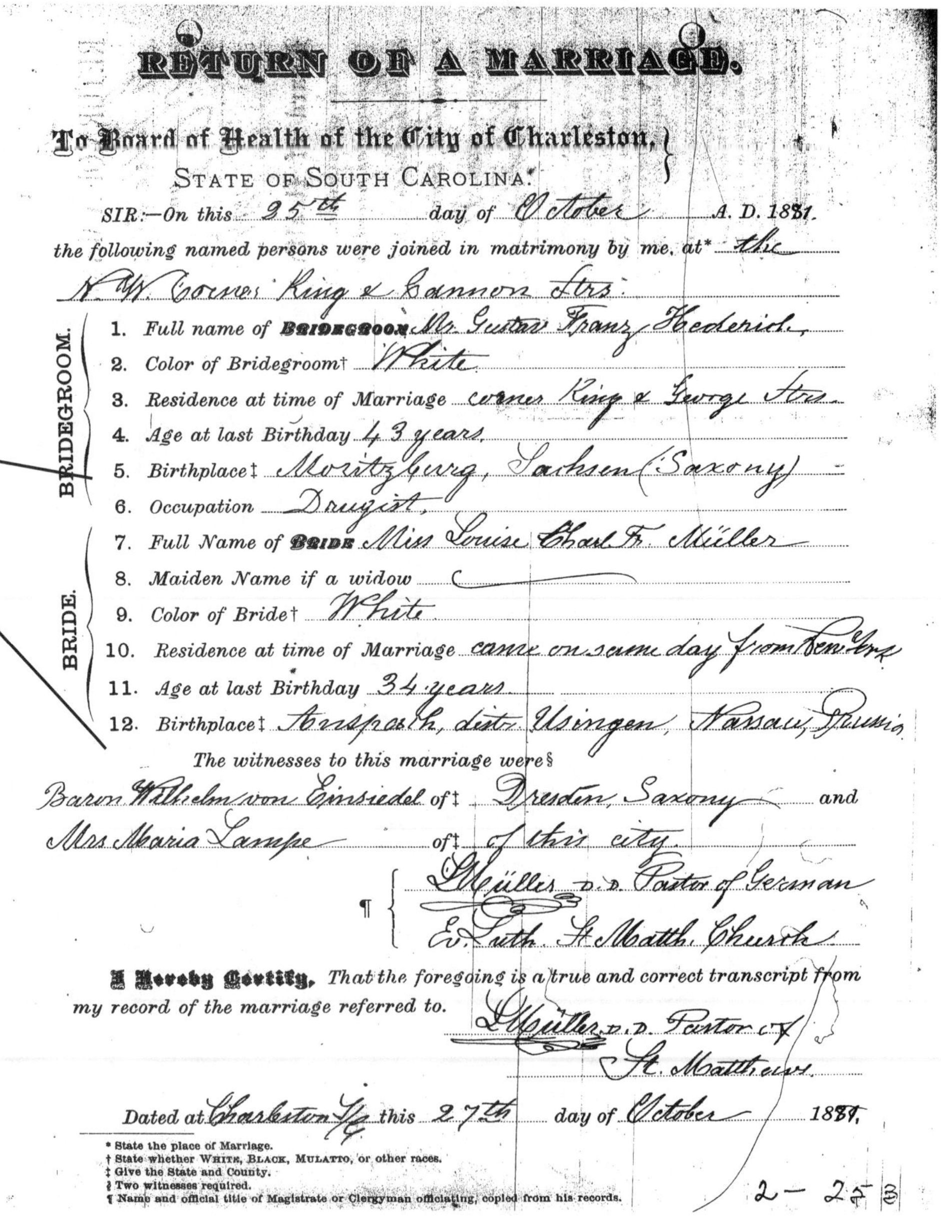

RETURN OF A MARRIAGE.

To Board of Health of the City of Charleston,
STATE OF SOUTH CAROLINA.

SIR:—On this 25th day of October A. D. 1881.
the following named persons were joined in matrimony by me, at* the N.W. Corner King & Cannon Strs.

BRIDEGROOM.
1. Full name of **BRIDEGROOM** Mr. Gustav Franz Hederich.
2. Color of Bridegroom† White
3. Residence at time of Marriage corner King & George Strs.
4. Age at last Birthday 43 years.
5. Birthplace‡ Moritzburg, Sachsen (Saxony)
6. Occupation Druggist.

BRIDE.
7. Full Name of **BRIDE** Miss Louise Charl. F. Müller
8. Maiden Name if a widow
9. Color of Bride† White
10. Residence at time of Marriage came on same day from New York
11. Age at last Birthday 34 years
12. Birthplace‡ Anspach, dist. Usingen, Nassau, Prussia

The witnesses to this marriage were§
Baron Wilhelm von Einsiedel of‡ Dresden, Saxony and
Mrs. Maria Lampe of‡ of this city.

¶ { Müller, D.D. Pastor of German
Ev. Luth. St. Matth. Church

I Hereby Certify, That the foregoing is a true and correct transcript from my record of the marriage referred to. Müller, D.D. Pastor of St. Matthews.

Dated at Charleston S.C. this 27th day of October 1881.

* State the place of Marriage.
† State whether WHITE, BLACK, MULATTO, or other races.
‡ Give the State and County.
§ Two witnesses required.
¶ Name and official title of Magistrate or Clergyman officiating, copied from his records.

2 – 25 3

Indiana, Kansas, Michigan, Missouri, Nebraska, Oregon, Texas, and Wisconsin. After 1906, citizenship was required before an immigrant could vote. Generally, voters' records are kept at the county or city level, with some states having statewide lists of voters kept in the secretary of state's office. Voter records may give naturalization information. Records may be extant only for the past five to seven years; however, some counties may have records from the twentieth century or earlier. (See Figure 5-17 on page 85.)

To utilize any of these original, contemporary records and others to their fullest potential, you should also familiarize yourself with the purpose and limitations of the record collection, as well as the social history of your ethnic

GREAT REGISTER, SACRAMENTO COUNTY.

Voter's records may detail the country of origin.

They may also give the date, place, and court where an immigrant became naturalized.

No.	NAME.	Age	Country of Nativity.	Occupation.	Local Residence.	NATURALIZED. Date.	NATURALIZED. Place.	NATURALIZED. By what Court.	Date of Registration.	Sworn
5044	Martin, Isaac	36	Ohio	Miner	Granite Township				July 15, 1867	Sworn
			Maryland	Laborer	Sacramento do				July 25, 1867	"
			Ireland	Laborer	Sacramento do	Aug. 5, 1867	Sacramento Co., Cal	District	Aug. 5, 1867	"
			Russia	Merchant	Sacramento do	Nov. 3, 1866	San Francisco, Cal.	12th Dist.	Aug. 20, 1867	"
			England	Farmer	Georgiana do	Sept. 5, 1859	San Francisco, Cal.	U.S.District	Aug. 30, 1867	"
			Ireland	Laborer	Sacramento do	Sept. 3, 1867	Sacramento Co., Cal	District	Sept 3, 1867	"
6038	Mayhew, Leo	49	Canada	Farmer	Brighton do	May 26, 1865	Sacramento Co., Cal	District	Sept. 3, 1867	"
6186	Maroney, Stephen	23	Pennsylvania	Carpenter	Sacramento do				March 9, 1868	"
			Ireland	Plasterer	Sacramento do	Sept. 4, 1838	Baltimore	District	March 9, 1868	"
			New York	Farmer	Natoma do				May 5, 1868	"
			New York	Clerk	Sacramento do				Sept 8, 1868	"
			Mississippi	Dep. Clk. Sup. Ct.	Sacramento do				Sept. 8, 1868	"
			Massachusetts	Clerk	Sacramento do				Sept. 15, 1868	"
			Rhode Island	Farmer	Sacramento do				Sept. 17, 1868	"
			Poland	Merchant	Sacramento do				Sept. 18, 1868	"
			Missouri	Teamster	Sacramento do				Sept. 19, 1868	"
6936	Maury, Alexander Henry	53	Rhode Island	Miner	Granite				Sept. 22, 1868	"
6971	Mann, Simon†	21	Ireland	Laborer	Sacramento do				Sept. 22, 1868	"
7025	Mahoney, Jeremiah	30	New York	Foreman	Sacramento do				Sept. 24, 1868	"
7059	Maynard, George "A."	28	Vermont	Painter	Sacramento do				Sept. 25, 1868	"
7106	Mangen, Peter "F."	43	Ireland	Horse shoer	Sacramento do	Sept. 26, 1868	Sacramento Co., Cal	District	Sept. 26, 1868	"
7202	Martfelt, William	44	Germany	Physician	Sacramento do	Sept. 28, 1868	Sacramento Co., Cal	District	Sept. 28, 1868	"
7248	Mahrt, Charles†	36	Germany	Butcher	Sacramento do				Sept. 29, 1868	"
7389	Martin, Hugh	25	Ireland	Laborer	Sacramento do	Sept. 25, 1866	Pennsylvania	U.S. Circuit	Sept. 30, 1868	"
7456	Mauldin, Benjamin Francis	54	Maryland	Merchant	Sacramento do				Oct. 1, 1868	"
7530	Massey, Richard Lee	28	Massachusetts	Painter	Sacramento do				Oct. 2, 1868	"
7535	Magee, James Bington	22	Ohio	Harness maker	Sacramento do				Oct. 2, 1868	"
7548	Marshall, Charles	52	Rhode Island	Cook	Sacramento do				Oct. 3, 1868	"
7586	Mason, Lewis Smith	64	Ohio	Book canvasser	Sacramento do				Oct. 8, 1868	"
7703	Marcuse, Max	22	Germany	Clerk	Sacramento do	Oct. 5, 1868	Sacramento Co., Cal	District	Oct. 5, 1868	"
7751	Maley, William	32	Ireland	Horse shoer	Sacramento do	Oct. 6, 1868	Sacramento Co., Cal	District	Oct. 6, 1868	"
7830	Major, Samuel Edward	47	Pennsylvania	Machinist	Lee do				Oct. 14, 1868	"
7878	Maranski, Julian‖	53	Poland	Merchant	Sacramento do				Oct. 19, 1868	"
7934	Martin, Alfred Alonzo	24	New Jersey	Teamster	Sacramento do				Oct. 26, 1868	"
7965	Martin, John Corbley	60	United States	Farmer	Franklin do				Oct. 29, 1868	"
8032	Maney, Cornelius	25	Ireland	Hostler	Sacramento do	Oct. 3, 1868	Sacramento Co., Cal	District	Nov. 2, 1868	"
8100	Martin, John	24	Arkansas	Laborer	Brighton do				Nov. 2, 1868	"
8123	Martin, John	28	Massachusetts	Watchman	Sacramento do				July 14, 1869	"
8284	Marrity, James Edward**	33	Ireland	Machinist	Sacramento co				July 31, 1869	"
8359	Marshall, Oscar	21	Iowa	Student	Sacramento do				July 30, 1869	"
8446	Maupin, Samuel Ford	49	Virginia	Shepherd	Cosumnes do				Aug. 10, 1869	"
8493	Manuel, Francisco**	26	Western Isles	Merchant	Sacramento do				Aug. 13, 1869	"
8553	Manning, John**	26	United States	Laborer	Sacramento do				Aug. 17, 1869	"
8595	Mallins, John**	28	Missouri	Farmer	Sacramento do				Aug. 23, 1869	"
8675	Maloney, Daniel**	35	Ireland	Laborer	Sacramento do				Aug. 23, 1869	"
8678	Maxwell, James	31	England	Hostler	Sacramento do	Sept. 23, 1868	San Francisco, Cal	U.S. Dist't	Aug. 25, 1869	"
8733	Mahoney, William	28	Pennsylvania	Laborer	Dry Creek do				Aug. 25, 1869	"
8736	Maxfield, George**	22	Missouri	Laborer	Dry Creek do				Aug. 25, 1869	"
8737	Maxfield, George**	53	Kentucky	Farmer	Dry Creek do				Aug. 25, 1869	"
8738	Maxfield, Robert Banks**	28	Kentucky	Farmer	Dry Creek do				Aug. 25, 1869	"

Figure 5-17
California's Great Register, 1871, Sacramento, FHL 978917.

group of interest that would affect your research in a particular set of documents. For instance, the draft registration records of World War I (discussed earlier in this chapter) dealt with a specific time period and age group of men. Without knowing the purpose and limitations of this source, some genealogists may overlook these documents, reasoning that an alien would not be included. But this is not the case.

While the sources mentioned above will give you clues or, in some cases, direct information about your immigrant ancestors, the federal government created several types of records specifically dealing with immigration and naturalization.

SIX

Naturalization, Immigration, and Emigration Records

T hroughout most of U.S. history, the federal government created records to keep track of foreign nationals entering and residing in America, primarily naturalization records and passenger arrival lists. While you no doubt would love to jump right to passenger arrival lists, unless you know the date of arrival and name of the ship, you need to get that information from somewhere. For some, it will come from information on the naturalization record, so this is how I've arranged the discussion. In other words, as with other aspects of your genealogical research, you will be working backward in time, starting with the immigrant's naturalization, then moving to the time of arrival (passenger lists or border crossings), then ultimately back to the port of departure in the homeland (emigration lists).

NATURALIZATION RECORDS

Depending on the time of your ancestor's arrival, naturalization records can give you the precise date and port of arrival, as well as the name of the ship, port of departure, and immigrant's date and place of birth. Some records, however, may only give you a year when the immigrant arrived. Regardless, the naturalization record is worth seeking for any and all information it may give you.

Between 1776 and 1790, each state established laws, procedures, and residency requirements for aliens to become naturalized citizens. After 1790, when the first federal naturalization law was passed, a series of acts changed restrictions and requirements over the centuries. **An abridged overview of the naturalization laws follow; however, for more detailed coverage, see John J. Newman, *American Naturalization Processes and Procedures, 1790–1985*, and Loretto Dennis Szucs, *They Became Americans: Finding Naturalization Records and Ethnic Origins*.**

In 1790, the applicant for citizenship had to be a free white male, twenty-one years of age or older, who had lived in the United States for two years and

For More Info

in the state in which he applied for one year. The applicant could have applied in any court of public record—federal, state, or local—in any one of the states.

In 1795, a two-step process was created to gain U.S. citizenship. First, a declaration of intention needed to be filed and a minimum of three years later, the alien could petition for naturalization. At that time, eligibility was extended to free white females, twenty-one years old, and the U.S. residency requirement was raised to five years. In 1798, the residency requirement was extended to fourteen years. In 1801, it was reduced back to five years, where it has remained since.

The 1795 law stipulated that applicants had to declare their intent at least three years prior to naturalization, but in 1824, this requirement was amended to two years. The 1824 law also stipulated that the naturalization process could be effected in one step, where the applicant was under the age of eighteen when he or she immigrated and had resided in the United States for three full years before turning twenty-one and petitioning for citizenship. This was known as "minor naturalization."

A nationality act of 1870, approved on 14 July of that year, allowed for naturalization of those of African nativity or descent, although ratification of the Fourteenth Amendment to the U.S. Constitution in 1868 made former slaves citizens. Asians could not become American citizens from 1882 until 1943. Copies of alien naturalization files, known as the "A-Files" (1943 to the present), are held by the Immigration and Naturalization Service. They may be obtained through a Freedom of Information/Privacy Act request, using Form G639 (see page 92). In 1910, Asian Indians were eligible for a short time; however, the Supreme Court ruled them ineligible in 1923. Filipinos and Asian Indians were banned from citizenship until 1946. Laws passed in 1887 and 1924 made American Indians citizens.

Though it was required, prior to 1903, some courts did not have an applicant file a petition (application) for naturalization. A special form was created in 1903 by the U.S. Department of Justice, but not all courts used it. The nineteenth-century records may contain some or all of the following data: the applicant's name, country of birth, date of application, and signature. Some give the date and port of arrival, occupation, residence, age, birthplace, and date of birth.

As with any bureaucratic process, people found ways to avoid legally becoming a citizen. For example, a person might obtain several copies of his declaration and then sell them at election time, so aliens could vote. Also, more aliens applied at county and state courts than federal because the fee was usually less and standards may not have been as stringent.

The Bureau of Immigration and Naturalization, now known as the Immigration and Naturalization Service, was established in 1906, and copies of all naturalizations made after this date in courts around the country were forwarded to that agency. Becoming a naturalized citizen became standardized and involved the process of filing a declaration of intention (first papers), then, after fulfilling the residency requirement, filing a petition for naturalization, which required the applicant's signature (second or final papers).

48

Shows the county in Ireland where John was born and the year.

UNITED STATES OF AMERICA.

STATE OF NEW YORK----ORANGE COUNTY, ss:

— On this *3rd* day of *August* , in the year of our Lord one thousand eight hundred and ninety *six* , I, *John Simpson* , an Alien, formerly a resident of *Ireland* , and now a resident of *Newburgh* , in the County of Orange, and State aforesaid do, upon oath, declare that I was born in *County Antrim Ireland* on or about the year 18 *76* ; that I emigrated to the United States of America and landed at the Port of *New York* on or about the month of *June* , in the year 18 *86* ; that it is, bona fide, my intention to become a CITIZEN OF THE UNITED STATES OF AMERICA, and to _____ nce and fidelity to any and every Foreign Prince, Potentate, State or Sovereignty whatsoever, and particula_____ elity to _____

From this record we learn the port and the month and year of arrival. Assuming this is accurate information, at least it narrows the search to a month and year for his passenger arrival list.

Victoria, Queen of the United _____ d Ireland _____ of whom I am now a Subject.

Subscribed and sworn to this *3rd* of *August* A. D. 18*96*, before _____

Geo A. Price
Depty _____ Clerk of Orange County.

_____ idence : No. *62 Hasbrouck* Street, *Newburgh* N. Y.

John Simpson

Figure 6-1
Declaration of intention for John Simpson, Orange County, New York, FHL 1298783, item 5, 1895–1906. Pre-1906 naturalization records often give only scanty information.

\di'fin\ *vb*

Definitions

\di'fin\ *vb*

Definitions

In the first papers, or declaration of intention, an alien renounced his allegiance to his homeland and declared his intention to become a U.S. citizen. The declaration needed to be submitted between two and seven years before the petition. The post-1906 declarations of intention included the applicant's name, age, occupation, and personal description; date and place of birth; citizenship; present address and last foreign address; vessel and port of embarkation; U.S. port and date of arrival; date of application; and signature (see Figure 6-3 on page 90).

In the naturalization petition (second or final papers), an immigrant who had already filed the intention papers and had met the residency requirements made a formal application for citizenship. Information on the petition included name, residence, occupation, date and place of birth, citizenship, and personal description of applicant; date of emigration; ports of embarkation and arrival; marital status (with wife's name and date of birth, if married); names, dates, places

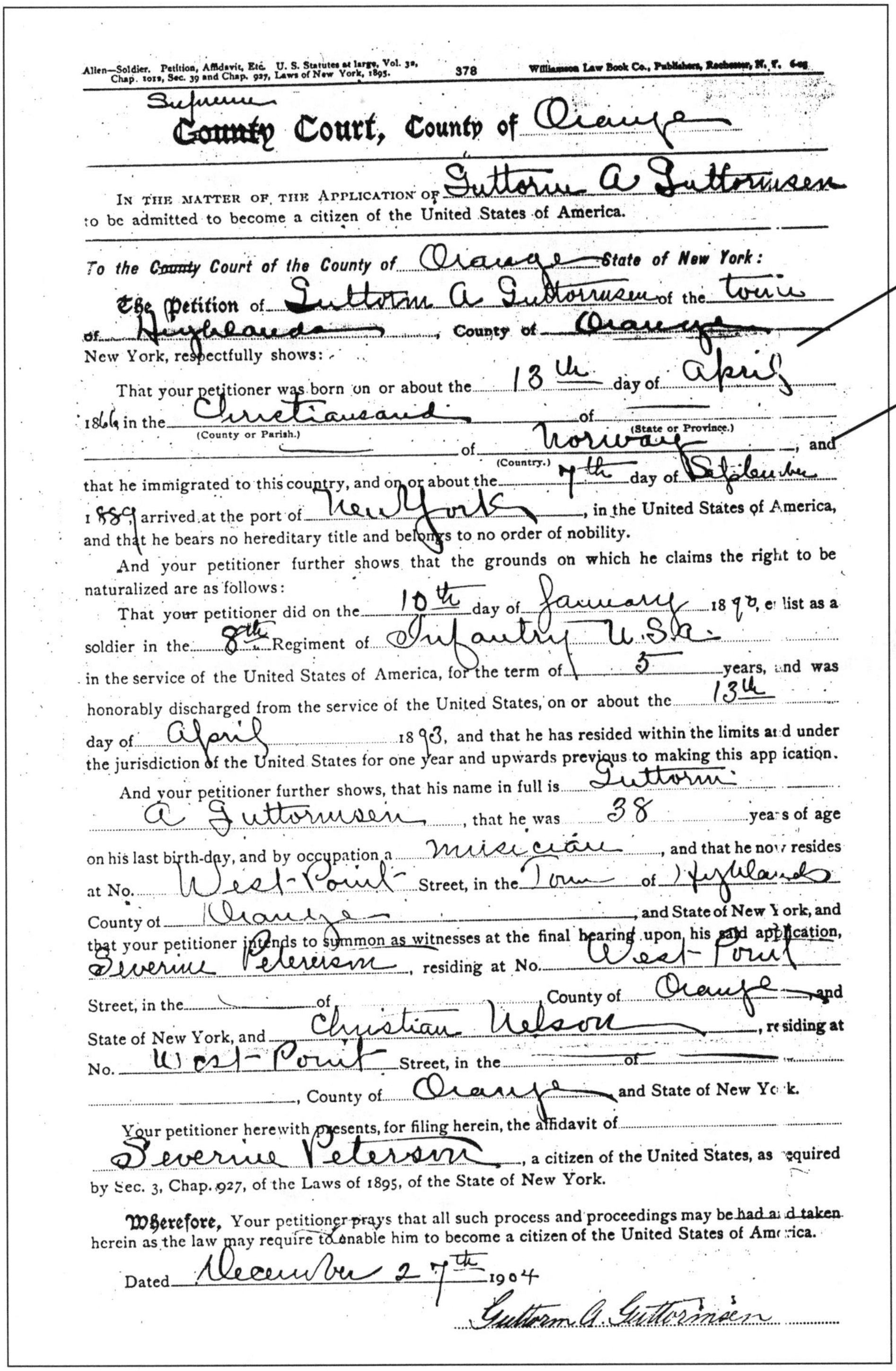

Allen—Soldier. Petition, Affidavit, Etc. U. S. Statutes at large, Vol. 32, Chap. 1012, Sec. 39 and Chap. 927, Laws of New York, 1895. 378 Williamson Law Book Co., Publishers, Rochester, N. Y. 6-03

Supreme ~~County~~ Court, County of Orange

In the matter of the Application of Guttorm A Guttormsen to be admitted to become a citizen of the United States of America.

To the ~~County~~ Court of the County of Orange State of New York:

The Petition of Guttorm A Guttormsen of the town of Highlands, County of Orange, New York, respectfully shows:

That your petitioner was born on or about the 13th day of April 1866 in the Christiansand (County or Parish.) of (State or Province.) of Norway (Country.), and that he immigrated to this country, and on or about the 7th day of September 1889 arrived at the port of New York, in the United States of America, and that he bears no hereditary title and belongs to no order of nobility.

And your petitioner further shows that the grounds on which he claims the right to be naturalized are as follows:

That your petitioner did on the 10th day of January 1890, enlist as a soldier in the 8th Regiment of Infantry U.S.A. in the service of the United States of America, for the term of 5 years, and was honorably discharged from the service of the United States, on or about the 13th day of April 1893, and that he has resided within the limits and under the jurisdiction of the United States for one year and upwards previous to making this application.

And your petitioner further shows, that his name in full is Guttorm A Guttormsen, that he was 38 years of age on his last birth-day, and by occupation a musician, and that he now resides at No. West-Point Street, in the Town of Highlands, County of Orange, and State of New York, and that your petitioner intends to summon as witnesses at the final hearing upon his said application, Severine Petersen, residing at No. West-Point Street, in the of, County of Orange and State of New York, and Christian Nelson, residing at No. West-Point Street, in the of, County of Orange and State of New York.

Your petitioner herewith presents, for filing herein, the affidavit of Severine Petersen, a citizen of the United States, as required by Sec. 3, Chap. 927, of the Laws of 1895, of the State of New York.

Wherefore, Your petitioner prays that all such process and proceedings may be had and taken herein as the law may require to enable him to become a citizen of the United States of America.

Dated December 27th 1904

Guttorm A. Guttormsen

Figure 6-2
Petition for naturalization of Guttorm A. Guttormsen, Orange County, New York, FHL 1298782. Effective 17 July 1862, citizenship was granted to any alien who was age twenty-one or older, and who had enlisted in the armies of the United States, either as part of the regular or volunteer forces, and who had been or was eligible to be honorably discharged. The alien could bypass the first step of filing a declaration of intention and only needed to file a petition for naturalization. This incentive for aliens to perform military service was repeated after the Civil War, such as in the Spanish-American War of 1898, the Philippine Insurrection of 1900–1901, and World War I. A copy of the immigrant's naturalization papers should also be among his military service records.

of birth, and residence of applicant's children; date at which U.S. residence commenced; time of residence in state; name changes; and signature (see Figure 6-4 on page 91). After 1929, photographs were included on the declaration and final certificate. In the deposition that accompanied the petition, witnesses signed in support of the applicant.

The naturalization law of 1906 stated that after the petition had been filed,

Figure 6-3
Declaration of intention for Salvatore Ebetino, 27 February 1914, case number 8062, Supreme Court of New York, Westchester County; Westchester County Records Center and Archives, Elmsford, New York.

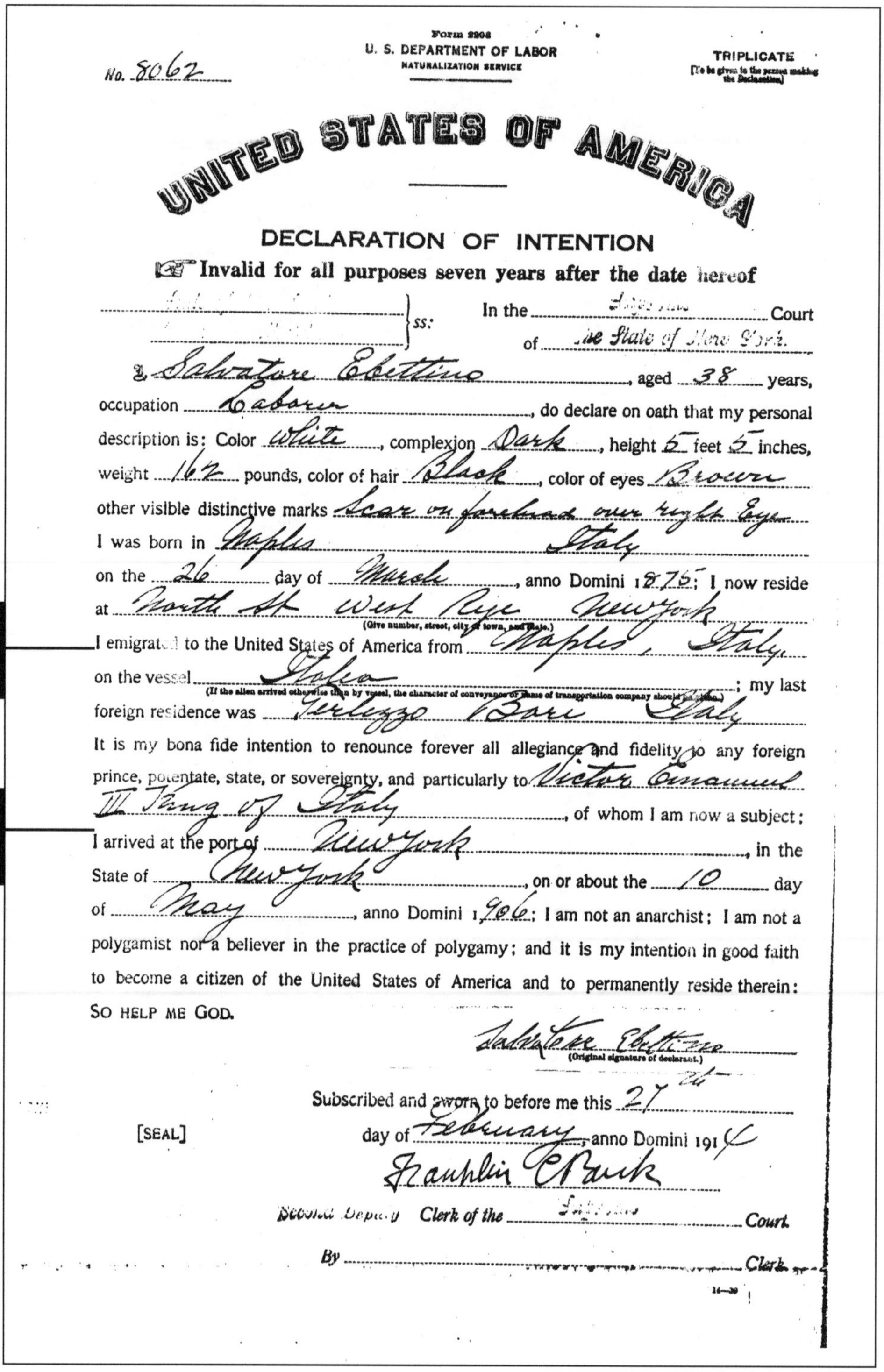
Form 2202
U. S. DEPARTMENT OF LABOR
NATURALIZATION SERVICE

No. 8062

TRIPLICATE
[To be given to the person making the Declaration]

UNITED STATES OF AMERICA

DECLARATION OF INTENTION

Invalid for all purposes seven years after the date hereof

ss: In the Supreme Court of the State of New York.

I, Salvatore Ebettino, aged 38 years, occupation Laborer, do declare on oath that my personal description is: Color White, complexion Dark, height 5 feet 5 inches, weight 162 pounds, color of hair Black, color of eyes Brown other visible distinctive marks Scar on forehead over right Eye I was born in Naples Italy on the 26 day of March, anno Domini 1875; I now reside at North St West Rye New York (Give number, street, city or town, and State.) I emigrated to the United States of America from Naples, Italy, on the vessel Italia (If the alien arrived otherwise than by vessel, the character of conveyance or name of transportation company should be given.); my last foreign residence was Terlizzo Bari Italy It is my bona fide intention to renounce forever all allegiance and fidelity to any foreign prince, potentate, state, or sovereignty, and particularly to Victor Emanuel III King of Italy, of whom I am now a subject; I arrived at the port of New York, in the State of New York, on or about the 10 day of May, anno Domini 1906; I am not an anarchist; I am not a polygamist nor a believer in the practice of polygamy; and it is my intention in good faith to become a citizen of the United States of America and to permanently reside therein: SO HELP ME GOD.

Salvatore Ebettino
(Original signature of declarant.)

Subscribed and sworn to before me this 27th day of February, anno Domini 1914

[SEAL]

Franklin C Burk
Second Deputy Clerk of the Supreme Court.

By .... Clerk.

Gives the port of departure and the name of the vessel.

Gives the port of arrival and the date.

there would be a ninety-day wait before the hearing and citizenship was granted or denied. There were also no naturalization hearings thirty days prior to any general election within the court's area of jurisdiction. The new U.S. citizen was given a certificate of citizenship bearing the seal of the naturalizing court. This

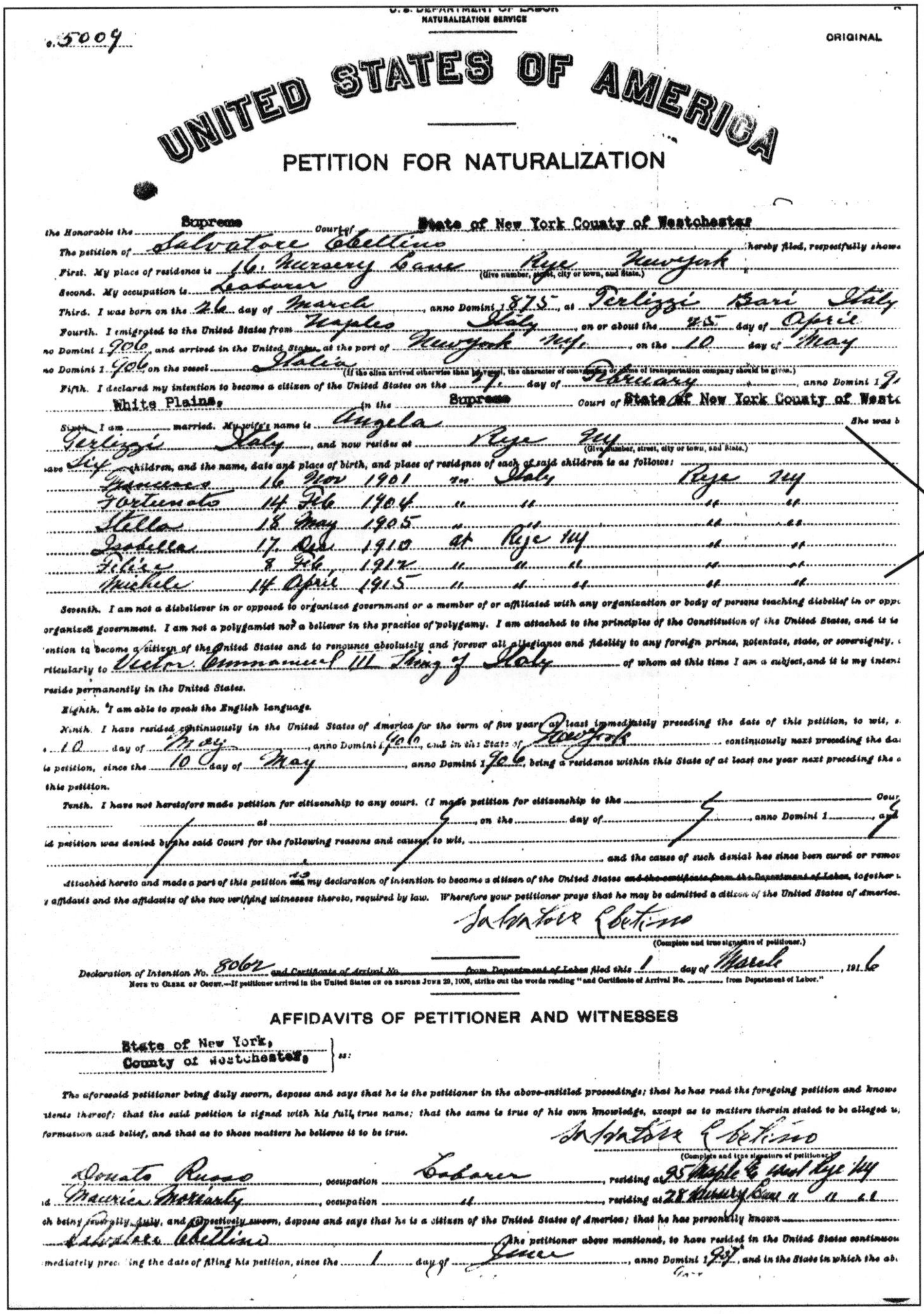
U.S. DEPARTMENT OF LABOR
NATURALIZATION SERVICE

No. 5009 ORIGINAL

UNITED STATES OF AMERICA

PETITION FOR NATURALIZATION

To the Honorable the Supreme Court of State of New York County of Westchester

The petition of Salvatore Ebetino hereby filed, respectfully shows:

First. My place of residence is 16 Nursery Lane Rye New York (Give number, street, city or town, and State.)

Second. My occupation is Laborer

Third. I was born on the 26 day of March anno Domini 1875 at Terlizzi Bari Italy

Fourth. I emigrated to the United States from Naples Italy on or about the 25 day of April anno Domini 1906, and arrived in the United States, at the port of New York N.Y. on the 10 day of May anno Domini 1906 on the vessel Italia (If the alien arrived otherwise than by vessel, the character of conveyance or name of transportation company should be given.)

Fifth. I declared my intention to become a citizen of the United States on the 27 day of February anno Domini 19.. at White Plains, in the Supreme Court of State of New York County of Westc...

Sixth. I am married. My wife's name is Angela She was b... Terlizzi Italy and now resides at Rye NY (Give number, street, city or town, and State.) I have Six children, and the name, date and place of birth, and place of residence of each of said children is as follows:

Francesco 16 Nov 1901 in Italy Rye NY
Fortunato 14 Feb 1904 " " " "
Stella 18 May 1905 " " " "
Isobella 17 Dec 1910 at Rye NY " "
Felice 8 Feb 1912 " " " "
Michele 14 April 1915 " " " " "

Seventh. I am not a disbeliever in or opposed to organized government or a member of or affiliated with any organization or body of persons teaching disbelief in or opp... organized government. I am not a polygamist nor a believer in the practice of polygamy. I am attached to the principles of the Constitution of the United States, and it is ... ...ention to become a citizen of the United States and to renounce absolutely and forever all allegiance and fidelity to any foreign prince, potentate, state, or sovereignty, ...rticularly to Victor Emmanuel III King of Italy of whom at this time I am a subject, and it is my inten... reside permanently in the United States.

Eighth. I am able to speak the English language.

Ninth. I have resided continuously in the United States of America for the term of five years at least immediately preceding the date of this petition, to wit, ... 10 day of May, anno Domini 1906, and in the State of New York continuously next preceding the da... ...is petition, since the 10 day of May, anno Domini 1906, being a residence within this State of at least one year next preceding the ... this petition.

Tenth. I have not heretofore made petition for citizenship to any court. (I made petition for citizenship to the ... Court at ... on the ... day of ... anno Domini 1... and ...id petition was denied by the said Court for the following reasons and causes, to wit, ... and the cause of such denial has since been cured or remov...

Attached hereto and made a part of this petition are my declaration of intention to become a citizen of the United States and the certificate from the Department of Labor, together ... affidavit and the affidavits of the two verifying witnesses thereto, required by law. Wherefore your petitioner prays that he may be admitted a citizen of the United States of America.

Salvatore Ebetino
(Complete and true signature of petitioner.)

Declaration of Intention No. 8062 and Certificate of Arrival No. .... from Department of Labor filed this 1 day of March, 1916

Note to Clerk of Court.—If petitioner arrived in the United States on or before June 29, 1906, strike out the words reading "and Certificate of Arrival No. .... from Department of Labor."

AFFIDAVITS OF PETITIONER AND WITNESSES

State of New York,
County of Westchester, ss:

The aforesaid petitioner being duly sworn, deposes and says that he is the petitioner in the above-entitled proceedings; that he has read the foregoing petition and knows ...tents thereof; that the said petition is signed with his full, true name; that the same is true of his own knowledge, except as to matters therein stated to be alleged u... ...formation and belief, and that as to those matters he believes it to be true.

Salvatore Ebetino
(Complete and true signature of petitioner.)

Donato Russo, occupation Laborer, residing at 95 Maple Av West Rye NY
Maurice Moriarty, occupation ", residing at 28 Nursery Lane " " "

...ch being severally, duly, and respectively sworn, deposes and says that he is a citizen of the United States of America; that he has personally known Salvatore Ebetino the petitioner above mentioned, to have resided in the United States continuou... ...mediately preceding the date of filing his petition, since the 1 day of June, anno Domini 1907, and in the State in which the ab...

Figure 6-4
Petition for naturalization for Salvatore Ebetino, 1 March 1916, number 5009, Supreme Court of New York, Westchester County; Westchester County Records Center and Archives, Elmsford, New York.

Before 1922, women and children became citizens when the husband/father did, so you may find information about the petitioner's wife and children.

document may be preserved and handed down from generation to generation in many American families.

Between 1855 and 1922, an alien wife automatically became a citizen when her husband did or when she married an American citizen. This was called "derivative" citizenship. Conversely, a congressional act of 1907 declared that if an American woman married an alien, she lost her citizenship and took on the nationality of her husband. She was then no longer eligible for U.S. citizenship unless her husband applied and was accepted. After 1922, the law was

For More Info

For more on laws affecting the citizenship of women, see Marian L. Smith, "Women and Naturalization, ca. 1802–1940," in *Prologue* 30 (Summer 1998): 146–153.

changed to allow women to obtain citizenship independently, and they did not lose it when they married aliens. Since the first federal naturalization law of 1790, children (under the age of twenty-one) enjoyed derivative citizenship when the father became naturalized.

To obtain naturalization records, check at courthouses—municipal, county, state, and federal—where the immigrant arrived and/or settled. These records as well as indexes may have also been microfilmed by the Family History Library. Also check city, county, and state archives. Naturalizations made in municipal courts may be found in the town halls or city archives of some major cities, such as Baltimore, Chicago, and St. Louis. If these avenues fail, write to the Immigration and Naturalization Service, 425 I Street NW, Washington, DC 20536. On the envelope, write "FOIA/PA request," as well as in your letter. This means you are making the request under the Freedom of Information Act/Privacy Act.

As you will learn from reading social histories, members of some ethnic groups were slow to become naturalized, if at all, or were not allowed to do so. Typically, those men who were birds of passage—Italians, Greeks, and Poles—did not rush to become American citizens. In many cases, their goal was not to permanently settle in America; it was to earn money and return to their homeland and buy land there. This may be a reason you would not find a naturalization record for your ancestor, or you will find one several years after your ancestor arrived.

Certificates of Arrival

Between 1906 and the early 1940s, the Bureau of Immigration and Naturalization (or INS) may have created a certificate of arrival for your ancestor. These certificates were created when an applicant applied for citizenship and officials checked the ship's manifest to verify legal admission. If the arrival record was found, the INS issued a certificate of arrival and sent it back to the court where the alien applied for citizenship. This certificate, which, if created and extant, should be on file with the naturalization record. It will list the port of entry, the date, and the name of the ship. You may also find a manifest number, such as 1-39-5235, giving the list number, group number, and volume number of the manifest.

Naturalization Stub Books

Although largely unindexed and arranged by filing date, surviving naturalization certificate stub books are another useful source. Most courts did not keep a copy of the naturalization certificate given to the new citizen, but they may have retained the "stubs" attached to the certificates that were bound in volumes. While these records vary in content over the years and from one court to another, they may contain the date the alien declared his intention to become a citizen, his age, and the names and ages of his wife and children. Look for these stub books in the courts of various jurisdictions that handled naturalizations and in archives and historical societies.

ALIEN REGISTRATIONS

Aliens were required to register their current addresses and places of employment with the federal government between 1940 and about 1982. The Alien Registration Act of 1940 required aliens to report their address and employment, and to report any change of address immediately. In 1952, this changed to reporting their address annually. The address reporting ended in the 1980s, and only the last/most recent address might remain on file. Requests may be made through the Freedom of Information Act and by writing to the Immigration and Naturalization Service in Washington, D.C. Alien registration cards may often be found among family papers and keepsakes. (See Figure 6-5 below.)

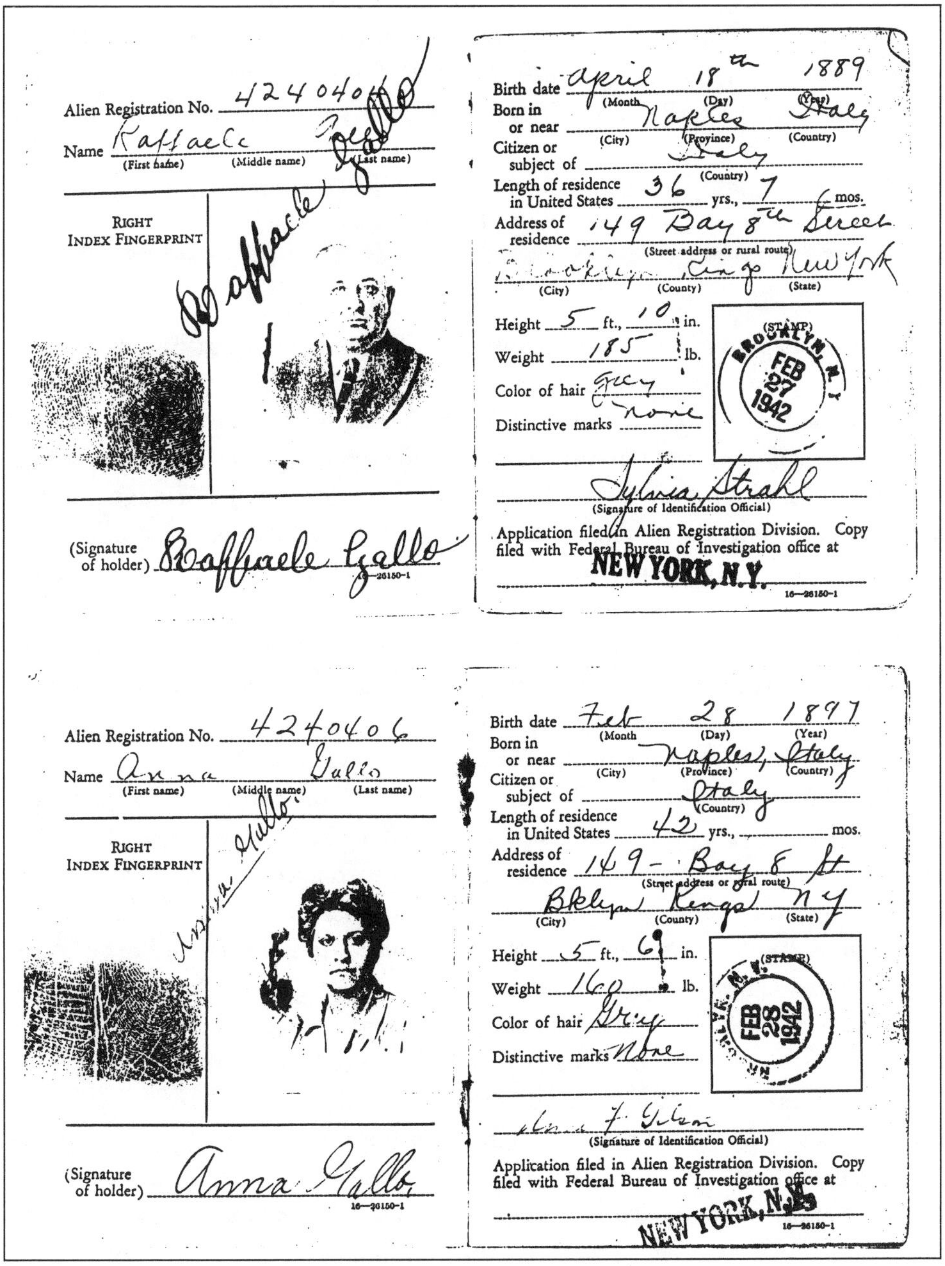
Alien Registration No. 4240400
Name Raffaele Gallo (First name) (Middle name) (Last name)
RIGHT INDEX FINGERPRINT
(Signature of holder) Raffaele Gallo
16—26150-1

Birth date April 18th 1889 (Month) (Day) (Year)
Born in or near Naples Italy (City) (Province) (Country)
Citizen or subject of Italy (Country)
Length of residence in United States 36 yrs., 7 mos.
Address of residence 149 Bay 8th Street (Street address or rural route)
Brooklyn Kings New York (City) (County) (State)
Height 5 ft., 10 in.
Weight 185 lb.
Color of hair Grey
Distinctive marks None
(STAMP) BROOKLYN, N.Y. FEB 27 1942
Sylvia Strahl (Signature of Identification Official)
Application filed in Alien Registration Division. Copy filed with Federal Bureau of Investigation office at NEW YORK, N.Y.
16—26150-1

Alien Registration No. 4240406
Name Anna Gallo (First name) (Middle name) (Last name)
RIGHT INDEX FINGERPRINT
(Signature of holder) Anna Gallo
16—26150-1

Birth date Feb 28 1897 (Month) (Day) (Year)
Born in or near Naples, Italy (City) (Province) (Country)
Citizen or subject of Italy (Country)
Length of residence in United States 42 yrs., mos.
Address of residence 149 - Bay 8 St (Street address or rural route)
Bklyn Kings NY (City) (County) (State)
Height 5 ft., 6 in.
Weight 160 lb.
Color of hair Grey
Distinctive marks None
(STAMP) FEB 28 1942
(Signature of Identification Official)
Application filed in Alien Registration Division. Copy filed with Federal Bureau of Investigation office at NEW YORK, N.Y.
16—26150-1

Figure 6-5
Aliens were required to register their current addresses and places of employment with the federal government between 1940 and 1982. Look for alien registration cards among family papers. The Gallo registration cards are courtesy of Anita Lustenberger, Irvington, New York.

PUBLISHED PASSENGER LISTS AND INDEXES

The federal government did not begin keeping a record of passenger arrivals until 1820, but many pre-1820 passenger lists created by state or local authorities have been published in a multitude of works. We will begin our examination of immigrant arrival information with these published works and then move on to the unpublished original federal records.

More and more published works appear on passenger arrivals each year, and many are listed in the bibliography. Only selected and representative examples will be mentioned here. Most of the surviving early American passenger lists have been published. P. William Filby and his coeditors provide indexes to these as well as other evidence of immigration taken from sources in their multivolume work, *Passenger and Immigration Lists Index: A Guide to Published Arrival Records of About 500,000 Passengers Who Came to the United States and Canada in the 17th, 18th, and 19th Centuries*. *Passenger and Immigration Lists Index*, or PILI, was first published in 1981, and there are currently nineteen supplements, covering more than 3,050,000 persons. Remember, the information in these volumes comes from published sources, not original records. At first glance, the entries in PILI look rather cryptic:

Fryer, George; Virginia, 1623 **9180.10** p34

There is an explanation at the beginning of each volume, but here is what it means: name of the immigrant as spelled in the original published source; place of arrival, naturalization, or other record of immigration; year of arrival, naturalization, or other record of immigration; code referring to the source in which the record was found (codes are identified in each volume); and page number on which that particular name is listed in the cited source. Keep in mind that the date associated with an ancestor's name may not be the date of arrival, but the date an ancestor was first mentioned in a record as being in America. You must either check each volume, or you can speed your search by checking Family Tree Maker's CD #354, *Family Archives: Passenger and Immigration Lists Index, 1538–1940* (1999 update).

Several works deal with arrivals of indentured servants and convicts, for example, Peter Wilson Coldham's *The Complete Book of Emigrants in Bondage, 1614–1775* and *Emigrants in Chains, 1607–1776*. In the latter book, there are brief biographical sketches on some of the transported felons. Other books focus on specific ethnic arrivals, such as Ira A. Glazier and P. William Filby's *The Famine Immigrants: Lists of Irish Immigrants Arriving at the Port of New York, 1846–1851* (six volumes); *Germans to America: Lists of Passengers Arriving at U.S. Ports, 1850–1891* (sixty volumes); and *Italians to America: Lists of Passengers Arriving at U.S. Ports, 1880–1899* (twelve volumes projected). (See bibliographies of each ethnic group in Part II for additional ethnic arrival lists.)

The series of Glazier and Filby's *Italians to America*, for example, covers the major American ports of arrival. Data were taken from the original passenger lists kept at the Balch Institute, which are not available for public research since microfilm copies may be accessed via the National Archives or Family History

Sources

Library. These lists were compiled at the port of embarkation and filed once the ship docked in America. Most of the lists deal with ships that left ports in Italy—Naples, Genoa, and Palermo—but Glazier and Filby also included those Italians sailing on ships that departed from other European ports. Along with a surname index to every volume, the information contained gives the name of the vessel, ports of departure and arrival, date of arrival, name of passenger, age, sex, occupation, village or province of origin, and destination (when available). Most of the arrival lists for the 1880s contain scanty information; places of origin may simply be recorded as "Italy." Under the column "village or province of origin," a listing of "unknown" is typical.

Multivolume indexes such as these offer convenient access to previously unindexed records; be aware, however, that they are not without error. For example, in a random comparison of a ship's list transcribed in *Italians to America* with the original list on microfilm available through the National Archives, I noted several transcription errors. For the ship *Utopia*, which left Naples and arrived at New York on 23 April 1883, I found twenty-five-year-old E. Cassiere, a female passenger, recorded as a servant in *Italians to America*; on the original list (National Archives microfilm M237, roll 464), she was a maid. Ant. Gersosimo was listed in the book as one-year-old; on the microfilmed list, he was fifteen months old. G. Mennella, a male aged forty-four, was of "unknown" occupation in Glazier and Filby's work; on the microcopy, his occupation was "interpreter." Sav. Rubetro appeared as a forty-eight-year-old laborer on both the transcription and the original, but the transcription omitted his death aboard the *Utopia* on 21 April 1883 from pneumonia. This is an important detail if Sav. Rubetro is *your* ancestor. These examples reinforce the standard rule: You should always go beyond the convenience of a published source to verify its accuracy against the original record.

Along with the Ellis Island project to transcribe and make available passenger arrival lists for the Port of New York, 1892–1924, there is an Immigrant Ships Transcribers Guild posted on the Internet at <http://istg.rootsweb.com/> (see chapter four).

So did I check Filby's *Passenger and Immigration Lists Index* and the other pertinent sources for Cornelius Carmack's arrival? Yes. Did I find an entry for him? No.

MORTON ALLAN DIRECTORY

The Morton Allan Directory of European Passenger Steamship Arrivals for the Years 1890 to 1930 at the Port of New York and for the Years 1904 to 1926 at the Ports of New York, Philadelphia, Boston, and Baltimore can be an extremely helpful source if your ancestors arrived during these time periods and through one of these ports. However, **it is not complete regarding steamships arriving from Europe, and it does not list ships arriving from places other than Europe.**

Suppose from family stories or a naturalization record you learn that your ancestor arrived in 1896 at the Port of New York on the ship *Rotterdam*. Sadly,

Warning

For More Info

See Gordon L. Remington, "Feast or Famine: Problems in the Genealogical Use of *The Famine Immigrants* and *Germans to America*," in *National Genealogical Society Quarterly* 78 (June 1990): 135–146.

Warning

there is no index yet to New York passenger arrival lists for 1896. You could search all passenger lists for that year to find the *Rotterdam*'s list, but you would be cranking through more rolls of microfilm than you'd care to count. To narrow your search, you need a precise date or at least a month. Turn to the *Morton Allan Directory,* which can be found in most genealogical libraries.

This book is arranged by year, then the shipping lines and routes, listing ships and their dates of arrival to a particular port. Turning to 1896, you can scan the lists of ships' names and find that the *Rotterdam* docked in New York nine times that year. You can then search each date's lists—a more manageable task—or try to narrow the time frame even more—spring, summer, fall, winter—from family information or details found in other records. Sometimes, a record will give you a precise arrival date, but the date could be off by a few days, so double-check the date in the *Morton Allan Directory.* This directory also gives the dates the ships were scheduled to arrive, not the actual arrival date. Delays of a few days were common.

INFORMATION ON PASSENGER SHIPS

For details on the ships themselves, including sketches and photographs of vessels, the following books are helpful: Michael J. Anuta's *Ships of Our Ancestors*; Eugene W. Smith's *Passenger Ships of the World Past and Present*; Arnold Kludas' *Great Passenger Ships of the World* (five volumes). The National Maritime Museum, J. Porter Shaw Library (Building E, Fort Mason Center, San Francisco, CA 94123) and The Mariner's Museum (100 Museum Drive, Newport News, VA 23606) provide assistance in obtaining photographs and sketches of ships to include when publishing a family history. Other maritime museums offering assistance are Mystic Seaport Museum, 50 Greenmanville Avenue, Mystic, CT 06355; Peabody Museum, East India Square, Salem, MA 01970; Steamship Historical Society of America, Langsdale Library, University of Baltimore, 1420 Maryland Avenue, Baltimore, MD 21201.

PORTS OF ARRIVAL

In the eighteenth century, Philadelphia saw the lion's share of immigration. In the nineteenth century, the five major ports of arrival receiving significant numbers of newcomers were Baltimore, Boston, New Orleans, New York, and Philadelphia, with New York receiving three-quarters of all arrivals by the 1880s. Also in use throughout the nineteenth and well into the twentieth century, and for which some records survive, were about ninety-six other ports on the Atlantic, Pacific, and Gulf coasts, and the Great Lakes.

Prior to the mid-nineteenth century, there were no immigrant inspection stations. Then in 1855, Castle Garden, located on an island off the southern tip of Manhattan, opened. Here, short inspections and medical examinations of arriving passengers took place. Castle Garden gave way to Ellis Island in 1892. The two most famous inspection stations were New York's Ellis Island (1892–1957) and San Francisco's Angel Island (1910–1940). New York was

For More Info

For the immigrant experience aboard ship, see Edwin C. Guillet, *The Great Migration: The Atlantic Crossing by Sailing-Ship Since 1770*; Terry Coleman, *Going to America*; and Mary J. Shapiro, *Gateway to Liberty: The Story of the Statue of Liberty and Ellis Island.*

For More Info

For more on the immigrant experience through Ellis Island and Castle Garden, see Peter Morton Coan, *Ellis Island Interviews: In Their Own Words*; Mary J. Shapiro, *Gateway to Liberty: The Story of the Statue of Liberty and Ellis Island*; and Virginia Yans-McLaughlin and Marjorie Lightman, *Ellis Island and the Peopling of America: The Official Guide.* For information on other ports of arrival, see Bernard Marinbach, *Galveston: Ellis Island of the West*; and M. Mark Stolarik, editor, *Forgotten Doors: The Other Ports of Entry to the United States.*

the busiest port, receiving up to five million immigrants in a single year. Keep in mind that some arriving vessels docked at more than one port, stopping first in Boston, for example, and then making a final arrival in New York, so check indexes for all ports if you are having trouble finding your ancestors.

SHIPS' MANIFESTS

Now we turn to the original arrival records kept by the federal government, beginning in 1820, and the indexes to them. **This is an overview of passenger lists; for more in-depth study on this subject, see John Colletta's** *They Came in Ships* **and Michael Tepper's** *American Passenger Arrival Records.*

Most original passenger arrival lists, 1820–1957 (with some gaps), have been microfilmed and are available through the National Archives as well as through the Family History Library and its Family History Centers. The regional records services facilities of the National Archives have films for the ports in their jursidiction. The guide, *Immigrant and Passenger Arrivals: A Select Catalog of National Archives Microfilm Publications*, details more fully the availability of records and indexes for each port. This catalog is available via the National Archives' Web site at <http://www.nara.gov/publications/microfilm/immigrant/immpass.html/>, or at most genealogical libraries. You may also purchase a copy from the National Archives (see Appendix B).

For More Info

Customs Lists (1820–ca. 1891)

Passenger lists from 1820 to about 1891 were known as Customs Lists. They were usually printed in the United States, completed by ship company personnel at the port of departure, and maintained primarily for statistical purposes; therefore, they contain scanty information: name of ship and its master; port of embarkation; date and port of arrival; each passenger's name, sex, age, occupation, and nationality. (See Figure 6-6 on page 98.)

Immigration Passenger Lists (ca. 1891–1954)

Arrival records created from about 1891 to the 1950s are referred to as Immigration Passenger Lists. Like Customs Lists, these were printed in the United States, but completed at the port of departure, then filed in America after the ship docked. The information provided in Immigration Passenger Lists varied over the decades. As the influx of immigrants became greater, more details were recorded, for example, in 1893, there were twenty-one columns of information; in 1906, twenty-eight; in 1907, twenty-nine; and in 1917, thirty-three. All of these details are valuable to your research, but in particular, items such as the last residence; the final destination in the United States; if going to join a relative, the relative's name and address; a personal description; the place of birth; and the name and address of the closest living relative in the native country, will give you information you may not find anywhere else.

Prints of microfilmed passenger lists may be obtained by mail from the National Archives for a modest fee, using NATF Form 81. Forms may be requested by E-mail at inquire@nara.gov or by letter to the National Archives and Records

Figure 6-6
Customs list, *Utopia*, arriving at the Port of New York, 23 April 1883, NARA microfilm M237, roll 464.

The following annotations appear on the figure:

> **Early passenger arrival lists give scanty information, and usually only the country of origin is given, not a precise location.**

> **If a passenger died at sea, you'll typically find the date and cause of death. Sav. Ruberto, age 48, died on 21 April 1883, of pneumonia.**

For More Info

What do those numbers and annotations made on your ancestor's passenger arrival list mean? See Marian L. Smith, "Interpreting U.S. Immigration Manifest Annotations," *Avotaynu: The International Review of Jewish Genealogy* 12 (Spring 1996): 10–13.

Administration, 700 Pennsylvania Avenue NW, Washington, DC 20408. (You may also find copies of National Archives request forms at the regional records services facilities.) The National Archives will not do research for you, however. The minimum information required for a search of the index is: (1) the full name of the person, (2) the port of arrival, and (3) the month and year of arrival. Additional facts, such as the passenger's age and names of accompanying passengers, are also helpful. If the list is not indexed, more specific information is needed, such as the exact date of arrival and the name of the ship.

Ships' arrivals on microfilm are also available through the Family History Library or its centers, and you can make prints there as well. Or check with a National Archives regional records services facilities that would have films for its corresponding port, such as NARA's Northeast Region in New York City for the Port of New York passenger arrival lists. And once the Ellis Island database is available on the Internet (see chapter four), you will be able to make prints using your home computer.

Births, Deaths, and Marriages at Sea and Stowaways

All of his life, Albert Trimigliozzi believed he was born in Norwich, Connecticut, on 24 January 1913. He even had a birth certificate to prove it. The problem was his parents hadn't arrived in America until 29 January 1913. On the passenger arrival list, next to his parents' names, there are a few cryptic notations, but nothing to indicate that a child had been born at sea. On the very last page of the entire manifest, however, a passenger was added:

> Trimigliozzi, Albano (born at sea) 24th January 1913, Father & Mother
> manifested on page 7, lines 4 & 5, final destination: Norwich, Conn.

Births, deaths, and marriages occurring during the voyage and discovered stowaways will very likely be recorded on the last page of the passenger list. Only cryptic notations may be made next to the original entry of the passenger, so be sure to check the last page of the lists for a given ship and the list of detainees (see below). Lines drawn through passengers' names indicated that they never boarded the ship. Émigrés may have purchased a ticket (hence the manifest entry) but did not show up the day the ship departed.

Record of Detained Aliens

Beginning about 1903, the passenger arrival lists began to include a supplemental section for detainees. Many immigrants were detained for short periods of time at the port of arrival until relatives came to claim them; this was particularly true of unescorted women arrivals, whether or not they were accompanied by children.

These lists of detainees, or Record of Detained Aliens, that have survived were microfilmed with their corresponding passenger lists at the end of the lists of arrivals. These contain the name of each detainee, the cause for the detention, and the date and time of discharge. The number of meals the detainee was fed during detention was also recorded. If the émigré was deported before being released from the immigrant receiving station, these records stated the reason and the date deported. The abbreviations "L.P.C." meant "likely public charge" and "L.C.D." meant "loathsome contagious disease," two main causes for deportation.

Also check subsequent passenger lists and indexes for aliens who were deported but may have reentered the country at a future date when they might have been able to pass inspection. Another common way for aliens to reimmigrate was to save enough money and reenter as a first or second class passenger, who underwent less stringent exams aboard ship.

Microfilm Source

Record of Aliens Held for Special Inquiry

Following the Record of Detained Aliens will be a page or pages of the Record of Aliens Held for Special Inquiry. On this form, the cause of the detention or rejection was noted, actions taken by the Board of Special Inquiry, the date of the hearings, the number of meals eaten during detention, and if deported, the date, name of vessel, and port from which they returned to their native land (see Figure 6-7 on page 100). If the rejected immigrant was waiting for someone, the form will also include the name and address of the American contact. (See Deportations later in this chapter.)

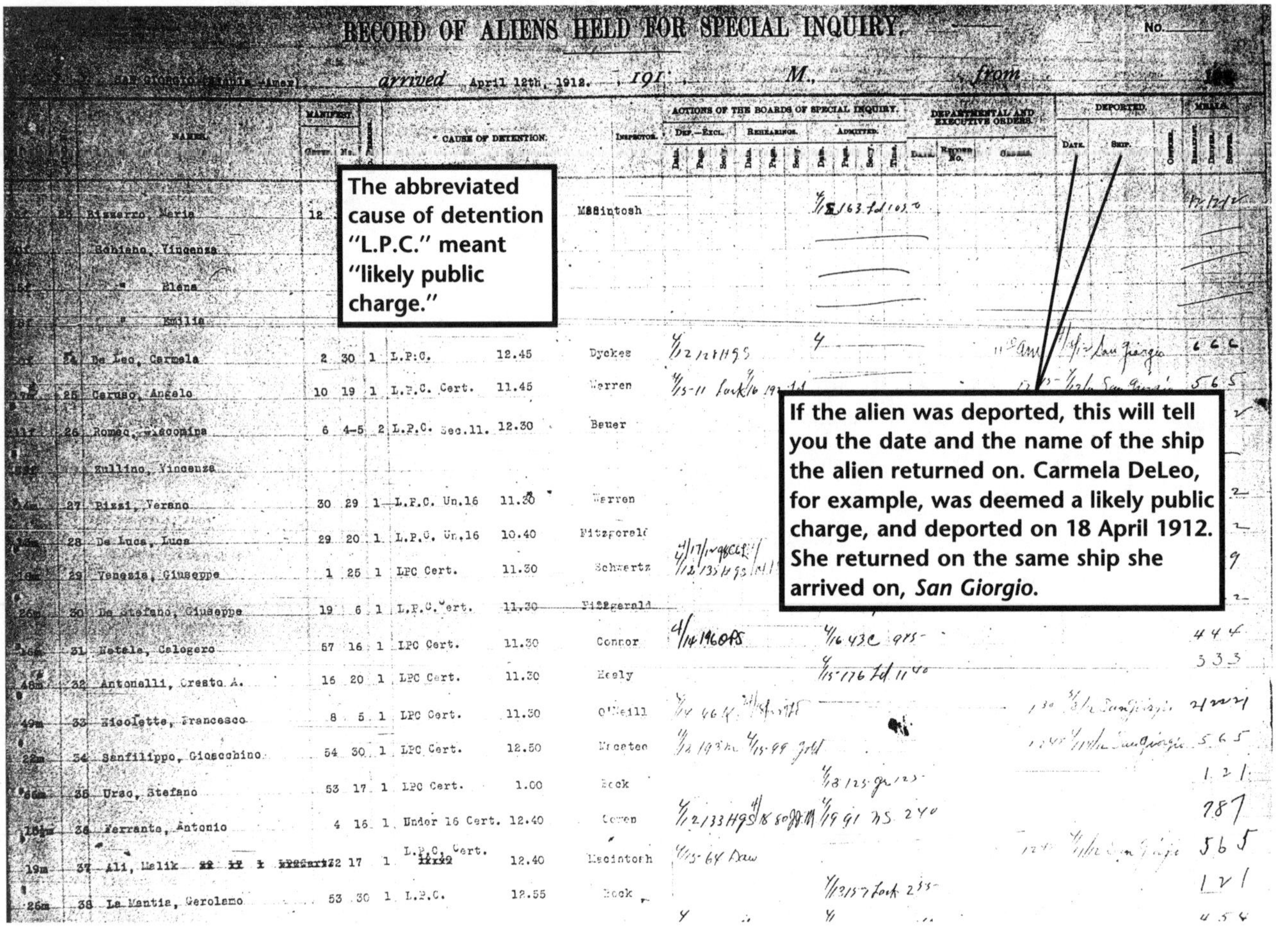

RECORD OF ALIENS HELD FOR SPECIAL INQUIRY.

arrived April 12th, 1912.

> The abbreviated cause of detention "L.P.C." meant "likely public charge."

> If the alien was deported, this will tell you the date and the name of the ship the alien returned on. Carmela DeLeo, for example, was deemed a likely public charge, and deported on 18 April 1912. She returned on the same ship she arrived on, *San Giorgio*.

Figure 6-7
Record of Aliens Held for Special Inquiry, *San Giorgo*, arriving at the Port of New York, 12 April 1912, NARA microfilm T715, roll 1840, volume 4077. Look at the end of the list for each ship to find the Record of Aliens Held for Special Inquiry and the Record of Detained Aliens.

USING INDEXES TO PASSENGER ARRIVAL LISTS

Research Tip

To identify an immigrant in an index or passenger list, you must have enough information (e.g., birth date, town of origin) from other sources and know the full original name of the immigrant. A foreign name that seems unique in America may be as common as John Smith in the homeland. Knowing approximately how old the immigrant was upon arrival will help you eliminate others by the same name in the index. Knowing the town of origin or names of relatives or neighbors in America with whom your ancestor may have traveled will help you eliminate other passengers of the same name. Keep in mind that names were often recorded as they were heard. Many emigrants were illiterate and did not know how to spell their names, even if asked. Ship company clerks often recorded the name as they heard it, so check for spelling variations.

Of the five major ports, here are time periods with indexes:

Baltimore	1820–1897, 1897–1952
Boston	1848–1891, 1902–1906, 1906–1920

New Orleans	1853–1899, 1900–1952
New York	1820–1846, 1897–1902, 1902–1943, 1944–1948
Philadelphia	1800–1906, 1883–1948

You have no doubt noticed that there are several gaps in these indexes, and I bet your ancestors arrived during one of those gaps, right? Before you panic, check to see if there is a published index for the ancestor's ethnic group that covers the time period, for example, if your ancestor was German, check the *Germans to America* series mentioned earlier. If you do not find published sources, then you will have to narrow your search through other records (censuses, city directories, naturalizations, and so forth).

All of the indexes to the five major ports are on cards, which have been microfilmed. Some of these indexes will be alphabetical; others will use the Soundex code, described in chapter five. The alphabetical ones may not be in strict alphabetical order, however, or may be misfiled. Here is how they are supposed to be arranged for the Port of New York:

Microfilm Source

1897–1902	Alphabetical by surname, then by given name
1902–1943	Surnames A-D, arranged by Soundex code, then alphabetically by the first letter or first two letters of the given name, then by date of arrival (or volume number when date is not given) Surnames D-Z, arranged by Soundex code, then alphabetically by given name, followed by those whose age was not given (for the years 1903–1910), then by age at arrival

If you do not find your ancestor, check for him or her by initials instead of a full given name (Patrick Murphy as P. Murphy), and check for variant spellings. Women belonging to some ethnic groups (typically Italian and French) will likely be recorded under their maiden names, not their married surnames. If you do not know the female ancestor's maiden name but she traveled with either her husband or children, look for them in the index. The children should be recorded under their father's surname.

The index cards on microfilm will have different looks, depending on the arrival year. Some of the cards have all the fields written out and are straightforward, giving name, age, group number, list number, sex, citizenship, steamer, line, date, and port. But other cards may baffle you. Identifying the name is no problem, but what are all those other numbers? The Soundex code number is always in the upper left corner. (See Figure 6-8 and 6-9 on page 102.)

Below is a guide to the other information during different years, and which primarily pertains to the cards for the Port of New York. Other ports may have their own irregularities.

December 1903–June 1910	name, group number, list number, vessel, date of arrival
July 1910–1937	name, age/sex, list number, group number, volume number

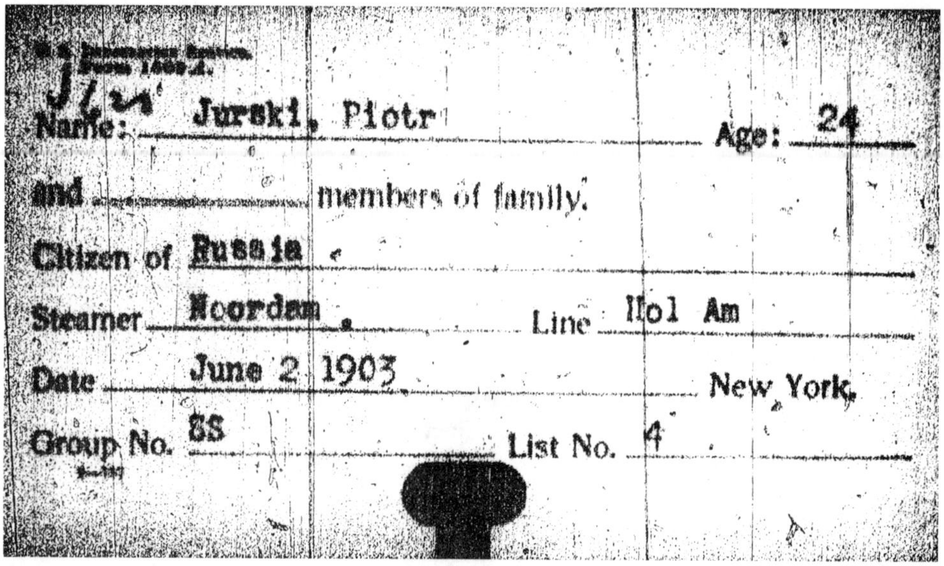

Figure 6-8
Index (Soundex) to passenger lists of vessels arriving at New York, New York, 1 July 1902–31 December 1943. Copy all the information from the Soundex card and consult with the librarian or the NARA publication *Immigrant and Passenger Arrivals: A Select Catalog of the National Archives Microfilm Publications*, second edition, to find the roll of microfilm you need for the passenger arrival list.

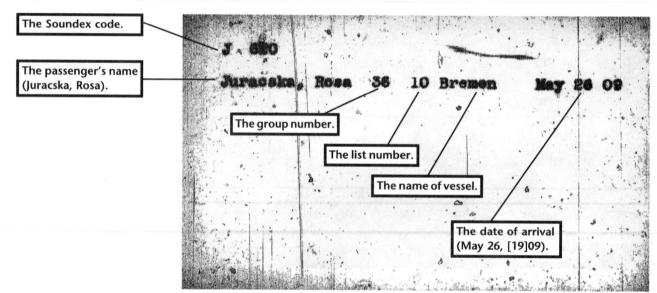

Figure 6-9
Index (Soundex) to passenger lists of vessels arriving at New York, New York, 1 July 1902–31 December 1943. Once you have the information from the card, consult with the librarian or the NARA publication *Immigrant and Passenger Arrivals: A Select Catalog of the National Archives Microfilm Publications*, second edition, to find the roll of microfilm you need for the passenger arrival list.

1937–June 1942	(top line after Soundex code) month/year (center line) name, age/sex, list number, group number, volume number (bottom line) vessel
July 1942–December 1943	(top line) Soundex code, vessel or plane, date (center line) name, age/sex, list number, group number, volume number

Copy all of the information from the index card. The date of arrival is given on cards prior to June 1910, so let's look at these first. The microfilm rolls for the passenger lists will be catalogued differently in different repositories, so check with the librarian to find the roll with the date you need from the information on the index. Regardless of how the films are catalogued, however, they are all publications of the National Archives, and the arrival lists are microfilmed in rough chronological order and some lists may be out of order.

Step By Step

After putting the roll on the reader, you will find that typically two to three "volumes" are filmed on one roll. A title sheet precedes each volume, giving you the volume number, the dates of arrival, the names of the steamships in the order they have been microfilmed, the ports of departure, and how many sheets each manifest contains (see Figure 6–10 on page 104).

Once you find the ship's list, use the other information from the index card to find the exact page. The "list number" on the index card refers to the line number on the manifest, running down the left side of the sheet. The group number is the tricky one. You will probably note several numbers on each passenger list page: there are stamped numbers, numbers handwritten in grease pencil, numbers on the bottom of the page, and numbers at the top. Once again, the placement of the group number varied, depending on the year. Here is the breakdown for the Port of New York:

LOCATION OF GROUP NUMBER ON THE PASSENGER LIST

1897–1902 usually top right corner

1902–1908 usually in grease pencil or stamped numbers at top left

1908–1943 usually stamped numbers at bottom left

To decipher the information on the cards after 1910, on which no date appears, you will need to do an extra step. **Consult the finding aid *Immigrant and Passenger Arrivals: A Select Catalog of the National Archives Microfilm Publications* to find the appropriate volume number, which will list the date of arrival for that volume, along with the National Archives microfilm roll number.** If you are at the Family History Library in Salt Lake City, then consult the immigration finding aid binders in the reference section of the United States/Canada floor. Look for the volume number, which gives you the date of arrival, followed by the library's microfilm call number.

Research Tip

There is another set of indexes for the Port of New York called Book Indexes to New York Passenger Lists, 1906–1942, which has been microfilmed by the National Archives and is also available through the Family History Library. These alphabetical book indexes were compiled by steamship companies at the same time they prepared the passenger list, so they are grouped by the shipping line, then arranged chronologically by date of arrival. The drawback, of course, is you must know the name of the ship and the date of arrival, then find the name of the shipping line through the *Morton Allan Directory* in order to use these indexes.

Following is a step-by-step case study using passenger lists so that you can see what information can be found on some passenger lists (ships' manifests).

Figure 6-10
Usually two or three "volumes" of lists are on each roll of microfilm. The title sheet to each volume precedes the lists it covers. Volume 4183 of NARA microfilm T715, roll 1883, contains the arrival list, among others, for the *Titanic*. The notation reads, "The *Carpathia* was eastward bound when she rescued the *Titanic* passengers, and returned to N.Y. to land them. Apr. 18-1912."

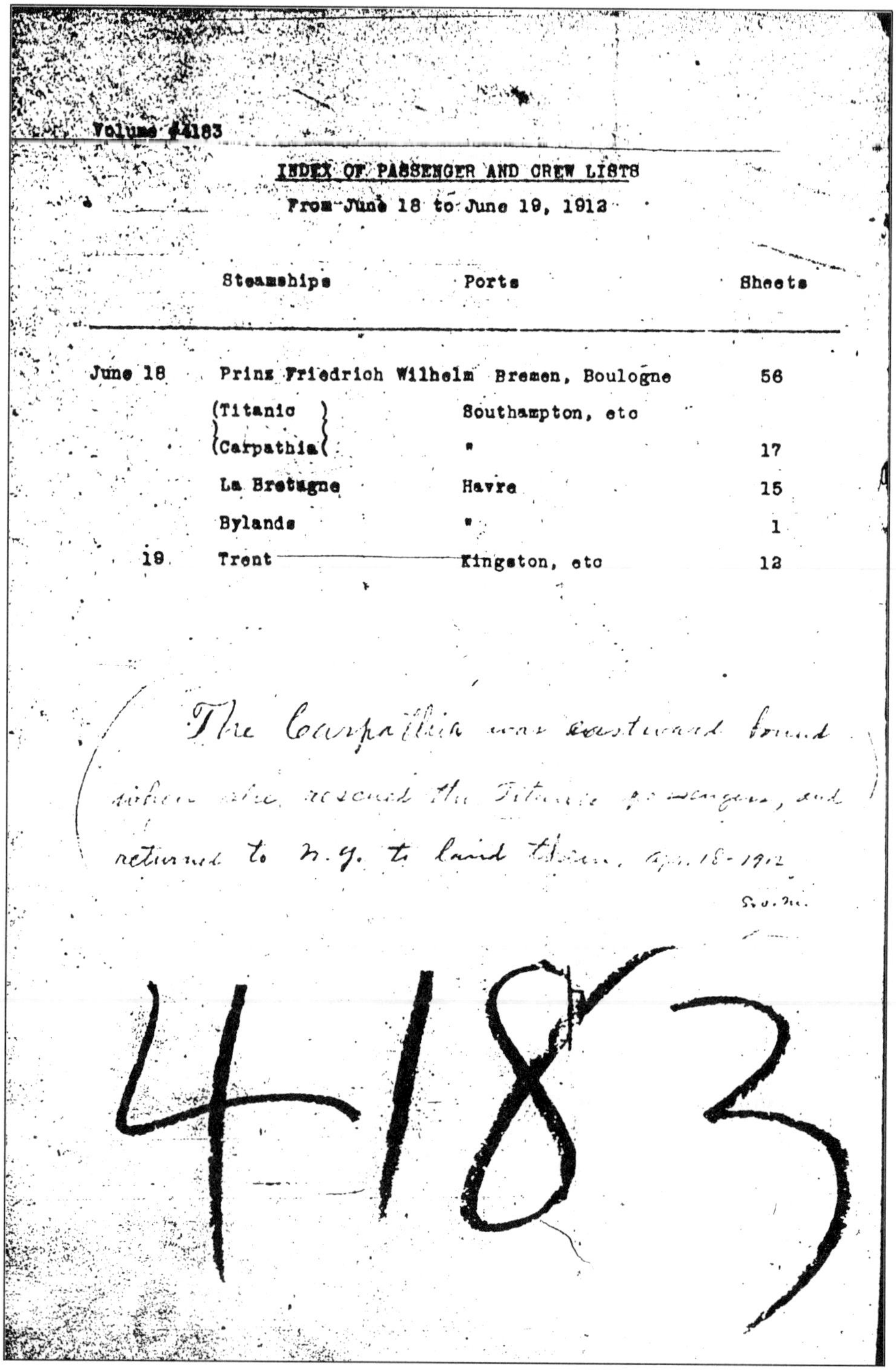

Volume 4183

INDEX OF PASSENGER AND CREW LISTS
From June 18 to June 19, 1912

Steamships	Ports	Sheets
June 18	Prinz Friedrich Wilhelm	Bremen, Boulogne	56
(Titanic)	Southampton, etc	
(Carpathia(	"	17
La Bretagne	Havre	15
Bylands	"	1
19	Trent	Kingston, etc	12

The Carpathia was eastward bound when she rescued the Titanic passengers, and returned to N.Y. to land them. Apr. 18-1912.

4183

CASE STUDY IN USING PASSENGER LISTS AND INDEXES

Ester Ahlquist came to the United States in 1912 through the Port of New York. Family members remember it was April of 1912 because that was the same month and year the *Titanic* sank, but Ester's ship docked sometime after the

USING PASSENGER LISTS AND WORLD WAR I DRAFT REGISTRATIONS TO FIND THE VILLAGE OF ORIGIN

All I knew about my father's father, Isaac Fineberg, was that he had come from "Russia," sometime before 1900. Talking to my relatives was of little value. All they could contribute was that Zaydie (Yiddish for grandfather) had come, not from Russia, but from Lithuania. Actually, Lithuania was part of Russia at that time. Zaydie had told us little about his life in Russia, except how he was in the army before he left for America. After he passed away, I found his naturalization papers among his documents. Zaydie was naturalized in October 1900 in Flemingsburg, Kentucky. These papers were handwritten and didn't give much information.

Even so, the little information I retrieved from his papers gave me someplace to start. For example, I learned that he had come to America at least nine years prior and had declared his intention to become a citizen in Baltimore, Maryland. Knowing his hatred for the Czar of Russia, I guessed that he didn't waste time in declaring his intention to become an American citizen. So now I had a rough year—1890—to start my search for the date of his arrival in America.

I assumed that he probably landed in Baltimore, since that is where he declared his intention to become a citizen and because we had many relatives there. I also assumed that Zaydie left from a popular port in Europe. There were two main ports from which Jews of eastern Europe left for America: Bremen and Hamburg.

But I wasn't looking for Isaac Fineberg; I knew from family stories that Isaac Fineberg was actually Isaac Meister when he left Lithuania. In the Soundex cards for Baltimore arrivals I found not one, but two Isaac Meisters, both coming to Baltimore from Hamburg within months of each other. (I have since learned that these Isaac Meisters were first cousins.)

Now I had to examine the passenger lists for both. The first Isaac Meister came to Baltimore on the *Auguste* in early 1891. He sailed alone, and there was no other information I could gather from the passenger list. When you are researching a list or census, always look above or below the name you are seeking for other names that might be familiar. In this case, there was nothing that would give me a clue as to whether or not this was my grandfather. After making notes, I went on to the next Isaac Meister.

The second Issac Meister arrived in Baltimore aboard the *Munchen* in April 1891. When I found his name on the passenger list, I knew immediately that this was my grandfather. Directly above his name was the name of his father-in-law, Fichel Sterisick. I now knew when my grandfather came to Baltimore, but I still didn't know from where in Lithuania he had come.

USING PASSENGER LISTS AND WORLD WAR I DRAFT REGISTRATIONS TO FIND THE VILLAGE OF ORIGIN—Continued

When you speak to people from Lithuania, unless they came from a big city such as Vilnius or Kaunas, they will always say they came from the Gubernia of Kovna. That is like saying you came from the state of New York or California. So for his place of origin, I took a different approach. My father and his brother had registered for the draft during World War I. The registrations show the date and place of birth of the registrant. I obtained copies of both my father's and his brother's draft registrations. Not only did I get their places of birth, but I was also able to verify their dates of birth. Both my father and his brother were born in a small town called Pokrijus, Lithuania. Now I knew where Isaac Meister had lived before he came to America.

—Robert Fineberg

world-known disaster. She was from Sweden, around seventeen or eighteen when she emigrated, and she came alone, as did so many young Swedish women of her time.

The first step was to Soundex Ester's last name, Ahlquist, as A422, so I could check the index to New York passenger lists. Among the index cards were two possible matches (see Figure 6-11):

| Ahlquist, Ester | 17f | 16 | 25 | 4085 |
| Ahlquist, Ester | 17f | 9 | 91 | 6633 |

Figure 6-11
Index (Soundex) to passenger lists of vessels arriving at New York, New York, for Ester Ahlquist's passenger arrival list.

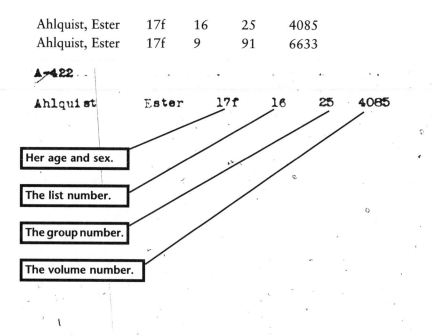

A-422

Ahlquist   Ester   17f   16   25   4085

Her age and sex.

The list number.

The group number.

The volume number.

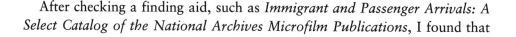

After checking a finding aid, such as *Immigrant and Passenger Arrivals: A Select Catalog of the National Archives Microfilm Publications*, I found that

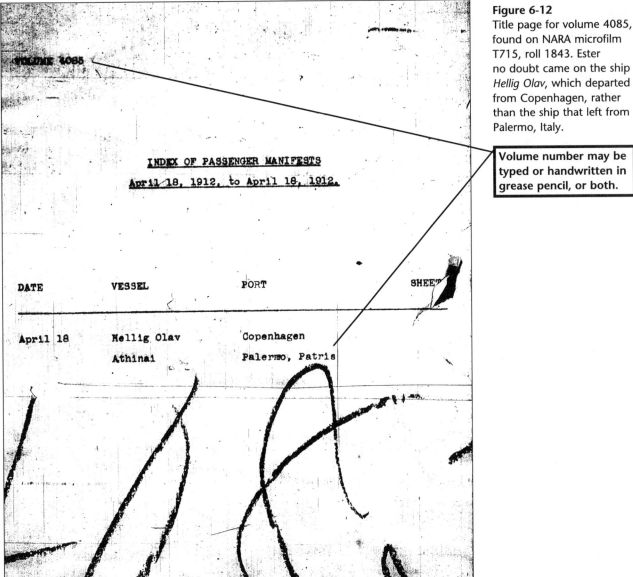

volume 4085 is for ships arriving on 18 April 1912, but volume 6633 is for vessels arriving on 27 November 1920. Obviously, the first listing is the one I need.

After finding the appropriate microfilm and putting it on the microfilm reader, I came to a title page (see Figure 6-12 above), showing two ships in that volume, docking at New York: *Hellig Olav* from Copenhagen and *Athinai* from Palermo, Italy. Since Ester's Swedish, the ship she came on was more than likely the ship from Copenhagen.

The two other numbers on the index card were 16 and 25. For the year 1912, these numbers are the list and group numbers, respectively. The list number will be the column of vertical numbers on the left side of the page; the group number is the one I need to seek on the many pages of the passenger list. Also for 1912, this group number is usually going to appear as a stamped number on the

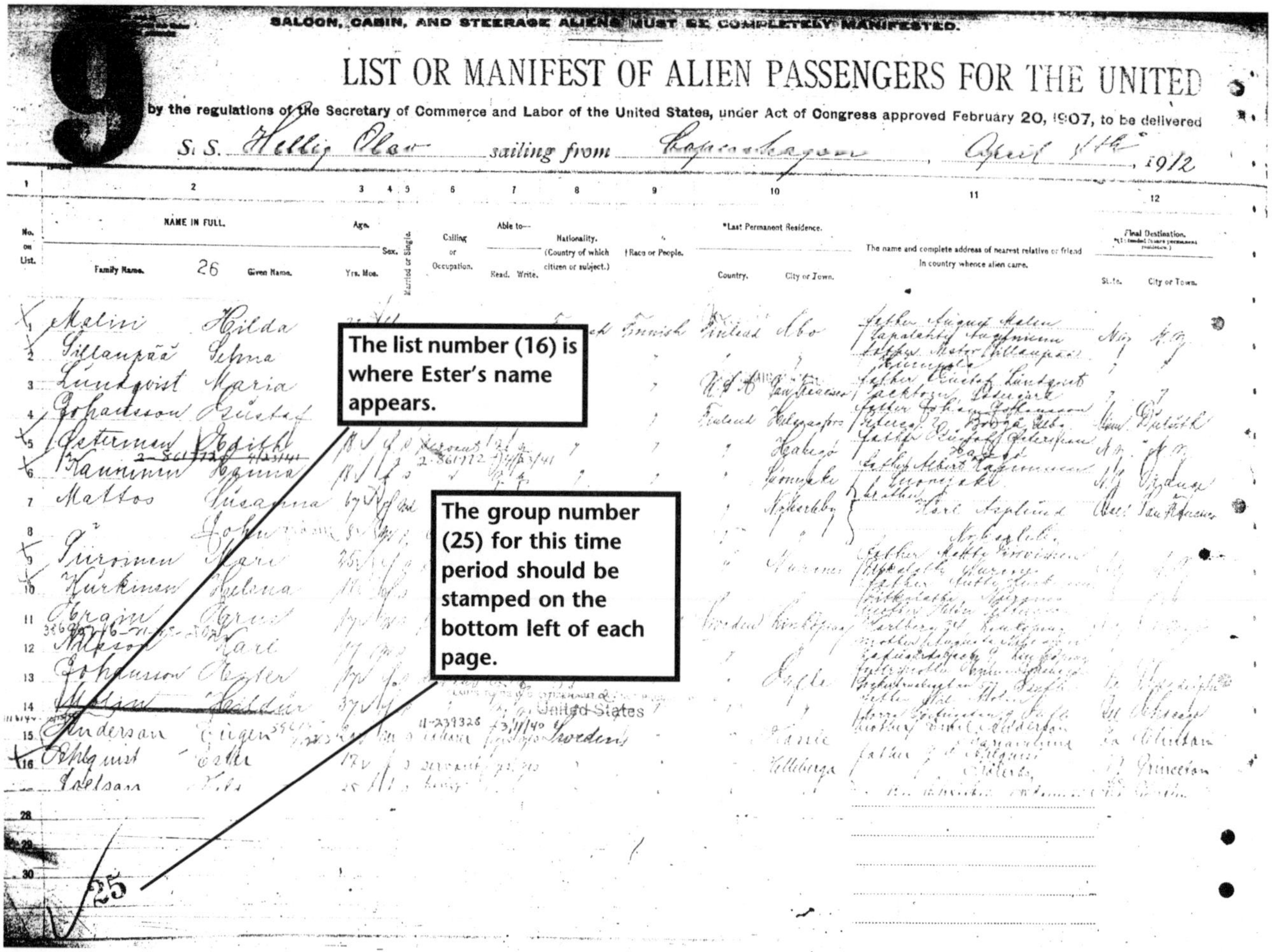

Figure 6-13

In 1912, when Ester's ship arrived in New York, the group number (25) should be stamped on the bottom left of each passenger list. Once I find this number, I will go to the list (or line) number 16, and that's where Ester's name appears.

bottom left of each sheet (see Figure 6-13 above). After I find number 25, I then look at the list numbers for number 16. Sure enough, there's Ester in the third class, or steerage compartment (see Figure 6-14 on page 109). Here is what the passenger list information showed:

- The ship left Copenhagen on 4 April 1912, and docked at the Port of New York on 18 April 1912
- Name: Ahlquist, Ester
- Age: 17
- Sex: f[emale]
- Married or single: single
- Occupation: servant
- Able to read and write: yes
- Nationality: Sweden
- Race or people: Scandinavian [denoted by ditto marks]
- Last Permanent Residence: Country—Sweden [denoted by ditto marks]; City or Town—Helleberga [Hallsberg?]

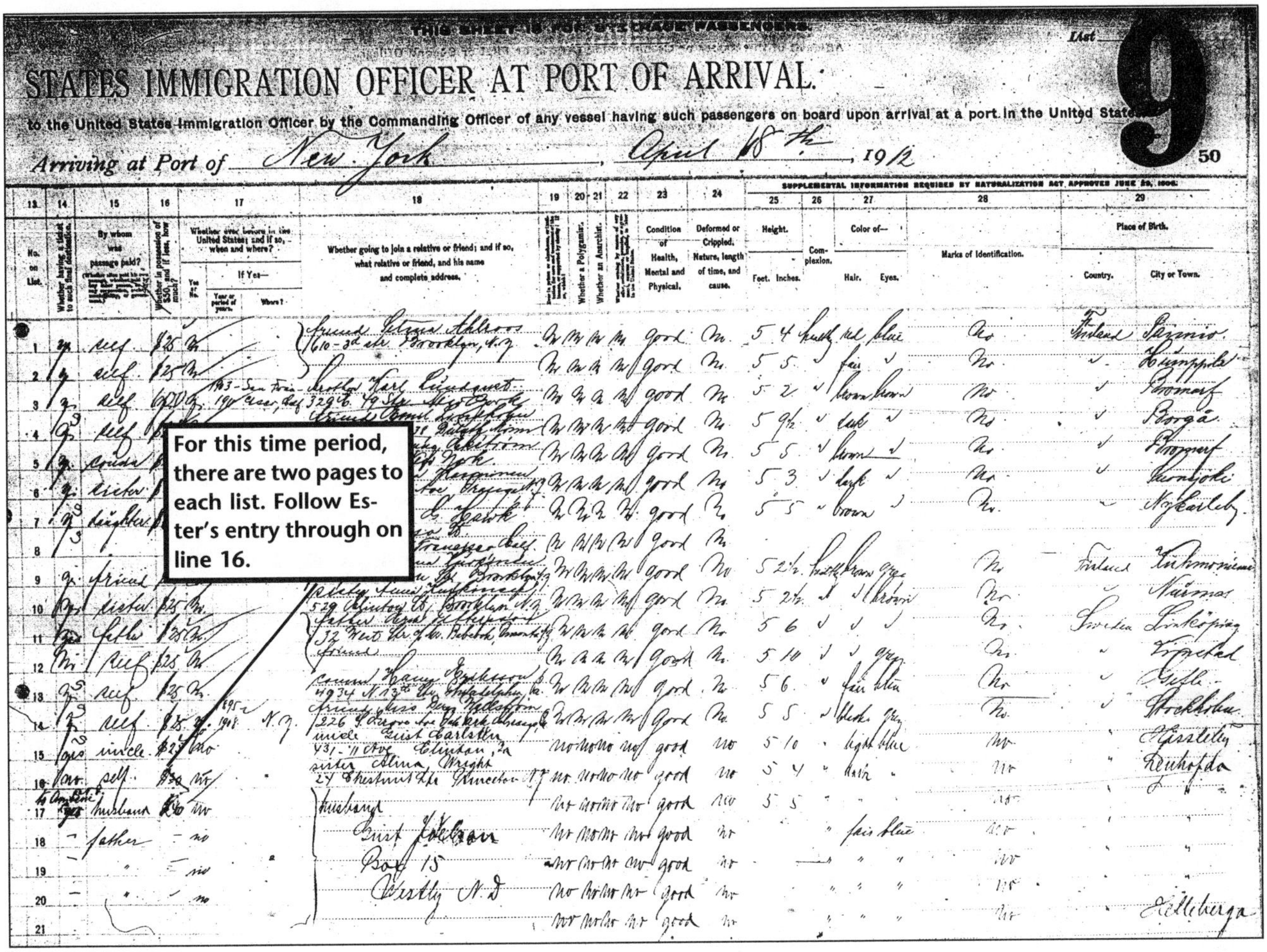

Figure 6-14
The second page of Ester's passenger arrival list gives more information.

- Name and complete address of nearest relative or friend in the county whence alien came: father, Y.G. Ahlquist, Moleras
- Final destination: State—NJ [New Jersey]; City or Town—Princeton [page two of manifest]
- Whether having a ticket to such final destination: no
- By whom was passage paid: self
- Whether in possession of $50, and if less, how much: $30
- Whether ever in the United States, and if so, when and where: no [if she had answered yes, I would check for another passenger list]
- Whether going to join a relative or friend, and if so, what relative or friend, and his name and complete address: sister, Alina Wright, 24 Chestnut [unreadable], Princeton, NJ
- Ever in prison, almshouse, . . . : no
- Whether a polygamist: no
- Whether an anarchist: no
- Whether entering by reason of any offer . . . : no
- Condition of health, mental and physical: good

- Deformed or crippled: no
- Height: 5′4″
- Complexion: healthy
- Color of hair: dark; eyes: blue
- Marks of identification: no
- Place of birth: Country—Sweden; City or Town—Lenhofda [Lenhovda?]

Before I make a photocopy of the pages or put the film away, I next check the end of the lists to see if Ester is on the Record of Detained Aliens. She should be, since most unescorted women arriving in the early twentieth century were detained until someone arrived to claim them. She's there on line 9, and there is more information about her (see Figure 6-15 below):

- Name: Ahlquist, Ester
- Manifest: Group: 9, Line: 16 (see Figures 6-13 and 6-14)
- Number of aliens: One year old or under: [none], Older than one year: 1
- Cause of detention: To sister
- Disposition: Sister, Alrma [or Almira] Wright, 24 Chestnut St., Princeton, NJ

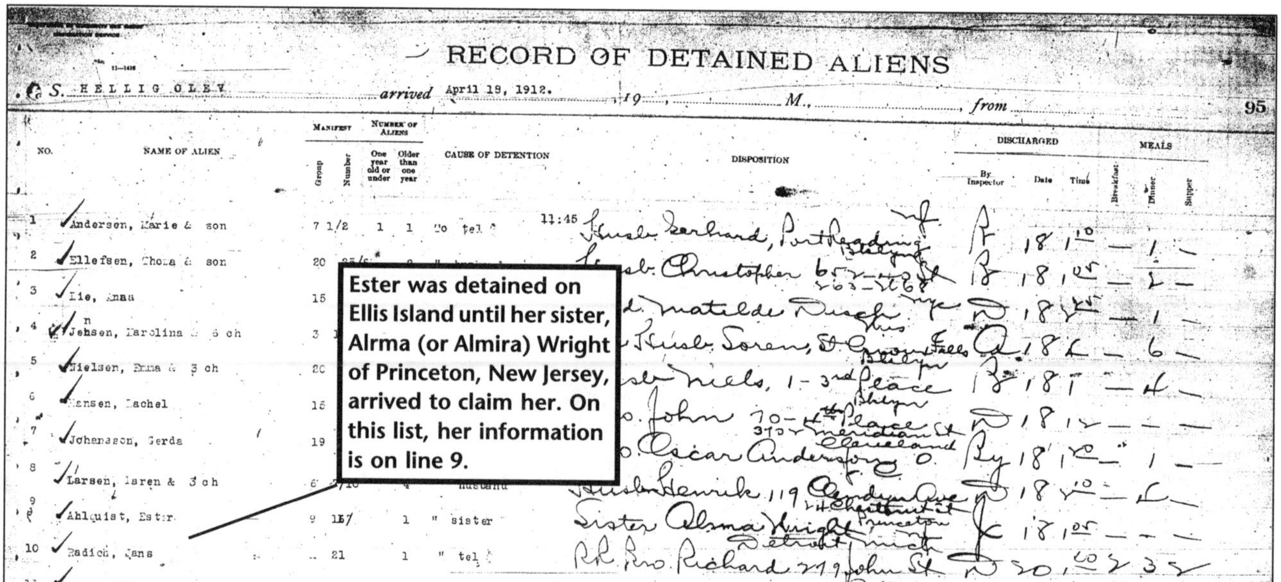
RECORD OF DETAINED ALIENS

S.S. HELLIG OLEV arrived April 19, 1912. 95

NO.	NAME OF ALIEN	Manifest Group	Manifest Number	One year old or under	Older than one year	CAUSE OF DETENTION
1	Andersen, Marie & son	7	1/2	1	1	To tel
2	Ellefsen, Thora & son	20	[illegible]			
3	Lie, Anna	15				
4	Jensen, Karolina & 6 ch	3				
5	Nielsen, Emma & 3 ch	20				
6	Hansen, Rachel	15				
7	Johansson, Gerda	19				
8	Larsen, Karen & 3 ch	6	2/10		4	husband
9	Ahlquist, Ester	9	16		1	" sister
10	Radich, Jans		21		1	" tel
11	Olsen, Eliz	6	16		1	" friend
12	Johnson, Anna	22	12		1	" friend
13	Kriansen, Harriet	12	11		1	" sister
14	Hedin, Elis	16	1		1	" brother
15	Tonnesen, Cordia	20	16		1	" sister
16	Andreasen, Agnes and					
17	Bodholt, Katline	1	5/6		2	" friend
18	Larsen, Anna	6	13		1	" frien
19	Westberg, Marianna	16	11		1	" friend
20	Ostensen, Alma		7		1	" frien

Figure 6-15
Record of Detained Aliens, *Hellig Olav*, NARA microfilm T715, roll 1843, volume 4085.

- Discharged: By inspector "J," Date: 18 [April], Time: 1:05
- Meals: [none]

Technique

I now wanted to know what the ship *Hellig Olav*, on which Ester spent two weeks of her life, looked like, as well as some information about the vessel in order to write about it. Turning to Arnold Kludas's *Great Passenger Ships of the World*, volume one: 1858–1912, I found a photograph and the following information on the *Hellig Olav*:

> Builders: Stephen, Glasgow
> Yard no: 399
> 10,085 GRT; 158.5 × 17.8 m/520 × 58.2 ft; III exp eng, Stephen; Twin screw; 8,500 IHP; 15, max 16 kn; Passengers: 130 1st class, 140 2nd class, 900 steerage.
> 1902 Dec 16: Launched
> 1903 Mar 17: Delivered
> Mar 26: Maiden voyage Copenhagen-New York
> 1931: Laid up
> 1933 Dec: Sold for breaking up
> 1934: Broken up by Hughes, Bolckow & Co., Blyth

Eugene W. Smith's *Passenger Ships of the World Past and Present* gave similar and some additional information:

> *Hellig Olav* (1902) Scandinavian-American Line.
> Built by Alexander Stephen & Sons, Ltd., Glasgow, Scotland. Tonnage: 9,939. Dimensions: 500′ × 58′ (515′ o.l.). Twin-screw, 16 knots. Triple expansion engines. Two masts and one funnel. Passengers: 130 first, 140 second, 900 third. Service: Copenhagen-Oslo-New York. Final Atlantic crossing in 1931. Scrapped in 1934. Sister ships: *Oscar II* and *United States*.

I wish I could tell you that finding every ancestor's passenger list is going to be as easy and legible as in this example, but I'm afraid that's not always the case. You may come upon microfilm that is difficult, if not impossible, to read. And, unfortunately, the originals of the passengers lists for the peak Ellis Island years (1892–1924) were destroyed after microfilming in the 1940s. Originals of the extant earlier lists are housed at the Balch Institute in Philadelphia, but they are not available for public research (see Appendix A). (See Marian Smith, "The Creation and Destruction of Ellis Island Immigration Manifests.")

DEPORTATIONS, EXCLUSIONS, AND QUOTA LAWS

In 1891, the federal government took over control of national immigration policy and enacted laws governing the deportation of aliens. A few earlier acts, and subsequent acts, excluded or limited the number of aliens allowed to enter and reside in the United States (see Chronology of American Immigration Policy, 1882–1960 on page 112). New aliens deemed to be members of one of the excluded classes were briefly detained at the port until their case

CHRONOLOGY OF AMERICAN IMMIGRATION POLICY, 1882–1960

1875   excluded criminals and women "brought for lewd and immoral purposes"

1882   excluded lunatics, idiots, convicts, or those likely to become a public charge; Chinese Exclusion Act; fifty cent head tax paid by transportation company

1885   excluded contract laborers

1891   excluded those infected with a "loathsome" or contagious disease, paupers, offenders of "moral turpitude," polygamists

1894   head tax increased to one dollar

1903   excluded anarchists, prostitutes and their procurers, epileptics, insane persons, professional beggars; head tax increased to two dollars

1907   excluded the "feeble-minded," children under sixteen traveling alone, anyone with a physical or mental handicap that might hinder ability to earn a living; Gentlemen's Agreement excluding Japanese laborers; head tax increased to four dollars (skilled workers and whole families exempted from this tax)

1917   literacy requirement; exclusion of persons coming from Asia and the Pacific Islands; head tax increased to eight dollars; made it a misdemeanor to bring in or harbor aliens not duly admitted by immigration officers; Mexican workers effectively restricted by head tax, literacy test, and limit of six months stay for contracted employees

1921   first quota law (temporary), annual admission of certain ethnic groups based on a percentage of those nationalities in the 1910 census

1924   National Origins Act (second quota law), annual admission of certain ethnic groups based on 2 percent of those nationalities in the 1890 census, until 1927, when it would change to a ratio using the 1920 census; exempted Western Hemisphere countries from quotas; émigrés also needed a visa from the U.S. embassy in their country of origin before leaving

1929   penalties and restrictions on the return of previously deported aliens

1943   Chinese Exclusion Act was repealed; nationality law changed to allow Chinese to become citizens; authorized and financed "bracero" program to bring temporary Mexican farm workers to the United States

1945   exempted war brides of GIs from quotas

1946   facilitated admission of alien fiancés and fiancées pending marriage to U.S. military service personnel, with visiting time extended in 1947

1947   relaxed quotas and other restrictions of displaced persons from World War II, particularly favoring Polish, Czechoslovakian, Hungarian, Romanian, and Yugoslavian immigrants

1948   made it a felony to bring in or harbor aliens not duly admitted by immigration officers

1951   authorized Migratory Labor Agreement to continue "bracero" program importing Mexican farm laborers for ten years

1950   additional categories and extensions for displaced persons and war orphans; excluded "subversives" with any communist associations

1952   revised quotas; removed racial barriers to naturalization; increased family preferences; excluded more classes such as subversives, lepers, drug addicts, and dealers; abolished head tax but increased various fees

1953   provided nonquota visas for refugees from Germany, Austria, and Italy; admitted children adopted by citizens serving abroad

1954   strengthened laws to deport communists; admitted sheepherders

1957   permitted enlistment of aliens of U.S. Army

1958   permitted emergency admission of Hungarian refugees

1959   extended access for orphans to be adopted; revised laws to allow entry for family members with tuberculosis

1960   expanded refugee access; excluded convicted users of marijuana

Source: E.P. Hutchinson, *Legislative History of American Immigration Policy, 1798-1965* (Philadelphia: University of Pennsylvania Press, 1981); Nicolás Kanellos with Christelia Pérez, *Chronology of Hispanic-American History, From Pre-Columbian Times to the Present* (New York: Gale Research, 1995).

was decided, then sent back to the country of origin on the next returning ship of the same line—that is, they were barred from entry. Other aliens were admitted but were later charged with violation of one or another immigration law; if the charges were proved to the satisfaction of an examining board, they were deported.

Once an immigrant was admitted, the statute of limitations varied for discovery of a prior transgression or commitment of a new one, depending on the legislative act then in effect. Beginning in 1891, deportation was limited to within one year after the immigrant had been admitted. An act of 1917, however, stated that "at any time within five years of entry, any alien who at the time of entry was a member of one or more of the classes excluded by law [or] any alien who shall be found in the United States in violation of this act . . . shall, upon warrant of the Attorney General, be taken into custody and deported." Another act the following year amended this to remove the five-year limitation. From 1892 to 1930, nearly 135,000 immigrants were deported. If you lose track of an immigrant or if a family story tells of a relative returning to the homeland, it may be because he or she was deported. (**For information on Chinese exclusion records, see Asians in Part II.**)

See Also

An alien who was barred or deported could return to America once the reason entry was denied was corrected. So, for example, if an alien had a contagious disease, was sent back to the homeland, sought medical care, and became disease-free, he could return again. Some saved enough money to travel in first or second class when they remigrated, where the inspections were not as strict as those for steerage or third class passengers.

Existing records for barring or deporting aliens varied according to the situation:

- In open-and-shut cases involving barred aliens (prior to 1903), no special records were created. Only a notation was made on the original passenger list next to that person's name. By 1903, the name was added to a new list created at the inspection station, called the Record of Aliens Held for Special Inquiry. These appendixes (when extant) are included in the microfilm publication of the various ship rolls, and each appears following the passenger list to which it pertains.

- Whether a Board of Special Inquiry admitted or deported an immigrant, the best you may find is the information on the Record of Aliens Held for Special Inquiry. Surviving records of appeals to the Board of Special Inquiry decision, which are in the custody of the National Archives in Washington, DC, are extremely difficult to use because there is no finding aide or name index, and there are more than eight thousand boxes of records.

- For an alien already in the United States who was admitted but later threatened with deportation after identification as a member of an excluded class, a file was created. The U.S. Immigration and Naturalization Service pursued the case within administrative (as opposed to criminal) proceedings. Once again, these files are among the thousands of boxes of unindexed records. If you find among family papers a reference or file number for such a case, your hope of gaining access to the records will be slightly better.

A helpful guide, "INS Genealogy Correspondence Resource Guide," containing instructions and record request Form G-639, may be obtained by writing to the Immigration and Naturalization Service, History Office, Room 1100, 425 I Street, N.W., Washington, DC 20536, or by E-mail at INS.History@usdoj.gov. Another informative publication offered for free (while quantities last) by the INS is *An Immigrant Nation: United States Regulation of Immigration, 1798–1991*. The INS Historical Reference Library, located in the INS building in Washington, is for research assistance; it does not have or release any records.

VISAS AND PASSPORTS

Records of the Visa Office from 1910 to 1940 are open to the public. They are located in National Archives II in College Park, Maryland (see Appendix B). The records are arranged chronologically in ten-year groupings, then alphabetically by surname.

Except for brief periods during wartime, 19 August 1861 to 17 March 1862 and 22 May 1918 to 1921 (Civil War and World War I), passports were not required of U.S. citizens who traveled out of the country prior to 1941. Many Americans, however, for their own security, obtained them. Passports were, and still are, issued by the Department of State, and those issued from 1791 to 1925 have been transferred to the National Archives. The originals are housed at the National Archives II. They are on microfilm and there are indexes and registers to help you find them. The Family History Library also has this on microfilm.

Applications contain little information, but from 1906 to 1925, they included the name of the applicant; date and place of birth; name, date, and place of birth of spouse or children; residence and occupation at the time of application; immediate travel plans; physical description; and a photograph. Passport applications of naturalized citizens included information about their immigration and naturalization, plus the date and port of arrival, name of the ship, and date and court of naturalization (see Figure 6-16 on page 115).

For passports after 1925, write to the Passport Office, Department of State, Washington, DC 20520. If the applicant of the passport is still alive, you will need a letter from the applicant; if the person is deceased, you need to provide a copy of the death certificate and state your relationship to the deceased.

CANADIAN BORDER CROSSINGS

Many immigrant families arrived through Canadian ports, some settling for a time in Canada before coming to the United States. No records were kept by the United States on those who crossed the border until 1895, when the U.S.

Application for Passport.—Naturalized.

W. Reid Gould, Law Blank Publisher and Stationer, 168 Nassau St., N. Y.

No. 3869

Issued Dec. 1. 1877

UNITED STATES OF AMERICA.

STATE OF *New York*
COUNTY OF *New York* } ss.

I, *Merchor Fee* do swear that I was born in *Bagla Island of Cuba* on or about the *Twenty seventh* day of *September* 1844 that I am a NATURALIZED AND LOYAL CITIZEN OF THE UNITED STATES, and about to travel abroad; and further, that I am the **Identical Person** described in the Certificate of Naturalization, herewith presented *and which herewith accompanies this my Application for a Passport to the Island of Cuba and other Spanish Countries abroad*

Sworn to before me, this 30th day of November 1877
Mitchell Hershfield
Notary Public.
N. Y. City & County

Merchol Fee

Description of *Merchor Fee*
Merchor
Age: *Thirty three* years,
Stature: *Five feet, 3 3/8* inches, Eng.
Forehead: *Moderate*
Eyes: *Brown, dark brown*
Nose: *Straight, Moderate*

Mouth: *Moderate size*
Chin: *Moderate size*
Hair: *dark brown*
Complexion: *dark*
Face: *Moderate size*
Side Whiskers & Mustachio dark brown color

I, *Merchor Fee* do solemnly swear that I will support, protect and defend the Constitution and Government of the United States against all enemies, whether domestic or foreign; and that I will bear true faith, allegiance, and loyalty to the same, any ordinance, resolution or law of any State, Convention or Legislature to the contrary notwithstanding; and further, that I do this with a full determination, pledge and purpose, without any mental reservation or evasion whatsoever; and further, that I will well and faithfully perform all the duties which may be required of me by law. So help me God.

Sworn to before me this 30th day of November 1877
Mitchell Hershfield
Notary Public
N. Y. City & County

Merchol Fee

...a imposed by law, will be required, in U. S. currency, with each application.
...ife, minor children and servants expect to travel together, a single passport for the whole will suffice.
...on in the party a separate passport will be required.
...t of State, Passport Bureau, Washington, D. C.

Figure 6-16
Application for a passport for Merchor Fee, 1 December 1877, NARA microfilm M1372, roll 220, volume 487, number 3869. As well as giving a personal description, it gives his place and date of birth.

Written on the side of this document is the court in which he became naturalized and the date (Court of Common Pleas, City & County of New York, 27 November 1877).

government realized that about 40 percent of those who arrived in Canada had as their final destination the United States. Joint immigrant inspection between Canada and the United States created two sets of records: passenger lists and inspection cards. Records from all ports of entry within the INS Montreal district were centralized at the district headquarters in Montreal (later St. Albans, Vermont). **The records and Soundex have been microfilmed** and are available

Microfilm Source

at the National Archives, at all of the regional records services facilities of the National Archives, and through the Family History Library.

- Soundex Index to Canadian Border Entries Through the St. Albans, Vermont, District, 1895–1924
- Soundex Index to Entries Into the St. Albans, Vermont, District Through Canadian Pacific and Atlantic Ports, 1924–1952
- Alphabetical Index to Canadian Border Entries Through Small Ports in Vermont, 1895–1924
- Manifests of Passengers Arriving in the St. Albans, Vermont, District Through Canadian Pacific and Atlantic Ports, 1895–1921
- Manifests of Passengers Arriving in the St. Albans, Vermont, District Through Canadian Pacific and Atlantic Ports, 1921–1954 (not available at the Family History Library)
- Manifests of Passengers Arriving in the St. Albans, Vermont, District Through Canadian Pacific Ports, 1929–1949

For More Info

For more information, see Constance Potter, "St. Albans Passenger Arrival Records," in *Prologue* 22 (Spring 1990): 90-93.

Like the Soundex cards for ships' passenger arrival lists to the United States, the index cards for Canadian border crossings are on microfilm and arranged by the Soundex code, then alphabetically by the passenger's first name. Each card contains an abstract of the information found on the manifest (see Figure 6-17 on page 117). The Soundex covering 1895–1924 also includes names of people who crossed through other U.S. borders within the Montreal district: Washington, Montana, Michigan, New York, North Dakota, and Minnesota.

The actual manifests, 1895–1954, contain two types of lists: a traditional passenger arrival list of seaports, and monthly lists of names of aliens crossing the land border, usually on trains (see Figure 6-18 on page 118. The monthly lists are arranged by month and year, then alphabetically by the name of the port, then by the name of the railway.

MEXICAN BORDER CROSSINGS

For More Info

For a listing of microfilmed records for Mexican border crossings, see the three-part article by Claire Prechtel-Kluskens, "Mexican Border Crossing Records," in *NGS Newsletter* 25 (May-June 1999): 156–157, 159; (July-August 1999): 182–183; (September-October 1999): 278–281.

Until the early twentieth century, no records of border crossings from Mexico into the United States were kept. The Immigration and Naturalization Service records from 1903 to 1953, documenting people coming into the country from Mexico, are becoming available as microfilm publications at the National Archives. Many have been published already. These records also contain information on U.S. citizens living in Mexico. There is no centralized Soundex, but many have alphabetical arrangements. Microfilms of Mexican "ports" may be viewed at the National Archives in Washington, DC.

EMIGRATION LISTS

Just as lists were made of people coming into America (immigrants), lists were also made of people leaving a country (emigrants). These records of departure, or emigration lists, have not all survived, but some have, and some are available

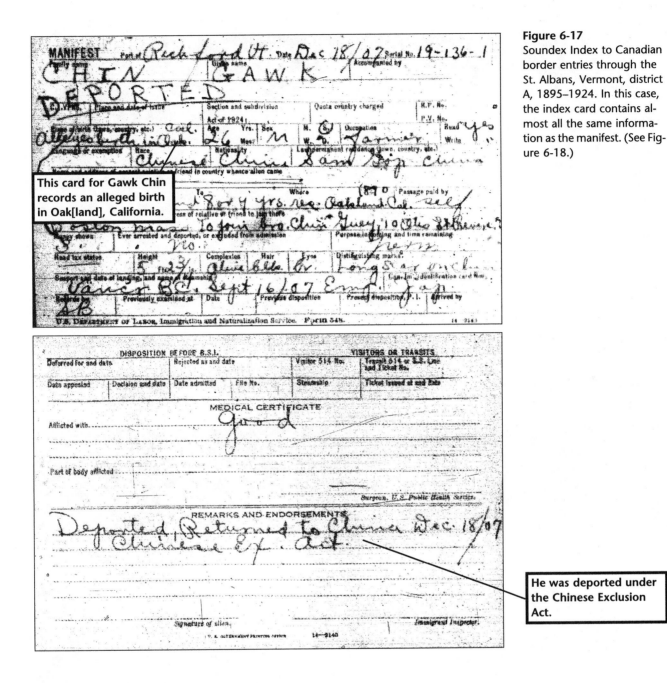

Figure 6-17
Soundex Index to Canadian border entries through the St. Albans, Vermont, district A, 1895–1924. In this case, the index card contains almost all the same information as the manifest. (See Figure 6-18.)

This card for Gawk Chin records an alleged birth in Oak[land], California.

He was deported under the Chinese Exclusion Act.

through the Family History Library. Among these records you may find letters of manumission, sale of property, letters of recommendation, and a permit to emigrate. To begin this type of research, you usually need to know from which port your ancestors left. Certainly, if you have found the passenger arrival record in America, this will tell you. If not, then you will have to learn that information from other research, or by developing and testing some theories. For example, by reading social histories of Italians, you would learn that a quarter of all Italian emigrants left from the Port of Naples, so that would be a good starting place.

Of the four busiest ports of departure in 1907, here is a breakdown of the major ethnic groups they served:

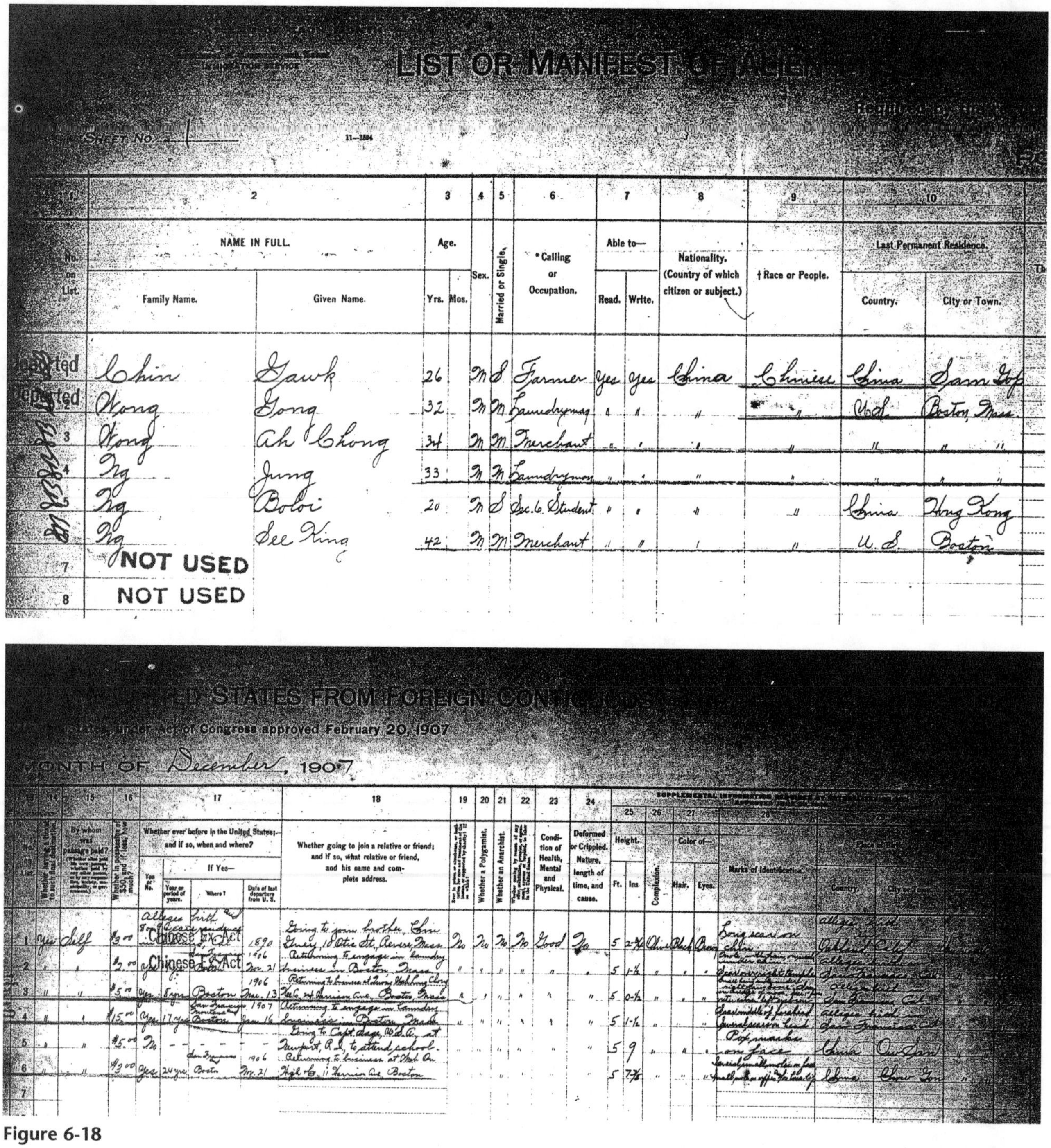
LIST OR MANIFEST OF ALIEN

SHEET No. 1

No. on List	Family Name	Given Name	Age Yrs.	Mos.	Sex	Married or Single	Calling or Occupation	Read	Write	Nationality (Country of which citizen or subject.)	Race or People	Last Permanent Residence: Country	City or Town
Deported 1	Chin	Gawk	26		M	S	Farmer	Yes	Yes	China	Chinese	China	Sam Gop
Deported 2	Wong	Gong	32		M	M	Laundryman	"	"	"	"	U.S.	Boston, Mass.
3	Wong	Ah Chong	34		M	M	Merchant	"	"	"	"	"	"
4	Ng	Jung	33		M	M	Laundryman	"	"	"	"	"	"
5	Ng	Boloi	20		M	S	Sec. 6 Student	"	"	"	"	China	Hong Kong
6	Ng	See King	42		M	M	Merchant	"	"	"	"	U. S.	Boston
7	NOT USED												
8	NOT USED												

UNITED STATES FROM FOREIGN CONTIGUOUS

under Act of Congress approved February 20, 1907

MONTH OF December, 1907

Figure 6-18

Manifests of passengers arriving in the St. Albans, Vermont, district through Canadian Pacific and Atlantic ports, 1895–1921. Port of Richford, Vermont, 18 December 1907, FHL 1561154.

Naples	Italians, Greeks, and Syrians
Bremen	Poles, Czechs, Croats, Slovaks, and other Slavs
Liverpool	Irish, British, Swedes, Norwegians, Eastern European Jews
Hamburg	Eastern European Jews, Scandinavians

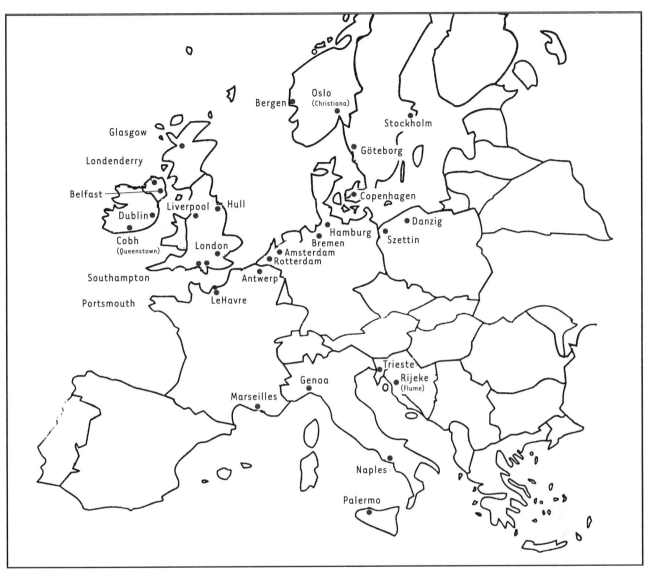

Figure 6-19

Some emigration lists have been published, such as *Wuerttemberg Emigration Index*, compiled by Trudy Schenk and Ruth Froelke. (See the resources listed in the Germanic Peoples section.) This seven-volume set contains information on thousands of people who applied to emigrate from Wuerttemberg, Germany, between 1750 and 1900. Each entry contains information such as place and date of birth, month and year of application, and destination in America.

Other lists may be available on microfilm, such as the Hamburg Passenger Lists, 1850–1934. These lists contain the names of millions of emigrants who left through the Port of Hamburg, Germany, roughly a third of all those who left from central and eastern Europe in this time period. There are two sections to these lists: the Direct Lists and the Indirect Lists, both of which are indexed. The Direct Lists name passengers who left Hamburg and sailed directly to America without stopping at other European ports. The Indirect Lists cover

For More Info

For more information, see John Colletta, *They Came in Ships*, and the resource guide, "The Hamburg Passenger Lists, 1850–1934," available through the Family History Library and its centers.

those passengers (about 20 percent) who stopped at other European ports before sailing to their final destination. Both the lists and the indexes are available through the Family History Library.

Another example of a type of emigration record is the Danish police records (found in the Family History Library Catalog under "Danish Emigration"). These volumes recorded information about Danish emigrants who left between 1869 and 1914, documenting approximately 300,000 names. The volumes provide the name, sex, and age for each emigrant, plus the month and year of departure, whether traveling alone or in a group, the person's occupation, the place of last residence (usually the parish of birth), and a specific destination in America—not just "USA" or the name of a state.

Once you have bridged the ocean or crossed America's borders, having a precise location in the Old Country, then you are ready to begin researching in your ancestor's homeland.

SEVEN

Starting Foreign Research

T he first step in bridging the ocean or crossing the border and starting your research in foreign sources is to thoroughly exhaust all American records. (This point is repeated for those of you who skipped the beginning of the book and feel you are ready to dive into foreign research. Be careful—you might drown if you try to cross the ocean before you are thoroughly prepared!) Collect every possible document created by, for, and about your immigrant ancestor in America. If you follow the premise of working from the known to the unknown, or working backward in time, then researching immigrants in any time period should be no different. You need to begin the search with their lives in America and know them intimately before you can identify them and their relatives in foreign records. More importantly, you need to know the emigrant's *place* of origin to begin. Knowing that great-great-grandpa came from Holland is no more helpful to you than knowing he settled in America. Searching American records and studying the social history that applies to the ethnic group and time period of interest should either reveal your immigrant ancestor's native town, or at least supply you with some clues of places to start your search.

GUIDES ON FOREIGN RESEARCH

Once you have identified the place of origin, the next step is to study genealogical guides published about that foreign country. These will tell you what records are available and how to access them. At the end of each ethnic group's section in the second part of this book, I have listed guides to help you. Additionally, the Family History Library publishes Source Guides for many foreign countries and all U.S. states. These are available for a small fee through the library's centers or from the main library. The outlines are also available on CD-ROM (Family History SourceGuide) and from the Family History Library's Web site, <http://www.familysearch.org/sg/>.

Technique

Money Saver

FOREIGN SOURCES AVAILABLE IN AMERICA

After you determine what types of records the foreign county has available for research, then **check to see if any of these sources have been published or microfilmed and are available in America.** This will save you countless hours and dollars, whether your eventual goal is to make a trip to your ancestral village, conduct research through correspondence, or hire a researcher in the homeland. The Family History Library has microfilmed records from all over the world—not every record for every country has been microfilmed, of course, but you would be surprised at what is available.

When you find your immigrant ancestor's name in foreign records, you need to ascertain whether this person is indeed your ancestor or another individual with the same name—a task no different than when searching American records. This is a main reason for knowing your ancestors better than they knew themselves, which is not really a difficult assignment, just time-consuming.

Research Tip

To determine if you have the right person, ask yourself these questions:

- Does the age/birthdate match what I know about my ancestor from American sources?
- Are the names found among those in the foreign records and in conjunction with my immigrant ancestor the same as neighbors and acquaintances in America?
- Are there listings in foreign records with my immigrant ancestor's name for the time *after* he or she left for America?
- What were the names of my immigrant ancestor's parents? siblings? children? Do these match in foreign records?
- What were the naming patterns of the ethnic group that would help me determine names of parents and siblings who did not emigrate?

Case Study

An example will illustrate one case. All you may know about an ancestor, Giovanni Spada, is that he was born about 1845 in Molfetta, Italy. In searching the Family History Library's microfilmed birth records for that town, you discovered three children named Giovanni Spada born between the years 1842 and 1846. If you have done your homework in not only American genealogical records, but also Italian-American social history sources, you will learn that Italians typically followed a particular naming pattern. They named the first son after the paternal grandfather and the first daughter after the paternal grandmother. From genealogical data, you know that your Giovanni's first son was named Luigi (no doubt in honor of Giovanni's father) and his first daughter was Lucia (no doubt in honor of Giovanni's mother).

The three Giovanni babies recorded in the Italian birth records show the following parents:

Giovanni, born 1842; parents: Francesco and Maria
Giovanni, born 1844; parents: Nicolo and Caterina
Giovanni, born 1846; parents: Luigi and Lucia

Which is most likely to be your Giovanni, and which one will you pursue further research first? Obviously, the third one.

There is no doubt; the more you know about your immigrant ancestors in American records, the easier it will be to identify them in foreign records.

MEETING THE FOREIGN LANGUAGE CHALLENGE

In order to read records written in a foreign language, you may only need to use a foreign-language/English dictionary and have a general familiarity with certain key terms and phrases. The Family History Library has foreign language guides with terms and phrases pertinent to genealogical research. These are available for a small fee.

For other records, however, you may need the assistance of a translator. **Foreign records are not only written in a foreign language, including Latin, but are often handwritten in an archaic script with abbreviations and may be written in a dialect.** Translators may be found by looking in the yellow pages for foreign language schools, by checking with local colleges and universities, and by looking in genealogical magazines and directories, such as the *Directory of Professional Genealogists*, published biennially by the Association of Professional Genealogists (see Appendix B) and available online at <www.apgen.org>. You will also find translators advertising in ethnic genealogical societies' newsletters. Addresses of some of these societies may be found in each ethnic group section in this book, but also consult Elizabeth Petty Bentley's *The Genealogist's Address Book*. Many ethnic societies have members who are more than willing to help fellow members translate documents and letters. Someone who immigrated from your ancestor's homeland may be able to help, as well as a foreign language teacher at a local high school or a teacher or student in a college or university's foreign language department. Also check with Catholic priests, if the document is in Latin, since they may be able to offer assistance.

WRITING FOR RECORDS

Before you make an out-of-the-country trip or hire someone in another country, you may want to try writing for records. The genealogical guidebooks written about foreign records will tell you what sources are likely obtainable through correspondence. These guides may also provide form letter translations, or you may acquire form letters from the Family History Library. There are also computer translating programs available in the major languages: Spanish, French, German, and Italian. You can type the responses you receive, and the program will translate them into English. Be aware, however, that the translating capability of the software is limited. These programs will do simple translations of current languages, not complex historical text. For example, you will want to use formal English and avoid using idioms. Do not write, "It happens once in a blue moon." Instead, write, "It rarely happens." While the translations may not be perfect, they are somewhat understandable.

When you write for foreign records, include two postal International Reply

Definitions

A naming practice common to many ethnic groups is the use of "necronyms," naming a newborn after a previously deceased child. The name was used as a tribute to the deceased child and to the name.

Warning

Case Study

USING FOREIGN MICROFILMS

Several years ago, I visited a Family History Center, where I started to look for records of my grandfather, who, according to family stories, had come to America from the Gubernia of Kovna in Lithuania. I had been told that the various churches in the towns were responsible for maintaining vital records. This meant that if Jewish couples were married, a child was born, a brit was held, or a death occurred, the church should have a record of the event.

I looked through the indexes for the Gubernia of Kovna and came across a microfilm of church records for a time period that would have included the years my grandfather's family lived in Lithuania. When the film arrived, I went to the library to look at it. I was expecting to find all kinds of information about my family. When I placed the film on the reader, however, all I found was something in a foreign language. Of course. The records were from the mid-1800s, when that part of Lithuania was actually part of Poland. Naturally, the records were in Polish, but I thought they'd be in English! Since the library would hold the film for three weeks, I had time to figure something out.

At that time, my next-door neighbor had a cleaning lady who was from Poland. She spoke very little English, but I was able to explain to her my problem. She agreed to go to the library with me and translate the film. A couple of days later, we went to the library, I placed the film on the reader, and waited for the translation to begin. Alas, the woman explained to me that the Polish on the film was not the same Polish that she spoke. Evidently, the film was in a different dialect, and she couldn't read a word of it.

Today, I could turn to an ethnic genealogical society, such as the Polish Genealogical Society of America (Chicago, Illinois), which offers translation services. So now I have a new resource to help me learn whether or not these microfilmed church records hold any information about my Jewish ancestors.

—Robert Fineberg

Important

Coupons with each request instead of a self-addressed stamped envelope. Foreign post offices will not accept U.S. stamps, and their envelope sizes may be different from ours. Depending on the country, sending an international or U.S. postal money order may be sufficient rather than exchanging currency. If you do need to exchange currency, however, you can check the Universal Currency Converter site on the Internet at <http://www.xe.net/ucc/> to see the current exchange rate and to convert the amount you will need to send. Foreign guidebooks and talking with others who have requested records by mail will tell you about how much money you need to send.

WRITING LETTERS TO FORMER ADDRESSES AND PEOPLE IN THE TELEPHONE BOOK WITH YOUR SURNAME

If you have old letters in your possession written from someone in the Old Country to your relatives, even though that person may not still be alive, try writing to the current resident of that address, simply addressing the envelope to "Current Resident." In the letter, which should be in the native language, say that you are searching for relatives of the person who used to live at this address. Ask the current resident if she or he knows the family in question, and where you might get in touch with relatives. Mail it, then don't expect an answer. Forget that you even sent it, partly because you may never receive an answer, and partly because it will be such a surprise if you do! I know of at least two people who have tried this and received wonderfully unexpected results from it.

In my own case, I wrote letters to everyone with the surname DeBartolo who lived in the village where my ancestors came from. I found about a dozen DeBartolos listed in the telephone directory for Terlizzi, Italy. (To order foreign telephone directories, call AT&T at (800) 432-6600 or (888) 582-3688. The operator will give you a price and take credit card orders.) I had a letter translated into Italian, saying that I was researching my family history and looking for relatives of my grandparents and great-grandparents (giving their names), who had come to America in the early 1900s. Out of a dozen letters, with return International Reply Coupons, I received one response. Though this gentleman was not related to my family, he referred me to someone who was also gathering genealogical data on the DeBartolos—a Frank DeBartolo, who lives in Florida!

HIRING A RESEARCHER

Look for the names of American and foreign researchers who specialize in your ethnic/immigrant group in the same places you would find a translator: genealogical magazines, ethnic genealogical society newsletters, and professional genealogists' directories. **If possible, get a recommendation from someone who has used a researcher in the country where you will be hiring someone.** Again, this would be another advantage of joining an ethnic genealogical society. The Association of Professional Genealogist's *Directory of Professional Genealogists* lists contact information for American researchers specializing in ethnic groups, as well as foreign professional genealogists' organizations from which you can obtain a roster of their members. Also seek the rosters of the Board for Certification of Genealogists and the Accredited Genealogists, which list ethnic specialists (see Appendix B).

Initially, supply the researcher with clear, concise instructions on what you seek, giving as much information as you can on the ancestors you're looking for. This will help the researcher give you a better estimate of how much time

Tip

Case Study

BRIDGING THE OCEAN WITH LETTERS

My knowledge of my family consisted of my mother, father, two older brothers, three older sisters, three elderly aunts, and one uncle. With the exception of my brothers and sisters, all were emigrants from "the Old Country" of Russia. I never met any of my grandparents. Both of my parents, at the age of twenty and as newlyweds, left their families and friends, never to see them again. Once my parents were in the United States, rarely, if ever, did they discuss their family. I later found this to be typical of many German Russians. So to the best of my knowledge, my family was the only Kissler family in the United States.

The records of my family included a few notations in a German Bible, my father's Russian passport, and a number of old photographs. A valuable resource was a series of letters to my father from his brother David in Russia from about 1956 to 1965. Prior to that time, no communications were permitted due to the edict of Stalin to deport all Germans to the slave labor camps of Siberia in 1941 until the disbanding of the camps in 1955.

After my parents died, a number of early photographs and the letters written to my father by his brother David came into my possession. After having the letters translated from German into English, I decided to copy the "Russian" address from one of the envelopes and to have a letter written in Russian to anyone that might have knowledge of the Kissler family from Russia. I sent the letter in 1990 with the expectation that it would probably find its way to the "dead letter file."

Naturally, I was surprised when I received a response written in Russian and from a Waldimir Kissler, the youngest son of David Kissler—a first cousin. Shortly thereafter, I received additional letters from other Kissler family members in Russia and the former Soviet Union. As a result of these letters and at the invitation of our relatives, my wife and I decided to visit the villages and homes of our relatives in Russia, including Frank, Russia, the birthplace of my parents. During these visits, we shared family and historical information with my newly found relatives. I was shocked when Waldimir brought forth a photograph album, which had the fiftieth wedding anniversary photo of my mother and father that they had sent from the United States, as well as a number of photos of my immediate Kissler family.

—Clarence D. Kissler

and expense will be involved. In this inquiry letter, ask for the following information:

- the researcher's qualifications and to what professional organizations he/she belongs
- research costs (hourly fee and what expenses the researcher anticipates);

WRITING TO A FIFTY-YEAR-OLD ADDRESS IN ITALY

I was working for a client, whom I'll call Francis, whose parents and oldest sister were all born in Italy, but Francis knew nothing about her parents' siblings or their parents (her grandparents). Francis could remember her mother sending packages to family in Italy. She believed it was to her mother's stepsister or half-sister, but this was all she knew. After Francis's mother died in 1950, Francis found an unused mailing tag and sent a letter to the address. She received a response in Italian. Neither Francis nor her sisters could read Italian, but it was obvious from the name and address on the letter that it was not from Maria Rossi, whom she believed may be an aunt. They never had the letter translated.

Nearly fifty years later, I encouraged her to have the letter translated. The letter was from an admirer, not even from anyone belonging to Maria's family. The gentleman mentioned that Maria was Francis's aunt, but no other family information was included other than to say he had seen Francis's picture and had heard about her from her aunt. The admirer never mentioned why he was answering the letter and not Maria.

Since we had little information about the family in Italy, with my client's permission, I wrote to the address again on her behalf. I do not write, read, or speak Italian, but I felt any correspondence should be written in Italian. A friend and colleague had a computer program that could translate a basic letter from English to Italian. The letter was addressed to "Resident or Family of Maria Rossi" at the address that was nearly fifty years old. I included a self-addressed envelope. Here is what I wrote:

> Dear Resident,
>
> Maria Rossi lived at this address. Maria was my mother's sister. My mother, Angela, married Mario Umberto, and they immigrated to the United States. I know nothing about my family in Italy. I would like to find my family in Italy and learn more about them. Do you know any of Maria Rossi's family? If you do, please give them this letter. Thank you.

Not long after I sent the letter, my client received a response from Maria's granddaughter, Teresa. Teresa wrote in broken English on behalf of her father and uncles, sons of Maria. Teresa said that her father and uncles remembered "with great affection and gratitude" the help Angela had provided during the war. Teresa also stated that the family had tried to contact Angela's family when no news was received from Angela. Teresa said she would write "family stories" if Francis wished to correspond, and that Francis could write in English and Teresa would translate for the family in Italy. Who knew that a fifty-year-old address might be the ticket to reconnecting to family in Italy!

—Marcia K. Wyett, CGRS

some researchers may have to travel to your ancestral village to conduct research, so there may also be the expense of travel, lodging, and meals
- how often you can expect research reports
- how much of a retainer you need to send, and in what type of currency (U.S. dollars by check or money order, or foreign currency)

MAKING A TRIP TO THE ANCESTRAL HOMELAND

I made my first trip to my ancestors' village in Italy in March 1999. I talked with everyone I could think of who had been to Italy or to my particular village to get their advice and recommendations, and I still wasn't adequately prepared. You almost need to plan on two trips: one to get your feet wet, the second to really get down to business.

No matter how much time you plan for research, it will never be enough. Just as it took you some time to learn to use American records with proficiency, it will take you time to learn the intricacies of foreign records and what will be available for you to search. Take into account that for most foreign countries, the records won't be in English. Even in English-speaking countries, you could find yourself trying to translate Latin or Gaelic. If you haven't studied some of the records on microfilm before you leave on your trip, you may be in for a big surprise. Even if the records for your ancestral village have not been filmed, look at records from neighboring villages for an idea of what records of that area look like, and what type of records you may find.

Timesaver

Have specific research goals in mind or written out before you leave. Don't go expecting to get your family tree back to the Middle Ages in just a few days of research. Decide which families are most important to your current research and focus on them. Then if you have more time, you can look for more. You certainly do not want to waste valuable time looking at records that you could have viewed in America, so do your homework!

Every country and municipality is different when it comes to availability and types of records and whether you will be allowed to search the records yourself. For example, in Terlizzi, population of about 2,500, I was given carte blanche to the civil vital records and could go through the indexes and records to my heart's content. In Potenza, just fifteen miles away and with a population of about 100,000, the clerk wouldn't even let me breathe on the record books. If you are in a situation where you cannot look at the documents yourself, have specific goals in mind and a list of names and dates, so the clerk can easily look things up for you, assuming that person is willing to do so. Remember, it is especially hard to sweet talk the clerk into looking up records, or possibly allowing you to look at the records, if you don't speak the language.

After your trip, always send a thank-you note and small gift to the record clerks that helped you while you were researching, even if they weren't all that helpful. If you utilized church records, you might want to send a donation. If you ever need to write for records, you can always remind them of your visit and the gift you sent, and this may get you a better and faster response through the mail. They are more likely to remember you when you make that second visit, too.

Tip

OTHER THINGS I LEARNED ON MY TRIP TO ITALY
(Which May Apply to Other Countries)

Friend's Advice: The civil vital records office is in the center of town by the main cathedral.

Reality: Since the time my friend had been there, the civil vital records office had moved to another location that was nowhere near the center of town or the main cathedral. Make sure you know how to ask where the records office is and be able to understand enough of the language to absorb directions.

Friend's Advice: Bring very little cash (i.e., foreign currency). Rely on your ATM card.

Reality: I tried my ATM card on three or four different ATM machines in two different cities in Italy and never could get it to work.

Friend's Advice: Use your credit card.

Reality: I did. And so did someone else. On the second credit card statement I received when I got home, there were two restaurant charges made nine days after I left Italy and in a city that I had never visited. Although my credit card was never out of my sight, and it came home with me, someone used the number to have some lovely dinners. Additionally, some places would not take credit cards, especially if the amount I was spending was small or the place was a small establishment (shop or restaurant).

Friend's Advice: Take American Express Traveler's Cheques.

Reality: While we have all been told that traveler's checks are as good as cash, they aren't. At the bank in small-town Terlizzi, you would have thought I had printed the traveler's checks on my laser printer that morning. It took the bank manager forty-five minutes to examine them, find and figure out the exchange rate, and cash my traveler's checks. It was a waste of good research time. In Rome, however, there was a special window for traveler's checks and currency exchanges, and it took all of five minutes. If you're visiting a tourist area, cash your traveler's checks at a bank there, not in a small ancestral village.

Friend's Advice: Everything closes between 1 P.M. and 5 P.M.

Reality: Yep. Everything did close during those hours. Even most of the restaurants. If you find this to be true in your ancestral village, plan to accomplish other activities during these down times, such as walking or touring the village, locating former residences of your ancestors, or visiting the cemetery.

Friend's Advice: Learn the language.

Reality: I didn't. After all, everyone speaks *some* English nowadays, don't they? If you are visiting a tiny ancestral village far from any major cities, don't expect

OTHER THINGS I LEARNED ON MY TRIP TO ITALY—Continued

anyone to speak English, except maybe the third grader at the candy counter, assuming English is part of their required curriculum. Fortunately, my friend had learned the language better than I had, but I had practiced over and over again in Italian something far more important than "Where is the bathroom?" and that was, "I am researching the history of my family: DeBartolo and Vallarelli. Where are the birth, marriage, and death records?"

Friend's Advice: Rent a car. Driving over there isn't that bad.

Reality: The cab driver we rode with passed on hills and around curves, ignored stop signs, and drove 50 MPH within the city limits and 95 MPH on the *autostrada*. We even passed a police car as we were leaving town, but the two officers were fast asleep with their chins on their chests. I still haven't decided if I stood a better chance of survival by being in a rented vehicle and driving on the same road with the taxis or simply being a helpless passenger.

WHAT TO DO IF YOU CAN'T FIND ARRIVAL AND NATURALIZATION RECORDS

or You Can't Bridge the Ocean or Land Border

Sadly, bridging the ocean or land border may be difficult. According to the 1900 census and the passenger list of him returning from a trip to Ireland, my great-grandfather David Norris was naturalized. But I have yet to find a record of this event. I also know from census records that his wife, Delia (Gordon) Norris, came to this country from Ireland with her twin sister about 1885, yet I have not found a record of their arrival that would lead me to a place in Ireland. I do know where my Italian great-grandfather came from, but I haven't a clue if he ever became a citizen because I cannot find a record of him becoming naturalized. That could be because he never did; he was a bird of passage. And I am still stymied over Cornelius Carmack. Was he the immigrant? If so, when did he arrive? And was he Scotch-Irish as everything thus far seems to point?

When you get blocked by these brick walls, you have several options. One is to set the problem aside for awhile and work on other lines. When you come back to it, your research knowledge will have changed and you will have gained more experience as a researcher. There may also be new sources available for you to check that weren't available when you were originally researching the problem. Finally, you may have been overlooking some clues because you were too close to the problem at the time. Picking up your notes and photocopies months and sometimes years later, you may discover a possible solution staring you in the face.

Sometimes the answer to your research problem may require more advanced methods of research. In the case of Cornelius Carmack, my next step may be

Brick Wall Buster

to read all the deeds in Cecil County, Maryland, starting with the earliest date I know he was there and working backward to see if he witnessed any documents that would place him in the county earlier than 1718. Or I might try researching his neighbors in Frederick County, Maryland, where I know he owned land, and see if I can determine the origins of Cornelius's neighbors. The records created on these people may give me some clues. These research strategies are, of course, extremely time-consuming and arduous. Or I may decide that I have gotten as close as I will ever get to finding the origins of Cornelius Carmack. Presently, I am quite content with my hypothesis that he was likely Scotch-Irish.

In some cases, you may never find that magical date of arrival, that passenger list, or that naturalization record, but you can get awfully close. You may not find a precise location in the Old Country. I know that is frustrating and disappointing, and I do not mean to discourage you. This is not to say, however, that all of your research has been in vain. In the process, you have gathered the facts and story of someone's *life*. I may not know where Cornelius came from or when, but along the way, I learned about everyday life in colonial Maryland, about the Scotch-Irish, and a little something about Irish and Scottish names; and I found a wonderful document for Cornelius—an inventory of his estate after he died. He owned tools, kitchen ware, bushels of rye and Indian corn, a bed, swine, an old saddle, some tanned leather, a plow, a saw, and more. I also learned that his son, Cornelius, apparently used the name McCarmack, perhaps to distinguish him from his father, since they lived in the same community. All of this information makes Cornelius Sr. a person, not just a name on a chart.

In Part III, I'll show you how you can compile what you've found on your immigrant ancestors into a valuable, narrative family history. Remember, every immigrant's story deserves to be documented and recorded because every immigrant's story is the history of America. But for now, turn to the introduction of Part II, then read about the ethnic/immigrant groups to which your ancestors belonged.

PART TWO

Major Ethnic Groups
in America:
Historical Overviews

Exploring Your Heritage

One cursory look at the list of American ethnic groups in chapter two emphasizes the impossibility of discussing each group within this book. The decision regarding which groups to include was not easy, so I established the following criteria. I began with a list of ethnic groups based on the percentage of those with foreign ancestry as reported in the 1990 census.

PERCENTAGE OF U.S. POPULATION WITH EUROPEAN ANCESTRY
1990 Census

German	23% or 58 million
Irish	16% or 39 million
English	13% or 33 million
African American	10% or 24 million
Italian	6% or 15 million
Mexican	5% or 12 million
French	4% or 10 million
Polish	4% or 9 million
American Indian	4% or 9 million
Dutch	3% or 6 million
Scotch-Irish	2% or 6 million
Scottish	2% or 5 million
Swedish	2% or 5 million
Norwegian	2% or 4 million

Source: Census Questionnaire Content, 1990, Bureau of the Census, <http://www.census.gov>.
Note: These statistics are not entirely accurate. People of mixed heritage may have only reported one ethnic background. About 30 percent of the people wrote in a second ancestry and about 10 percent did not report any ancestry.

I also used a cutoff date of those groups who had immigrated in significant numbers prior to World War II. My reasoning was twofold: (1) The rate of immigration by then had declined significantly due to the quota laws established in the 1920s and the Great Depression of the 1930s; and (2) I presumed that most readers with ancestors who came after World War II still have living relatives with whom they could talk and learn who was in the immigrant generation, when they came, and from where they came. (I realize this will not be true in every case, of course.) Finally, I included certain groups based on my knowledge of genealogical interest in that group, or based on the availability of significant published and other resources to advance genealogical research. Unfortunately, for some groups, such as Portuguese, Russians, and a few others, you will notice that there is a dearth of published genealogical research materials, showing where there are holes in resources to help researchers. Certainly, if you descend from an ethnic group not discussed here, you can apply the same research techniques as discussed in this book and search out available information and sources.

Some groups in this part receive more attention than others. This is because more is available about some groups in a social history context. While no ethnic heritage is less important than another, examining the most populous groups will illustrate that the socio-historical patterns and traits are distinctive for each group, leading you to specific research strategies in any situation. If, for example, you learn that nearly half of all French Canadians were not likely to become naturalized citizens, this may explain why you have been unable to locate a naturalization record for your ancestor. Or, if you have not yet identified the immigrant generation, learning the migration patterns and folkways may help you determine it. Or suppose all you know about an immigrant ancestor is that he was "German." By reading the overviews of the Germanic groups and learning the immigration and settlement patterns of each, you can at least determine a possible group upon which to focus the beginning of your research.

Besides gravitating toward genealogical resources, study the ethnic social history, which will lead you to original and published sources. Social histories provide the general, common experience for an ethnic group; it is then up to you to determine whether your ancestors were typical or atypical of the people and time period based on your genealogical research. The bonus is that social history will give life to sterile names, dates, and places when you are ready to write your family history (see Part III).

For each ethnic group and subgroup, I have tried to identify the following:

Important

- typical immigration experience, i.e., periods of emigration, ports of departure and arrival
- settlement and migration patterns in America
- resources for further research in America and in the native homeland. Please note that these resources are select and not all-inclusive. There are many excellent histories of ethnic groups or neighborhoods in American cities, which I encourage you to seek, but it would be impossible to list all of these for each group. Regarding the organizations and Internet sites, I tried to include organizations of a national scope and the most popular Web sites. But there are more than those listed, so also see sources such as Elizabeth Petty Bentley, *The Genealogist's Address Book*, latest edition,

and Cyndi Howells, *Cyndi's List: A Comprehensive List of 40,000 Genealogy Sites on the Internet.*

When possible, I tried to include some cultural traits, folkways, and customs that have a bearing on genealogical research. These may include, but are not limited to naming patterns, marriage customs and patterns, family patterns, religious affiliations, and behavioral patterns (e.g., overall health, diet, divorce rates, and educational levels). The sections on African Americans and American Indians deviate from the historical overview in that I also include some commonly used sources specific to these two groups and some special research strategies.

I compiled most of the information in the ethnic sections from these sources:

- *Harvard Encyclopedia of American Ethnic Groups*, edited by Stephan Thernstrom and Ann Orlov
- *Coming to America: A History of Immigration and Ethnicity in American Life,* by Roger Daniels
- *Ethnicity and Family Therapy*, second edition, edited by Monica McGoldrick, Joe Giordano, and John K. Pearce
- *Ethnic Families in America: Patterns and Variations*, fourth edition, by Charles Mindel, Robert W. Habenstein, and Roosevelt Wright Jr.
- *We Who Built America*, by Carl Wittke

For the sections on English and Scotch-Irish, I also relied heavily upon *Albion's Seed: Four British Folkways in America*, by David Hackett Fischer.

I'll be the first to admit that I do not have research expertise in all of these groups, so I have made every effort to ensure the accuracy of each overview by consulting with as many specialists as I could. (Please see the acknowledgments.) Remember, this book is not intended to have the answers to all of your ethnic/immigrant research problems. It is meant to be a springboard to help you get started. Once you have explored the general records discussed in Part I and read the overview of the ethnic group from this section, then you should move on to more specialized resources that will help you find sources specific to your group of interest. Learning never stops when you are researching your ancestors.

African Americans

Some Africans came to the North American continent as explorers and were free; a few came as indentured servants and eventually became free after working off their debt. The vast majority of Africans who came to this country were brought in chains.

The slave trade involved the kidnapping and transportation of nearly ten million blacks between about 1701 and 1810. Slightly less than half that number were sent to British North America and Louisiana; the rest were shipped to the Caribbean Islands. Even though the slave trade was outlawed in 1807, a small number of blacks were still imported. Slavery existed in every colony and Canada, although it eventually became predominant in the southern colonies and states. Northern merchants, however, also profited from slavery: the southern cotton planters, northern textile manufacturers, and New England shippers had a symbiotic relationship.

Enslaved and free Africans are the ancestors of more than 10 percent of the population today, or roughly twenty millions Americans. Unfortunately, there are few surviving letters, diaries, or reminiscences of blacks comparable to those from the colonial English or other groups to document their thoughts and feelings. Most of the contemporary documents were written by whites—slave traders, masters, and other white observers.

We usually do not even know the original names of enslaved Africans, only what their masters later called them. Nor can we usually determine their origins accurately. While some slave traders did not care much where their human cargo came from and did not bother to record it, others traveled to specific ports to obtain Africans from specific tribes. Most of the slaves to British North America appear to have come from a narrow strip along the West African coast. About half, according to Thomas C. Holt in Thernstrom's *Harvard Encyclopedia of American Ethnic Groups* (pp. 7–8), originated from the areas presently occupied by Angola and southern Nigera; about one-eighth each from Ghana, Senegal and Gambia, and Sierra Leone; a few others from the Benin area and Mozambique. Some colonists preferred Africans from specific areas: South Carolinians wanted Senegambians, especially the Bambara and Malinké but did not want blacks from Biafra, known as the Ibo. Virginians felt differently and ended up with the larger portion of Biafrans.

Even most of African culture did not survive intact, since distinct groups were not allowed to cluster, as other ethnic groups had, in enclaves. It is a testimonial to these cultures that music, dance, food, language, and religious ceremonies survived at all. Those Africans from Spanish colonies and the Caribbean, however, were influenced more by Spanish culture; those from French or Dutch colonies exhibited characteristics of those cultures. This mixing even created new subcultures.

Oral History

Aspects that have survived are a heavy reliance on oral traditions, making oral history interviewing a vital part of tracing African heritage, and the fostering of extended family groups. Kinship ties by blood and marriage were (and are) extremely valued among African Americans, as evidenced by the search for family members after emancipation and for couples to make their marriages legal.

In historical records, you will no doubt find the term "mulatto." It was used to denote those of African and European heritage. The term "quadroon" was someone who was one-fourth black, being the child of a mulatto and a white. In some societies, such as that of New Orleans, even classifications such as "octoroon" were common. According to Holt in the *Harvard Encyclopedia of American Ethnic Groups* (p. 9), "Laws to prohibit intermarriage between whites and blacks indicate not only the growth and codification of racist fears, but also the existence of considerable interracial contact" between white men and black women, and between white women and black men. (For more information on black-white relations, see Joel Williamson, *New People: Miscegenation and Mulattoes in the United States*; Catherine Clinton and Michele Gillespie, editors, *The Devil's Lane: Sex and Race in the Early South*; and Martha Hodes, *White Women, Black Men: Illicit Sex in the 19th-Century South*.)

In 1860, the census indicated 200,112 free blacks in the North, and 287,958 free blacks in the South, totaling 488,070 free persons of color. Migration of free blacks to the north began after World War I, but more than 90 percent of former slaves remained in the South until after World War II. For the first fifty years after emancipation, most blacks worked as laborers or sharecroppers on plantations.

Origins of surnames of former slaves are complicated, and many used the name of their former owners. According to Holt in *Harvard Encyclopedia of American Ethnic Groups* (p. 11), however, "Despite forced migrations and separations, slaves carefully passed on the surnames of their black family of origin and declined to take the names of their various subsequent owners. The large percentage of sons named for their fathers suggests the important status of the male parent. . . . Children were named for grandparents, uncles, and aunts; and the practice of addressing elders as 'auntie' and 'uncle' was quite likely a slave invention to show respect."

Slaves who managed to escape tended to flee to southern cities, rather than to northern states or Canada. Slave uprisings and revolts were not common but did occur. During the American Revolution, the British commanders offered freedom to southern black slaves who would flee their masters' plantations. There were no age or sex restrictions, so many men and women took their children and fled. When the British left an American port, they took large numbers of former slaves. Approximately ten thousand blacks left from Savannah and Charleston. Some left from the Port of New York and sailed to Nova Scotia, landing near Birchtown.

WHERE DID THEY GO?
Black Migration Routes to and From Nova Scotia From 1782 to 1890

1782–1784	Black loyalists from New York to Birchtown/Shelburne and Halifax
1792	Black loyalists from Halifax to Sierra Leone in Africa
1813–1815	Black refugees from Delaware and Chesapeake Bay
1821	Black refugees from Halifax to Trinidad
1890s	Black workers from the Caribbean to Cape Breton Island

Source: Nova Scotia Economic Development and Tourism as cited in "Ancestral Quest: Two women hunt for clues to lives of black Loyalists," *The* [Colorado Springs] *Gazette*, 15 February 1999, pp. A1, A3.

British commander Sir Guy Carleton ordered an enumeration of all blacks who sought the army's protection. In the process, the army obtained crude biographical details of the former slaves to determine whether they would be allowed to leave with the troops for England and Nova Scotia. According to Mary Beth Norton in *Liberty's Daughters* (pp. 209–212), "Blacks who had belonged to loyalists were excluded from the promise of freedom offered by the British during the war, as were any who had joined the British after November 1782," so these runaways were returned to their masters. All others were liberated. Some slaves also gained their freedom in fighting for the colonists. (For more information on blacks during the Revolution, see Mary Beth Norton's "The Fate of Some Black Loyalists of the American Revolution," *Journal of Negro History*; Benjamin Quarles's *The Negro in the American Revolution*; and Graham Russell Hodges's *The Black Loyalist Directory: African Americans in Exile After the American Revolution*.)

SLAVE SCHEDULES

While free blacks before and after the Emancipation Proclamation of 1863 usually appear by name in traditional records such as censuses, population schedules usually do not list the names of slaves. Population schedules of 1790–1840 contain columns for recording slaves in sex and age categories, but not by name. In 1850 and 1860, separate slave schedules were enumerated, giving the slave owner's name, each slave's color (black or mulatto), sex, and age (see Figure II-1 on page 139). This is why it is important to know the name of the slave owner, which may have been passed down through oral history. If you have an ancestor, either free or slave, who died during the census years of 1850 and 1860 (1 June through 31 May in 1849–1850 and 1859–1860), the mortality schedule recorded the names of blacks and mulattos who died during that year. These names may not appear in many of the general indexes to these enumerations.

COURT RECORDS

Other types of records where you might find mention of slaves, often by name, are deeds and wills. These documents, recorded mostly in county courthouses, show slaves being sold or transferred from one owner to another. In wills and probate records, you will often find slaves bequeathed to children and grandchildren. Daughters typically received slaves from their parents, rather than land. Some testators gave slaves their freedom upon their death, such as by the will of Derrick Kroesen of Bucks County, Pennsylvania, in 1783:

> Item: It is my will that my Negro man Striffin, after my decease, he paying the sum of fifty pounds lawful money, he likewise shall be free and it is my will that my Negro girl Liddy, after my decease, she paying the sum of thirty pounds lawful money, she shall likewise be free with all her waring apperl [*sic*]. . . . (Warren D. Cruise, *The Croesen Families of America, Volume 1* [Baltimore, Md.: Gateway Press, 1998], 303–304.)

Sometimes you will find detailed information, as in the will of Mary Bryant of New York, dated 13 February 1797:

> . . . also £100 further part thereof in trust to receive the interest thereof and pay the same to Catharine Bell, negro woman and heretofore my slave, at present residing in the Island of St. Christopher in the West Indies. . . .

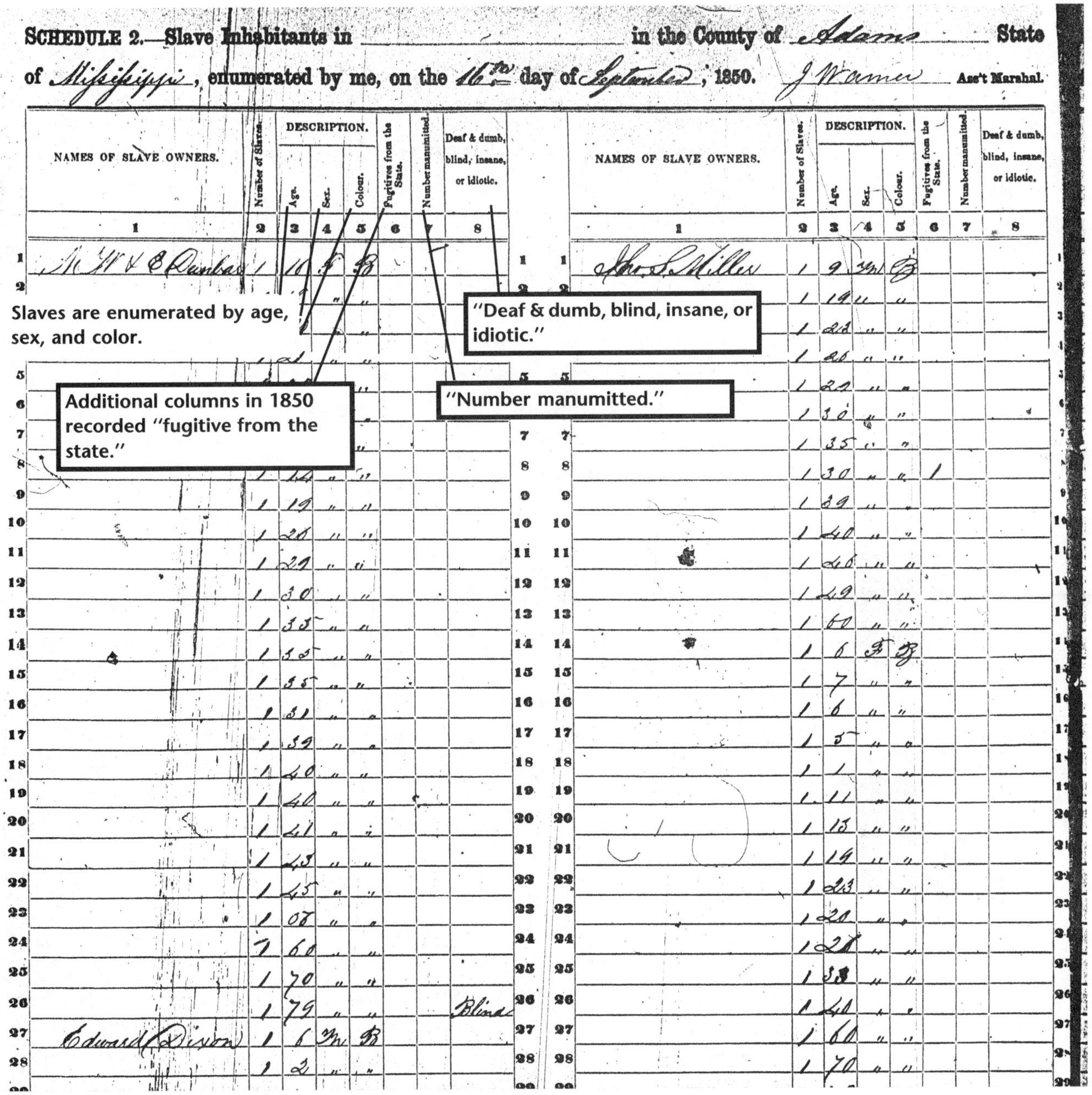

Figure II-1
1850 slave schedule, Mississippi, Adams County, NARA microfilm M432, roll 368. Only the slave owners' names are given.

(*Collections of the New-York Historical Society for the Year 1906. Abstracts of Wills—Liber 42.* [New York: The New York Genealogical and Biographical Society, 1907], 110–112.)

Slaves may also be mentioned or named in probate inventories or distributions.

SOME RESEARCH STRATEGIES

Deeds and wills that list unusual first names of slaves, such as Truelove, Tulip, and Travers, may be helpful in tracing their whereabouts after the Civil War.

As indicated above, slaves did not always take the surnames of their masters. Look at the 1870 census for blacks by their first names in the area in which they lived during and prior to the war. Remember, too, that free blacks may have owned black slaves.

Research Tip

It is also extremely important for descendants of slaves to learn the state laws of inheritance during a given time period and whether the slaves were considered real or personal property. For example, Maryland and South Carolina slaves were considered personal property; in Virginia in 1705, the law was changed to make slaves real property for purposes of inheritance. When a white woman married, all of her property, real and personal, became her husband's. But what happened to the slaves when he died? If there is a surviving will, perhaps it will tell you. But what if there was no will? Did the slaves become her property, or were they distributed to other heirs? Did she gain absolute title, meaning she could bequeath them to whomever she wanted at her death? Or did she receive only a life interest, which terminated upon her death? And what happened if the widow remarried and then she died? Did the slaves go to the second husband and his heirs, or to her heirs from her first marriage? As you can see, this can be a complex problem, but in cases where you cannot find a will that tells you who inherited your ancestors, you must study the laws of inheritance to determine in which direction your research should go.

Along with the deeds and wills of whites who owned slaves, newspapers are another valuable source for tracing African-American families. Owners may have advertised for runaway slaves, giving physical descriptions. Some of these advertisements have been published in Lathan A. Windley's *Runaway Slave Advertisements: A Documentary History From the 1730s to 1790.*

Sources

Plantation records, if still in existence, might be another helpful source. Some slave owners recorded not only the sales and ownership of their slaves, but births, marriages, and deaths. These records may be found among manuscript collections in state libraries and archives (check the *National Union Catalog of Manuscript Collections*). Some have been microfilmed and made available at the Family History Library or through a Family History Center. In particular, see the microfilmed collection titled *A Guide to Records of Ante-Bellum Southern Plantations From the Revolution Through the Civil War*, compiled by Martin P. Schipper (Frederick, Md.: University Publications of America, 1985–1995.) Also look for published sources, such as *South Central Kentucky Vital Statistics: Births and Deaths for Slaves and Black Families*, by Michelle Bartley Gorin.

After slaves were emancipated, segregation increased, even in records, such as marriage records. Even city directories may have a separate section in the back that lists people of color. For the time period after the war, also look for slave narratives and autobiographies, such as the nineteen volume set with twenty volumes in its supplements, edited by George P. Rawick, *The American Slave: A Composite Autobiography.*

Sources

A few other records to consider are Civil War pension records, records of the "Freedmen's Bureau," and signature cards for the Freedman's Savings and Trust

Company. More than 100,000 African-American men served in the war. Because slave marriages were not considered legal, Congress made an adjustment in the requirement for presenting a legal document when a black veteran or his widow applied for a pension. These records contain a wealth of information on the veteran, his widow, and their families. (See Military Records in chapter five). The Bureau of Freedmen, Refugees and Abandoned Land, established in 1865, created bureau reports, aided in labor contract disputes and settlements that can aid in researching black ancestry, although they may not contain a great deal of genealogical information. These records are in the custody of the National Archives in Washington, DC. Rich in family information are the thousands of signature cards of depositors in the Freedman's Savings and Trust Company. These are available on microfilm through the National Archives and the Family History Library. See also the National Archives guide, *Black Studies: A Select Catalog of National Archives Microfilm Publications.*

Since they were excluded from white groups, black men and women formed their own organizations. For example, the National Association of Colored Women (NACW) was founded in 1896 and had more than three dozen chapters in twelve states and Washington, DC. By the early 1900s, black women had formed their own suffrage organizations in cities such as Tuskegee, St. Louis, Los Angeles, Memphis, Boston, Charleston, and New Orleans. There were also state-level associations.

Although African-American family history research is challenging, as you can see, there are many avenues to take and many resources to help in your search.

RESOURCES

Research Guides

Amico, Colete J. and Shirley J. Burton. "Freedmen's Bureau Records as a Family History Resource at the National Archives." Federation of Genealogical Societies' *Forum* (Winter 1989): 8–10.

Bradley, Frank. "Personal Property Taxes in Virginia: A Genealogical Goldmine." *Journal of the Afro-American Historical and Genealogical Society* 3 (Spring 1986): 125–136.

Byers, Paula K., ed. *African American Genealogical Sourcebook*. Detroit: Gale Research, 1995.

Cerny, Johni. "From Maria to Bill Cosby: A Case Study in Tracing Black Slave Ancestry." *National Genealogical Society Quarterly* 75 (March 1987): 5–14.

Crouch, Barry A. and Larry Madaras. "Reconstructing Black Families: Perspectives From the Texas Freedmen's Bureau Records." In *Our Family, Our Town: Essays on Family and Local History Sources in the National Archives*. Timothy Walch, ed. Washington, D.C.: National Archives and Records Administration, 1987.

Davis Jr., Robert Scott. "Documentation for Afro-American Families: Records of the Freedman's Savings and Trust Company." *National Genealogical Society Quarterly* 81 (March 1993): 24–25.

Greene, Robert Ewell. *Black Courage, 1775–1783: Documentation of Black Participation in the American Revolution.* Washington, D.C.: National Society, Daughters of the American Revolution 1984.

Hoff, Henry B. "A Colonial Black Family in New York and New Jersey: Peter Santomee and His Descendants." *Journal of Afro-American Historical and Genealogical Society* 9 (Fall 1988): 101–134, and "Additions and Corrections" in volume 10 (Winter 1989): 158–160.

Matthews, Harry Bradshaw. *African American Genealogical Research: How to Trace Your Family History.* Baldwin, N.Y: Matthews Heritage Services, 1992.

Mills, Gary B. "Tracing Free People of Color in the Antebellum South: Methods, Sources, and Perspectives." *National Genealogical Society Quarterly* 78 (December 1990): 262–278.

Sanborn, Melinde Lutz. "Angola and Elizabeth: An African Family in the Massachusetts Bay Colony." *The New England Quarterly* LXXII (March 1999): 119–129.

Smith, Gloria L. *Black Americana at Mount Vernon: Genealogy Techniques for Slave Group Research.* Tucson: the author, 1984.

Streets, David H. *Slave Genealogy: A Research Guide With Case Studies.* Bowie, Md.: Heritage Books, 1986.

Thackery, David T. *Afro-American Family History at the Newberry Library: A Research Guide and Bibliography.* Chicago: Newberry Library, 1988.

———. *Tracking Your African American Family History.* Salt Lake City: Ancestry, Inc., 1999.

Witcher, Curt. *Bibliography of Sources for Black Family History in the Allen County Public Library Genealogy Department.* Fort Wayne, Ind.: Allen County Public Library, 1986.

Woodtor, Dee Parmer. *Finding a Place Called Home: A Guide to African-American Genealogy and Historical Identity.* New York: Random House, 1999.

Social Histories and Historical Sources

Abrahams, Roger D. *Singing the Master: The Emergence of African American Culture in the Plantation South.* New York: Pantheon, 1992.

Ball, Edward. *Slaves in the Family.* New York: Farrar, Straus and Giroux, 1998.

Bean, Richard Nelson. *The British Trans-Atlantic Slave Trade, 1650–1775.* New York: Arno Press, 1975.

Blassingame, John W. *The Slave Community.* New York: Oxford University Press, 1972.

Campbell, Edward D. and Kym S. Rice. *Before Freedom Came: African-American Life in the Antebellum South.* Richmond, Va.: Museum of the Confederacy, 1991.

Campbell, Georgetta Merritt. *Extant Collections of Early Black Newspapers: A Research Guide to the Black Press, 1880–1915, With an Index to the Boston Guardian, 1902–1904.* Troy, N.Y.: Whitston Publishing Co., 1981.

Clinton, Catherine and Michele Gillespie, eds. *The Devil's Lane: Sex and Race in the Early South.* New York: Oxford University Press, 1997.

Crahan, Margaret and Franklin W. Knight. *Africa and the Caribbean: The Legacies of a Link*. Baltimore: Johns Hopkins University Press, 1979.

Curtin, Philip D. *The Atlantic Slave Trade: A Census*. Madison: University of Wisconsin Press, 1969.

Federal Writers' Project. *Slave Narratives*. 17 vols. Irvine, Calif.: Reprint Services, 1989.

Finkelman, Paul. *State Slavery Statutes*. Frederick, Md.: University Publications of America, 1989.

Forbes, Jack D. *Africans and Native Americans: The Language of Race and the Evolution of Red-Black Peoples*. Urbana, Ill.: University of Chicago Press, 1993.

Frankel, Noralee. "From Slave Women to Free Women: The National Archives and Black Women's History in the Civil War Era." *Prologue* 29 (Summer 1997): 100–101.

Franklin, John Hope and Alfred A. Moss Jr. *From Slavery to Freedom*, 7th ed. New York: McGraw-Hill, 1994.

Gutman, Herbert George. *The Black Family in Slavery and Freedom, 1750–1925*. New York: Pantheon Books, 1976.

Halliburton Jr., R. *Red Over Black: Black Slavery Among the Cherokee Indians*. Westport, Conn.: Greenwood Press, 1977.

Hodes, Martha. *White Women, Black Men: Illicit Sex in the 19th-Century South*. New Haven, Conn.: Yale University Press, 1997.

Jones, Jacqueline. *Labor of Love, Labor of Sorrow: Black Women, Work and the Family, From Slavery to the Present*. New York: Vintage Books, 1985.

Katz, William Loren. *Black Indians: A Hidden Heritage*. New York: Atheneum, 1986.

———. *Breaking the Chains: African-American Slave Resistance*. New York: Atheneum, 1990.

Miller, Joseph C., ed. *The African Past Speaks: Essays on Oral Tradition and History*. Hamden, Conn.: Archon, 1980.

Nash, Gary B. *Red, White, and Black: The Peoples of Early America*. Englewood Cliffs, N.J.: Prentice-Hall, 1974.

Norton, Mary Beth. "The Fate of Some Black Loyalists of the American Revolution." *Journal of Negro History* LVIII (1973): 402–426.

———. *Liberty's Daughters: The Revolutionary Experience of American Women, 1750–1800*. Ithaca, N.Y.: Cornell University Press, 1980.

Puckett, Newbell Niles. *Black Names in America: Origins and Usage*. Boston: G.K. Hall, 1975.

Quarles, Benjamin. *The Negro in the American Revolution*. Chapel Hill: University of North Carolina Press, 1961.

Rawick, George P., ed. *The American Slave: A Composite Autobiography*. 19 vols. Westport, Conn.: Greenwood Press, 1972. *Supplement, Series 1*, 10 vols., 1977; *Supplement, Series 2*, 10 vols., 1979.

White, Anne Terry. *Human Cargo: The Story of the Atlantic Slave Trade*. Champaign, Ill.: Garrard, 1972.

Williamson, Joel. *New People: Miscegenation and Mulattoes in the United*

States. Baton Rouge: Louisiana State University Press, 1995.

Windley, Lathan A. *Runaway Slave Advertisements: A Documentary History From the 1730s to 1790.* 4 vols. Westport, Conn.: Greenwood Press, 1983.

Winks, Robin W. *The Blacks in Canada: A History.* New Haven, Conn.: Yale University Press, 1971.

Wright, Donald R. *African Americans in the Colonial Era: From African Origins Through the American Revolution.* Arlington Heights, Ill.: Harlan Davidson, 1990.

———. *African Americans in the Early Republic, 1789–1831.* Arlington Heights, Ill.: Harlan Davidson, 1993.

Sources and Finding Aids

Abajian, James de T. *Blacks in Selected Newspapers, Censuses, and Other Sources: An Index to Names and Subjects.* 2 vols. Boston: G.K. Hall, 1985.

Bell, Barbara L. *Black Biographical Sources: An Annotated Bibliography.* New Haven, Conn.: Yale University Library, 1970.

Black Newspapers Index. Ann Arbor, Mich.: University Microfilms, 1987–.

Black Studies: A Select Catalog of National Archives Microfilm Publications. Washington, D.C.: National Archives, 1984. (Available online at http://www.nara.gov/publications/microfilm/blackstudies/blackstd.html.)

Eiccholz, Alice and James M. Rose. *Free Black Heads of Households in the New York State Federal Census, 1790–1830.* Detroit: Gale Research Co., 1981.

Eisenberg, Marcia J. "Birth Registrations of Children of Slaves." *Journal of the Afro-American Historical and Genealogical Society* 1 (1980).

Foner, Eric. *Freedom's Lawmakers: A Directory of Black Officeholders During Reconstruction,* rev. ed. Baton Rogue: Louisiana State University Press, 1996.

Ham, Debra Newman. *List of Free Black Heads of Families in the First Census of the United States, 1790.* Washington, D.C.: National Archives and Records Service, 1973.

Heinegg, Paul. *Free African Americans of North Carolina and Virginia,* 3rd ed. Baltimore: Clearfield Publishers, 1999.

Hodges, Graham Russell. *The Black Loyalist Directory: African Americans in Exile After the American Revolution.* New York: Garland Publishing, Inc., 1996.

Jacobs, Donald M. *Antebellum Black Newspapers: Indices to* New York Freedom's Journal *(1827-1829),* The Rights of All *(1829),* The Weekly Advocate *(1837), and* The Colored American *(1837-1841).* Westport, Conn.: Greenwood Press, 1976.

Lawson, Sandra M. *Generations Past: A Selected List of Sources for Afro-American Genealogical Research.* Washington, D.C.: Library of Congress, 1988.

Newman, Debra L. *Black History: A Guide to Civilian Records in the National Archives.* Washington, D.C.: National Archives Trust Fund Board, 1984.

————. *List of Black Servicemen Compiled From the War Department Collection of Revolutionary War Records.* Washington, D.C.: National Archives and Record Service, 1974.

Potts, Howard E. *A Comprehensive Name Index to the American Slave.* Westport, Conn.: Greenwood Press, 1985.

Schubert, Frank N. *On the Trail of the Buffalo Soldier: Biographies of the African-Americans in the U.S. Army, 1866–1917.* Wilmington, Del.: Scholarly Resources, 1994.

Smith, Billy G. and Richard Wojtowicz. *Blacks Who Stole Themselves: Advertisements for Runaways in the* Pennsylvania Gazette, *1728–1790.* Philadelphia: University of Pennsylvania Press, 1989.

Organizations, Periodicals, and Internet Sites
African-American Genealogical Societies Around the U.S.A.
  Web site: http://www.everton.com/oe2-7/afamlist.htm
Afro-American Historical and Genealogical Society, Inc.
  P.O. Box 73086, Washington, DC 20056-3086
  Web site: http://www.rootsweb.com/~mdaahgs/index.html
Freedmen's Bureau Records
  Web site: http://www.freedmensbureau.com

American Indians

When Europeans first colonized America, there were close to two thousand different cultures of people already residing on the North American continent. Europeans, however, destroyed entire communities and exterminated tribes inadvertently through disease, and deliberately through genocidal warfare. At least fifty groups are now extinct. In the 1840s, there were some 600,000 American Indians; by the next decade, the population had dropped to 250,000. Recent censuses, however, show that almost two million people claim American Indian ancestry, and that there are five hundred tribes and more than three hundred reservations. All tribes are different, having their own religious practices, customs, and family structures. Even tribes in the same geographic areas are distinct. Obviously, it is beyond the scope of this book to discuss all five hundred tribes and the nuances of their cultures.

Oral history interviewing will be extremely important to begin your research. Take note of the name of the tribe, whether the individual was living on a reservation and when, the Indian and English names, and any migratory (voluntary or involuntary) patterns. If you have stories of American Indian ancestry and have not been able to identify the tribe, ask what language your ancestors spoke, what religious beliefs and ceremonies they celebrated, and what the familial ties were. Then match these with published overviews of tribes, such as those found in encyclopedias of American Indian tribes. Also take note of where ancestral family members resided at different times, since this will be

Oral History

\di'fin\ vb

Definitions

NATION AND TRIBE

The term "nation" has been applied to American Indian groups that were land-controlling entities. Each nation had a common language or dialect and common set of customs. In the nineteenth century, the term "nation" was replaced with "tribe." By the middle of the twentieth century, American Indians began to reject the word "tribe," reverting to the word "nation." Some prefer to use "community" or "band." The Bureau of Indian Affairs, however, still uses "tribe." Usage of terms is not consistent and often involves political considerations.

---

important in locating records. Remember, however, that one of the most common family stories passed from one generation to the next is that of American Indian ancestry. Even more prevalent is the tradition of descent from an Indian princess (see chapter one). While many such tales may be just that, you will still want to investigate and establish whether or not the tradition is true. As with most family lore, there is usually a grain of truth couched somewhere within the story.

SOME RESEARCH STRATEGIES

Technique

According to Marsha Hoffman Rising, CG, FASG, **there are essentially four steps to American Indian research:**

1. Attempt to identify the individual with American Indian ancestry. Family traditions can be helpful, but it is not enough. Until the individual who was the tribal member is identified, research in Indian records is futile. Solid genealogical research should be conducted as usual until an individual is identified who shows tribal residence or association.

2. Identify the tribe. Learn its history, culture, traditions, and location.

3. Place the individual who you believe to bear the Indian ancestry to a specific location and document that the tribe lived there at the same time as your ancestor. If the family tradition says your ancestor was Cherokee and living in Colorado in 1860, but there were no Cherokee in Colorado in 1860, then you've got a questionable family legend. Or, if the ancestor crossed over into white society—through marriage, for instance—then it will be difficult to identify American Indian origins, since that person was probably passing for white.

4. Study the federal government's treaties with the tribe. The best way to document Indian lineage is to find the individual you believe to be your Indian ancestor applying for benefits or compensation from the federal government. Even Indians who were living in white society often identified with the tribe again if they could receive financial benefit for doing so. To find treaties, check Charles Joseph Kappler, *Indian Treaties, 1778–1883.*

Start researching American Indian origins the same way you would any other

TOP 25 AMERICAN INDIAN TRIBES FOR THE UNITED STATES Based on 1990 Census			
Tribe	Percent of American Indian Population	Tribe	Percent of American Indian Population
Cherokee	19	Tohono O'Odham	0.9
Navajo	11.6	Potawatomi	0.9
Sioux	5.5	Seminole	0.8
Chippewa	5.5	Pima	0.8
Choctaw	4.5	Tlingit	0.7
Pueblo	2.9	Alaskan Athabaskans	0.7
Apache	2.8	Cheyenne	0.6
Iroquois	2.7	Comanche	0.6
Lumbee	2.6	Paiute	0.6
Creek	2.4	Osage	0.5
Blackfoot	2.0	Puget Sound Salish	0.5
Canadian and Latin American	1.4	Yaqui	0.5
Chickasaw	1.1		

ancestry—begin with yourself and work backward, supporting each generation's facts with original documents before moving on to the next. **Generation skipping or hopping is a dangerous pitfall.** By not thoroughly researching each ancestral couple and their family, you may inadvertently latch onto the wrong ancestor.

Warning

After talking with relatives, check for home sources such as obituaries and other family records, then obtain vital records (births, marriages, and deaths) and search for possible published genealogies that may have been compiled about your family. Next search federal population censuses (see below).

Many records you need to consult for American Indian research exist in the National Archives and its regional records service facilities, particularly the one in Fort Worth, Texas (NARA's Southwest Region—see Appendix B). These records are collected under the Records of the Bureau of Indian Affairs, Record Group 75. The Office of Indian Trade was established in 1806, but these records deal primarily with correspondence about the U.S. government and Indian trading posts. Later records are more helpful to genealogists. In 1824, the Office of Indian Affairs became a separate agency within the War Department. This office was transferred in 1849 to the Department of the Interior, and was renamed in 1947 the Bureau of Indian Affairs.

FEDERAL CENSUSES

Little reference is made to American Indians in the regular federal population schedules until 1870. The 1870 federal population census was technically the first to designate Indians in the "color" column with an "I." Prior to that census year, enumerators for 1850 and 1860 were instructed to record only White ("W"), Black ("B"), or Mulatto ("M"), although you may find exceptions in these censuses where an "I" is recorded. Of course, you may also find them recorded as white or colored.

American Indians were supposed to be enumerated on the 1880 federal census the same way as the general population; however, some may have been missed. There was a special 1880 enumeration of Indians who lived near military installations in Washington and Dakota territories and in California, but these schedules may be incomplete. For the 1900 and 1910 censuses, there are special schedules found among the regular population schedules that enumerate American Indians. These are called "Inquiries Relating to Indians." In 1920, Indians were enumerated on the general population schedules and in a "Supplemental Schedule for Indian Population." These schedules are usually at the end of the censuses of the general population for each enumeration district.

From 1885 to 1940, Indian censuses were taken by agents on each federal reservation. For some reservations, censuses may have been taken every year for several years; for other reservations, there may not be any. Likewise, the information varies. These censuses are part of the National Archives Record Group 75, Microcopy M595, 692 rolls. An Indian Census Card Index for 1898 to 1906 was compiled by the Dawes Commission to verify rights to tribal status for the Five Civilized Tribes (Cherokee, Chickasaw, Choctaw, Creek, and Seminole). This is available at the Family History Library and at NARA's Southwest Region in Fort Worth, Texas.

From 1910 to 1939, the Bureau of Indian Affairs took Indian school censuses. Indian children—in most cases, against their parents' wishes—were required to attend school, usually at some distance, to become assimilated into white society. Again, the information varies, but you may find the names of children between the ages of six and eighteen years, their sex, tribe, degree of Indian blood, distance from home to school, parent or guardian, and attendance in school during the year. They may also include the maiden name of the mother. These schedules are housed in the National Archives's regional records service facilities for the region where the tribe was located. (See *American Indians: A Select Catalog of National Archives Microfilm Publications* and below for other guidebooks.)

If you discover colonial American Indian ancestry, you may also want to read "captivity narratives" written by white people who were kidnapped by various Indian tribes. Although these are no doubt biased by the white person's prejudices, many of these firsthand accounts discuss their observations of Indians and their daily lives. For references to some of these narratives, see June Namias's *White Captives: Gender and Ethnicity on the American Frontier* and Annette Kolodny's *The Land Before Her: Fantasy and Experience of the American Frontiers, 1630–1860*. A comprehensive collection is *The Garland Library of North American Indian Captivities*, 311 titles in 111 volumes, selected and arranged by Wilcomb E. Washburn. Also look for records of missionaries, priests, ministers, and fur traders.

American Indian research is not without its problems, but because of the wonderful emphasis on oral tradition, you have a good starting place. There are many people researching American Indian ancestry, and the following resources will help.

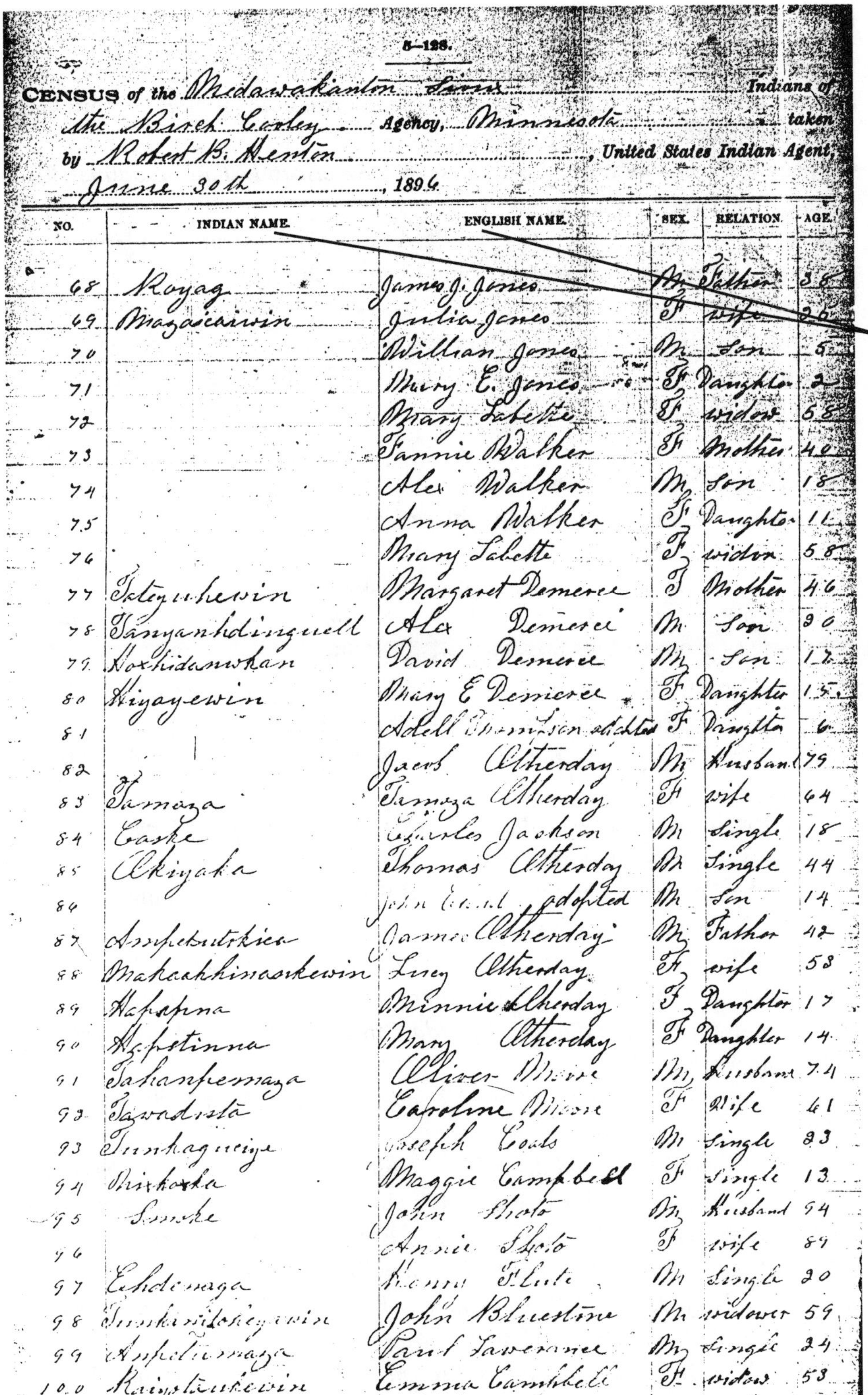

Figure II-2
Census of Medawakanton Sioux Indians of the Birch Cooley Agency, Minnesota, 30 June 1896, National Archives Microfilm 595, roll 2.

Many of the Indian census schedules give both the Indian name and the English name.

CENSUS of the *Medawakanton Sioux* Indians of the *Birch Cooley* Agency, *Minnesota* taken by *Robert B. Henton* United States Indian Agent; *June 30th*, 1896.

NO.	INDIAN NAME	ENGLISH NAME	SEX	RELATION	AGE
68	Koyag	James J. Jones	M	Father	36
69	Magawawin	Julia Jones	F	Wife	26
70		William Jones	M	Son	5
71		Mary E. Jones	F	Daughter	2
72		Mary Labette	F	Widow	68
73		Fannie Walker	F	Mother	40
74		Alex Walker	M	Son	18
75		Anna Walker	F	Daughter	11
76		Mary Labette	F	Widow	58
77	Ixteyuhewin	Margaret Demeree	F	Mother	46
78	Tanyanhdinguell	Alex Demeree	M	Son	20
79	Hoxhidanwhan	David Demeree	M	Son	12
80	Hiyayewin	Mary E. Demeree	F	Daughter	15
81		Adell Comisen	F	Daughter	6
82		Jacob Otherday	M	Husband	79
83	Tamaza	Tamaza Otherday	F	Wife	64
84	Caske	Charles Jackson	M	Single	18
85	Akiyaka	Thomas Otherday	M	Single	44
86		John Earl adopted	M	Son	14
87	Ampetutekiea	James Otherday	M	Father	42
88	Makahkinaskewin	Lucy Otherday	F	Wife	53
89	Ahapana	Minnie Otherday	F	Daughter	17
90	Axpetinna	Mary Otherday	F	Daughter	14
91	Tahanpemaza	Oliver Moore	M	Husband	74
92	Tawadota	Caroline Moore	F	Wife	41
93	Tunhagueiya	Joseph Coals	M	Single	23
94	Wixhoxka	Maggie Campbell	F	Single	13
95	Smoke	John Shoto	M	Husband	94
96		Annie Shoto	F	Wife	89
97	Echdemaza	Henry Flute	M	Single	20
98	Tunkanitokeywin	John Bluestone	M	Widower	59
99	Ampetumaza	Paul Lawrence	M	Single	24
100	Haiyotanwin	Emma Campbell	F	Widow	53

RESOURCES

Research Guides

Byers, Paula K., ed. *Native American Genealogical Sourcebook*. Detroit: Gale Research, 1995.

Carpenter, Cecelia Svinth. *How to Research American Indian Bloodlines*. Orting, Wash.: Heritage Quest, 1987.

McClure, Tony Mack. *Cherokee Proud: A Guide for Tracing and Honoring Your Cherokee Ancestors*. Somerville, Tenn.: Chunannee Books, 1997.

Witcher, Curt B. and George J. Nixon. "Tracking Native American Family History." In *The Source: A Guidebook of American Genealogy*, rev. ed. Loretto Dennis Szucs and Sandra Hargreaves Luebking, eds. Salt Lake City: Ancestry, Inc., 1997.

Social Histories and Historical Sources
(also look for histories on the specific tribe)

Bataille, Gretchen and Kathleen M. Sands. *Native American Women Telling Their Lives*. Lincoln: University of Nebraska Press, 1984.

Coward, John M. *The Newspaper Indian: Native American Identity in the Press, 1820–90*. Champaign: University of Illinois Press, 1999.

Foreman, Grant. *Indian Removal: The Emigration of the Five Civilized Tribes of Indians*. Norman: University of Oklahoma Press, 1932.

Green, Rayna. *Women in American Indian Society*. New York: Chelsea House, 1992.

Halliburton Jr., R. *Red Over Black: Black Slavery Among the Cherokee Indians*. Westport, Conn.: Greenwood Press, 1977.

Handbook of North American Indians. Multiple volumes. Washington, D.C.: The Smithsonian Institution, 1978–.

Jacobs, Wilbur R. *Dispossessing the American Indian: Indians and Whites on the Colonial Frontier*. New York: Charles Scribner's Sons, 1972.

Jennes, Diamond. *The Indians of Canada*, 7th ed. Buffalo, N.Y.: University of Toronto Press, 1977.

Katz, William Loren. *Black Indians: A Hidden Heritage*. New York: Atheneum, 1986.

Kolodny, Annette. *The Land Before Her: Fantasy and Experience of the American Frontiers, 1630–1860*. Chapel Hill: University of North Carolina, 1984.

Namias, June. *White Captives: Gender and Ethnicity on the American Frontier*. Chapel Hill: University of North Carolina Press, 1993.

Nash, Gary B. *Red, White, and Black: The Peoples of Early America*. Englewood Cliffs, N.J.: Prentice-Hall, 1974.

Otis, D.S. *The Dawes Act and the Allotment of Indian Land*. Norman: University of Oklahoma Press, 1973.

Prucha, Francis Paul. *The Churches and the Indian Schools, 1888–1912*. Lincoln: University of Nebraska Press, 1979.

Smith, Jane F. and Robert M. Kvasnicka. *Indian-White Relations: A Persistent Paradox*. Washington, D.C.: Howard University Press, 1981.

Thomas, David Hurst. *Native American Archaeology: A Guide to Exploring Ancient North American Cultures.* New York: Prentice-Hall, 1994.

Thornton, Russell. *The Cherokees: A Population History.* Lincoln: University of Nebraska Press, 1990.

Utley, Robert M. *The Indian Frontier of the American West, 1846–1890.* Albuquerque: University of New Mexico Press, 1984.

Vogel, Virgil J. *This Country Was Ours: A Documentary History of the American Indians.* New York: Harper & Row, 1972.

Washburn, Wilcomb E. *The Garland Library of North American Indian Captivities.* 311 titles in 111 vols. New York: Garland, 1976–1983.

Witmer, Linda F. *The Indian Industrial School: Carlise, Pennsylvania, 1879–1918.* Carlisle, Pa.: Cumberland County Historical Society, 1993.

Sources and Finding Aids

American Indians: A Select Catalog of National Archives Microfilm Publications. 2nd ed. Washington, D.C.: National Archives and Records Administration, 1995. (Available online at http://www.nara.gov/publications/micro film/amerindians/indians.html.)

Bantin, Philip C. and Mark G. Thiel. *Guide to Catholic Indian Mission and School Records in Midwest Repositories.* Milwaukee: Marquette University, 1984.

Barr, Charles Butler. *Guide to Sources of Indian Genealogy.* Independence, Mo.: the author, 1989.

Biographical Dictionary of Indians of the Americas. 2 vols. Newport Beach, Calif.: American Indian Publishing, 1983.

Bogle, Dixie. *Cherokee Nation Births and Deaths, 1884–1901.* Owensboro, Ky.: Cook & McDowell Publications, 1980.

———. *Cherokee Nation Marriages, 1884–1901.* Owensboro, Ky.: Cook & McDowell Publications, 1980.

Chepesiuk, Ron and Arnold Shankma. *American Indian Archival Material: Guide to Holdings in the Southeast.* Westport, Conn.: Greenwood Press, 1982.

Cohen, Felix. *Handbook of Federal Indian Law.* Albuquerque: University of New Mexico Press, 1971.

Confederation of American Indians. *Indian Reservations: A State and Federal Handbook.* Jefferson, N.C.: McFarland & Co., 1986.

Danky, James P., ed. *Native American Periodicals and Newspapers, 1828–1982: Bibliography, Publishing Record, and Holdings.* Westport, Conn.: Greenwood Press, 1984.

DeWitt, Donald L. *American Indian Resource Materials in the Western History Collections, University of Oklahoma.* Norman: University of Oklahoma Press, 1990.

Dictionary of Indian Tribes of the Americas. 4 vols. Newport Beach, Calif.: American Indian Publishing, 1980.

Ellsworth, Carole and Sue Emler. *1900 U.S. Census of the Cherokee Indian Nation.* 5 vols. Gore, Okla.: Oklahoma Roots Research, 1982–.

Fixico, Donald L. *Termination and Relocation: Federal Indian Policy,*

1945–1960. Albuquerque: University of New Mexico Press, 1986.

Fleck, John A. *Native American Archives: An Introduction.* Chicago: Society for American Archivists, 1984.

Goss, Joe R. *A Complete Roll of All Choctaw Claimants and Their Heirs Existing Under the Treaties Between the United States and the Choctaw Nation as Far as Shown by the Records of the United States and of the Choctaw Nation.* Conway, Ark.: Oldbuck Press, 1992.

Hill, Edward E. *Guide to Records in the National Archives of the United States Relating to American Indians.* Washington, D.C.: National Archives and Records Administration, 1981.

Hutchins, Alma. *Indian Territory Marriages, 1867–1898.* Tahlequah, Okla.: the author, 1988.

Index to the Final Rolls of Citizens and Freedmen of the Five Civilized Tribes in Indian Territory. Washington, D.C.: Government Printing Office, 1961.

Jordan, Jerry Wright. *Cherokee by Blood: Records of Eastern Cherokee Ancestry in U.S. Court of Claims, 1906–1910.* Bowie, Md.: Heritage Books, 1997.

Kappler, Charles Joseph. *Indian Treaties, 1778–1883.* New York: Interland, 1975.

Kutsche, Paul. *A Guide to Cherokee Documents in the Northeastern United States.* Metuchen, N.J.: Scarecrow Press, 1986.

Lists Showing the Degree of Indian Blood of Certain Persons Holding Land Upon the White Earth Indian Reservation in Minnesota and a List Showing the Date of Death of Certain Persons Who Held Land Upon Such Reservation. Hinton Roll. Washington, D.C.: U.S. Government Printing Office, 1911.

Marquis, Arnold. *A Guide to America's Indians: Ceremonials, Reservations, and Museums.* Norman: University of Oklahoma Press, 1974.

Maudlin, Dorothy J. *Federal Population Schedule of the United States Census, 1860, Indian Lands West of Arkansas.* Tulsa: Oklahoma Yesterday Press, 198–.

Oklahoma Historical Society. *The Native American Collection on CD-ROM.* Oklahoma City: 1998.

Olsen, Monty. *Choctaw Emigration Records* [1831–1856]. Calera, Okla.: Bryan County Heritage Assocation, 1990.

Silfer, David. *The Eastern Cherokees: A Census of the Cherokee Nation in North Carolina, Tennessee, Alabama, and Georgia in 1851.* New Orleans: Polyanthos, 1977.

Starr, Emmet McDonald. *Old Cherokee Families and Their Genealogy.* Norman: University of Oklahoma Foundation, 1968.

Svoboda, Joseph G. *Guide to American Indian Resource Materials in Great Plains Repositories.* Lincoln: University of Nebraska Center for Great Plains Studies, 1983.

Waldman, Carl. *Atlas of the North American Indian.* New York: Facts on File, 1985.

———. *Encyclopedia of Native American Tribes.* New York: Facts on File, 1988.

Watson, Larry S. *Cherokee Emigration Records, 1829–1835*. Laguna Hills, Calif.: Histree, 1990.

Witcher, Curt B. *A Bibliography of Sources for Native American Family History*. Fort Wayne, Ind.: Allen County Public Library, 1988.

Organizations, Periodicals, and Internet Sites

American Indian Tribal Directory
Web site: http://www.indians.org./tribes

Cherokee Indian Descendants Genealogical, Cultural, and Research Organization
1300 N. Hatchery Rd., Morgan, UT 84050   *Phone:* (801) 829-6758

Indian and Colonial Research Center
The Eva Butler Library, Main St., Rt. 27, P.O. Box 525, Old Mystic, CT 06372
Phone: (860) 536-9771

Indian Territory Genealogical Society
Tahlequah, OK 74465

The Lydia Adams Native American Ancestry Hunting Reading Room and Cultural Center
3308 Acapulco Dr., Riverview, FL 33569
Phone: (813) 653-0015   *E-mail:* laurie.duffy@pchelp.com   Publishes *Native American Ancestry Hunting to Help Unrecognized Native Americans Find and Build Upon Their Heritage and Reunite Present Day Relatives*

Asians

The term "Asian" applies to many different groups of people, but it is most commonly associated with people of East Asian ancestry—Chinese, Japanese, Filipino, and Korean—and those from southeast Asia—Indo-chinese, Burmese, Indonesians, and Thai. The term has also included practically all peoples from geographic Asia—Turkey, Persia, India, and Asia—as well as Pacific Islanders. For the purposes of this book, however, discussion will be limited to two groups: the Chinese and Japanese, who arrived in significant numbers before World War II.

Asian immigrants suffered more racism and exclusionary legislation than any other immigrant group. The main ports of entry were Oahu, Hawaii, and San Francisco. Those who arrived between 1910 and 1940 were processed at the Angel Island immigration station—Ellis Island's West Coast counterpart. Angel Island was at times crowded and resembled a prison with its barbed wires and sentries. Once in American cities, Asians lived in communities primarily because they were excluded elsewhere. The "second wave" of large Asian immigration occurred with the Immigration Act of 1965, which removed national origins quotas.

As with many ethnic groups, researchers need to consider regional differences of the homeland, such as language dialects, food preferences, religions, and marriages within the group, to aid them in pinpointing places of origin.

\di'fin\ *vb*

Definitions

CHINESE

The Chinese voluntarily immigrated to California during the gold rush years of 1848–1854. Ninety percent came from Guangdong Province in the southern part of China, and they were mostly males. By agreement with the Chinese government, railroad companies imported laborers in 1868. During the 1880s to 1890s the male-female ratio was twenty men to every female. Most settled in San Francisco and other urban areas of the West Coast in ethnic enclaves called "Chinatowns," although today, there are more Chinese in New York than in San Francisco. The Chinese were largely occupied in the mining industry, as laborers on the railroad, and in the service trades, such as restaurants and laundries, which became outlets for Chinese entrepreneurships. Some were successful businessmen before and after emigration. Roger Daniels, a leading historian in Asian-American studies, states in *Coming to America* (p. 240) that "there is no evidence that any coolies [Chinese slave laborers] were ever brought to the United States." Many Chinese borrowed money from fellow countrymen, who charged high interest rates, and came to America on a "credit-ticket system."

These men, or "sojourners," planned to stay in the United States only temporarily. Like other birds of passage, they saw America as an opportunity to make money and return to their homeland with a higher economic status. Increasingly, however, they stayed, and this tripped a negative backlash as sources of cheap labor. The Naturalization Act of 1870 made Asians ineligible for citizenship until 1943, when the restriction was lifted. The Chinese Exclusion Act of 1882 targeted Chinese and later other Asians, and limited immigration to only diplomats, scholars, travelers, and merchants. It froze Chinese immigration with its imbalanced sex ratio, making the group largely a male bachelor society. Some of these "bachelors," however, had wives and families in China, who were not allowed to immigrate. Chinese men who were laborers had essentially three options if they wished to have a family: return to China permanently, since the Scott Act of 1888 stipulated that once Chinese laborers left, they would be barred from reentering; if single, they could stay in America as single, since there were also laws in some states forbidding them to have interracial marriages; or if married, their families were prohibited from immigrating. Furthering the sex-ratio problem of the Chinese in America, the quota laws of the 1920s made it impossible for American citizens of Chinese ancestry to bring their wives and children here.

The San Francisco earthquake and subsequent fire of 1906 destroyed many birth records, affording the creation of fraudulent birth certificates whereby Chinese immigrants circumvented the Chinese Exclusion Act, making them American citizens "by birth," and giving them the freedom to return to China and bring their families. Other Chinese, with their new citizenship, then traveled to China to marry and have children. Those children, usually sons, who derived U.S. citizenship by virtue of their fathers' acquired citizenship status as "native borns," were free to enter the United States. Sometimes, the fraudulent papers were then sold to someone waiting to immigrate. The individual who immigrated with those papers was called a "paper son," and assumed the name and

For More Info

For more information on exclusions and restrictions on Asian Americans, see chapter five under Land Records and Military Records, and chapter six, under Naturalization Records and Deportations, Exclusions, and Quota Laws.

identity of the alleged individual. In 1959, the Immigration and Naturalization Service instituted a program whereby individuals could clear their immigration status through the "Confession and Amnesty" program. The Chinese Exclusion Act was repealed in 1943.

The family is the most important institution to the Chinese, although it was difficult to be a Chinese family in America until after immigration restrictions were repealed. Family clans united everyone with a common surname and presumably a common ancestor. Despite prejudice, more than any other ethnic group, the Chinese were able to maintain their Old World customs once they settled in their communities: cuisine, dress, religions (Buddhism, Taoism, and ancestor worship), languages (dialects), and marriage. Others assimilated into American society, adopting Western names, Christianity, interracial marriages, dress, and language. The Chinese have had a low rate of divorce and illegitimacy, and maintain close ties between generations. With succeeding generations, however, those demographics are beginning to reflect trends in American society.

Chinese Immigration Records, 1882–1925

Beyond searching for passenger arrival lists, most Chinese immigration case files are found in various regional records service facilities of the National Archives. (See Loretto Dennis Szucs and Sandra Hargreaves Luebking, *The Archives: A Guide to the National Archives Field Branches*.) Many files to 1908 are found in the Segregated Chinese Files at the National Archives in Washington, DC. These Chinese Immigration Records are part of Record Group 85, and contain items such as applications for residence certificates, correspondence relating to residence certificates, and correspondence relating to the use of Chinese identification certificates under the Chinese Exclusion Act. There are no complete indexes to these records. Copies of Chinese naturalization records from 1943 to the present are available from the Immigration and Naturalization Service through the Freedom of Information and Privacy Acts (see chapter six). The case files for participants of the Confession and Amnesty program are also included in naturalization records from the time Chinese were immigrants to when they became naturalized citizens.

Sources

JAPANESE

In the late 1860s and early 1870s, most Japanese migrants settled in Hawaii—a U.S. territory then—to work on sugar plantations. The major immigration wave to mainland United States occurred in the 1890s, when Japanese immigrants arrived through the ports of San Francisco and Seattle. Unlike the Chinese, the male to female ratio was better balanced, although males still outnumbered females. Mostly young men came between the 1890s and 1908 to work as agricultural laborers. A Gentlemen's Agreement of 1907–1908 was made between President Theodore Roosevelt and Japan to halt Japanese immigration to America. Japan stopped granting passports to laborers, but former American residents and parents, wives, and children of residents were allowed to enter, providing for family unification. This forced a change in the migration pattern

Important

THE "A-FILES" AND THEIR POSSIBLE DESTRUCTION

Since the 1940s, the Immigration and Naturalization Service (INS) has maintained Alien Registration Case Files, or "A-Files," on all known immigrants since the passage of the Alien Registration Act of 1940.

There are an estimated 1,000,000 cubic feet of A-Files classified as "temporary" under the INS's jurisdiction. As temporary records, the A-Files are kept for seventy-five years and then become eligible to be destroyed. Of those A-Files, 650,000 cubic feet are relatively current files in INS's own storage, and the remaining 350,000 cubic feet are relatively noncurrent files. INS contracts with the National Archives to store a majority of the noncurrent files at Lee's Summit, Missiouri, with approximately 35,000 cubic feet stored at NARA's San Bruno, California, records center. Access via electrostatic copies or personal review may be obtained through the INS by obtaining and sending a completed Freedom of Information Act Request on Form G-639.

Many A-Files contain valuable documents such as rare photos and family information for each immigrant from their investigation through naturalization. Sample files include Holocaust survivors, Chinese Americans in the Confession and Amnesty program, Japanese War Brides, and political refugees from World War II to the Vietnam War. NARA has the authority to designate any government records that are older than thirty years for its permanent historical collection.

Genealogists are urged to write the United States Archivist, 8601 Adelphi Road, Room 4100, College Park, MD 20740-6001; the Immigration and Naturalization Service Commissioner, 425 I Street, NW, Washington, DC 20536; and their local congressional representatives to support appropriate federal funding for NARA to preserve, enhance public use, and provide access to the older A-Files (thirty years or more).

—Jeanie Chooey Low

to a female mode when some twenty thousand adult Japanese women came to America between 1910 and 1920. Husbands were usually a decade older than their wives, and in the typical Japanese family of this period, children were born between 1918 and 1922.

During this time, some Japanese men returned to their homeland to acquire wives; many never left America's shores, however, but married in Japan by proxy. In 1921, the Japanese government agreed to a so-called ladies' agreement, and refused passports to "picture-brides," those women who married by proxy in Japan and met their husbands for the first time when they came to America.

In 1913, California limited Japanese immigrants' rights to own or lease farmland in the state. Because they were ineligible for citizenship, the California legislature also deemed them ineligible to own agricultural land. They could keep land they already owned prior to the passage of the act, but they could not bequeath or sell the land to one another.

Shortly after Japan bombed Pearl Harbor, setting off World War II, President Franklin D. Roosevelt signed Executive Order 9066 to relocate about 120,000 Japanese Americans, of whom about two-thirds were American citizens (Nisei), including school children. They were sent to internment camps, where they lived behind barbed wire and under military guard. The ten internment camps, their alternate names, and their state locations were

Gila River (Rivers)	Arizona
Granada (Amache)	Colorado
Heart Mountain	Wyoming
Jerome (Denson)	Arkansas
Manzanar	California
Minidoka (Hunt)	Idaho
Poston (Colorado River)	Arizona
Rohwer	Arkansas
Topaz (central Utah)	Utah
Tule Lake (Newell)	California

Many families were confined for more than two years until all of the camps were closed by 1946. (**See chapter five, Military Records, for relocation records.**)

Generational terms developed after Japanese began immigrating to the United States, which would help researchers know when they have reached the immigrant from Japan. Wesley Tak Matsui, in his essay on "Japanese Families" in McGodrick's *Ethnicity and Family Therapy* (p. 272), gives these distinctions: *Issei* were the first generation of immigrants, and *Nisei* were the second generation and the first generation born in America. Most *Nisei* were born between 1915 and 1935, assuming the *Issei* came during the window of opportunity for immigrants between 1905 and 1935. *Kibei* was a subset of the *Nisei*, who were born in America, sent to Japan for education, then returned to the United States. This was a popular practice among Japanese Americans between 1920 and 1940. *Sansei* are the third generation and tend to have been born between 1945 and 1965. *Yonsei* are the fourth generation, and *Gosei* refers to the fifth generation.

Although Asians have been in America since the mid-nineteenth century, there has been relatively little interest in Asian-American genealogy until recently. For successful Asian family history research, study the Chinese Exclusions Acts, learn what documents are available for you to research, and network with other Asian Americans who are researching their family history. As you can see, there are several resources below to get you started.

RESOURCES

Research Guides

Byers, Paula K., ed. *Asian American Genealogical Sourcebook*. Detroit: Gale Research, 1995.

See Also

For More Info

One of the best sources on Asian immigration is Ronald Takaki's *Strangers From a Different Shore: A History of Asian Americans.*

California State Archives. *Genealogical Research in the California State Archives*. Sacramento: Office of the Secretary of State, California State Archives, 1976.

Guber, Greg. "Looking East: The Realities of Genealogical Research in Japan." *Genealogical Journal* 8 (May-June 1979): 43–50.

Low, Jeanie W. Chooey. *China Connection: Finding Ancestral Roots for Chinese in America*. San Francisco: JWC Low Co., 1994.

Palmer, Spencer J., ed. *Studies in Asian Genealogy*. Provo, Utah: Brigham Young University Press, 1972.

Reed, Robert D. *How and Where to Research Your Ethnic-American Cultural Heritage—Chinese Americans*. Saratoga, Calif.: the author, 1979.

Tan, Thomas Tsu-wee. *Your Chinese Roots: The Overseas Chinese Story*. Union City, Calif.: Heian, 1986.

Social Histories and Historical Sources

Brandon, Alexandria. *Chinese Americans*. New York: Crestwood House, 1994.

Broom, Leonard and John I. Kitsuse. *The Managed Casualty: The Japanese Family in World War II*. Berkeley: University of California Press, 1956.

Brownstone, David. *The Chinese-American Heritage*. New York: Facts on File, 1988.

Chinn, Thomas, et al., ed. *A History of the Chinese in California: A Syllabus*. San Francisco: Chinese Historical Society of America, 1969.

Daley, William. *The Chinese Americans*. New York: Chelsea House, 1995.

Daniels, Roger. *Asian Americans: Chinese and Japanese in the United States Since 1850*. Seattle: University of Washington Press, 1988.

———. *Prisoners Without Trial: Japanese Americans in World War II*. New York: Hill and Wang, 1993.

Hong, Maria, ed. *Growing Up Asian American*. New York: William Morrow, 1993.

Hosokawa, Bill and Robert A. Wilson. *East to America: A History of the Japanese in the United States*. New York: William Morrow, 1980.

Jensen, Joan M. *Passage From India: Asian Indian Immigration in North America*. New Haven, Conn.: Yale University Press, 1988.

Kawaguchi, Gary. *Tracing Our Japanese Roots*. Santa Fe: John Muir Publications, 1995.

Kim, Hyung-Chan. *Dictionary of Asian American History*. Westport, Conn.: Greenwood Press, 1986.

Kitano, Harry. *The Japanese Americans*. New York: Chelsea House, 1988.

——— and Roger Daniels. *Asian Americans: Emerging Minorities*. Englewood Cliffs, N.J.: Prentice-Hall, 1988.

Lai, Him Mark, et al. *Island: Poetry and History of Chinese Immigrants on Angel Island, 1910–1940*. Seattle: University of Washington Press, 1980.

Lee, Kathleen. *Tracing Our Chinese Roots*. Santa Fe: John Muir Publications, 1994.

Mangiafico, Luciano. *Contemporary American Immigrants: Patterns of Filipino, Korean, and Chinese Settlement in the United States*. New York: Praeger, 1988.

McCunn, Ruthanne Lum. *Chinese American Portraits: Personal Histories, 1828–1988*. San Francisco: Chronicle Books, 1996.

———. *Chinese Proverbs*. San Francisco: Chronicle Books, 1991.

Niiya, Brian, ed. *Japanese American History: An A-to-Z Reference From 1868 to the Present*. New York: Facts on File, 1992.

Rolater, F.S. *Japanese Americans*. Vero Beach, Fla.: Rourke Publishing Group, 1992.

Takaki, Ronald. *Ethnic Islands: The Emergence of Urban Chinese America*. New York: Chelsea House, 1994.

———. *Journey to Gold Mountain: The Chinese in Nineteenth-Century America*. New York: Chelsea House, 1995.

———. *Strangers From a Different Shore: A History of Asian Americans*. Boston: Little, Brown and Co., 1989.

Wu, Dana Ying-Hui and Jeffrey Dao-Sheng Tung. *The Chinese-American Experience*. Brookfield, Conn.: Millbrook Press, 1993.

Yanagisako, Sylvia Junko. *Transforming the Past: Tradition and Kinship Among Japanese Americans*. Stanford, Calif.: Stanford University Press, 1985.

Yung, Judy. *Unbound Feet: A Social History of Chinese Women in San Francisco*. Berkeley: University of California Press, 1995.

———. *Unbound Voices: A Documentary History of Chinese Women in San Francisco*. Berkeley: University of California Press, 1999.

Sources and Finding Aids

Chao, Chen-chi. *Catalogue of Chinese Genealogies in Taiwan*. Taipei, China: 1986.

Lowell, Waverly B., comp. *Chinese Immigration and Chinese in the United States: Records in the Regional Archives of the National Archives and Records Administration*. Reference Information Paper 99. Washington, D.C.: National Archives and Records Administration, 1996.

Telford, Ted. *Chinese Genealogies at the Genealogical Society of Utah*. Taipei, China: Cheng-wen Publishing Co., 1983.

Organizations, Periodicals, and Internet Sites

Angel Island Immigration Station Foundation

P.O. Box 472243, San Francisco, CA 94147-2243

Phone: (415) 561-2160   *E-mail:* aiisf@earthlink.net

Asian Net Homepage

Web site: http://www.asiannet.com

Center for Chinese Research Materials

P.O. Box 3090, Oakton, VA 22124

Chinese Genealogy Surnames

Web site: http://www.geocities.com/Tokyo/3919

Chinese Historical and Cultural Project
  Web site: http://www.chcp.org

Chinese Historical Society of America
  965 Clay St., San Francisco, CA 94111
  Phone: (415) 391-1188   *Web site:* http://www.chsa.org
  Publishes *The Bulletin* and *Chinese America: History and Perspectives*

Japanese American History Archives
  1840 Sutter St., San Francisco, CA 94115   *Phone:* (415) 776-0661
  Web site: http://amacord.com/fillmore/museum/jt/jaha/jaha.html

Japanese American National Museum
  369 E. First St., Los Angeles, CA 90012   *Phone:* (213) 625-0414

National Japanese American Historical Society
  1684 Post St., San Francisco, CA 94115   *Phone:* (415) 921-5007
  Fax: (415) 921-5087   *E-mail:* njahs@njahs.org
  Web site: http://www.njahs.org

Organization of Chinese Americans
  10001 Connecticut Ave., NW, #707, Washington, DC 20036

Canadians

See the sections on English for British Canadians (those originating from the British Isles) and French for French Canadians, as well as other ethnic group sections. Like the United States, Canada has a wide ethnic distribution.

RESOURCES

Research Guides

Gagne, Peter. *Links to Your Canadian Past*. 3 vols. Pawtucket, R.I.: Quintin Publications, 1999.

Merriman, Brenda. *Genealogy in Ontario: Searching the Records*, 3rd ed. Toronto: Ontario Genealogical Society, 1996.

Punch, Terrence M., ed. *Genealogist's Handbook for Atlantic Canada Research*. Boston: New England Historical Society, 1989.

Social Histories and Historical Sources

Hansen, Marcus Lee and John Bartlett Brebner. *The Mingling of the Canadian and American Peoples*. New Haven, Conn.: Yale University Press, 1940.

Jennes, Diamond. *The Indians of Canada*, 7th ed. Buffalo, N.Y.: University of Toronto Press, 1977.

Truesdell, Leon E. *The Canadian-Born in the United States*. New Haven, Conn.: Yale University Press, 1943.

Winks, Robin W. *The Blacks in Canada: A History*. New Haven, Conn.: Yale University Press, 1971.

Sources and Finding Aids

Elliot, Noel Montgomery, ed. *The Atlantic Canadians, 1600–1900: An Alphabetical Directory of People, Places, and Vital Dates.* 3 vols. Toronto: The Genealogical Research Library, 1994.

————. *The French Canadians, 1600–1900: An Alphabetical Directory of People, Places, and Vital Dates.* 3 vols. Toronto: The Genealogical Research Library, 1992.

————. *The Central Canadians, 1600–1900: An Alphabetical Directory of People, Places, and Vital Dates.* 3 vols. Toronto: The Genealogical Research Library, 1994.

————. *The Western Canadians, 1600–1900: An Alphabetical Directory of People, Places, and Vital Dates.* 3 vols. Toronto: The Genealogical Research Library, 1994.

Organizations, Periodicals, and Internet Sites

American-Canadian Genealogical Society
P.O. Box 6478, Manchester, NH 03108-6478
E-mail: 102475.2260@compuserve.com   *Web site:* http://www.acgs.org

Czechs and Slovaks

Czechs (Bohemians) and Slovaks, along with the Poles, are West Slavs. The other two branches of Slavic are East Slavs (Russian, Belorussian, Ukrainian) and South Slavs (Bulgarians, Macedonians, Serbs, Croats, Slovenes). Slovaks and Czechs, as ethnic groups, are distinct and have separate historical developments.

The Czechs and Slovaks speak languages which are mutually understandable. Their religious and cultural lives are quite distinct and, aside from scattered individuals who arrived beginning at the time of the American Revolution, their immigration patterns to the United States are also quite different.

CZECHS (BOHEMIANS)

Soon after the abolition of serfdom in 1848, Czechs came to the United States in order to settle as farmers, especially where inexpensive land was now available in the upper Midwest—Wisconsin, Minnesota, Iowa, Nebraska, and the Dakotas—as well as in Kansas and Texas. They arrived in sailing ships, first through the port of Galveston, Texas, and by boat up the Mississippi. A few Czechs came as political refugees after the failed revolutions of 1848 in central Europe.

Immigrants settled in industrial centers, such as Cleveland, Chicago, and New York City, and worked in manufacturing, tobacco, and the garment industries. Women might also have been employed as domestic servants. In New York, a main occupation for men and women was cigarmaking; whereas, in Chicago, Czechs worked in the garment industry. But more than half of the Czech immigrants worked in agriculture, the majority owning their own farms.

Czechs tended to come as family groups and had a low return migration rate. Chain migration was common, where those already settled would encourage other family members or friends to join them. The group had an extraordinarily high literacy rate of 97 percent. Czechs usually had more savings than other immigrant groups who arrived in this country.

The Czechs divided into several sociointellectual groups. First, the Texas Czechs, farmers from the northern counties of Moravia, were canny, thrifty, and mostly Roman Catholic. Second, there were many farmers from southern and northeastern Bohemia, equally strong Roman Catholics. Third came the skilled tradesmen, industrial workers, and miners from central and western Bohemia. Among them were many freethinkers and intellectuals, some of them the political refugees of 1848, many of whom spoke German as well as Czech. Whereas Protestants were an extremely small minority in Bohemia because Catholicism was the state religion under the Habsburgs, many Czech Catholics were only nominally so and quickly became freethinkers or Protestants in this country.

Czechs were slower to assimilate into American society than some other groups. Until World War I, they preferred to marry within their own group. For example, as of late 1900, 92 percent of men and 93 percent of women born in Bohemia married other Czechs. As is common for many immigrant groups of this time period, the first generation had a higher birthrate than succeeding generations. This group was eager to educate their children and sent most to public schools, where they had a high attendance rate, so school records may be a helpful source to researchers. Children typically lived at home until they married.

The Czech people have a strong sense of heritage and perpetuated ties to the homeland, maintaining contact through letters even through both world wars. Look in family papers to see if any of these have survived, and ask relatives about family still in the Old Country. Since many Czechs Anglicized their names, oral history and home sources will be important to determine the spelling of the original name.

SLOVAKS

The Slovaks began to arrive, along with other ethnic groups from Hungary (including Magyars, ethnic Germans, Romanians, and others), from 1879 onward. They often had the goal of working as industrial laborers and miners to accumulate capital in order to return to upper Hungary to purchase farmland or a house. While sailing vessels before the Civil War had taken some six weeks for the voyage, steamships reduced the journey to ten days and made possible yearly or even seasonal travel. An estimated 50 percent of Slovaks who came to this country between 1880 and 1914 returned to Slovakia, so be sure to check for earlier and later passenger lists for those who were birds of passage. Many did eventually settle here, bringing their wives and children after World War I and before quota laws restricted immigration.

Slovaks tended to migrate in village chains and identified themselves in terms of their country of origin. Likewise, they tended to settle in these same groups. The vast majority settled in industrial cities of the Northeast and Midwest,

MAKING CZECH CONNECTIONS

Joseph Betlock had died at an early age, leaving a widow, Anna, and seven young children. When I started searching for Joseph's origins, I didn't have many clues. My grandfather, Willard Betlock, told me that Joseph was from Bohemia (now part of the Czech Republic) and that our surname, Betlock, had once been Betlach. But he couldn't provide me with any further details.

I knew that my great-grandfather, Joseph (the immigrant's second son), was born in Havana Township, Steele County, Minnesota, in 1881, so I began my search there. I wrote to the Steele County Historical Society in Owatonna and asked if they had any information about the family. I was delighted to receive a cemetery card for Joseph, noting that he was buried at the Bohemian National Cemetery in Owatonna. The card also contained a transcript of Joseph's death record: "Joseph Betlock d. 9 Oct 1889 age 31 9m 7d married farmer b. Bohemia father John mother Tracy both b. Bohemia." Now I had a birth date (figured from his age at death), a death date, and the first names of his parents. Granted, Tracy did not sound like a Bohemian name, but it was better to have "Tracy" than a blank on my chart.

Armed with a death date, I searched for Joseph's obituary, hoping it might provide additional details about his origins. Since I lived in Massachusetts, I didn't have access to nineteenth-century Minnesota newspapers, but I was able to borrow them on microfilm from the Minnesota Historical Society's interlibrary loan program. I didn't find an obituary for Joseph, but I found mention of his impending death. The *Owatonna People's Press* of 9 October 1889 reported, "The changeable weather which we are having this fall causes a great deal of sickness among our people. Mrs. Joseph Schlert, Joseph Betlock, and Gust Zimmerman are sick abed with typhoid fever. Mr. Betlock is not expected to live. The others are recovering." In fact, Joseph died the day the article was published.

My quest was at a standstill. Research in Bohemia seemed impossible, and I didn't know what to try. On my next trip to Minnesota, I made my first visit to Owatonna. I met some distant Betlock cousins, visited the Bohemian National Cemetery, and stopped by the Steele County Historical Society. When I spoke to a staff member about my search, he recalled that a woman in California had written to him about her Betlach family. By this time, I knew that she couldn't be descended from my Joseph and Anna, but I asked for her address to see if we could make a connection.

This Betlach researcher's avocation was placing "lost" Betlachs back on the family tree. Her interest in discovering her Betlach origins led her to invest considerable time and effort in documenting the family. All the Betlachs she had researched eventually traced back to Dolni Cermna, a village in an area

---

MAKING CZECH CONNECTIONS—Continued

east of Prague, near Poland. My California connection was confident that my Joseph came from there, too, and she sent the information I provided about Joseph to the Cermna village historian.

Six weeks later, I received a letter that confirmed my Joseph Betlach was a native of Dolni Cermna, Bohemia. According to Catholic church records, "Josef" was the youngest of Jan and Terezie Betlach's six children. The thing that really clinched it for me was Joseph's mother's name: Terezie. What would the name "Terezie" sound like to an American ear? Why, "Tracy," of course! And next to Joseph's name in the baptismal register was the notation "USA."

Not only did I find Joseph, his siblings, and his parents, but I also gained ten more generations of ancestors in Bohemia. My California pen pal and others in Cermna had been working on this family for a long time, and through the use of baptismal registers and land records, the family was solidly documented into the Middle Ages. Suddenly, the family that I knew the least about became the family that I knew the most about.

—Lynn Betlock

---

seeking jobs in the coal mines, steel mills, and oil refineries. At least half went to Pennsylvania, with the largest concentration in Pittsburgh. Other large communities of Slovaks are in Ohio, New York, New Jersey, Illinois, Connecticut, Indiana, and Michigan. Because of their choice of occupation and urban living conditions, the first two generations suffered from high rates of tuberculosis and industrial accidents.

Slovaks came from an agricultural country with strong folk traditions and religious beliefs. The majority were Roman Catholics, but there were smaller numbers of Evangelical Lutherans and Calvinists (Reform), along with a number of Byzantine Catholics. (Most of the latter were Rusyn, East Slavs who spoke a language closer to Ukrainian than to Slovak and lived in eastern Slovakia, Sub-Carpathian Rus, and southeastern Poland—all part of Austria-Hungary at the time.)

The first two generations stayed in tightly knit communities, which centered around work, church, family, and lodges. Like the Czechs, they formed fraternal benefit societies upon arrival, which served the need for companionship and insurance. In the late 1880s, forty Slovak lodges existed; by 1890, these had become national organizations. The National Slovak Society was formed in 1890 and required all of its members to become U.S. citizens.

The first two generations of Slovak families often lived together in one dwelling, which might also include boarders, either relatives or others from the same or neighboring villages in the Old Country. When the second generation married, a couple lived with the husband's parents until they could afford to purchase their own home, which was usually in the same neighborhood, if not next door. First-generation Slovaks married others from their ethnic group, preferably someone from the same or a neighboring village in the Old Country. The second generation also kept this practice, but mates came from neighboring Slovak-American communities. Offspring of prosperous first-generation Slovaks, however, might marry outside the group for status, preferring Irish partners who were already established in America. For her dowry, the bride danced with male guests at the wedding for a fee. Divorce was almost unknown in Slovak communities. The average number of children in the first generation was five, but as with other immigrant groups, the birthrate declined in later generations.

This ethnic group had little interest in education for their children and preferred to send them to parochial schools rather than public schools. Remnants of their peasant foodways are still present today. Soups are a popular main dish, and pastries, containing crushed poppy seeds or ground nuts, are served after a meal.

Do not be discouraged by the few resources listed below. Even though little is presently available for Czech and Slovak genealogists, there are plenty of researchers interested in these groups. Networking with others on the Internet may be your most valuable resource.

RESOURCES

Research Guides

Gardiner, Duncan. *German Towns in Slovakia and Upper Hungary: A Genealogical Gazetteer*, 3rd ed. Lakewood, Ohio: the author, 1993.

Schlyter, Daniel. *Czechoslovakia: A Handbook of Czechoslovak Genealogical Research*. Buffalo Grove, Ill.: Genun, 1985.

Social Histories and Historical Sources

Kann, Robert A. *A History of the Habsburg Empire, 1526–1918*, 2nd ed. Berkeley and Los Angeles: University of California Press, 1977.

Magocsi, Paul Robert. *Historical Atlas of East Central Europe*. Seattle: University of Washington, 1993.

———. *The Rusyns of Slovakia*. Fairview, N.J.: Carpatho-Rusyn Research Center, 1993.

Stolarik, Marian Mark. *The Slovak Americans*. New York: Chelsea House, 1988.

Sources and Finding Aids

Baca, Leo, comp. *Czech Immigration Passenger Lists*. 8 vols. Richardson, Tex.: the author, 1983–1999.

Organizations, Periodicals, and Internet Sites

Checklist of U.S. Sources Helpful in Identifying European Ancestral Villages
Web site: http://www.feefhs.org/frl/czs/dg-csar.html

Czech, Bohemian, and Moravian Genealogical Research Page
  E-mail: Czeching@iarelative.com
  Web site: http://www.iarelative.com/czech/
Czechoslovak Genealogical Society International
  P.O. Box 16225, St. Paul, MN 55116-0225   *Phone:* (612) 645-4585
  Web site: http://www.r/.orgcgsi
  Publishes *Nase Rodina (Our Family)* and *Rocenka*
The Eastern Slovakia, Slovak, and Carpatho-Rusyn Genealogical Research Page
  E-mail: ancestors@iarelative.com
  Web site: http://www.feefhs.org/iar/slovakia.html
Genealogical Research Through the Czech and Slovak Archives
  Web site: http://www.feefhs.org/frl/czs/dg-arch.html
Slovak-World Home Page
  E-mail: gecovic@fris.sk   *Web site:* http://www.fris.sk/Slovak-World

Dutch

Most of the Dutch who came to America originated from the two provinces of Holland (North and South), the other provinces of the present Netherlands, and the Flemish part of Belgium. They spoke Dutch, a Low German language. In colonial records, Frisians born in the Netherlands will probably be listed as Dutch; Dutch-speaking Flemings, however, might be listed as Dutch or after 1830, as Belgians. The colonial Dutch (including the Frisians and Flemings) referred to themselves as *Neder Duits*, or Low Dutch, and referred to Germans as *Hoog Duits*, or High Dutch. There were three distinct phases of Dutch immigration: during the commercial expansion of the seventeenth century; free immigration of the nineteenth and twentieth centuries; and planned immigration after WWII.

The famous Dutch West India Company created permanent trading posts on the Hudson, Delaware, and Connecticut rivers in 1624. It transported thirty families, mostly Walloons from the southern Netherlands, to the colonies and established Fort Orange. In 1625, New Amsterdam was the first permanent settlement on Manhattan. From 1655 to 1664, the Dutch owned the former colony of New Sweden (Delaware). The Dutch West India Company granted vast feudal estates to patroons, who would bring more immigrants to America. Most of the patroonships were short-lived, and by 1644, when the Dutch colony of New Netherland surrendered to the English, only one still existed, the huge Van Rensselaer grant. Later, some Dutch were granted manors by the English kings, but these were not patroonships.

In 1790, about 80 percent of all Dutch immigrants and descendants lived in New York and New Jersey, within 150 miles of New York City. There were small clusters elsewhere in the seventeenth and eighteenth centuries in Pennsylvania, Delaware, Maryland, Virginia, the Carolinas, and into western New England.

Most who came were rural folk—farmers, laborers, and artisans—with a strong desire to own their own agricultural land. Indeed, most pursued farming, so land records are important in tracing Dutch families. Once a family owned its own land, it typically remained in the family for generations. A married son or son-in-law assumed ownership when his father retired or died.

Few of the Dutch who came to America were illiterate since the Dutch stressed education. In the mid-1840s, groups of Dutch immigrated to America, influenced by mass German immigration, a potato crop failure, and a revolt against the Dutch Reformed church. After the American Civil War, the rate of emigration peaked and waned. Other peak years of Dutch arrivals were 1880–1893, 1903–1914, and 1920–1928.

The Dutch immigrants of the nineteenth and twentieth centuries primarily settled in the northern Midwest. By 1920, more than half of Dutch immigrants and the next generation lived in urban areas. The Pullman Company, the Paterson textile mills, and the lumber mills in rural Michigan and Wisconsin employed a large number of Dutch.

Until recently, the Dutch tended to marry within their own ethnic group, and divorce was rare. Large families were quite common, no doubt stemming from their agricultural background where many hands were needed to work the fields. In the nineteenth century, a dozen children was not unusual for a couple, but six children was more the norm.

Colonial Dutch surnames may pose a challenge for genealogists. In colonial America, the use of patronymics was common until around 1700. In the Netherlands, the use of patronymics died out more gradually and ended altogether by 1811. **Patronymics is where the surname is derived from the father's name,** usually by adding a suffix, e.g., Pietersen (son of Pieter), so the surname is liable to change in each generation. There were Dutch families, however, who had permanent surnames from an early date.

Firstborn children were usually given the names of grandparents; subsequent children were named for parents, then usually aunts and uncles. Women commonly used their maiden names after marriage or widowhood, e.g., Neeltje Jans, who was married to Garret Dircksen Croesen, was the daughter of Jan Pietersen. Use of the prefix "Van" before a name usually indicates where that person came from, e.g., Van Amsterdam.

The Dutch people remained clannish even among the fifth and sixth generations in America. Many Dutch went from cradle to grave without needing to leave their ethnic community. Those from particular areas in the Old County created segregated enclaves within larger Dutch communities. When families moved, they typically moved from one Dutch settlement to another. They also preferred to patronize Dutch-owned businesses.

Although the Dutch did not join many organizations, their socialization revolved around the church and its *dominie*. The majority of Dutch belonged to the Calvinistic Dutch Reformed church; less than 20 percent were Roman Catholic, Mennonites, or Jews. In the Dutch Reformed church, the *dominie* was a man of superior education. In colonial times, he was not only a spiritual adviser, but a promoter, realtor, banker, newspaper editor, and politician. The

Sources

Records of the Pullman Company may be obtained by writing to the South Suburban Genealogical and Historical Society, P.O. Box 96, South Holland, Illinois 60473.

\di'fin\ *vb*

Definitions

dominie conducted church services in the Dutch language, a practice that was not discontinued entirely until the early 1840s. The church, therefore, was a key factor in maintaining the language for several generations. In the United States, another major Dutch denomination developed: the Christian Reformed church. It originated in western Michigan in 1857.

The Dutch have had a low rate of social problems, such as alcoholism, neglect of the aged, poverty, malnutrition, illegitimacy, and crime. No doubt this is due to their clannish community and emphasis on church activities. The traditional Dutch diet has a heavy emphasis on bread, potatoes, vegetables, dairy, fish, and poultry. Until recently, it seldom included beef.

Because the Dutch have been in America since colonial times, genealogists have published a number of resources to aid researchers. Take advantage of these as you begin your search. (For an explanation of the "Pennsylvania Dutch," see Germanic Peoples.)

RESOURCES

Research Guides

Bailey, Rosalie Fellows. *Dutch Systems in Family Naming: New York-New Jersey.* National Genealogical Society Special Publication 12, 3rd printing. Washington, D.C.: National Genealogical Society, 1978.

Epperson, Gwenn F. *New Netherland Roots.* Baltimore: Genealogical Publishing Co., 1995.

Hart, Simon. *Bridging the Atlantic: Finding the Place of Origin of Your Germanic Ancestor—The Netherlands.* Salt Lake City: Genealogical Society of Utah, 1969.

Hoff, Henry B. "Researching New York Dutch Families: A Checklist Approach." *The New York Genealogical and Biographical Newsletter* 7:2 (Summer 1996): 12–14; 7:3 (Fall 1996): 27.

Social Histories and Historical Sources

DeJong, G.F. *The Dutch in America, 1609–1974.* Boston: Twayne Publishers, 1975.

Lucas, Henry S. *Netherlanders in America: Dutch Immigration to the United States and Canada, 1789–1950.* Ann Arbor, Mich.: 1955.

Swierenga, Robert P. *The Dutch in America: Immigration, Settlement, and Cultural Change.* New Brunswick, N.J.: Rutgers University Press, 1985.

Sources and Finding Aids

Collections of the New York Genealogical and Biographical Society, Baptisms From 1639 to 1800 in the Dutch Reformed Church, New York, New York. 2 vols. New York: New York Genealogical and Biographical Society, 1901–1902. Reprint, Hackensack, N.J.: Bergen Historic Books, 1999.

Collections of the New York Genealogical and Biographical Society, Marriages From 1639 to 1801 in the Dutch Reformed Church, New Amsterdam, New York. Originally published in New York in 1890. Reprint, 1940.

Doezma, Linda Pegman. *Dutch-Americans: A Guide to Manuscript Sources.* Detroit: Gale Publications, 1979.

Fernow, Berthold, ed. *The Records of New Amsterdam From 1653 to 1674 Anno Domini, Minutes of the Court of Burgonmasters and Schepens, 1653 to 1655.* 7 vols. New York: The Knickerbocker Press, 1897.

Gasero, Russell L. *Guide to Local Church Records in the Archives of the Reformed Church in America and to Genealogical Resources in the Gardner Sage Library, New Brunswick Theological Seminary.* New Brunswick, N.J.: Historical Society of the Reformed Church in America, 1979.

Gehring, Charles T. *A Guide to Dutch Manuscripts Relating to New Netherland in United States Repositories.* Albany, N.Y.: State Education Dept., 1978.

Swierenga, Robert P., comp. *Dutch Emigrants to the United States, South Africa, South America, and Southeast Asia, 1835–1880: An Alphabetical Listing by Household Heads and Independent Persons.* Wilmington, Del.: Scholarly Resources, 1983.

————. *Dutch Households in U.S. Population Censuses, 1850, 1860, 1870: An Alphabetical Listing by Family Heads.* 3 vols. Wilmington, Del.: Scholarly Resources, 1987.

————. *Dutch Immigrants in U.S. Ship Passenger Manifests, 1820–1880.* 2 vols. Wilmington, Del.: Scholarly Resources, 1983.

Van Laer, Arnold J.F., et al., trans. *The New York Historical Manuscripts: Dutch* (later title, *New Netherland Documents Series*). Multiple volumes. Baltimore: Genealogical Publishing Co.; and Syracuse, N.Y.: Syracuse University Press, 1974–.

Organizations, Periodicals, and Internet Sites

Dutch Family Heritage Society
2463 Ledgewood Dr., West Jordan, UT 84084
Phone: (801) 967-8400   *Fax:* (801) 963-4604
Publishes *Dutch Family Heritage Society Quarterly*

Historical Society of the Reformed Church of America
Gardner A. Sage Library, 21 Seminary Pl., New Brunswick, NJ 08901
Phone: (732) 246-1779

The Holland Page
Web site: http://ourworld.compuserve.com/homepages/paulvanv/

Holland Society of New York
122 E. Fifty-eighth St., New York, NY 10022-1939
Phone: (212) 758-1875   Publishes *de Halve Maen (The Half Moon)*

New Netherland Connections
Dorothy A. Koenig, Editor, 1232 Carlotta Ave., Berkeley, CA 94707
Phone: (510) 524-5796   *E-mail:* dkoenig@library.berkeley.edu

New Netherland Project and Friends of New Netherland
CEC Eighth Fl., Albany, NY 12230   *Phone:* Project (518) 474-6067
Friends (518) 486-4815   *Web site:* http://www.nnp.org

Publishes *de Nieu Nederlanse Marcurius* newsletter and the ongoing series of books *New Netherland Documents* (formerly *New York Historical Manuscripts: Dutch*).

English

Because colonial records may consider anyone who came from England, Scotland, Ireland, or Wales as British or English, it is all the more important to look at the social history and folkways to distinguish the correct ethnic background. Primarily there were three major groups of British arrivals in the seventeenth and early eighteenth centuries: the Puritans of New England, Anglican planters and indentured servants who settled in Virginia and Maryland, and Quakers who established themselves not only in New England, but also in the middle colonies. The folkways of these groups were distinct from one another.

Even these early immigrants did their best to maintain their customary foodways as did more recent immigrants, such as Italians and Chinese. For example, those from the south and west of England (Virginia planters) fried their foods, the northern Englanders (Quakers) boiled theirs, and those from East Anglia (Puritans) preferred baking. Thus, recipes and food preparation methods preferred in your family today, or recorded in letters and diaries, may reveal the origins of a colonial settler.

For More Info

For more on colonial English ancestors' everyday lives, see David Hackett Fischer, *Albion's Seed: Four British Folkways in America*; John Demos, *A Little Commonwealth: Family Life in Plymouth Colony*; and Eugene Aubrey Stratton, *Plymouth Colony: Its History and People, 1620–1691*.

THE PURITANS OF NEW ENGLAND

The arrival of the first Pilgrim settlers to Massachusetts in 1620 sparked an immigration wave known as the Great Migration of Puritans, between 1628 and 1642, which brought roughly fifty-eight thousand English to settle in Massachusetts. These colonists later spread to Connecticut, Rhode Island, New Hampshire, Vermont, Maine, and other colonies. In the Massachusetts Bay Colony, the arrivals came from all socioeconomic backgrounds and from almost all counties in England; but two-thirds originated from East Anglia, the West Country, and the London area. Few of these arrivals came as indentured servants; the majority emigrated in family groups.

The typical age for men to marry was twenty-six and for women, twenty-three. Marriages were generally not prearranged. Because of a high mortality rate among the first generation of arrivals, most marriages only lasted from seventeen to nineteen years. Divorces were granted rarely, but on the following grounds: physical abuse, adultery, desertion, cruelty, and a failure to provide.

For the immigrant generation, high infant and child mortality rates meant that most families only had two to four children survive past adolescence. Women bore on average about six to eight children, twenty to thirty months apart, with a woman's last child usually born after she was forty.

New England couples showed a strong preference for biblical and English child-naming—John, Joseph, Josiah, and Samuel for boys; Mary, Elizabeth, and Sarah for girls. The general naming descent pattern was to name firstborn children after the parents, and younger children after grandparents or other relatives. Necronyms (naming another baby after a couple's recently deceased child) were extremely common. So, two "Johns" on a list of births may indicate the earlier one had died by the birth of the second. (It could also mean that the second wife also wanted to name a son John, ending up with two half-siblings with the same name.) Puritans originating from Sussex, England, however, preferred "hortatory" forenames, for example, "Be-courteous."

Primogeniture (the legal practice of the first son inheriting the land and major portion of the father's estate) was not the overwhelming practice within this group. Many preferred giving the first son a double portion of the estate (double partible), so that other sons might also inherit.

For More Info

For more on inheritance practices, see Carole Shammas, Marylynn Salmon, and Michel Dahlin's *Inheritance in America: From Colonial Times to the Present.*

ANGLICAN PLANTERS AND INDENTURED SERVANTS TO THE CHESAPEAKE

In contrast to New England immigrants, the English who settled in the Chesapeake area of Virginia and Maryland were largely young single men, who may be classified as either cavaliers or indentured servants. The cavaliers were from English elite society and were generally younger sons who would not inherit land under English primogeniture, most arriving between 1640 and 1669. They originated from all parts of England, but many came from the south and west parts—the Weald of Kent to Devon and north of Warwickshire. They and their descendants became the prototypical southern planters.

The main influx to Virginia between 1620 and the 1680s, however, was composed of indentured servants whose passage was paid by the elite plantation owners wanting unskilled laborers. About fifteen hundred bonded laborers, mostly illiterate and unskilled, arrived each year. The indenture usually lasted between four and seven years, but it could be extended if the servant ran away and was captured, or if a woman became pregnant—an enforced punishment even though the owner may have been the father. (For more on indentured servants, see chapter five under Land Records.) Advertisements for runaway servants and slaves were common in colonial newspapers, often giving a physical description. These would be excellent sources to check if your ancestry includes indentured servants or slaves. Some of these advertisements have been abstracted and published.

While Puritan New England families were nuclear, those in Virginia and Maryland were extended; relatives of all types were referred to as "cousin." Marriages were commonly negotiated by parents based on social standing, and many were blood-cousin unions. The average age for marrying was twenty-four for men and about eighteen for women. Because of several religious holidays celebrated by the Church of England when marriages could not take place, early November and late December after Christmas were likely times to exchange wedding vows. Divorce was extremely uncommon and rarely granted, so marriages were more likely dissolved due to the death of a spouse, usually by the seventh anniversary.

Life expectancy for a seventeenth-century Chesapeake family was short because of disease and malnutrition: few survived to the age of sixty. Men lived until about age forty-three, and half the women only reached twenty. At least a quarter of the children did not reach their first birthday. Because almost two-thirds of all children were likely to lose one parent before their eighteenth birthdays, and almost one-third lost both parents by then, a descendant should check orphan and guardianship records.

Naming patterns also differed from Puritan settlers. Biblical forenames were less common in Virginia and Maryland. Preferred names were those of Teutonic warriors, Frankish knights, and English kings for sons: William, Robert, Richard, Edward, George, and Charles. They favored Christian saints' names and English folk names for daughters: Margaret, Jane, Catherine, Frances, Mary, Elizabeth, Anne, and Sarah. The basis for descent naming was the firstborn after the grandparents and secondborn after the parents. Using a surname as a forename was also common. Necronyms were used, but if the child given a repeated forename also died, the name was considered unlucky and not used again.

In the early days of the Virginia and Maryland colonies, the wills of many planters divided the estates among the children, with the first son inheriting the major portion. By the mid- to late 1700s, however, primogeniture revived. When a man died intestate (without a valid will), the laws of primogeniture were enforced. Knowledge of inheritance practices are vital to tracing property relationships in a southern plantation family.

QUAKERS TO NEW ENGLAND AND THE MIDDLE COLONIES

The Religious Society of Friends' migration to America began with a few individuals in the 1650s who settled in New England, but the greatest number of Quakers came between 1682 and 1685 to settle in the Delaware Valley (New Jersey, Pennsylvania, Delaware, and northern Maryland). By 1750, Quakers comprised the third largest religious group—mainly from converts—after Congregationalists (Puritans) and Anglicans (Church of England). While the majority of Quakers were of English origin, they might also come from other backgrounds: French, Dutch, German, Swedish, Danish, Finnish, Scottish, Irish, and Welsh. Those from England were likely to have originated from the counties of Chester, Lancaster, York, Derby, and Nottingham.

Quaker pacifism kept them from military participation in early wars, but their social activism led them to leave their mark in reform organizations, such as the abolition of slavery. Descendants of Quakers should investigate the many historical records maintained, particularly in Pennsylvania, by Quaker libraries, schools, and meetings.

Though the Quaker household consisted of the nuclear family, the extended family was just as important. Marriage outside the Quaker faith was strictly forbidden and meant being "read out of meeting" when it occurred. Men generally married around age twenty-seven; women at about twenty-four.

Firstborn children were generally named after grandparents. While Quakers preferred biblical forenames, they also chose from traditional English names: John, Joseph, and Samuel; Mary, Elizabeth, Sarah, and Ester/Hester and Anna/ Hannah. Christian virtues also provided forenames (grace names): Patience, Grace, Mercy, and Chastity. The typical inheritance pattern for Quakers was to divide two-thirds of the estate equally among the children, with the widow receiving one-third. Although daughters did not inherit land, at marriage they received a share of personal property.

LATER ENGLISH ARRIVALS

Of course, not all English arrived during the colonial period. English immigrants continued to come to America throughout the seventeenth, eighteenth, and nineteenth centuries. English immigration to America can be found in three major waves in the nineteenth century: the late 1840s and peaking in 1854; mid-1860s and peaking in 1873; and the largest movement, beginning in 1879 with peaks in 1882 and 1888. As with other time periods, emigrants came from all counties in England. Many gravitated toward farming; others were craftsmen. A number were also skilled industrial workers.

BRITISH CANADIANS

Not all those from the British Isles came directly to the United States. Many went to Canada first and then migrated southward across the border. British Canadians immigrated to this country most notably in the second half of the nineteenth century. Some of these have roots in colonial New England, however. During the 1760s and 1770s, small numbers of New England and New York colonists moved north to acquire land in Nova Scotia and Quebec. After the American Revolution, they were joined by about forty thousand Loyalists. A large number of immigrants from Britain arrived after 1815 (Presbyterians from Ulster and the Scottish Low-lands; Anglicans, Methodists, and Baptists from England; and Irish Catholics). Many of these took advantage of cheap fares to Canadian ports, then moved on to American destinations. (**See chapter six, Canadian Border Crossings.**) From 1850 to 1896, depression and economic change in Canada stimulated many more to move southward to the United States.

See Also

In the early years of migration into America, many were young, single males who moved on a seasonal basis in search of work. By the 1870s, however, the trend was for whole families to migrate. When single women migrated, they tended to settle in the nearest American cities.

In census records, it may be difficult to distinguish between British Canadians and French Canadians, since the birthplace may be listed as "Canada." Of course, names will give you a better idea, as will occupations. For example, those from Prince Edward Island preferred farming and land ownership; those from New Brunswick gravitated toward lumbering; and Nova Scotians sought work in the fishing industries. You may also find that British Canadians were slow to become naturalized, if at all. Many felt that they would return to Canada, or they alternated between the two countries.

If you have English ancestry that dates back to the founding of America, you have a wealth of resources to consult. Not every colonial English ancestor has been documented, of course, but no doubt you may tie into one that is. For those with later English arrivals, there are sources to help in your research, too.

RESOURCES

Research Guides

Fitzhugh, Terrick V.H. *The Dictionary of Genealogy*, 5th ed. Revised by Susan Lumas for the Society of Genealogists. London: A & C Black, 1998.

Herber, Mark. *Ancestral Trails: The Complete Guide to British Genealogy and Family History*. Baltimore: Genealogical Publishing Co., 1998.

Irvine, Sherry. *Your English Ancestry: A Guide for North Americans*, rev. ed. Salt Lake City: Ancestry, Inc., 1993.

Milner, Paul and Linda Jonas. *A Genealogist's Guide to Discovering Your English Ancestors*. Cincinnati: Betterway Books, 2000.

Moulton, Joy Wade. *Genealogical Resources in English Repositories*. Columbus, Ohio: Hampton House, 1988.

Pelling, George. *Beginning Your Family History in Great Britain*, 7th ed. revised and updated by Pauline Litton. Baltimore: Genealogical Publishing Co., 1999.

Reid, Judith Prowse. *Genealogical Research in England's Public Record Office: A Guide for North Americans*. Baltimore: Genealogical Publishing Co., 1996.

Rogers, Colin D. *The Family Tree Detective: Tracing Your Ancestors in England and Wales*, 3rd ed. Manchester, England: Manchester University Press, 1997.

Saul, Pauline A. and F.C. Markwell. *The A-Z Guide to Tracing Ancestors in Britain*. 4th ed. Baltimore: Genealogical Publishing Co., 1991.

Social Histories and Historical Sources

Bailyn, Bernard. *Voyagers to the West: A Passage in the Peopling of America on the Eve of the Revolution*. New York: Alfred A. Knopf, 1986.

Bell, James P. *Our Quaker Friends of Ye Olden Time*. Conway, Ark.: Oldbuck, Press, 1994.

Coldham, Peter Wilson. *Emigrants in Chains: A Social History of the Forced Emigration to the Americas of Felons, Destitute Children, Political and Religious Non-Conformists, Vagabonds, Beggars, and other Undesirables, 1607–1776*. Baltimore: Genealogical Publishing Co., 1992.

Cornelius, James M. *The English Americans*. New York: Chelsea House, 1990.

Cressy, David. *Coming Over: Migration and Communication Between England and New England in the Seventeenth Century*. Cambridge, England: Cambridge University Press, 1987.

Demos, John. *A Little Commonwealth: Family Life in Plymouth Colony*. New York: Oxford University Press, 1970.

Dumas, David W. "The Naming of Children in New England, 1780–1850," *New England Historical and Genealogical Register* 132 (1978).

Erickson, Charlotte. *Invisible Immigrants*. Ithaca, N.Y.: Cornell University Press, 1990.

Fischer, David Hackett. *Albion's Seed: Four British Folkways in America*. New York: Oxford University Press, 1989.

Green, Jack P., et al. "Forum: Albion's Seed: Four British Folkways in America—A Symposium," *William and Mary Quarterly*, 3rd series, vol. 48, no. 2 (April 1991): 224–308.

Norton, Mary Beth. *The British Americans: The Loyalist Exiles in England, 1774–1789*. Boston: Little, Brown, 1972.

Smith, Daniel Scott. "Child-Naming Practices, Kinship Ties, and Change in Family Attitudes in Higham, Massachusetts, 1641–1880." *Journal of Social History* 18 (1985).

Stratton, Eugene Aubrey. *Plymouth Colony: Its History and People, 1620–1691*. Salt Lake City: Ancestry, Inc., 1986.

Tyler, Lyon G. *England in America, 1580–1652*. New York: Cooper Square Publishers, 1968.

Sources and Finding Aids

Anderson, Robert Charles. *The Great Migration Begins: Immigrants to New England, 1620–1633*. 3 vols. Boston: New England Historic Genealogical Society, 1996.

Coldham, Peter Wilson. *American Loyalist Claims*. Washington, D.C.: National Genealogical Society, 1980.

———. *American Wills and Administrations in the Prerogative Court of Canterbury, 1610–1857*. Baltimore: Genealogical Publishing Co., 1989.

———. *American Wills Proved in London, 1611–1775*. Baltimore: Genealogical Publishing Co., 1992.

———. *The Bristol Registers of Prisoners Sent to Foreign Plantations: 1654–1686*. Baltimore: Genealogical Publishing Co., 1988.

———. *Child Apprentices in America From Christ's Hospital, 1617–1778*. Baltimore: Genealogical Publishing Co., 1990

———. *English Adventurers and Emigrants, 1609–1660*. Baltimore: Genealogical Publishing Co., 1984.

———. *English Adventurers and Emigrants, 1661–1733*. Baltimore: Genealogical Publishing Co., 1985.

———. *Emigrants From England to the American Colonies: 1773–1776*. Baltimore: Genealogical Publishing Co., 1988.

———. *The King's Passengers to Maryland and Virginia*. Westminster, Md.: Family Line Publications, 1997.

Dobson, David. *American Vital Records From The Gentleman's Magazine, 1731–1868*. Baltimore: Genealogical Publishing Co., 1987.

Hinshaw, William Wade. *Encyclopedia of American Quaker Genealogy*. Baltimore: Genealogical Publishing Co., 1991.

Hoff, Henry B. *English Origins of American Colonists*. Baltimore: Genealogical Publishing Co., 1991.

Hotten, John. *The Original List of Persons of Quality Who Went From Great Britain to the American Plantations, 1600–1700*. Baltimore: Genealogical Publishing Co., 1962.

Johnson, Lorand Victor. *Is This Your English Ancestor?* Shaker Heights, Ohio: the author, 1979.

Kaminkow, Jack and Marion J. Kaminkow. *A List of Emigrants From England to America, 1718–1759.* Baltimore: Magna Carta, 1981.

Roberts, Gary Boyd. *English Origins of New England Families.* Baltimore: Genealogical Publishing Co., 1985.

Schaefer, Christina K. *Instant Information on the Internet! A Genealogist's No-Frills Guide to the British Isles.* Baltimore: Genealogical Publishing Co., 1999.

Scott, Kenneth. *British Aliens in the United States During the War of 1812.* Baltimore: Genealogical Publishing Co., 1979.

Smith, Clifford Neal. *British and German Deserters, Discharges, and Prisoners of War Who May Have Remained in Canada and the United States, 1774–1783.* McNeal, Ark.: Westland Publications, 1988.

———. *British Deportees to America.* Dekalb, Ill.: Westland Publications, 1974.

Organizations, Periodicals, and Internet Sites

British Isles Family History Society—U.S.A.
2531 Sawtelle Blvd., PMB 134, Los Angeles, CA 90064-3163
Web site: http://www.rootsweb.com/~bifhsusa

Finding Your Quaker Roots
Web site: http://www.rootsweb.com/~quakers/quakfind.htm

International Society for British Genealogy and Family History
P.O. Box 3115, Salt Lake City, UT 84110-3115   *Phone:* (801) 272-2178
Web site: http://www.homestart.com/isbgfh   Publishes *Newsletter*

The Public Record Office Home Page
Web site: http://www.pro.gov.uk/

The Religious Society of Friends
Web site: http://www.quaker.org

The UK and Ireland Genealogical Information Service
Web site: http://www.genuki.org.uk

French

D istinct groups make up the majority of the French population in America: Catholic French directly from France, French Huguenots, French Louisianians, French Canadians, and Alsatians and Lorrainians. Immigrants from France began arriving in the seventeenth century and generally came in small numbers with a high return-migration rate, which explains why a family might have suddenly disappeared from the records. Most groups of French preferred city life, although a few French can be found scattered in rural areas of the Midwest, Maine, and Louisiana.

French cooking obviously had an influence on American foodways. The French introduced breads made with yeast instead of leaven, and soups, omelets, and artichokes, as well as fine wines.

FRENCH HUGUENOTS

French Huguenots were Calvinist Protestants who left France after 1685, when Louis XIV revoked the "Edict of Nantes," which had granted them the freedom to practice their religion. They headed first for Germany, Holland, or Switzerland (Protestant countries), and then eventually came to North America by the latter 1680s. The entire Huguenot immigration to America probably did not exceed fifteen thousand people, but it affected New England, the South and New York City, as Huguenots were educated entrepreneurs. About 150 Huguenot families came to Massachusetts around 1686–1687, and thirty of them obtained a land grant of twenty-five hundred acres near Worcester, Massachusetts, in 1687. Groups also settled in Maine and Rhode Island. Perhaps one of the best-known Huguenot settlements was Manakintown, Virginia, founded in 1700. This was the most populous Huguenot settlement in the British Colonies. Many Huguenots entered South Carolina through the Port of Charleston, giving that city a cultural complexion akin to that of her sister-city, New Orleans. Besides populating New England and the South, Huguenots also carried an elite French lifestyle into the upper circles of New York society. Huguenots tended to do well in Protestant British North America.

\di'fin\ *vb*

Definitions

FRENCH LOUISIANIANS

French Louisianians, living on the bayous of the lower Mississippi River, are referred to as Acadians or "Cajuns," since they immigrated from Acadia (Nova Scotia) in French Canada. They were expelled by the British in 1755, and by 1790, many had settled in Louisiana. Similar to the Scotch-Irish, Cajuns were isolated culturally, which caused them to develop distinct ethnic patterns, such as dialect and foodways. The majority of Cajuns were Roman Catholics, and extended family households consisting of aunts, uncles, and grandparents were typical. It was not uncommon for Cajun women to have ten to twelve children.

French immigrants to New Orleans, however, were a totally dissimilar group. They were aristocrats fleeing the "Reign of Terror" that followed the French Revolution of 1789, and escaping the 1791 slave revolt in Saint-Domingue (Haiti, today). These educated and cultivated French aristocrats had nothing in common (not even language) with the Cajuns, and there was no intercourse between the two groups.

"Creole" refers to Louisianians of French and Spanish descent or mixed European and African blood. They began calling themselves by this term to distinguish themselves from Anglo-Americans. Today, the word Creole most often refers to the Louisiana Creoles of color, who range in appearance from mulatto to white. Until the late nineteenth century, this group spoke mostly French.

\di'fin\ *vb*

Definitions

\di'fin\ *vb*

Definitions

FRENCH CANADIANS

The first French from Canada to figure in American history were fur traders and missionaries of the Great Lakes region, circa 1680s–1760s. They were relatively few in number, but some settled permanently down the Mississippi River. Those we now call French Canadians came from Quebec to settle in New England between the 1840s and 1920s, with two peak arrivals: between 1880 and 1895, and between 1923 and 1929. Besides settling in the New England states, other leading areas were Michigan, New York, Minnesota, Mississippi, Illinois, and Wisconsin. Unfortunately, the U.S. government did not keep regular immigration statistics before 1895 on this group as they migrated across a land border and not by ship, so their ethnic origin may not be distinct in many records. (See Canadian Border Crossings, chapter six.) Like some other immigrant groups, overpopulation in their homeland and job opportunities in the United States spurred French-Canadian migration.

A predominantly Catholic people, French Canadians felt a strong tie to their culture and heritage in Quebec, so they returned frequently—explaining gaps in research—and were reluctant to become American citizens. By 1930, only 47 percent of French Canadians became naturalized; this was less than any other major ethnic group. Because of their intense feelings of heritage, intermarriage with other ethnic or religious groups was not common. When they did intermarry, it was usually to other Canadians or English (usually Protestant), or to Irish, French, or German Catholics.

ALSATIANS AND LORRAINIANS

Immigrants from Alsace and Lorraine pose a ticklish "categorization" problem. The major immigration took place from about 1817 to 1871, when the provinces of Alsace and Lorraine were part of France and had been for almost two hundred years. Before Louis XIV conquered this area in the 1630s, however, it was Germanic, and from 1871 to 1919, these two provinces were once again a part of the German empire, as a result of the German victory (French defeat) in the Franco-Prussian War of 1870–1871. By that time, the major emigration out of this area was over. Alsatians and Lorrainians, therefore, were Germanic by heritage, language, cuisine, and folkways, yet at the same time, they were citizens of France. Though sources specific to Alsatians and Lorrainians are covered in the resources below, you should also check the resources in the Germanic Peoples section.

Alsatians—who originated in a province of France lying between the Vosges Mountains and the Rhine River—first started arriving in North America during the late eighteenth century. The early Alsatian immigrants were Protestant and settled among other German-speaking people from the Rhine. They were almost indistinguishable from the Palatines. Alsatians who came to America later were predominantly Catholic, however, although a significant number were Jews, and they arrived in clearly distinguishable waves between about 1820 and 1860. Lorrainians—Alsatians' neighbors to the northwest—followed a few years behind the Alsatians in coming to America, about 1828–1871.

Immigrants from Alsace and Lorraine tended to be stable, close-knit, middle-class families of the tradesman and merchant classes. Levi Straus of denim jeans fame is probably the best-known Alsatian Jew in American history.

USING PROBATE RECORDS IN FRANCO-AMERICAN RESEARCH

Growing up, there were two military pictures in my grandparents' living room. One showed my grandfather Eddie Morin and his brother Emile in their uniforms from the Merchant Marine where they had served during World War II. The other was a slim man in full dress uniform of the U.S. Army. I always wondered who the man was, but for some odd reason, never ventured to ask my grandmother about his identity.

Just before the turn of the century, my great-great-grandfather Onésime Morin brought his wife, Céline, and their children to the mill town of North Grosvenordale, a village in the town of Thompson, Connecticut. They were a typical, poor, Quebec family who had owned no property and had little personal effects. When dealing with ancestors who worked in New England's mills and lived in either rented apartments or company-owned housing, there is a tendency to assume that there will be no probate record. Nothing could be further from the truth. Onésime died in August 1902, five short months after his wife, and he did leave a probate record. While he owned no property in the United States, he did own a large farm in Quebec, which he left to his daughter. This and his personal property were all detailed in the probate record.

Even more intriguing, however, is the story of Mononcle Eloi (Mononcle is French for uncle). There was no marriage or death record for Eloi in North Grosvenordale, and I assumed he may have gone back to Quebec. Imagine my surprise when I found his name in the probate index for the town of Thompson. This record and additional research in military records unearthed a heartwarming story.

Eloi was born in St. Calixte de Kilkenny, Quebec, 10 September 1887. He never married. At the age of thirty, he was inducted into the U.S. Army at New London, Connecticut, on 1 May 1918. He served as a private in the American Expeditionary Forces from 15 June 1918 until he was killed in action 21 October 1918. Eloi was my grandfather Eddie's godfather. He left his military survivor's benefits to my grandfather. According to the probate record, they were set up in a trust fund, which he received when he turned eighteen. My grandfather was only three years old when his uncle died. He lost his father Anselme only two years later. The probate record is filled with letters and petitions from my great-grandmother for partial benefits of the trust fund to help take care of my grandfather, who was one of twelve children she was caring for.

Shortly after his eighteenth birthday, my grandfather married his sweetheart, Yvette Ruel, in 1933. And shortly thereafter, he received the benefit from the trust fund. He used the money to purchase a small house in a rural area outside of the mill town of Central Falls where he and his wife were living. They wanted to be able to raise their children outside of the city, in the quiet countryside. The picture in my grandparents' living room was that of Mononcle Eloi. My grandmother insisted on hanging it there in tribute and thanksgiving to the man who had made ownership of the house possible, and it hung there for almost fifty years, until long after her death.

—Michael Leclerc

Although there aren't as many sources for French genealogy as for some of the other groups, there are still resources to get you started. Determine from which French subculture your ancestors came, then study that culture.

RESOURCES

Research Guides

Boudreau, Rev. Dennis M. *Beginning Franco American Genealogy*. Pawtucket, R.I.: American French Genealogical Society, 1986.

Social Histories and Historical Sources

Baird, Charles W. *History of the Huguenot Emigration to America*. Baltimore: Genealogical Publishing Co., 1998.

Brasseaux, Carl A. *The Founding of New Acadia: The Beginnings of Acadian Life in Louisiana, 1765–1803*. Baton Rouge: Louisiana State University Press, 1987.

Butler, Jon. *The Huguenots in America: A Refugee People in New World Society*. Cambridge: Harvard University Press, 1983.

Houpert, Jean. *Les Lorrains en Amérique du Nord*. Sherbrooke, Quebec: Editions Naaman, 1985.

Laybourn, Norman. *L'Emigration des Alsaciens et des Lorrains du XVIIIe au XXe Siècle*. 2 vols. Strasbuorg, France: Association des publications près les universités de Strasbourg, 1986.

Maire, Camille. *L'Emigration des Lorrains en Amérique, 1815–1870*. Metz, France: Centre de Recherches, Relations Internationales, de l'Université de Metz, 1980.

Sources and Finding Aids

Burget, Annette K. *Eighteenth Century Emigrants From the Northern Alsace to America*. Camden, Maine: Picton Press, 1992.

Finnell, Arthur Louis. *Huguenot Genealogies: A Selected Preliminary List*. Baltimore: Clearfield Company, 1999.

Huguenot Settlers in America, 1600s–1900s. 16 books on CD-ROM. Baltimore: Genealogical Publishing Co., 1999.

White, Jeanne Sauve. *Guide to Quebec Catholic Parishes and Published Parish Marriage Records*. Baltimore: Clearfield Company, 1998.

Organizations, Periodicals, and Internet Sites

Acadian Genealogy Exchange
863 Wayman Branch Rd., Covington, KY 41015
Phone and Fax: (859) 356-9825.   Publishes *Acadian Genealogy Exchange*

American-Canadian Genealogical Society
P.O. Box 6478, Manchester, NH 03108-6478
E-mail: 102475.2260@compuserve.com   *Web site:* http://www.acgs.org

American-French Genealogical Society
P.O. Box 2113, Pawtucket, RI 02861-2113   *Phone and Fax:* (401) 765-6141
E-mail: afgs@ids.net   Publishes *Je Me Souviens*
Creole-American Genealogical Society, Inc.
P.O. Box 3215, Church Street Station, New York, NY 10008

Germanic Peoples

I f you have German ancestry, you are one of 58 million Americans who claimed that heritage in the 1990 census, surpassing Irish (39 million) and English (32 million). Germanic groups began arriving with the opening of Pennsylvania in 1683. Large-scale German immigration occurred in 1709 with about 13,000 people from the Palatinate, and between 1720 and the 1770s, but the main influx was between 1830 and 1880. Though Philadelphia was a major port of arrival, they also arrived through New York, Baltimore, Galveston, and Charleston. Settlement in America depended upon the time of arrival, transportation routes, and occupational goals.

One challenging aspect of tracing German ancestry is determining the more specific national background. In records, you may find your ancestors listed by their ethnicity—"German" or from "Germany"—and not their actual nationality. For example, someone who came from Austria may be listed as German, based on the language spoken. The same may be true for German speakers from Alsace, Lorraine, Switzerland, and Russia. Between the 1720s and 1880s, several different groups of Germanic peoples arrived in America: Germans, Alsatians and Lorrainians, Austrians, Luxembourgers, Swiss, and Germans from Russia. They were members of the Lutheran, Catholic, or Jewish faiths, or adherents of one or another of a dozen minor Protestant sects, such as Mennonites (including Amish), Moravians, Schwenkfelders, and Dunkards. You will also encounter further distinctions: Hessians, Palatines, and Salzburgers. Each had its own distinct cultural elements, and it would be impossible to discuss them all in detail here. But you may want to explore more fully the distinctions in the sources listed later in this section. Because there was no unified Germany as we know it until 1871, and the boundaries of the empire were under continual change, there was no unity based on religion, provincial origin, or class.

Another challenge of German research is posed by the group's recent history in America. During both world wars, there was much prejudice against Germans in America, which caused some people with German heritage to hide their origins (e.g., assuming an Anglicized name, suppressing language and cultural traits, claiming a different ethnicity). Even popular German food items took on new patriotic names during the wars: sauerkraut, for example, became "liberty cabbage." The family skeleton may be a relative who was a member of the Nazi party. As was discussed in chapter five under Military Records, you may find relocation records for German alien ancestors who were taken into custody and placed in internment camps.

Warning

GERMANS FROM IMPERIAL GERMANY

The states that combined to form Germany as we know it today

During the seventeenth century, many Germans arrived as indentured servants or redemptioners, with some members of the family arriving free. Philadelphia was the major port of arrival, with New York, Baltimore, and Charleston also receiving newcomers. Two-thirds to three-quarters traveled to America in family groups. Death during the ocean voyage in the 1740s was common among Germans, leaving many children orphaned by the time the ships reached America. The orphans may have been adopted by relatives already here or, if old enough, apprenticed to someone else to learn a trade, so look for court records that may document guardianships and indentures.

Colonial Germans tended to isolate themselves in farming communities with a common religious denomination (the most isolated were and continue to be the Amish). Most colonial Germans were, to some degree, pietist, and thus conservative socially, politically, and economically. Eventually, however, many of these groups spread out geographically. While Germans followed the Scotch-Irish in their geographic expansion, buying up clearings as the Scotch-Irish blazed farther and farther onto the frontier, the two groups generally did not intermarry.

Definitions

Palatines—those from the southwest region of Germany near the mouth of the Rhine River known as the Palatinate—began arriving in large numbers in 1709. These German Rhinelanders, favoring wooded areas, migrated to settle in the upper Mississippi and Ohio valleys and along the Hudson River in New York. At a later time (ca. 1830s and 1850s), they also pioneered the Pacific Northwest, and some went directly south into Texas. The name "Palatine" became so common in colonial America that it was used to refer to anyone who was a Protestant German immigrant. As with any mass emigration of people, they traveled on overcrowded, disease-ridden ships. Typhus fever became "Palatine fever" because it was so common among these travelers. Many died enroute, and according to Carl Wittke in *We Who Built America*, in 1710, of 2,814 who headed for America, 446 died on the way.

The term "Pennsylvania Dutch" refers to the large ethnic German settlements of southeastern Pennsylvania beginning in the 1680s. Yankee Americans probably developed the misnomer "Dutch" for these people because, to them, anyone Germanic was most like the Dutch of New York. It may also have been a corruption of the German's own word for their language: "*Deutsch*." That we still associate so many cultural characteristics with Pennsylvania Dutch—from hex signs to recipes—testifies to the strength of German-American culture in general.

Definitions

Hessians were German mercenary soldiers brought to America to fight for the British during the American Revolution, but not all originated from the area of Hesse. While many returned to Germany after the war, between 5,000 and 12,000 soldiers stayed in America, settling in German-populated areas like Pennsylvania. Even some Hessian prisoners of war stayed in America after their release. The Continental Congress of 1776 enticed Hessians to switch their allegiance from the British Crown to the Americans by promising them fifty acres of land for soldiers, more for officers.

ALSATIANS AND LORRAINIANS

Although a Germanic people, immigrants from the two provinces of Alsace and Lorraine were citizens of France and are discussed under the section for French.

AUSTRIANS

Arriving between the 1830s and 1850s, Austrians settled in the Midwest among other German speakers. Some of these immigrants originated from the province of Burgenland. During the 1880–1920 period, millions arrived from "Austria," according to immigration statistics. A few were Austrians, others were from other countries within the Austro-Hungarian Empire. You need to look at all available sources for your ancestors to discover more precise places of origin. Ethnic Austrians were relatively uncommon among immigrants because Upper and Lower Austria had few displaced farmers or artisans. Immigrants from Austria were more liable to be from Galicia, Hungary, Bosnia, Croatia, Hercegovina, and Dalmatia. (See also the section on Czechs.)

LUXEMBOURGERS

The main influx of Luxembourgers was between the 1840s and 1910s. During this time, Luxembourg was part of Zollverein under the policies of Prussia. Many settled in Chicago; others went to Iowa or along the Mississippi River in the Midwest. Almost all Luxembourgers were Catholic.

SWISS

Swiss immigrants may be designated in records as German, French, or Italian, depending on their mother tongue. About 72 percent spoke the German language, about 20 percent French, and about 6 percent Italian. The majority of Swiss arrived between 1820 and 1900, although some twelve thousand from the German cantons of Switzerland had already arrived by 1750. Those who settled in Pennsylvania blended into the Germanic communities already established there. Some Anglicized their surnames: from Gallman to Coleman or Stauffer to Stover.

GERMANS FROM RUSSIA

Before these people began arriving in the United States, they had migrated from Germany into Russia (ca. 1762), where they lived for more than a century. Also known as Volga Germans for the river valley where they had settled, they fled Russian religious and political persecution between the 1870s and 1910s and headed for North America. Most were Evangelical Lutherans, but some were Roman Catholics. They preferred isolated, austere settlements on the midwestern plains of North Dakota, South Dakota, Nebraska, and Colorado, where the climate and terrain resembled the rich agricultural territory they knew in

Case Study

FINDING GREAT-GRANDFATHER OTTO'S GERMAN BIRTHPLACE

The family story was very romantic. My great-grandfather, Ottomar C. Senftleben, growing up in Germany, was greatly opposed to war and abhorred the idea he might be drafted into the Kaiser's army. As a young man, he stowed away on a steamer bound for America and on arrival, changed his surname to Waldau. For his actions, Otto's father disowned him and he had to secretly correspond with his mother through her neighbor.

In the family Bible that Otto purchased and presented to his wife at their first Christmas in 1883, he entered his date and detailed place of birth:

> O. C. Waldau June 16. 1856. Erfurt, Provinz Sachsen, Koenigreich Prussen. Germany

What more could a curious great-grandson want? My desire to trace Otto's background began about 1960, when Erfurt was somewhat inaccessible in East Germany. My German high school teacher assisted me with a letter to the appropriate local agency, but the long-awaited reply was disappointing: No record of Otto could be found.

I knew Otto's approximate age of twenty at the time of his arrival through the Port of New York, but it fell into that abyss of unindexed passenger lists. His naturalization record provided no other details, and he arrived as a minor, so there was no chance of additional information in a declaration of intention. His marriage and death certificates and obituary tell nothing about his specific place of birth or his parents' names.

In 1977, I met a German genealogist (Frederick Wollmershauser), who was visiting America, and discussed my problem with him. He agreed to help, and through a series of contacts, he also had a search made in Erfurt records, but again, nothing about Otto was found.

He then suggested the Hamburg Passenger lists [see page 119]—as yet not available in this country—and had them checked for me. The lists are indexed, and knowing Otto arrived about the mid-1870s, I quickly learned he was in the lists. Otto C. Senftleben, age nineteen, merchant's clerk, had lower berth 279 aboard the *Gellert*, which left Hamburg 29 March 1876. He was not a stowaway after all. Unlike the New York arrival list for him (now easily found, arriving 12 April 1876), the Hamburg record showed his specific residence: Ingersleben.

Ingersleben is a tiny village just outside the city of Erfurt, and a subsequent search of the church records there not only turned up Otto's birth and notice of his immigration, but also record of his ancestors there back to the 1600s.

—Roger D. Joslyn, CG, FASG

Russia. They specialized in growing sugar beets, so western states encouraged them to come to America for that purpose.

GERMAN JEWS AND POLES FROM GERMANY

Between 1877 and 1887, another major influx of Germans arrived, with 1881 being the peak year. Many of these arrivals were Jews who came from southwest Germany, Prussia (German-occupied Poland), and Austria. The Germans who were already here did not identify with these latecomers. These arrivals settled primarily in port cities, and many continued to marry only within their own group as late as the 1960s. (See the section on Polish and Jewish groups.)

All of the eighteenth- and nineteenth-century German settlements tended to be "nuclear clusters," whose populations were born, married, and died within the settlement, making neighborhood and community research all the more crucial. The Germans assimilated slowly into American culture, gradually marrying outside of their groups. A great emphasis was placed on education, hence the origins of American kindergartens and the blackboard. School records would be a source not to overlook.

Most German arrivals before the 1880s engaged in agricultural occupations such as farming and had large families, since children were an economic asset for farmers. Land ownership was a goal of many, so land records are going to be an important source. Few settled in New England or were slaveholders, although Germans and Alsatians settled in the South. Some of these immigrants became merchants who established businesses up and down the Mississippi and Ohio rivers.

According to Carl Wittke in *We Who Built America*, between 176,000 and 216,000 men who served in the Union Army during the Civil War were German by birth, and this figure does not take into account those soldiers of German heritage from border countries, such as Switzerland, France, and Austria. Many of them, no doubt, were enticed to serve by the promise of quicker processing of American citizenship (see Military Records in chapter five). Many others, however, were already naturalized and identified strongly with the culture—North and South—of their adopted land. Estimates of those of German origin serving for the Confederacy are about seventy thousand.

A highly literate people, Germans published, between 1732 and 1800, at least thirty-eight German newspapers in America. During the nineteenth century, German-language newspapers abounded, sometimes two or three in a major city like Cincinnati, St. Louis, or Buffalo.

Culinary specialties were an important aspect of German-American culture, which also had an influence on the American diet. Sauerkraut, hamburgers, pretzels, and frankfurters are popular German foods in our culture today. And would America have had the major brewing industries it has today had it not been for German beer? Looking at recipes and eating patterns handed down in your family and comparing them with the diets of your ancestors may yield some interesting insights.

Although family patterns differ according to the time of immigration, region

Sources

See Karl J.R. Arndt and May E. Olson, eds., *German-American Newspapers and Periodicals, 1732–1955: History and Bibliography*.

of origin, economic class, and religious affiliation, there are still some common traits that have endured through the generations, helping you to identify German origins. Watch for naming patterns, too. Germans usually give their children two given names, which can be used interchangeably: Johann Karl Schmidt, Johann K. Schmidt, Karl Schmidt, Karl Johann Schmidt, J.K. Schmidt, and so on. It would not be unusual to find several children in one family with the same first baptismal name, but distinct middle names by which they were known. Once again, by studying the different cultural backgrounds and characteristics of your German relatives, it will assist you in selecting appropriate research strategies.

There are many people researching their Germanic ancestry, which is emphasized by some of the resources listed below. Germanic research may be challenging, but you're not alone. Thousands of genealogists have walked the same road as you. Learn from their research experiences.

RESOURCES

Research Guides

Anderson, S. Chris and Ernest Thode. *A Genealogist's Guide to Discovering Your Germanic Ancestors*. Cincinnati: Betterway Books, 2000.

Arndt, Karl J.R. "How to Find Your Hessian Ancestor." *Genealogical Journal* 6 (1977): 15–18.

Bentz, Edna. *If I Can, You Can Decipher Germanic Records*. San Diego, Calif.: the author, 1988.

Hansen, Kevan. *Finding Your German Ancestors: A Beginner's Guide*. Salt Lake City: Ancestry, Inc., 1999.

Heisey, John W. *German for Genealogy: A Translator's Handbook*. Indianapolis: Heritage House, 1985.

Jensen, Larry O. and Norman J. Storrer. *A Genealogical Handbook of German Research*. Pleasant Grove, Utah: the authors, 1977.

Miller, Michael M. *Researching the Germans From Russia*. Fargo: North Dakota Institute for Regional Studies, 1987.

Riemer, Shirley J. *The German Research Companion*. Sacramento, Calif.: Lorelei Press, 1997.

Rubincam, Milton. "New Light on the Hessians in the Revolutionary War." *Genealogical Journal* 5 (1976): 92–95.

Smith, Clifford Neal. *Encyclopedia of German-American Genealogical Research*. New York: R.R. Bowker, 1976.

Smith, Kenneth L. *Going to Germany: A Guide to Traveling and Doing Genealogical Research in West Germany*. Columbus, Ohio: the author, 1987.

———. *Writing to Germany: A Guide to Genealogical Correspondence With German Sources*. Columbus, Ohio: the author, 1984.

Wellauer, Maralyn A. *Tracing Your Swiss Roots*. Milwaukee: the author, 1979.

Social Histories and Historical Sources

Billigmeier, Robert H. *Americans From Germany: A Study in Cultural Diversity*. Belmont, Calif.: Wadsworth, 1974.

Brancaforte, Charlotte L., ed. *The German Forty-Eighters in the United States.* New York: Peter Lang Publishing, 1989.

Galich, Anne. *The German Americans.* New York: Chelsea House, 1989.

Haller, Charles R. *Across the Atlantic and Beyond: The Migration of German and Swiss Immigrants to America.* Bowie, Md.: Heritage Books, 1993.

Hostetler, John A. *Amish Society*, 3rd ed. Baltimore: Johns Hopkins University Press, 1980.

Kloss, Heinz. *Atlas of 19th and Early 20th Century German-American Settlements.* Marburg, West Germany: 1974.

O'Connor, Richard. *The German-Americans.* Boston: Little, Brown, 1968.

Owen, Robert Edward, ed. *Luxembourgers to the New World.* 2 vols. Esch-sur-Alyette, Luxembourg: Editions-Reliures Schortgen, 1987.

Parsons, William T. *Pennsylvania Dutch.* Boston: Twayne Publishers, 1976.

Redekop, Calvin. *Mennonite Society.* Baltimore: Johns Hopkins University Press, 1989.

Rippley, La Vern J. *The German Americans.* Lanham, Md.: University Press of America, 1984.

———— and Robert J. Paulson. *The German-Bohemians: The Quiet Immigrants.* New Ulm, Minn.: German-Bohemian Society, 1995.

Sallet, Richard. *Russian-German Settlements in the United States.* Fargo: North Dakota Institute for Regional Studies, 1974.

Smith, C.H. *The Story of the Mennonites.* Newton, Kans.: Mennonite Publication Office, 1950.

Walker, Mack. *Germany and the Emigration, 1816–1885.* Cambridge: Harvard University Press, 1964.

Wittke, Carl. *The German Language Press in America.* Lexington: University of Kentucky Press, 1957.

————. *The Germans in America.* New York: Teachers College Press, 1967.

Sources and Finding Aids

Arndt, Karl J.R. and May E. Olson, eds. *German-American Newspapers and Periodicals, 1732–1955: History and Bibliography.* Heidelberg, West Germany: 1961.

Brandt, Edward R., et al. *Germanic Genealogy: A Guide to Worldwide Sources and Migration Patterns.* St. Paul, Minn.: Germanic Genealogy Society, 1995.

Burgert, Annette K. *Early Pennsylvania Pioneers From Mutterstadt in the Palatinate.* Worthington, Ohio: AKB Publications, 1983.

————. *Eighteenth Century Emigrants.* 2 vols. *Volume 1: The Northern Kraichgau; Volume 2: The Western Palatine.* Birdsboro, Pa.: The Pennsylvania German Society, 1985.

————. *Eighteenth Century Pennsylvania Emigrants From Hassloch and Boehl in the Palatinate.* Worthington, Ohio: AKB Publications, 1983.

————. *Eighteenth and Nineteenth Century Emigrants From Lachen-Speyerdorf in the Palatinate.* Myerstown, Pa.: AKB Publications, 1989.

————. *Pennsylvania Pioneers From Wolfsweiler Parish, Saarland, Germany.* Worthington, Ohio: AKB Publications, 1983.

Gardiner, Duncan B. *German Towns in Slovakia and Upper Hungary: A Genealogical Gazetteer.* Lakewood, Ohio: the author, 1988.

Glazier, Ira A. *Migration From the Russian Empire: Lists of Passengers Arriving at the Port of New York, 1875–1910.* Wilmington, Del.: Scholarly Resources, 1995–.

——— and P. William Filby. *Germans to America: Lists of Passengers Arriving at U.S. Ports, 1850–1855* (Ongoing). Wilmington, Del.: Scholarly Resources, 1988–.

Grubb, Farley. *German Immigrant Servant Contracts: Registered at the Port of Philadelphia, 1817–1831.* Baltimore: Genealogical Publishing Co., 1994.

Guth, Hermann and Gertrud Guth, et al. *Palatine Mennonite Census Lists, 1664–1793.* Elverson, Pa: Mennonite Family History, 1987.

Hacker, Werner. *Eighteenth Century Register of Emigrants From Southwest Germany.* Apollo, Pa: Closson Press, 1994.

Hall, Charles M. *The Atlantic Bridge to Germany.* 8 vols. Logan, Utah: Everton Publishers, 1974.

Hope, Anne and Joerg Nagler. *Guide to German Historical Sources in North American Libraries and Archives.* Washington, D.C.: German Historical Institute, 1991.

Index to Mennonite Immigrants on United States Passenger Lists, 1872–1904. North Newton, Kans.: Mennonite Library and Archives, 1986.

Irish, Donna R. *Pennsylvania German Marriages.* Baltimore: Genealogical Publishing Co., 1982.

Jones, George F. *German American Names.* 2nd ed. Baltimore: Genealogical Publishing Co., 1995.

Jones, Henry Z. *More Palatine Families: Some Immigrants to the Middle Colonies and Their European Origins Plus New Discoveries on German Families Who Arrived in Colonial New York in 1710.* Universal City, Calif.: the author, 1991.

———. *The Palatine Families of Ireland.* Camden, Maine: Picton Press, 1990.

———. *The Palatine Families of New York: A Study of the German Immigrants Who Arrived in Colonial New York in 1710.* 2 vols. Universal City, Calif.: the author, 1985.

——— and Annette Kunselman Burgett. *Westerwald to America: Some Eighteenth Century German Immigrants.* Camden, Maine: Picton Press, 1989.

Keresztesi, Michael and Gary R. Cocozzoli. *German-American History and Life: A Guide to Information Sources.* Detroit: Gale Research, 1980.

Le Van, Russell George. *Early Immigrants From Germany and Switzerland to Eastern Pennsylvania.* Baltimore: Gateway Press, 1990.

Pennsylvania German Church Records of Births, Baptisms, Marriages, Burials, etc. 3 vols. Baltimore: Genealogical Publishing Co., 1983.

Register and Guide to the Hamburg Passenger Lists, 1850–1934. Research Paper Series C, no. 30. The Genealogical Department of the Church of Jesus Christ of Latter-day Saints.

Remington, Gordon L. "Feast or Famine: Problems in the Genealogical Use of *The Famine Immigrants* and *Germans to America.*" *National Genealogical Society Quarterly* 78 (June 1990): 135–146.

Ritz, Albrecht. *Immigrants to America and Central Europe From Beihingen am Neckar, Baden-Württemberg, Germany: 1727–1934.* McNeal, Ariz.: Westland Publications, 1980.

Rupp, I. Daniel. *A Collection of Upwards of Thirty Thousand Names of German, Swiss, Dutch, French, and Other Immigrants in Pennsylvania From 1727 to 1776,* 2nd ed. Baltimore: Genealogical Publishing Co., 1965.

Schenk, Trudy, Ruth Froelke, and Inge Bork. *Wuerttemberg Emigration Index.* 7 vols. Salt Lake City: Ancestry, Inc., 1986–.

Smith, Clifford Neal. *British and German Deserters, Discharges, and Prisoners of War Who May Have Remained in Canada and the United States, 1774–1783.* McNeal, Ariz.: Westland Publications, 1988.

———. *Eighteenth-Century Emigrants From Kreis Simmern (Hünsruck), Rheinland-Pfalz, Niederrhein, and North America.* McNeal, Ariz.: Westland Publications, 1982.

———. *Emigrants From Saxony (Grandduchy of Sachsen-Weimar-Eisenach) to America, 1854–1859.* McNeal, Ariz.: Westland Publications, 1974.

———. *Emigrants From the Former Amt Damme, Oldenburg (Now Niedersachsen), Germany, Mainly to the United States, 1830–1849.* McNeal, Ariz.: Westland Publications, 1981.

———. *Emigrants From the Island of Foehr (Formerly Denmark, Now Schleswig-Holstein, Germany) to Australia, Canada, Chile, the United States, and the West Indies, 1850–1875.* McNeal, Ariz.: Westland Publications, 1983.

———. *Emigrants From the Principality of Hessen Hanau, Germany, 1741–1767.* McNeal, Ariz.: Westland Publications, 1979.

———. *Emigrants From the West German Fuerstenberg Territories (Baden and the Palatinate to America and Central Europe 1712, 1737, 1787).* McNeal, Ariz.: Westland Publications, 1981.

———. *From Bremen to America in 1850: Fourteen Rare Emigrant Ship Lists.* McNeal, Ariz.: Westland Publications, 1987.

———. *German Revolutionists of 1848: Among Whom Many Immigrants to America.* McNeal, Ariz.: Westland Publications, 1985.

———. *Missing Young Men of Württemberg, Germany, 1807: Some Possible Immigrants to America.* McNeal, Ariz.: Westland Publications, 1983.

———. *Reconstructed Passenger Lists for 1850: Hamburg to Australia, Brazil, Canada, Chile, and the United States.* McNeal, Ariz.: Westland Publications, 1980.

———. *Reconstructed Passenger Lists for 1851 via Hamburg: Emigrants From Germany, Austria, Bohemia, Hungary, Poland, Russia, Scandinavia, and Switzerland to Australia, Brazil, Canada, Chile, the United States, and Venezuela.* McNeal, Ariz.: Westland Publications, 1986.

Strassburger, Ralph Beaver. *Pennsylvania German Pioneers.* 3 vols. Norristown, Pa.: Pennsylvania German Society, 1934.

Tepper, Michael. *Emigrants to Pennsylvania, 1641–1819.* Baltimore: Genealogical Publishing Co., 1978.

Tolzmann, Don Heinrich, ed. *German Immigration to America: The First Wave.* Bowie, Md.: Heritage Books, 1993.

Thode, Ernest. *Address Book for Germanic Genealogy*. Baltimore: Genealogical Publishing Co., 1997.

———. *Atlas for Germanic Genealogy*, 2nd ed. Indianapolis: Heritage House, 1983.

———. *German-English Genealogical Dictionary*. Baltimore: Genealogical Publishing Co., 1992.

Wellauer, Marilyn. *A List of Evangelical Communities in the Province of Pommern (Pomerania), Germany, as They Existed Before World War I*. Milwaukee: the author, 1979.

Yoder, Don, ed. *Pennsylvania German Immigrants 1709–1786*. Baltimore: Genealogical Publishing Co., 1980.

———. *Rhineland Emigrants: Lists of German Settlers in Colonial America*. Baltimore: Genealogical Publishing Co., 1981.

Zimmerman, Gary J. and Marion Wolfert. *German Immigrants: Lists of Passengers From Bremen to New York, 1847–1871*. 4 vols. Baltimore: Genealogical Publishing Co., 1985–93.

Organizations, Periodicals, and Internet Sites
American Historical Society of Germans From Russia
  631 D St., Lincoln, NE 68502-1199
  Phone: (402) 474-3363; (402) 474-7229   *E-mail:* ahsgr@aol.com
  Web site: http://www.ahsgr.org   Publishes *Clues, Journal*, and *Newsletter*
German Genealogical Digest
  P.O. Box 112054, Salt Lake City, UT 84147
  Web site: http://www.feefhs.org/pub/frg-ggdp.html
German Genealogical Society of America
  P.O. Box 291818, Los Angeles, CA 90029   *Phone:* (909) 593-0509
  Publishes *Newsletter*
German Genealogy Homepage
  Web site: http://www.genealogy.net/gene/
German Genealogy Links
  Web site: http://www.geocities.com/SiliconValley/Haven/1538/german.html
Germanic Genealogical Society
  P.O. Box 16312, St. Paul, MN 55116-0312   *Phone:* (612) 777-6463
  Publishes *G.G.S. Newsletter*
German Research Association, Inc.
  P.O. Box 711600, San Diego, CA 92171-1600
  Web site: http://www.feefhs.org/gra/frg-gra.html
  Publishes *The German Connection*
German Society of Pennsylvania
  611 Spring Garden St., Philadelphia, PA 19123   *Phone:* (215) 627-2332
  E-mail: germanscty@aol.com   *Web site:* http://www.german-society.org
Immigrant Genealogical Society
  P.O. Box 7369, Burbank, CA 91510-7369   *Phone:* (818) 848-3122
  Web site: http://www.feefhs.org/igs/frqigs.html   Publishes *German American Genealogy* and *Immigrant Genealogical Society Newsletter*

Mennonite Historical Library

Goshen College, Goshen, IN 46526   *Phone:* (219) 535-7418

Fax: (219) 535-7438   *E-mail:* anetss@goshen.edu

Publishes *Mennonite Quarterly Review*

Palatines to America

Capital University, Box 101AB, Columbus, OH 43209-2394

Phone and Fax: (614) 236-8281   *E-mail:* pal-am@juno.com

Web site: http://www.genealogy.org/~palam/

Pennsylvania German Society

P.O. Box 397, Birdsboro, PA 19508-0397   *Phone:* (215) 582-1441

Publishes *Proceedings* and *Der Reggeboge (The Rainbow)*

The Swiss Connection

2845 N. Seventy-second St., Milwaukee, WI 53210

Phone: (414) 778-1224

Fax: (414) 778-2109   *E-mail:* swissmis@interserv.com

Greeks

Few Greeks came to America in its early history, and those who did come were individuals—sailors, explorers, students, cotton merchants, gold miners—not families or communities of people. Heavy Greek immigration began in the 1890s. During this time, more Greeks lived outside of Greece in the Balkans, Turkey, Egypt, and along the Mediterranean than lived in Greece. The Spartans came first, then Arcadians, then Greeks from central Greece, Crete, the Aegean and Ionian islands, the Dodecanese islands, Asian and European Turkey (during the 1890s, two-thirds of the immigrants from Turkey were Greek), Cyprus, the Balkan countries, and Egypt. The majority of arrivals in the 1900–1920s came from small villages in the Peloponnesus in southern Greece. Some also came from the Greek islands, many of them settling on the west coast of Florida and pursuing sponge fishing around Tarpon Springs.

Greek arrivals were heavily male—young men and boys—who were unskilled laborers. About half were birds of passage. Like Italians, their goal was to earn enough money to return home and buy land. **Many made the Atlantic crossing three or four times before deciding whether to bring their families and settle in America,** so passenger arrival lists are important to Greek researchers. Perhaps a third or more of the Greek birds of passage opted to remain in their homelands, but more than half of Greek immigrants decided to stay in America, preferring to settle in cities of the northeast and north-central states, such as New York, Chicago, and Lowell, Massachusetts. A significant number also went to California.

The vast majority of Greeks pursued urban occupations and shunned farming. Large numbers became small businessmen, especially restaurateurs, although few had run restaurants in their homeland. In America, they offered inexpensive, basic dishes in restaurants that became known as "greasy spoons." They learned quickly that opening a restaurant did not require a large amount of capital, and it became a family business, providing service to low-income

Reminder

patrons. Greeks also opened confectioneries and ice cream parlors, with Chicago becoming the center of Greek candy business.

Immigrants attended the Greek Orthodox church, which they established as families began settling in America. Church officials in Greece did not send clergy, however; the laity established the church first, and then requested a priest for the parish.

Sources

Immigrant Greeks were joiners, belonging to clubs, organizations, and fraternal lodges, all of which may have extant records. Two major post-World War I Greek-American organizations were the American Hellenic Educational Progressive Association (AHEPA), founded in 1922, and the Greek American Progressive Association (GAPA), founded in 1923. During oral history interviews with elder relatives, ask if family members belonged to either of these groups or others, since they will reveal quite a bit about your ancestors' characters. The AHEPA preached a doctrine of Americanization and nonsectarianism; the GAPA was antiassimilationist and believed that all Greeks should learn and use the Greek language, cultivate Greek heritage, and adhere to the Greek Orthodox church.

Another important social institution for Greek men was the coffeehouse. It was equivalent to saloons for Germans and pubs for Irish and English. Only men were allowed, and the coffeehouse was the center of a Greek community. The owner provided decks of cards, and the men played card games, debated issues, and drank coffee and spirits.

Since so few Greek women came in the early years of mass Greek immigration, a substantial number of Greek men married outside their ethnic group. Most, however, preferred to marry women of their own nationality, thus many returned to their homeland for a bride or sought a mate through family or friends. For the immigrant generation, arranged marriages were common. The couple had little or no courtship, and romance was not a factor. The union was an alliance of families. Husbands were usually much older than their wives, and the young bride typically lived with her husband's family in the first years of marriage. It was the woman's responsibility, married or not, to look after her aging parents.

Education and achievement were important in Greek immigrant families, and children were expected to do well in school. Name-day celebrations received more attention than birthdays. Children were named in honor of a saint, and it was the patron saint's day that was celebrated.

Because the Greeks are a fairly recent immigrant group, there has not yet been a lot of interest in Greek-American genealogy. This is common with many recent groups, and as the group becomes more assimilated into American society and, unfortunately, in danger of losing its distinct culture, more people become interested in preserving their heritage through family history research. Don't let the lack of apparent resources discourage you. Let it be a challenge to you to start the trend of preserving this group's heritage.

RESOURCES

Research Guides

Bywater, Lica Catsakis and Daniel M. Schyter. *Greek Genealogical Research.* Salt Lake City: Family History Library, 1992.

Social Histories and Historical Sources

Fairchild, Henry Pratt. *Greek Immigration to the United States*. New Haven, Conn.: Yale University Press, 1911.

Saloutos, Theodore. *The Greeks in the United States*. Cambridge: Harvard University Press, 1964.

Scourby, Alice. *The Greek-Americans*. Boston: Twayne Publishers, 1984.

Sources and Finding Aids

Voultsos, Mary, comp. *Greek Immigrant Passengers, 1885–1910*. 5 vols. Worcester, Mass.: the author, 1992.

Organizations, Periodicals, and Internet Sites

Greek Family Heritage Committee

75-21 177th St., Flushing, NY 11366   *Phone:* (718) 591-9342

E-mail: alonakia@worldnet.att.net

Hungarians

Since the Magyars (Hungarians) settled in Central Europe in the tenth century, Hungary (called Magyarorszag in Hungarian) stretched from Poland in the north to Belgrade in the south and included the large province of Transylvania, now a large segment of Romania. The Ottoman Turks invaded and occupied most of Lower Hungary (1526–1683) and gradually depopulated parts of it. After the Turks were driven back, many areas were repopulated from other areas of the Habsburg Empire and by the late 1700s, Magyars were less than 50 percent of the population of Hungary. The other significant minorities were Slovaks, Romanians, Germans, Serbs, Croats, Rusyns, and Jews. When the peace settlement after World War I redrew the boundaries of Austria-Hungary mostly along ethnic lines, Hungary lost two-thirds of its territory and population. For this reason, the country we now know as Hungary is almost totally Magyar and there are significant Magyar minorities in Romania, Slovakia, and northern Yugoslavia. Before World War I, immigrants to the United States from Hungary of some non-Magyar ethnic groups were recorded as Hungarians because they stated that their native country was Hungary.

The major wave of about 1.7 million Hungarian immigrants to the United States began in 1880, although some four thousand political refugees arrived after the Revolution of 1848 and a small number had come as early as the American Revolution.

Males under thirty were the predominant Hungarian immigrants; more than two-thirds came looking for jobs with better wages than in their homeland. Almost 90 percent of them were literate, but they came largely to work in industries and took dangerous jobs, such as coal mining and steel industries. They found work in western Pennsylvania, eastern Ohio, West Virginia, and northern Illinois and Indiana. Cleveland had Hungarian benevolent and community societies by 1881.

Because it was not their intent to stay in America, they were birds of passage, with nearly half returning to their homeland. Some eventually came back to America, however. Once here, they moved frequently, seeking temporary employment, not permanent residences. Even when they brought their families over, this group had a high mobility rate. As is common with birds of passage, only a small percentage before World War I became naturalized.

The majority of Hungarian immigrants were Catholic, but there were also some Protestants, and about 5 percent were Jews. While their churches were an important social and religious institution, they also formed hundreds of fraternal organizations, beginning in the 1890s. These played a key role in the assimilation process, and if these records still exist, they may provide a valuable aspect to your family history.

To Hungarians, the family has two meanings: the nuclear family and the extended family, which is referred to as the "sib." This was a network of aunts, uncles, cousins, and godparents, who may or may not be relatives by blood.

In 1910, many Hungarian couples took in boarders who were male Hungarian immigrants. Because the husband worked, the Hungarian wife did the chores and served as the boardinghouse manager. She shopped for food, did laundry, and kept track of the boarders' expenses. The Hungarian diet favored meat, with few dairy products or fruits and vegetables.

Unfortunately, Hungarian genealogical research in America has not yet become popular, which is so often the case with recent immigrant groups. The longer the group is in the United States, the more preserving ethnic heritage becomes important. Keep on the lookout for more sources to become available, and utilize the current few to your best advantage.

RESOURCES

Research Guides
Suess, Jared H. *Handy Guide to Hungarian Genealogical Records.* Logan, Utah: Everton Publishers, 1980.

Social Histories and Historical Sources
Lengyel, Emil. *Americans From Hungary.* Westport, Conn.: Greenwood Press, 1975.
Vardy, Steven Bela. *The Hungarian Americans.* New York: Chelsea House, 1990.

Organizations, Periodicals, and Internet Sites
Family History in Hungary
   Web site: http://user.itl.net/~glen/FamilyHistoryinHungary.html
Hungarian Genealogy Newsletter
   P.O. Box 13548, St. Louis, MO 63138
Hungarian Genealogical Society of Greater Cleveland
   7830 Sugar Bush Ln., Gates Mills, OH 44040
   Web site: http://www.community.cleveland.com/cc/hungariangenealogy

Irish

In proportion to its total population," wrote Carl Wittke, "Ireland has lost more of its sons and daughters to emigration than any other country." From 1820 through 1920, more than 4.25 million Irish immigrants came to the United States.

Historians consider the Catholic Irish to be the first ethnic minority to settle in American cities in great numbers. Some Irish settled in Liverpool, England, for a time before coming to America, removing them two or three generations from their ancestral land. In American records, therefore, they may appear as English or British. The Irish of the colonial period came as indentured servants, redemptioners, convicts, and paying passengers.

The majority of Irish who began immigrating in mass numbers in 1815 were farmers and laborers. Although not all who left southern Ireland were Catholic, about 50 to 60 percent were. The rest consisted of Irish Quakers, Presbyterians, Episcopalians, and other faiths, with some coming through Canada. The Irish of the early nineteenth century came primarily as intact families, but by 1835, single women constituted 48 percent of the immigrants. The Great Famine of the 1840s–1850s forced many to leave Ireland. About 120,000 arrived between 1845 and 1846, and between 1847 and 1854, 1.25 million Irish came from southern and western Ireland. Sixty-six percent were between the ages of fifteen and thirty-five. Most came in cargo ships, many during the mid-1830s, arriving at the Canadian port of Quebec. In 1847, about 20 percent died enroute. The loss of life during the voyage was so huge that Americans almost automatically assumed that an orphan in the 1840s was Irish. If records have survived for orphanages, they may be helpful, but these records—although historical—may also have restricted access.

Many Irish were so poor that once they arrived in America, they could not afford to migrate elsewhere, so they settled in the port cities and in nearby towns where unskilled labor was needed. Other major cities of settlement were Lawrence, Lowell, Fall River, and Worcester, Massachusetts; Troy, New York; Jersey City, New Jersey; and Hartford, Connecticut. The massive canal building of the 1820s to 1840s was done by Irish immigrant labor, and the Irish also sought work in western mining. Additionally, the police forces of major port cities, such as Boston, took a significant Irish brogue during the nineteenth century. Conversely, many Irish also took advantage of land grants and pursued farming.

During the famine years, the average life expectancy of an urban Irish American was forty because of illness, alcohol-related diseases, hard labor, and poor living conditions in ethnic enclaves. Irish-born females were prone to tuberculosis and ailments of the circulatory system. The infant mortality rate was higher than in any other immigrant group. Those who had settled outside of the heavily populated cities had better health.

The Irish made the Catholic church a powerful institution in America. Neighborhood communities and activities revolved around the parish and the church

Tip

calendar. Look for parish histories, giving you a flavor of your ancestor's parish and the counties in Ireland the parishioners may have represented. Marriage and burial records may provide names of parents and birthplaces. Witnesses, such as godparents, may give you further clues to family and friends in Ireland. Instead of sending their children to public schools, the Irish were more likely to enroll them in parochial schools.

The Irish were likely to leave a record trail of donations and remittances in honor of family members back in Ireland. Taking care of their own, the Irish formed aid societies, trade associations, fraternal organizations, their own welfare system, and homes for the aged.

The average marriage age for the immigrant generation was thirty-five for men and thirty-one for women. The Irish typically did not practice primogeniture in Ireland, and many fathers did not decide until late in life which of their sons would inherit property. Generally, the son who inherited land had the best means of support to marry. (Certainly, there are also cases of daughters taking over rent and tax payments after the parents' deaths.) As a result, the Irish had the lowest rate and oldest age of marriage in the world. Because of the decline in dowries resulting from the famine years, the arrivals after the 1880s were largely young, single females who sought work as domestic servants. More Irish females than women in any other ethnic group in America remained unmarried. Unmarried women were allowed to work, and they enjoyed their independence; thus, Irish men were more likely to marry outside the ethnic group. For the second-generation Irish, the average marrying age was twenty-six for men and twenty-three for women. An engagement period of a year or more was the norm. Divorces were extremely uncommon.

At the peak of Irish immigration in 1855, many households consisted of parents, siblings, nieces, nephews, some in-laws, grandparents, and some non-relative boarders. The Irish used necronyms and saints' names. The traditional pattern, although never a hard-and-fast rule, was to name the first son after the father's father, the second son after the mother's father, the first daughter after the father's mother, and the second daughter after the mother's mother.

If you are one of the many thousands researching Irish ancestry, you have some wonderful resources to aid your search. Irish research is extremely popular in America, and you will no doubt meet people within your local genealogical society who are also tracing their Irish roots. Look to these people for more help with your own search.

RESOURCES

Research Guides

Begley, Donal F., ed. *Irish Genealogy: A Record Finder.* Dublin, Ireland: Heraldic Artists, 1987.

Betit, Kyle J. and Dwight A. Radford. *Ireland: A Genealogical Guide.* Salt Lake City: The Irish at Home and Abroad, 1998.

Falley, Margaret Dickson. *Irish and Scotch-Irish Ancestral Research: A Guide to the Genealogical Records, Methods and Sources in Ireland.* 2 vols. Originally published in 1962. Reprint, Baltimore: Genealogical Publishing Co., 1988.

Grenham, John. *Tracing Your Irish Ancestors.* Dublin, Ireland: Gill and Macmillan, 1999.

Mac Conghail, Máire and Paul Gorry. *Tracing Irish Ancestors.* Glasgow, Scotland: HarperCollins, 1997.

Maxwell, Ian. *Tracing Your Ancestors in Northern Ireland: A Guide to Ancestry Research in the Public Record Office of Northern Ireland.* Edinburgh, Scotland: The Stationery Office, 1997.

Mitchell, Brian. *Pocket Guide to Irish Genealogy.* Baltimore: Genealogical Publishing Co., 1991.

Ryan, James G. *Irish Records: Sources for Family and Local History*, rev. ed. Salt Lake City: Ancestry, Inc., 1997.

Social Histories and Historical Sources

Delaney, Mary Murray. *Of Irish Ways.* New York: Harper and Row, 1973.

Diner, Hasia R. *Erin's Daughters in America: Irish Immigrant Women in the Nineteenth Century.* Baltimore: Johns Hopkins University Press, 1983.

Fallows, Marjorie R. *Irish Americans: Identity and Assimilation.* Englewood Cliffs, N.J.: Prentice-Hall, 1979

Fitzgerald, Margaret E. and Joseph A. King. *The Uncounted Irish: In Canada and the United States.* Toronto: P.D. Meany, 1990.

Fitzgibbon, Theodora. *Irish Traditional Food.* Dublin, Ireland: Gill and Macmillan, 1991.

Handlin, Oscar. *Boston's Immigrants.* New York: Atheneum, 1968.

Maguire, John F. *The Irish in America.* New York: Arno Press, 1974.

Miller, Kerby A. *Emigrants and Exiles: Ireland and the Irish Exodus to North America.* New York: Oxford University Press, 1985.

Nolan, Janet A. *Ourselves Alone: Women's Emigration From Ireland, 1885–1920.* Lexington: The University Press of Kentucky, 1989.

Watts, J.F. *The Irish Americans.* New York: Chelsea House, 1988.

Wittke, Carl. *The Irish in America.* New York: Russell and Russell Publishers, 1970.

Sources and Finding Aids

Flanagan, Deirdre and Laurence Flanagan. *Irish Place Names.* Dublin, Ireland: Gill and Macmillan, 1994.

General Alphabetical Index to the Townlands and Towns, Parishes, and Baronies of Ireland. Originally published in 1861. Reprint, Baltimore: Genealogical Publishing Co., 1995.

Glazier, Ira A. *The Famine Immigrants: Lists of Irish Immigrants Arriving at the Port of New York, 1846–1851.* 7 vols. Baltimore: Genealogical Publishing Co., 1983–1986.

Hackett, J. Dominick and Charles M. Early. *Passenger Lists From Ireland.* Baltimore: Clearfield Co., 1994.

Harris, Ruth-Ann M., Donald M. Jacobs, et al., eds. *The Search for Missing Friends: Irish Immigrant Advertisements Placed in the* Boston Pilot. 7 vols. Boston: New England Historic Genealogical Society, 1989–1999.

MacLysaght, Edward. *The Surnames of Ireland*, 6th ed. Dublin, Ireland: Irish Academic Press, 1991.

Mitchell, Brian. *Irish Emigration Lists, 1833–1839*. Baltimore: Genealogical Publishing Co., 1989.

———. *Irish Passenger Lists, 1847–1871: Lists of Passengers Sailing From Londonderry to America on Ships of the J. & J. Cooke Line and the McCorkell Line*. Baltimore: Genealogical Publishing Co., 1988.

O'Brien, Michael J. *The Irish in America: Immigration, Land, Probate, Administrations, Birth, Marriage, and Burial Records of the Irish in America and About the Eighteenth Century*. Baltimore: Clearfield Co., 1990.

———. *Irish Settlers in America*. 2 vols. Baltimore: Genealogical Publishing Co., 1979.

Ó Corráin, Donnchadh and Fidelma Macquire. *Irish Names*. Dublin, Ireland: The Lilliput Press, 1990.

Remington, Gordon L. "Feast or Famine: Problems in the Genealogical Use of *The Famine Immigrants* and *Germans to America*." *National Genealogical Society Quarterly* 78 (June 1990): 135–146.

Organizations, Periodicals, and Internet Sites
American Irish Historical Society
991 Fifth Ave., New York, NY 10028 *Phone:* (212) 288-2263
Web site: http://www.aihs.org
Familia: Ulster Genealogical Review
Ulster Historical and Genealogical Guild, Ulster Historical Foundation, 12 College Sq. E., Belfast BT1 6DD, Northern Ireland
Web site: http://www.uhf.org.uk/
Irish American Magazine
P.O. Box 200, Congers, NY 10920-9929
Irish Ancestors
Web site: http://scripts.ireland.com/ancestor/index.html
Irish Genealogical Foundation
P.O. Box 7575, Kansas City, MO 64116 *Phone:* (816) 454-2410
E-mail: Irelande@compuserve.com
Web site: http://www.irishroots.com Publishes *Journal of Irish Families*
Irish Family History Foundation
Web site: http://www.mayo-ireland.ie/roots/htm
Irish Genealogical Society, International
P.O. Box 16585, St. Paul, MN 55116-0585 *Phone:* (612) 595-9347
E-mail: raymarsh@minn.net *Web site:* http://www.rootsweb.com/~irish/index.html Publishes *The Septs.*
Irish Roots
Belgrave Publications, Belgrave Ave., Cork, Ireland
E-mail: irishrts@iol.ie *Web site:* http://www.iol.ie/~irishrts/

The Irish at Home and Abroad
Six volumes published between 1993 and 1999; available in many genealogical libraries

Italians

Northern Italians began arriving in small numbers in the colonial period. Because Italy was not unified until the 1860s, its people considered themselves citizens of a village or region, rather than a nation; therefore, they were usually recorded in colonial America by their region of origin, Genoese or Florentine, rather than "Italian." Italian immigrants of the American colonial and early national periods tended to be skilled artisans and scholars, and many were Protestant.

By contrast, in the late nineteenth and early twentieth centuries, Italian immigrants were mostly peasants and unskilled laborers from southern Italy, especially the regions of Abruzzi, Molise, Apulia, Basilicata, Calabria, Campania, parts of Latium, and the island of Sicily. They displaced the Irish immigrants of the nineteenth century in urban ghettos, the largest settlements being in New York City, San Francisco, and New Orleans.

Southern Italians had a high return migration rate: 30 percent went back to Italy within five years of arrival in America. The goal for the Italian man was to earn enough money in the United States to be able to return home and buy land. Those who decided to stay in America sent for their families generally after three to five years. Some traveled back and forth to Italy several times before bringing relatives, so once you identify an Italian man in passenger lists, check for earlier and subsequent voyages. Since settling in the United States was not the goal of many Italians, this group was also unlikely or slow to become naturalized.

Reminder

Though Italy was unified by the time mass numbers of southern Italians began emigrating, they still considered themselves citizens of a town and were regionalistic. Since dialects varied from village to village and often were incomprehensible to the residents of other regions, Italian newcomers clustered in America with fellow villagers. Italian immigrants were predominantly Catholic, although some Italian Jews also emigrated and a small number of Italian Protestants. Women and children attended church, but not men. Only three life events mandated their attendance: baptisms, marriages, and funerals. In retirement, however, Italian men might attend religious services more regularly.

Italians almost invariably married within their own ethnic group, which remained the dominant pattern into the second generation. They generally sought mates from the same village first, or the same province second. Southern Italians preferred marrying other ethnic groups rather than form a north/south Italian mixed marriage. Divorce, separation, and desertion were rare. The traditional naming pattern was the first son after the father's father, the second son after the mother's father, the third son after the father, the first daughter after the father's mother, the second daughter after the mother's mother, and the third daughter after the mother. Necronyms were common.

If you have trouble locating your Italian families on census enumerations, one reason may be the group's high mobility rate. During their first few years in the United States, Italian families, and particularly unmarried Italian men, might change residences three or four times. Italians and other immigrants who lived in tenement apartments moved on average of once every ten years, either to better their living quarters or because landlords raised the rent. Another explanation may be Italian character. Because they emphasized family loyalty, southern Italians had a great distrust for outsiders, especially government agents, such as census takers. They also viewed education as a threat to family unity and economy. School records may be helpful since children of Italian immigrants had a high rate of truancy and drop outs. Records will reflect such activities.

During World War II, thousands of Italians and Italian-Americans were held at holding facilities or relocated to internment camps. With Franklin D. Roosevelt's signing of Executive Order 9066 in February 1942, some Italians and Italian-Americans were sent and held, ironically, at Ellis Island, while many others were interned at Fort Missoula, Montana, or camps in Bismark (Fort Lincoln), North Dakota, Crystal City and San Antonio, Texas, and McAllister, Oklahoma. (See also chapter five) Though Italians across the country were targeted, restrictions were heaviest on the fifty-two thousand Italian aliens living along the Pacific Coast, particularly northern California. Considered "enemy aliens," they were required to register at local post offices, carry photo identification cards, and surrender contraband items such as guns, radios, cameras, and signaling devices. They were also subjected to tight curfews and were not allowed to travel more than five miles from their homes. Anyone found in violation of any of these restrictions was arrested. About ten thousand Italians and Italian Americans were forced to evacuate restricted areas, and consequently lost their homes and businesses. Restrictions were in effect for about nine months and were lifted on Columbus Day 1942; those being held in internment camps, however, were not released until late 1943. In November 1999, HR 2442, the "Wartime Violation of Italian-Americans Civil Liberties Act," was passed, and as a result, perhaps more restricted records of this event will be opened to the public.

In Italian culture, food was a crucial element in family celebrations and daily life. Food represented the family, being a product of the father who earned the money or grew the crops, and the mother who prepared the dishes. Italian food is regional and may lead to the area of origin. For example, in northern Italy, the main staples were polenta and risotto; in southern Italy, it was pasta. In the region of Apulia, the primary dish was fish—eel in particular. By contrast, in Campania, mussels and clams were preferred. In comparing the family recipes and food preferences, one may trace family origins to a specific region in Italy. The variety and highly developed nature of Italian cuisine allowed many immigrant families to prosper as proprietors of restaurants, bakeries, and pastry shops.

It has only been within the past five years or so that Italian Americans have become interested in their ancestry and have started producing more research guides and finding aids. Take advantage of these to begin your search, as well as networking with others pursuing Italian genealogy.

RESOURCES

Research Guides

Carmack, Sharon DeBartolo. "Book Review: *Italians to America: Lists of Passengers Arriving at U.S. Ports, 1880–1899.*" *National Genealogical Society Quarterly* 81 (December 1993).

———. *Italian-American Family History: A Guide to Researching and Writing About Your Heritage.* Baltimore: Genealogical Publishing Co., 1997.

Cole, Trafford R. *Italian Genealogical Records: How to Use Italian Civil, Ecclesiastical, and Other Records in Family History Research.* Salt Lake City: Ancestry, Inc., 1995.

Colletta, John Philip. *Finding Italian Roots: The Complete Guide for Americans.* Baltimore: Genealogical Publishing Co., 1996.

Nelson, Lynn. *A Genealogist's Guide to Discovering Your Italian Ancestors.* Cincinnati: Betterway Books, 1997.

Social Histories and Historical Sources

Caroli, Betty Boyd. *Italian Repatriation From the United States, 1900–1914.* New York: Center for Migration Studies, 1973.

Fox, Stephen. *The Unknown Internment: An Oral History of the Relocation of Italian Americans During World War II.* Boston: Twayne Publishers, 1990.

Gambino, Richard. *Blood of My Blood: The Dilemma of the Italian-Americans.* New York: Doubleday, 1974.

"Italian Americans in World War II: *Una Storia Segreta* (A Secret Story)," aired 16 February 2000. The History Channel.

LaGumina, Salvatore J., Frank J. Cavaioli, Salvatore Primeggia, and Joseph A. Varacalli, eds. *The Italian American Experience: An Encyclopedia.* New York: Garland Publishing Co., 2000.

Malpezzi, Frances M. and William M. Clements. *Italian-American Folklore.* Little Rock, Ark.: August House Publishers, 1992.

Mangione, Jerre and Ben Morreale. *La Storia: Five Centuries of the Italian American Experience.* New York: HarperCollins, 1992.

Rolle, Andrew. *The Immigrant Upraised: Italian Adventurers and Colonists in an Expanding America.* Norman: University of Oklahoma Press, 1968.

Williams, Phyllis. *South Italian Folkways in Europe and America.* New Haven, Conn.: Yale University Press, 1938.

Sources and Finding Aids

Andreozzi, John. *Guide to Records of the Order of the Sons of Italy in America.* St. Paul, Minn.: Immigration History Research Center, 1988.

Fucilla, Joseph G. *Our Italian Surnames.* Baltimore: Genealogical Publishing Co., 1998.

Glazier, Ira and P. William Filby. *Italians to America: Lists of Passengers Arriving at U.S. Ports, 1880–1899.* 12 vols. projected. Wilmington, Del.: Scholarly Resources, 1992.

Organizations, Periodicals, and Internet Sites
American Italian Heritage Association
P.O. Box 3136, Albany, NY 12203-3136
Publishes *American Italian Heritage Digest*
Italian Genealogical Group
P.O. Box 626, Bethpage, NY 11714-0626
Web site: http://www.italiangen.org. Publishes *Newsletter*
Italian Genealogical Society of America
P.O. Box 8571, Cranston, RI 02920-8571   Publishes *Lo Specchio*
National Italian American Foundation
1860 Nineteenth St., NW, Washington, DC 20009-5501
Web site: http://www.niaf.org   Publishes *Ambassador* and *Newsletter*
Pursuing Our Italian Names Together
P.O. Box 14966, Las Vegas, NV 89114-4966
E-mail: POINTer01@aol.com   *Web Site:* http://www.members.aol.com/pointhompg/home.htm   Publishes *Pointers*
Virtual Italia
Web site: http://www.virtualitalia.com

Jews

T o be Jewish in America is to be a member of a religious faith, the followers of Judaism, but also importantly, it means to share a sense of 'peoplehood,' an ethnicity, with a vast number of people sharing a distinct cultural heritage," explain the authors of "The Jewish-American Family," in *Ethnic Families in America* (page 422). Though the duality of this group causes confusion in whether to present them as a religious group or an ethnic group, for the purposes of family history research, they are here as an ethnic/immigrant group. Keep in mind that Judaism is practiced by people of many nationalities; there are Italian Jews, French Jews, Polish Jews, German Jews, and so on. Jews classify themselves based on historical origin as Sephardic (pre-Inquisition Spain), Ashkenazic (Germany and Eastern Europe), Oriental (Iran, Iraq, India, and China), or Ethiopian (African).

Roughly 46 percent of the world's Jews reside in the United States today, and they have had a presence in America since the colonial period. The earliest settlement of Jews in America dates from 1654 in what was then the colony of New Amsterdam (New York today). The late Rabbi Malcolm H. Stern estimates that fewer than fifteen thousand Jews immigrated in the colonial and early national periods from various places around the world. His comprehensive work, *First American Jewish Families*, documents about fifty thousand Jews and their descendants who resided in America before 1838.

Sephardic Jews are those descended from Spanish Jews expelled from Spain in 1492. They fled to the Mediterranean countries and Holland, and may have been among the earliest settlers of the New World, mostly as crypto-Jews. **Ashkenazic Jews are the Jews whose origins were medieval Germany, who then migrated to the countries of Eastern Europe** (see discussion below). Almost all Jewish Americans are Sephardic or Ashkenazic.

\di'fin\ *vb*

Definitions

GERMAN JEWS, 1830–1880

Most of the Jews arriving between 1830 and 1880 were from Bavaria, Baden, Württemberg, and Posen (as well as Alsace; see the section on the French). Between 1848 and 1855, 62 percent of the Württemberg emigrants were between the ages of eleven and twenty; 70 percent were under thirty-one. Families typically sent a single son, who would arrange for the rest of the family to follow.

German Jews tended to leave from the ports of Hamburg (see the section on emigration lists in chapter six) and Bremen, and to settle in the port cities of the United States, but Cincinnati boasts the oldest Jewish community west of the Alleghenies. Most of the new arrivals became peddlers, since this required no initial capital. When peddlers accumulated enough money, they purchased a wagon, and eventually a store. Such is the origin of the great clothing and department stores, such as Bloomingdale's, Bamberger's, Nieman-Marcus, Macy's, The May Company, and Sears and Roebuck. Other occupations common among German Jews were fruit and grocery vendors, junk dealers, and pawnbrokers, as well as work in the clothing industry. Few Jews went into farming, as they had been prohibited from owning land in most European countries, so had no agricultural skills. Nevertheless, Jews did settle in the South (particularly in Texas), where they practiced their trades and businesses. Wherever they congregated in significant numbers, Jews started mutual-aid societies, fraternal organizations, and synagogues.

EASTERN EUROPEAN JEWS, 1881–1924

The largest wave of Jewish immigration was that of the eastern European Jews, when nearly three million immigrated between 1881 and 1924. Of this influx, 75 percent came from the Russian Pale (a broad swath of territory running from the Baltic Sea down to the Black Sea); 18 percent from Galicia, Bukovina, and Hungary, all regions of Austria-Hungary; and 4 percent from Romania. It is estimated that more than 90 percent of America's Jews today descend from these eastern European Jews.

To get to America, Jews typically traveled to wherever there was a port offering inexpensive fares. Hamburg and Bremen were the most popular, but also Rotterdam, Amsterdam, or Antwerp. The main port of arrival for this group was New York, coming through Ellis Island.

Although these immigrants were also young people interested in permanent settlement as were the German Jews, there was a higher incidence of family migration and a low return migration rate, since Russian Jews simply could not go back. Their exodus was prompted by the pogroms and intolerable treatment of Jews under the tsars. While German Jews also suffered discrimination before the Nazi era, they could return to their homelands if they wished. Also, German Jews were financially able to travel; Russian Jews were penniless. The typical Russian Jewish father was in his twenties or thirties at the time of immigration.

Of the 1.5 million who came through New York between 1881 and 1911, 70 percent settled there. They clustered in ethnic enclaves in Manhattan's Lower East Side and lived in crowded tenement apartments, which could be a breeding ground for filth and disease (see chapter two). The other two large Jewish populations were in Chicago and Philadelphia.

Most Eastern European Jews were skilled tradespeople and petty merchants, and by 1900, one out of three Russian Jews worked in some branch of the garment industry. Women were allowed to work outside the home, so many of them, both married and single, worked in garment factories. Jews were also active in labor unions, which may have surviving records found in repositories such as the Immigration History Research Center in Minneapolis, Minnesota.

The synagogue (Orthodox, Conservative, and Reform) was the heart and soul of the Jewish community, and learning was highly valued. Many also belonged to landsmanshaftn societies (organizations of people from the same ancestral town). There was great pressure for families to remain intact, so Jews had a low divorce rate. Ashkenazic Jews traditionally name their children after deceased relatives. Sephardic Jews traditionally name their children after grandparents, whether living or dead.

The Jewish-American genealogical community is large and extremely active, offering organizations, publications, and conferences. As you will see from the resources below, there is a wealth of material to help you with your search. There are many Jewish genealogical societies across the nation. Visit the International Association of Jewish Genealogical Societies Web site at <http://iajgs.org> for more information.

RESOURCES

Research Guides

Guzik, Estelle, ed. *Genealogical Resources in the New York Metropolitan Area.* New York: Jewish Genealogical Society, 1989. (A revised edition is due in 2000.)

Kurzweil, Arthur. *From Generation to Generation: How to Trace Your Jewish Genealogy and Personal History,* rev. ed. New York: HarperCollins, 1994.

———— and Miriam Weiner. *The Encyclopedia of Jewish Genealogy. Volume 1: Sources in the United States and Canada.* Northvale, N.J.: Jason Aronson, 1991.

Mokotoff, Gary. *How to Document and Locate Victims of the Holocaust.* Teaneck, N.J.: Avotaynu, 1996.

———. "Tracking Jewish-American Family History." In *The Source: A Guidebook of American Genealogy*, rev. ed. Loretto Dennis Szucs and Sandra Hargreaves Luebking, eds. Salt Lake City: Ancestry, Inc., 1997.

——— and Warren Blatt. *Getting Started in Jewish Genealogy*. Bergenfield, N.J.: Avotaynu, 1999.

Rottenberg, Dan. *Finding Our Fathers: A Guidebook to Jewish Genealogy*. Baltimore: Genealogical Publishing Co., 1977.

Weiner, Miriam. *Jewish Roots in Poland: Pages From the Past and Archival Inventories*. Secaucus, N.J.: Routes to Roots Foundation, 1997.

———. *Jewish Roots in Ukraine and Moldova: Pages From the Past and Archival Inventories*. Secaucus, N.J.: Routes to Roots Foundation, 1999.

Wynne, Suzan F. *Finding Your Jewish Roots in Galicia: A Resource Guide*. Teaneck, N.J.: Avotaynu, 1998.

Social Histories and Historical Sources

Angel, Marc D. *La America: The Sephardic Experience in the United States*. Philadelphia: Jewish Publication Service, 1982.

Brownstone, David M. *The Jewish-American Heritage*. New York: Facts on File, 1988.

Cohen, Naomi W. *Encounter With Emancipation: German Jews in the United States, 1830–1914*. Philadelphia: Jewish Publication Service, 1985.

Dawidowicz, Lucy S. *The War Against Jews, 1933–1945*. New York: Bantam Books, 1976.

Dinnerstein, Leonard. *Anti-Semitism in America*. London: Oxford University Press, 1994.

Eisenberg, Azriel, ed. *The Lost Generation: Children in the Holocaust*. New York: Pilgrim Press, 1982.

Eliach, Yaffa. *Hasidic Tales of the Holocaust*. London: Oxford University Press, 1982.

Evans, Eli N. *The Lonely Days Were Sundays: Reflections of a Jewish Southern*. Jackson: University of Mississippi Press, 1993.

Feingold, Harry I. *Zion in America: The Jewish Experience From Colonial Times to the Present*. New York: Hippocrene Books, 1981.

Howe, Irving. *The World of Our Fathers*. New York: Harcourt Brace Jovanovich, 1976.

Karp, Abraham J. *Golden Door to America: The Jewish Immigrant Experience*. New York: Viking Press, 1976.

———. *Haven and Home: A History of the Jews in America*. New York: Schocken Books, 1985.

Metzker, Isaac, ed. *A Bintel Brief: Sixty Years of Letters From the Lower East Side to the* Jewish Daily Forward. New York: Behrman House, 1982.

Muggamin, Howard. *The Jewish Americans*. New York: Chelsea House, 1995.

Press, D. *Jewish Americans*. North Bellmore, N.Y.: Benchmark Books, 1995.

Rischin, Moses. *The Promised City: New York's Jews, 1870–1914*. Cambridge: Harvard University Press, 1977.

Rochlin, Harriet and Fred Rochlin. *Pioneer Jews: A New Life in the American West.* Boston: Houghton-Mifflin, 1984.

Schooner, Allon, comp. *Portal to America: The Lower East Side, 1870–1925.* New York: Holt, Rinehart & Winston, 1967.

Weinberg, Sydney Stahl. *The World of Our Mothers: The Lives of Jewish Immigrant Women.* New York: Schocken Books, 1988.

Sources and Finding Aids

Beider, Alexander. *A Dictionary of Jewish Surnames From the Kingdom of Poland.* Teaneck, N.J.: Avotaynu, 1996.

———. *A Dictionary of Jewish Surnames From the Russian Empire.* Teaneck, N.J.: Avotaynu, 1993.

Feldblyum, Boris. *Russian-Jewish Given Names: Their Origins and Variants.* Teaneck, N.J.: Avotaynu, 1998.

Gorr, Shmuel. *Jewish Personal Names: Their Origin, Derivation, and Diminutive Forms.* Teaneck, N.J.: Avotaynu, 1992.

Mokotoff, Gary and Sallyann Amdur-Sack. *Where Once We Walked: A Guide to the Jewish Communities Destroyed in the Holocaust.* Teaneck, N.J.: Avotaynu, 1991.

Stern, Malcolm H. *First American Jewish Families.* Baltimore: Ottenheimer Publications, 1991.

Zubatsky, David S. and Irwin M. Berent. *Sourcebook for Jewish Genealogy and Family Histories.* 2 vols. Teaneck, N.J.: Avotaynu, 1996.

Organizations, Periodicals, and Internet Sites

American Jewish Archives
3101 Clifton Ave., Cincinnati, OH 45220
Phone: (513) 221-1875, ext. 403   *Web Site:* http://www.huc.edu/aja
Publishes *American Jewish Archives*

American Jewish Historical Society
15 W. Sixteenth St., New York, NY 10011   *Phone:* (212) 294-6160
Fax: (212) 294-6161   *E-mail:* ajhs@ajhs.org
Web Site: http://www.ajhs.org   Publishes *American Jewish History*

Avotaynu, Inc.
155 N. Washington Ave., Bergenfield, NJ 07621   *Phone:* (201) 387-7200
Fax: (201) 387-2855   *E-mail:* info@avotaynu.com
Web site: http://www.avotaynu.com   Publishes *Avotaynu, The International Review of Jewish Genealogy*

Hebrew Immigrant Aid Society
333 Seventh Ave., New York, NY 10001

International Association of Jewish Genealogical Societies
Web site: http://iajgs.org

JewishGen: The Principal Presence of Jewish Genealogy on the Internet
Web site: http://www.jewishgen.org

Leo Baeck Institute

   129 W. Seventy-third St., New York, NY 10021   *Phone:* (212) 744-6400

   Web site: http://www.users.interport.net/~lbi1/

U.S. Holocaust Museum

   100 Raoul Wallenberg Pl., SW, Washington, DC 20024-2150

   Phone: (202) 488-0400   *Fax:* (202) 488-2690

   Registry: (202) 828-9583   *Web site:* http://www.ushmm.org

YIVO Institute for Jewish Research

   15 W. Sixteenth St., New York, NY 10011   *Phone:* (212) 246-6080

   Web site: http://www.baruch.cuny.edu/yivo/

Poles

While the first Polish immigrants came as early as the founding at Jamestown, significant numbers did not begin arriving until the 1830s, with German Poles arriving between 1850 and the early 1890s. Large waves left from the Prussian part of Poland in the 1870s, and emigration fever spread into Russian and Austrian Poland after 1890. In 1900, Poles surpassed the number of Irish arrivals to become the third largest immigrant group (Germans were the largest; Italians second). The majority arrived through the Port of New York, regardless of their final destination. Like southern Italian immigrants, most of the emigrating Poles were landless peasants. As the nation of Poland was divided in the eighteenth century, Poles came from three European empires: Prussia (20 percent), Austria (35 percent), and Russia (45 percent). In American records, they were labeled according to their mother tongue—Polish—regardless of their geographic origin.

This ethnic group also had a high return migration rate of about 30 to 40 percent. Three out of every ten Austrian and Russian Poles intended to earn enough money in America to return home and buy land, whereas German Poles intended to stay in America. Those who did stay settled in midwestern agricultural areas like Illinois, Indiana, Minnesota, and Wisconsin; major cities where factories provided jobs, such as Chicago, Detroit, Cleveland, Pittsburgh, Milwaukee, and Buffalo; and states prominent in mining or steel industries, such as Pennsylvania. Immigrant Poles were the group least likely to be self-employed.

Reminder

Like many immigrant groups at the turn of the century, Poles seldom arrived or lived as isolated individuals. They came to join friends, former neighbors, or relatives already established in America. Like Italians, Poles valued work over education. Large families were advantageous as there were more people to contribute to the family economy. The Poles' major source of status was property—in order to get property, one had to work. By the early 1900s, one-third of all Polish Americans already owned real estate, so land records are important to Polish research.

Shunning the established Irish and German Roman Catholic churches, Poles founded their own parishes where they could worship in their own language, or they traveled great distances to attend a Polish Roman Catholic church rather than an Irish or German one around the corner. These institutions became central to their cultural life; the more affluent Poles preferred to send their children to Polish parochial schools instead of public schools. The immigrant and second generations commonly joined ethnic, religious, and fraternal organizations. Women were active in voluntary associations as well, so the records of Polish clubs and societies are valuable for documenting women's activities. This group was the most likely to Americanize their surnames. In Detroit in 1963, for example, of about 300,000 Polish Americans, three thousand had modified surnames.

Poles are another recent immigrant group who, with the fall of communism and the opening of Eastern European archives and records, are now taking an active interest in family history research. Though there may seem like few resources at this writing, watch for more to become available in the future.

RESOURCES

Research Guides

Chorzempa, Rosemary A. *Polish Roots*. Baltimore: Genealogical Publishing Co., 1993.

Frazin, Judith R. *A Translation Guide to 19th-Century Polish-Language Civil-Registration Documents*. 2nd ed. Northbrook, Ill.: Jewish Genealogical Society of Illinois, 1989.

Hoskins, Janina W. *Polish Genealogy and Heraldry: An Introduction to Research*. New York: Hippocrene Books, 1990.

Wellauer, Maralyn A. *Tracing Your Polish Roots*. Milwaukee: the author, 1991.

Social Histories and Historical Sources

Baker, T. Lindsay. *The First Polish Americans: Silesian Settlements in Texas*. College Station: Texas A & M University Press, 1979.

Brozek, Andrzej. *Polish Americans, 1854–1939*. Warsaw, Poland: Interpress, 1985.

Bukowczyk, John J. *And My Children Did Not Know Me: A History of the Polish-Americans*. Bloomington: Indiana University Press, 1987.

Dubnow, S.M. *History of the Jews in Russia and Poland From the Earliest Times Until the Present Day*. 3 vols. Philadelphia: Jewish Publication Society of America, 1916.

Friedel, Mieczyslaw W. *This Polish Blood in America's Veins: Sketches From the Life of Polish Immigrants and Their Descendants in America, Illustrating a Part of American History Unknown to Most Americans*. New York: Vantage Press, 1987.

Galazka, Jacek and Albert Juszczak. *Polish Heritage Travel Guide to the U.S.A. and Canada*. Cornwall Bridge, Conn.: Polish Heritage Publications, 1992.

Greene, Victor. *For God and Country: The Rise of Polish and Lithuanian Ethnic Consciousness in America, 1860–1910*. Madison: The State History Society of Wisconsin, 1975.

POLISH ARMY IN FRANCE

With the onset of World War I, and even as early as 1912, serious ambitions of an independent Poland were being flamed by those Poles (Polonia) living outside of the partitioned homeland. Unable to actively recruit volunteers in Europe, thoughts of building a Polish army made up of Poles living abroad were started in 1916.

Since the United States felt uncomfortable having a foreign army recruited on its soil, and because its ally, Russia, was against such a Polish Army, no support for its formation was forthcoming. Not until the Bolshevik Revolution and subsequent involvement of U.S. troops in Europe did the U.S. government finally approve of recruiting in the States. Unfortunately, American resources were destined for its own troops, so the Polish Army in France, as it was called, needed to seek out financial and technical support from other countries, those being Canada and France.

This army of approximately 25,000 drawn from about 40,000 volunteers was raised from recruiting centers basically in the Northeast, Great Lakes areas, and Canada, and was trained by Canadian officers at Camp Borden and Niagara-on-the-Lake Ontario. It was outfitted by the French as they arrived in Europe, starting in early 1918. Under General Jozef Haller, these troops were also known as Haller's Army, as well as the Blue Army for the French uniforms they were issued and which were adapted to a Polish style. These troops saw action in France until the Armistice in November of 1918 and were then shipped to Poland to continue the war on the eastern front, combating the Bolsheviks until January 1921 during the Polish-Soviet War.

These recruitment papers, yielding valuable genealogical information, are currently stored at the Polish Museum of America in Chicago. The forms, which give vital statistics as well as physical identifying information and next of kin in both North America and Europe, may be the only papers these resident aliens filed during their stay in North America. The timing of these papers was between the 1910 and 1920 censuses and were predominantly of immigrant, minimally educated workers, who may have only planned on staying in North America to make enough money to return to a comfortable living in Poland.

A computerized database is being formed of these records, as well as inclusion of military records from Canada, France, and Poland. If you would like to find out more information on any of these troops, as well as submit additional information on soldiers known to be in this volunteer fighting force, please send a SASE or E-mail to Dr. Paul S. Valasek, 2643 West 51st Street, Chicago, IL 60632-1559; Phone: (773) 776-5551; E-mail: paval56@aol.com.

—Paul S. Valasek

———. *A Passion for Polka: Old-Time Ethnic Music in America*. Berkeley: University of California Press, 1992.

Grzelonski, Bogdan. *Poles in the United States of America, 1776–1865*. Warsaw, Poland: Interpress, 1976.

Haiman, Miecislaus. *Polish Past in America, 1608–1865*. Chicago: Polish Museum of America, 1974.

Kajencki, Francis Casimir, ed. *Poles in the 19th-Century Southwest*. El Paso, Tex.: Southwest Polonia Press, 1990.

Kowalik, Jan. *The Polish Press in America*. San Francisco: R & E Research Associates, 1978.

Kuniczak, W.S. *My Name Is Million: An Illustrated History of the Poles in America*. Garden City, N.Y.: Doubleday, 1978.

Lopata, Helena Z. *Polish Americans: Status Competition in an Ethnic Community*. Englewood Cliffs, N.J.: Prentice-Hall, 1976.

Miaso, Jozef. *The History of the Education of Polish Immigrants in the United States*. New York: Kosciuszko Foundation, 1977.

Olszyk, Edmund G. *The Polish Press in America*. Milwaukee: Marquette University Press, 1940.

Pawlowska, Harriet M. *Merrily We Sing: 105 Polish Folksongs*. Detroit: Wayne State University Press, 1983.

Pierce, Richard L. *The Polish in America*. Chicago: Claretian Publications, 1972.

Polzin, Theresita. *The Polish Americans: When and Whither*. Pulaski, Wis.: Franciscan Publishers, 1973.

Pula, James S. *Polish Americans: An Ethnic Community*. New York: Twayne Publishers, 1995.

Renkiewicz, Frank A. *The Polish Presence in Canada and America*. Toronto: Multicultural History Society of Ontario, 1982.

Thomas, William I. and Florian Znaniecki. *The Polish Peasant in Europe and America*. Urbana: University of Illinois Press, 1984.

Toor, Rachel. *The Polish Americans*. New York: Chelsea House, 1988.

Wrobel, Paul. *Our Way: Family, Parish, and Neighborhood in a Polish American Community*. Notre Dame, Ind.: University of Notre Dame Press, 1979.

Wytrwal, Joseph A. *America's Polish Heritage: A Social History of the Poles in America*. Detroit: Endurance Press, 1961.

Sources and Finding Aids

Hoffman, William F. and George W. Helon. *First Names of the Polish Commonwealth: Origins and Meanings*. Chicago: Polish Genealogical Society of America, 1998.

———. *Polish Surnames: Origins and Meanings*. Chicago: Polish Genealogical Society of America, 1993.

Lenius, Brian J. *Genealogical Gazetteer of Galicia*, 3rd ed. Anola, Manitoba: the author, 1999.

Ortell, Gerald A. *Polish Parish Records of the Roman Catholic Church: Their*

Use and Understanding in Genealogical Research. Chicago: Polish Genealogical Society of America, 1996.

Organizations, Periodicals, and Internet Sites
Polish American Historical Association
St. Mary's College, Orchard Lake, MI 48324   *Phone:* (248) 683-1743
Fax: (248) 683-0402
Polish Genealogical Society of America
984 N. Milwaukee Ave., Chicago, IL 60622-4101
E-mail: pgsamerica@aol.com
Web site: http://www.members.aol.com/pgsamerica   Publishes *PGSA*
Newsletter and *Rodziny: PGSA Journal*
PolishRoots
Web site: http://www.polishroots.com

Portuguese

Portuguese immigration occurred in two major waves before World War II. The first was in the early 1830s, when Portuguese whalers were needed in New England, California, and Hawaii. These were male immigrants who initially left their families behind and visited them sporadically. Almost all were Azorean men from the west-central and western islands of São Jorge, Pico, Faial, and Flores, who settled in the whaling ports of New Bedford and Edgartown, Massachusetts; Sag Harbor and Cold Spring Harbor on Long Island; and in Stonington, Connecticut. Large numbers of these men eventually sent for their wives and families.

The second wave began in the 1890s, when entire families came from the Azores, Madeira, the Cape Verde Islands, continental Portugal, and China; few Portuguese-speaking Brazilians came to America. Portuguese immigrants worked in the textile mills and leather factories, and concentrated in Providence, Fall River, Lowell, Lawrence, and New Bedford. Internal migration took Portuguese families to the Newark-Elizabeth areas of New Jersey and later Yonkers, Mineola, and elsewhere around New York City.

Many of the first- and second-generation immigrants returned to Portugal during the depression years. Portuguese parents were slow to put their children in public schools, and when they did, they usually only permitted them to remain in school during the elementary grades. Virtually all Portuguese immigrants were Roman Catholic, and like other ethnic groups, they established fraternal benefit societies.

Even though the Portuguese have been in America since the 1830s, they are essentially a recent immigrant group. And like other recent immigrant groups, there is little initial interest in family history research thus far. But don't let the lack of resources discourage you. You could be breaking new ground by not only researching your own Portuguese ancestry, but compiling research material to help others.

RESOURCES

Social Histories and Historical Sources

Baganha, Maria. *Portuguese Emigration to the United States, 1820–1930*. New York: Garland Publishing, 1990.

Pap, Leo. *The Portuguese-Americans*. Boston: Twayne Publishers, 1981.

Williams, Jerry. *And Yet They Came: Portuguese Immigration From the Azores to the United States*. Staten Island, N.Y.: Center for Migration Studies, 1983.

Organizations, Periodicals, and Internet Sites

American-Portuguese Genealogical and Historical Society
P.O. Box 644, Taunton, MA 02780-0644   Publishes *Bulletinboard*

Portuguese Genealogical Society of Hawaii
810 N. Vineyard Blvd., Rm. 11, Honolulu, HI 96817
Phone: (808) 841-5044   Publishes *A Nossa Herança* (Our Portuguese Heritage)

Portuguese Historical and Cultural Society
P.O. Box 161900, Sacramento, CA 95816   *Phone:* (916) 392-1048
Publishes *O Progresso*

Russians

T he problem in dealing with Russian immigrants is that historical records and statistics may not have differentiated between those we call "Russians" and the Jews, Poles, Lithuanians, Latvians, and Estonians who emigrated from the old Czarist Empire. (See the sections on Germans From Russia and Russian Jews.) For this discussion, "Russian" also refers to the Belorussians and Ukrainians. Ukrainian may also refer to Rusyns, Ruthenians, Carpatho-Russians, Little Russians, Lemkos, Hutsuls, and Bojkos, but these groups are distinct from the major population of Ukrainians.

The first Russians in America came to Alaska and the upper west coast of California in the mid-1700s. By the early nineteenth century, there were more than twenty-five Russian settlements in Alaska, down the coast through Fort Ross, which is about one hundred miles north of San Francisco. These settlements were mostly forts or stockades to protect fur traders. When the United States bought Alaska from Russia in 1867, about half of the Russians went back to their native country, but many also moved to California.

Immigration to the East Coast from Russia began on an individual basis in the late 1700s, but large numbers began arriving during the 1880s. These were impoverished peasants, mostly unskilled and unmarried, who were birds of passage. By 1910, more than ninety thousand Russians had settled in the United States, with one-fourth originating from Galicia, and many of the rest from the Belorussian regions of the Russian Empire. The second wave of Russian immigration was from 1920 to 1940, with people fleeing the

Soviet regime. These immigrants were of a higher educational and professional level.

Settlement on the East Coast for those who came in the late nineteenth and early twentieth centuries was typical of other immigrants from eastern and southern Europe: They arrived at the Port of New York (some came through Boston), then they settled in nearby states where they could get jobs in the mines or industries. Pennsylvania, New York, New Jersey, Connecticut, and Ohio drew large concentrations of Russians. Most found employment in the coal mines, iron and steel mills, slaughterhouses, and meat-packing industry. Those who settled on the Pacific Coast worked for the railroad, in coal mining, lumber, sugar-beet refineries, and canneries.

Most were members of the Orthodox Christian church or the Byzantine Greek Catholic rites, and like other immigrants, they established their own fraternal benefit societies.

You will notice that there are not as many resources for Russian research as there are for some other groups. But there are a number of people interested in researching Russian heritage, so joining one of the societies below and networking with others on the Internet could be your best resource in finding help for Russian genealogy.

RESOURCES

Social Histories and Historical Sources
Eubank, N. *The Russians in America.* Minneapolis: Lerner Publications, 1973.
Magocsi, Paul R. *The Russian Americans.* New York: Chelsea House, 1989.

Sources and Finding Aids
Glazier, Ira A. *Migration From the Russian Empire: Lists of Passengers Arriving at the Port of New York, 1875–1910.* Wilmington, Del.: Scholarly Resources, 1995–.

Organizations, Periodicals, and Internet Sites
Along the Galician Grapevine
    P.O. Box 194, Butterfield, MN 56120-0194   *E-mail:* gvtl@rconnect.com
    Web site: http://feefhs.org/gal/agg/frg-agg.html
The Carpatho-Rusyn Society
    125 Westland Dr., Pittsburgh, PA 15217
Russian-American Genealogical Archival Source
    1929 Eighteenth St., NW, Washington, DC 20009-1719
    E-mail: ragas02@infonet.ee
    Web site: http://www.feefhs.org/ragas/frgragas.html   Publishes *RAGAS Resources*
Russian-Baltic Information Center
    907 Mission Ave., San Rafael, CA 94901   *Phone:* (415) 453-3579
    E-mail: enute@igc.apc.org   *Web site:* http://feefhs.org/blitz/frgblitz.html

Russian Heritage Society
P.O. Box 364, Agoura Hills, CA 91376-0364   *Phone:* (818) 991-0242
Web site: http://feefhs.org/frg-rhs.html
Ukrainian Genealogical and Heraldic Society
573 N.W. 102nd St., Miami Shores, FL 33138.

Scandinavians

T he Scandinavian peoples consist of five nationalities: Swedes, Norwegians, Danes, Finns, and Icelanders. They were all generally rural people who favored the northerly parts of the Midwest, the Great Plains, and Canada (Icelanders). Scandinavians were excellent examples of people who moved to places of terrain and climate similar to their homelands (geographic affinity). In many cases, they were simply young people moving a longer distance than previous generations had done to start their own farms. All Scandinavians were Lutheran by law from the time of the Reformation until about 1850, when religious freedom was granted. The majority of the population in each Scandinavian country remained Lutheran after 1850.

SWEDES

In colonial America, there were small Swedish settlements in Delaware and New Jersey, starting in 1638–1639. Most Swedish immigrants, however, arrived in family groups beginning in the 1860s. After 1900, the Swedish immigration consisted of single men and women. Most of those who arrived before the turn of the century were farmers and rural laborers who settled in the Midwest, especially Iowa, Illinois, Wisconsin, and Minnesota. From there, many migrated west to North and South Dakota, Nebraska, and Kansas, seeking better farmland. **Numerous Swedish immigrants and Norwegians, too, took advantage of the Homestead Act of 1862 and settled on quarter sections of the public domain** in all of these states. By the early twentieth century, the trend for newcomers was to settle in urban areas: the two largest settlements were in Chicago and Minneapolis. In these cities, a large demand for labor in the textile industries and for Swedish maids attracted single women, ages fifteen to twenty-nine.

A predominately Lutheran people, the Swedes were slow to marry outside their group. When intermarriage did occur, it was likely to be with a Norwegian, but the strongest desire was to marry a fellow Lutheran. Otherwise, Swedes were eager to assimilate into American culture, so they sent their children to public schools. They had a high naturalization rate, since securing the patent to their homesteads at the end of five years was contingent upon their completing the naturalization process.

Important

NORWEGIANS

Norwegian immigration occurred primarily between 1840 and 1915, with settlement in the upper Midwest states of Illinois, Wisconsin, Minnesota, the Dakotas, and south to Iowa. Like the Swedes, the highest concentration of urban settlers was in Chicago and Minneapolis. Norwegians moved to America primarily because their population outstripped tillable Norwegian land. As with all immigrant groups, the Norwegians, who were predominantly Lutheran, settled in areas with people from their homeland. Norwegians were particularly exclusive in their rural enclaves, retention of culture, marriage practices, and organizations.

They established *bygdelag*, which were social organizations for people originating from the same *bygd* (region) in Norway. The first of these organizations was founded in 1902 and by 1916, more than forty existed. One of the goals of the *bygdelag* was to compile genealogies and keep an archive of family histories. For more information on these groups, see Odd S. Lovoll, *A Folk Epic: The Bygdelag in America.*

Swedes and Norwegians had a reputation for being levelheaded, frugal, serious individualists who placed great stock in self-sufficiency, physical fitness, and education. They participated early on in the political process, running the affairs of their communities with the same staunch pragmatism they exercised in running their parishes.

\di'fin\ *vb*

Definitions

DANES

Large-scale immigration of Danes began in the 1870s, with the peak periods being 1881–1893 and 1903–1905. Missionaries of the Church of Jesus Christ of Latter-day Saints arrived in Denmark in 1850 and converted many Danes. Most of these converts came to America and settled in Utah between 1852 and 1930, the majority coming between 1872 and 1894. Other Danish areas of settlement included Illinois, Kansas, Nebraska, North Dakota, South Dakota, Oregon, Wisconsin, Iowa, and Minnesota.

Before the turn of the century, Danish emigrants consisted mostly of family groups, with an adult age range of twenty-five to thirty-nine. After 1890, single Danes from age fifteen to twenty-four were more common. The origins of these groups were two-fifths from Jutland, one-fifth from Copenhagen, and two-fifths from other areas of Denmark.

In America, Danes were less liable to concentrate in enclaves than other groups, with notable exceptions in Iowa, Wisconsin, and Minnesota. In keeping with this trend, Danes also intermarried more, assimilated more quickly, and formed fewer separate institutions than Swedes or Norwegians. Perhaps the explanation is that the Danes who came to America were more often job-seeking individuals with prepaid tickets and predetermined destinations. **(See Danish emigration records in chapter six.)**

See Also

FINNS

While Finnish immigration occurred as early as the 1630s, and thousands arrived in the late nineteenth century, the peak arrival period for this group was between 1899 and World War I. During this time, young unmarried adults between sixteen and thirty made up three-fourths of the emigrants. Many who came before 1891 departed from European ports, such as Liverpool, rather than the Finnish port of Hanko. After arriving in America—usually at the port of New York—almost half settled in Michigan and Minnesota, but some moved several times, looking for better job opportunities. Although there was an imbalance in the sex ratio, since more single men immigrated than single women, Finns still did not usually marry outside their group. As workers, Finns were particularly active in labor union movements and American socialism.

ICELANDERS

Though small in immigration numbers compared to the rest of the Scandinavian countries, Icelanders did and do contribute greatly to the communities in which they live. Almost 100 percent of Icelanders who immigrated in the mid-1800s were converts to the Mormon church and settled almost exclusively in the Spanish Fork, Utah, area. Another wave of immigration began in the 1870s and continued intermittently into the early 1900s. The majority of those Icelandic immigrants settled in the Canadian province of Manitoba.

There is quite a bit of interest in Scandinavian genealogy, and you should have no trouble in finding resources and people to help you with your search.

RESOURCES

Research Guides

Carlberg, Nancy Ellen. *Beginning Norwegian Research*. Anaheim, Calif.: Carlberg Press, 1991.

Choquette, Margarita, et al. *The Beginner's Guide to Finnish Genealogical Research*. Bountiful, Utah: Thomsen's Genealogical Center, 1985.

Dickson, Charles. "Scandinavian-American Archives." *Ancestry* 16 (May-June 1998): 20–25.

Hjelm, Dennis J. *Especially for Swedes*. Basset, Idaho.: the author, 1985.

Johansson, Carl-Erik. *Cradled in Sweden*. Logan, Utah: Everton Publishers, 1972. Revised 1995.

———. *Thus They Wrote: A Guide to the Gothic Script of Scandinavia*. Provo, Utah: Brigham Young University Press, 1970.

———. *Tracing Your Icelandic Family Tree*. Winnipeg, Manitoba: the author, 1975.

Olsen, Nils William. *Tracing Your Swedish Ancestry*. Sweden: Swedish Institute, 1982.

Price, Barbara. "Swedish Naming Patterns." *Ancestry* 16 (May-June 1998): 26.

Smith, Frank and Finn A. Thomsen. *Genealogical Guidebook and Atlas of Norway*. Logan, Utah: Everton Publishers, 1979.

Thomsen, Finn A. *Scandinavian Genealogical Research Manual*. 3 vols. Bounti-
    ful, Utah: Thomsen's Genealogical Center, 1980.
Wellauer, Maralyn A. *Tracing Your Norwegian Roots*. Milwaukee: the author,
    1979.
Vincent, Timothy Laitila and Rick Tapio. *Finnish Genealogical Research*. New
    Brighton, Minn.: Finnish Americana, 1994.

Social Histories and Historical Sources
Andersen, Arlow William. *The Norwegian-Americans*. Boston: Twayne Pub-
    lishers, 1975.
Babcock, Kendric Charles. *The Scandinavian Element in the United States*.
    Originally published in 1914. New York: Arno Press, 1969.
Benson, Adolph B. and Naboth Hedin. *Swedes in America, 1638–1938*. New
    Haven, Conn.: Yale University Press, 1938.
Bergmann, Leola. *Americans From Norway*. Philadelphia: Lippincott, 1950.
Blegen, Theodore. *Norwegian Immigration to America, 1825–1860*. Originally
    published in 1931. New York: Arno Press, 1969.
Flom, George T. *History of Norwegian Immigration to the United States From
    the Earliest Beginnings Down to the Year 1848*. Originally published in
    1909. Reprint, Bowie, Md.: Heritage Books, 1992.
Friis, Erik J., ed. *The Scandinavian Presence in North America*. New York:
    Harper's Magazine Press, 1973.
Gesme, Ann Urness. *Between Rocks and Hard Places: Traditions, Customs,
    and Conditions in Norway During the 1800s, Emigration From Norway,
    the Immigrant Community in America*. Cedar Rapids, Iowa: Gesme Enter-
    prises, 1993.
Hillbrand, Percie V. *The Norwegians in America*. Minneapolis: Lerner Publica-
    tions, 1967.
Hvidt, Kristian. *Flight to America: The Social Background of 300,000 Danish
    Emigrants*. New York: Academic Press, 1975.
Janson, Florence Edith. *The Background of Swedish Immigration, 1840–1930*.
    Originally published in 1931. New York: Arno Press, 1970.
Lovoll, Odd S. *A Folk Epic: The Bygdelag in America*. Boston: Twayne Publish-
    ers, 1975.
———. *The Promise of America: A History of the Norwegian-American Peo-
    ple*. Minneapolis: University of Minnesota Press, 1984.
Lowell, Briant Lindsay. *Scandinavian Exodus: Demography and Social Devel-
    opment of 19th-Century Rural Communities*. Boulder, Colo.: Westview
    Press, 1987.
Mortensen, Enok. *Danish American Life*. New York: Arno Press, 1978.
Ross, Carl and K. Marianne Wargelin Brown, eds. *Women Who Dared: The
    History of Finnish American Women*. St. Paul, Minn.: Immigration History
    Research Center, 1986.
Semmingsen, Ingrid. *Norway to America: A History of Migration*. Minneapolis:
    University of Minnesota Press, 1978.

Wakin, Edward. *The Scandinavians in America*. Chicago: Claretian Publications, 1974.

Wargelin, John. *The Americanization of the Finns*. Hancock, Mich.: Finnish Lutheran Book Concern, 1924.

Sources and Finding Aids

Guide to Swedish-American Archival and Manuscript Sources in the United States. Chicago: Swedish-American Historical Society, 1983.

Index to Emigrants From Sweden to New York, 1851–1869. Salt Lake City: Genealogical Society of Utah, 1987–1988.

Naeseth, Gerhard B. *Norwegian Immigrants to the United States: A Biographical Directory, 1825–1850*. Madison, Wis.: the author, 1993.

Olsen, Nils William. *Swedish Passenger Arrivals in the United States, 1820–1885*. Stockholm, Sweden: The Royal Library of Sweden, 1995.

Smith, Frank and Finn A. Thomsen. *Genealogical Guidebook and Atlas of Denmark*. Salt Lake City: Bookcraft, 1969.

Organizations, Periodicals, and Internet Sites

Danish-American Genealogical Group
c/o Minnesota Genealogy Society, P.O. Box 16069,
St. Paul, MN 55116-0069   *E-mail:* mgsdec@mtn.org

Danish American Heritage Society
29681 Dane Ln., Junction City, OR 97448   *Phone:* (541) 998-8562
Publishes *The Bridge* and *Newsletter*

Danish Emigration Archives
E-mail: emiarch@vip.cybercity.dk
Web site: http://www.emiarch.dk/home.php3

Evangelical Lutheran Church in America Archives
8765 W. Higgins Rd., Chicago, IL 60631-4198
Phone: (800) 638-3522, ext. 2818, or (847) 690-9410
Fax: (847) 690-9502   *E-mail:* Joel_Thoreson@elca.org
Web site: http://ww.elca.org

Finland Historical Society
P.O. Box 583, Finland, MN 55603   *Phone:* (218) 353-7393

Finnish Genealogy Group
2119 Twenty-first Ave. S., Minneapolis, MN 55404
Phone: (612) 333-6028
Publishes *Newsletter*

Norwegian-American Genealogical Association
5768 Olson Memorial Hwy., Golden Valley, MN 55422
Phone: (612) 595-9347
Web site: http://www.mtn.org/mgs/branches/naga/nagaindx.htm

Norwegian-American Genealogical Society
502 W. Water St., Decorah, IA 52101

Norwegian-American Historical Association

St. Olaf College, Northfield, MN 55057   *Phone:* (507) 646-3221

E-mail: naha@stolaf.edu

Norwegian Genealogical Group

1046 Nineteenth Ave., SE, Minneapolis, MN 55414.

Swedish Genealogical Group

%Minnesota Genealogy Society, P.O. Box 16069, St. Paul, MN 55116-0069

E-mail: phyllis.pladsen@sparecom.mn.org

Swenson Swedish Immigration Research Center

Augustana College, Rock Island, IL 61201-2273

Phone and Fax: (309) 794-7204   *E-mail:* sag@augustana.edu.

Web site: http://www.augustana.edu/administration/swenson

Publishes *Swedish American Genealogist*

Vesterheim Genealogical Center and Naeseth Library

415 W. Main St., Madison, WI 53703   *Phone:* (608) 255-2224

Fax: (608) 255-6842   *Web site:* http://www.vesterheim.org/

Publishes *Norwegian Tracks*

Vesterheim Norwegian-American Museum

P.O. Box 379, Decorah, IA 52101

Scots and Scotch-Irish
SCOTS

Although this ethnic group has almost entirely assimilated into American society, descendants maintain evidence of Scottish culture. In many states and localities, Scottish-American clubs sponsor and promote Scottish games, highland dancing, and clan tartans. The Scots who emigrated formed three distinct groups:

- *Lowland Scots* from the south and east of Scotland and of mixed British heritage. They spoke broad Scots (a heavily accented English dialect).
- *Highland Scots* from the center and west of Scotland. They were the clan warriors, purely Celtic, and spoke Gaelic. Scottish clans were more common in the Highlands. Although members of a clan may have the same surname and loyalty to a chief, not everyone was descended from the chief's ancestry—they just took his name.
- *Scotch-Irish* Presbyterians from the Scottish lowlands who were forced to settle in Ulster (Northern Ireland). Later in America, there was little connection between the Scotch-Irish and the Scots or Irish.

In historical records, it may be difficult to distinguish the Scots from the Scotch-Irish; therefore, it is important to learn how the social and familial characteristics of the Scots differ from those of the Scotch-Irish. For example, the Scots were less liable to isolate themselves on the frontier than the Scotch-Irish;

they preferred established business districts. Scots directly from Scotland, and their descendants, often pursued Scottish folkways and foodways with nostalgia for the Highlands, while the Scotch-Irish created their own unique group culture on the frontier.

Short-lived Scottish colonies were established early in Nova Scotia (1629), New Jersey (1683), South Carolina (1684), and Darien (New Caledonia) in present-day Panama (1686). Before the 1730s, many Scots were sent to America as punishment; they were criminals, or religious or political dissenters. After 1730, there were voluntary migrations, and many Scots came as indentured servants particularly to tobacco country, with the main influx between 1763 and 1775. Overpopulation and land unsuitable for farming were major push factors for the Scots. Seventy percent came as family groups, and the age ranges were broad: 25 percent were under fifteen; 40 percent were over twenty-five.

They settled in the southern and mid-Atlantic states as well as in New England. The Cape Fear Valley of North Carolina, the Mohawk Valley of New York, and Georgia had substantial Highland Scots settlements. Those who were sent to the colonies as criminals usually went to Massachusetts, New Jersey, Maryland, Virginia, and the Carolinas. Most were Presbyterian and acculturated quickly. A high percentage of those who put down roots in port cities were merchants and sea traders. During the Revolution, many were loyalists who fled to Canada or returned to their home in Scotland. So if your Scottish ancestral family has disappeared from the records, recheck the sources and those for neighbors, looking for clues that might lead to these countries.

Many Scottish, as well as English, Welsh, and Cornish peoples, also arrived between the 1800s and 1850s, with some settling in Canada for a few decades before coming to the United States. The Scots generally fled Scotland for Canada in the 1800s because of "the Clearances," when landlords discarded thousands of tenant farmers from their ancestral homes. Look for these Scots in Canadian and Maritime provinces that became Scottish frontier farm colonies, such as Upper Canada (Ontario), Nova Scotia, and Cape Breton. Some homeland connections in Cape Breton, for example, are so strong that once you know the community in which they settled in Cape Breton, you can usually identify which of the islands off the coast of Scotland the family came from. Like other immigrant groups, they migrated and settled as communities.

SCOTCH-IRISH PRESBYTERIANS

During the 1830s and 1840s, American Protestants whose Scottish ancestors had come from Northern Ireland fifty to one hundred years before wanted to emphasize their cultural distinction, so they referred to themselves as "Scotch-Irish." When the Catholic Irish began arriving in mass numbers, the Scotch-Irish felt an even greater need to differentiate themselves. This immigrant group consisted primarily of Presbyterians, with some Quakers and Anglicans, although once in America, they may have joined other denominations. Their ancestors from the Scottish lowlands had been forced to settle in the north of

Ireland (Ulster) in the seventeenth century. **While many genealogists and historians differ over the politically correct label for this group—Scotch-Irish, Scots-Irish, Ulster Scots, etc.—one cannot ignore that this group is culturally distinct from both the Irish and Scots**; therefore, I'll use the historical term "Scotch-Irish" here.

\di'fin\ *vb*

Definitions

There was no steady flow of immigration for the Scotch-Irish; instead, historians have isolated five "pulses" of arrival: 1717–1718, 1725–1729, 1740–1741, 1754–1755, and 1771–1775, with the latter years as the peak. It was common for the Scotch-Irish to arrive in groups from the same area of Ulster, so it is important to identify where neighbors, friends, and other family members also came from. Many who arrived in the earlier years were young and single, and established themselves as small farmers; others were skilled craftsmen. Some came as indentured servants; others preferred being "redemptioners." Redemptioners, upon arrival in the colonies, had a short time period—usually a week or two—to find a sponsor to pay their passage debts. In return, they worked off the debts their redeemer had paid.

A highly mobile people, the Scotch-Irish did not prefer to settle in the New England area (there was a major settlement in Londonderry, New Hampshire, however)—although there were a few settlements in the northern states—favoring, instead, the middle colonies, particularly Pennsylvania. There, the Quakers tolerated them as a frontier buffer colony. From Pennsylvania, the common migratory route during the 1730s and 1740s was to the Cumberland and Shenandoah valleys, along the Great Wagon Road. The heaviest populated area of Scotch-Irish was in Augusta and Rockingham counties in Virginia. By the 1760s, many Scotch-Irish moved into the backcountry of North and South Carolina, Tennessee, and Kentucky. As frontiersmen, they were often the trailblazers, clearing and cultivating the frontier for other settlers. Their migration pattern from Northern Ireland to America and within American borders tended to be a movement of clans. Families had common identities: they carried the same surname, they claimed descent from common ancestors, and they joined forces if there was a threat of danger. Clan warfare was the cultural source for frontier family feuds.

Scotch-Irish women generally married at age nineteen, men at age twenty-one. Scotch-Irish had a unique courting and marriage custom based on their ancestral folkways. Bridal abduction—either voluntary, involuntary, or a mock ritual—was practiced even after this group immigrated to America. President Andrew Jackson abducted his wife, Rachel Donelson Robards, who went voluntarily. The problem was Rachel was married to another man at the time, albeit unhappily, and Jackson was arrested.

Early Scotch-Irish immigrants might prefer to name their children after Teutonic warriors, Scottish kings, or border saints: John, Robert, Richard, Andrew, Patrick, and David. Sometimes Celtic forenames were used: Ewen/Owen, Barry, and Roy. Commonly, the first son was named after the father's father, and the second after the mother's father. First daughters were named after the mother's mother, the second daughter after the father's mother, and the third son or daughter after the parents.

Like the Irish and English, the Scots and Scotch-Irish have a healthy interest in preserving their family history. There are hundreds of people researching Scots and Scotch-Irish genealogy. Although Scotch-Irish research, in particular, may be difficult, you should have no trouble finding other researchers to network with and to learn from.

RESOURCES

Research Guides

Bede, Tim. *MacRoots: How to Trace Your Scottish Ancestors*. Edinburgh, Scotland: Macdonald, 1982.

Cory, Kathleen B. *Tracing Your Scottish Ancestry*. Baltimore: Genealogical Publishing Co., 1990.

Coppage, A. Maxim. *Searching for Scottish Ancestors*. Utica, Ky.: McDowell Publications, 1983.

Cox, Michael. *Exploring Scottish History: A Directory of Resource Centres for Scottish Local and National History in Scotland*. Edinburgh, Scotland: Scottish Library Association and Scottish Local History Forum, 1992.

Falley, Margaret Dickson. *Irish and Scotch-Irish Ancestral Research: A Guide to the Genealogical Records, Methods, and Sources in Ireland*. 2 vols. Originally published in 1962. Baltimore: Genealogical Publishing Co., 1988.

Goldie, Douglas Bruce. *In Search of Hamish McBagpipes: A Concise Guide to Scottish Genealogy*. Bowie, Md.: Heritage Books, Inc., 1992.

Hamilton-Edwards, Gerald. *In Search of Scottish Ancestry*. Chichester, Sussex, England: Phillimore, 1973.

Irvine, Sherry. *Your Scottish Ancestry: A Guide for North Americans*. Salt Lake City: Ancestry, Inc., 1997.

James, Alwyn. *Scottish Roots: A Step-by-Step Guide for Ancestor Hunters*. Gretna, La.: Pelican Publication, 1982.

Moody, David. *Scottish Family History*. Baltimore: Genealogical Publishing Co., 1990.

Sinclair, Cecil. *Tracing Your Scottish Ancestors: A Guide to Ancestry Research in the Scottish Record Office*. Edinburgh, Scotland: HMSO, 1990.

———. *Tracing Scottish Local History: A Guide to Local History Research in the Scottish Record Office*, rev. ed. Edinburgh, Scotland: HMSO, 1996.

Social Histories and Historical Sources

Adams, Ian H. and Meredyth Somerville. *Cargoes of Despair and Hope: Scottish Emigration to North America, 1603–1803*. Edinburgh, Scotland: J. Donald, 1993.

Aman, Catherine. *The Scottish Americans*. New York: Chelsea House, 1991.

Blethen, Tyler, Curtis Wood, and H. Tyler Blethen. *Ulster and North America: Transatlantic Perspectives on the Scotch-Irish*. Tuscaloosa: University of Alabama Press, 1997.

Bolton, Charles Knowles. *Scotch Irish Pioneers in Ulster and America*. Originally published in 1910. Reprint, Baltimore: Genealogical Publishing Co., 1967.

Brownstein, Robin. *The Scotch-Irish Americans*. New York: Chelsea House, 1988.

Buchanan, Frederick Stewart. *A Good Time Coming: Mormon Letters to Scotland*. Salt Lake City: University of Utah Press, 1988.

Dickson, R.J. *Ulster Emigration to Colonial America, 1718–1775*. Originally published by Routledge and Keegan in 1966. Reprint, Belfast, Northern Ireland: Ulster Historical Foundation, 1996.

Dobson, David. *Scottish Emigration to Colonial America, 1607–1785*. Athens, Ga.: The University of Georgia Press, 1994.

Dunaway, Wayland F. *The Scotch Irish of Colonial Pennsylvania*. Originally published in 1944. Reprint, Baltimore: Genealogical Publishing Co., 1985.

Fischer, David Hackett. *Albion's Seed: Four British Folkways in America*. New York: Oxford University Press, 1989.

Ford, Henry Jones. *The Scotch-Irish in America*. Originally published by Princeton University Press in 1915. Reprint, Baltimore: Genealogical Publishing Co., 1995.

Graham, Ian Charles Cargill. *Colonists From Scotland: Emigration to North America, 1707–1783*. Originally published by American Historical Association in 1956. Reprint, Baltimore: Clearfield Co., 1994.

Green, E.R.R. ed. *Essays in Scotch-Irish History*. Originally published by Routledge and Keegan in 1969. Reprint, Belfast, Northern Ireland: Ulster Historical Foundation, 1992.

Hanna, Charles A. *The Scotch-Irish or the Scot in North Britain, North Ireland, and North America*. 2 vols. Originally published in 1902. Reprint, Baltimore: Genealogical Publishing Co., 1995.

Karras, Alan L. *Sojourners in the Sun: Scottish Migrants in Jamaica and the Chesapeake, 1740–1800*. Ithaca, N.Y.: Cornell University Press, 1992.

Landsman, Ned C. *Scotland and Its First American Colony, 1683–1765*. Princeton, N.J.: Princeton University Press, 1985.

Lehmann, William C. *Scottish and Scotch-Irish Contributions to Early American Life and Culture*. Port Washington, N.Y.: National University Publications, 1978.

Leyburn, James G. *The Scotch-Irish: A Social History*. Chapel Hill: University of North Carolina Press, 1962.

MacKay, Donald. *Scotland Farewell: The People of the Hector*, rev. ed. Toronto: National Heritage/ National Inc, 1996.

MacLean, J.P. *An Historical Account of the Settlements of Scotch Highlanders in America*. Originally published in 1900. Reprint, Baltimore: Clearfield, 1996.

McLean, Marianne. *The People of Glengarry: Highlanders in Transition, 1745–1820*. Montreal, Quebec: McGill-Queen's University Press, 1991.

Meyer, Duane. *The Highland Scots of North Carolina: 1732–1776*. Chapel Hill: University of North Carolina Press, 1957.

Rethford, Wayne and June Skinner Sawyers. *The Scots of Chicago: Quiet Immigrants and Their New Society*. Dubuque, Iowa: Kendall/Hunt Publishing Co., 1997.

Smith, Abbot E. *Colonists in Bondage*. Chapel Hill: University of North Carolina Press, 1947.

McWhiney, Grady. *Cracker Culture: Celtic Ways in the Old South*. Tuscaloosa: University of Alabama Press, 1988.

Sources and Finding Aids

Chalkley, Lyman. *Chronicles of the Scotch-Irish Settlement in Virginia*. 3 vols. Originally published in 1988; Reprint, Baltimore: Genealogical Publishing Co., 1998.

Dobson, David. *Directory of Scots Banished to the American Plantations, 1650–1775*. Baltimore: Genealogical Publishing Co., 1983.

———. *Directory of Scots in the Carolinas, 1680–1830*. Baltimore: Genealogical Publishing Co., 1986.

———. *Directory of Scottish Settlers in North America, 1625–1825*. 6 vols. Baltimore: Genealogical Publishing Co., 1984.

———. *The Original Scots Colonists of Early America, 1612–1783*. Baltimore: Genealogical Publishing Co., 1989.

———. *The Original Scots Colonists of Early America, Supplement: 1607–1707*. Baltimore: Genealogical Publishing Co., 1998.

———. *Scots on the Chesapeake, 1607–1830*. Baltimore: Genealogical Publishing Co., 1992.

———. *Scottish-American Court Records, 1733–1783*. Baltimore: Genealogical Publishing Co., 1991.

———. *Scottish-American Heirs: 1683–1883*. Baltimore: Genealogical Publishing Co., 1990.

———. *Scottish-American Wills: 1650–1900*. Baltimore: Genealogical Publishing Co., 1991.

———. *Ships From Scotland to America, 1628–1828*. Baltimore: Genealogical Publishing Co., 1998.

Ferguson, Joan P.S. *Scottish Family Histories Held in Scottish Libraries*. Edinburgh, Scotland: Scottish Central Library, 1968.

MacDonald, Micheil. *Clans of Scotland*. Conway, Ark.: Oldbuck Press, 1993.

Scottish Tartans Society. *The Guide to Scottish Tartans*. London: Shepheard-Walwyn, 1977.

Stuart, Margaret. *Scottish Family History: A Guide to Works of Reference on the History and Genealogy of Scottish Families*. Originally published inEdinburgh, Scotland, in 1930. Reprint, Baltimore, Md.: Genealogical Publishing Co., 1994

Way, George of Plean and Romilly Squire. *Scottish Clan and Family Encyclopedia*. Glasgow, Scotland: HarperCollins, 1994.

Whyte, Donald. *A Dictionary of Scottish Emigrants to Canada Before Confederation*. Toronto: Ontario Genealogical Society, 1986.

———. *A Dictionary of Scottish Emigrants to the U.S.A.* Baltimore: Magna Carta, 1986.

Organizations, Periodicals, and Internet Sites
Ellen Payne Odom Genealogy Library
P.O. Box 1110, Moultrie, GA 31776-1110

Phone: (912) 985-6540   *Fax:* (912) 985-0936
Web site: http://www.teleport.com/~binder/famtree.shtml
Publishes *The Family Tree: The Ellen Payne Odom Genealogy Library*
Link O Mania Scotland on the Web
Web site: http://www.link-o-mania.com/scotgen.htm
The Scotch-Irish Foundation
P.O. Box 181, Bryn Mawr, PA 19010   *Phone:* (609) 429-5747
Fax: (609) 354-0848.   Publishes *Library and Archives Catalogue*

Spanish-Speaking Peoples

Quotes

According to Nydia Garcia-Preto, who wrote an overview of Latino families in *Ethnicity and Family Therapy* (p. 142), **"Hispanic or Latino are adjectives used to describe people who come from different countries with different cultures and sociopolitical histories, and who in their countries of origin would never describe themselves that way.** They are Cubans, Chicanos, Mexicans, Puerto Ricans, Argentineans, Colombians, Dominicans, Brazilians, Guatemalans, Costa Ricans, Nicaraguans, Salvadorians, and the other nationalities that comprise South America, Central America, and the Caribbean." After these groups arrived in America, they became categorized collectively as "Hispanic," a label made popular by the U.S. Census Bureau. Just as the labels "American Indian" and "African American" lump members of distinct cultures into one group, it also strips these groups of their ethnic identity and nationality. Such collective designations tend to hide the diverse ethnic identities and nationalities that exist within these groups. Like the American Indians, Spaniards and Mexicans were here long before the first Anglo settlements at Jamestown and Plymouth Colony; yet they, too, became a displaced group (although not exterminated as were some American Indian tribes).

The three largest Hispanic groups in our country are Mexican Americans, Puerto Ricans, and Cubans. Although lacking notable numbers of immigrants because of their long history in America, the Spanish (Europeans) are also included in this discussion. **(See chapter six, Mexican Border Crossings.)**

See Also

SPANISH

Spanish conquistadors, all men, began arriving in America in the sixteenth century and intermarried with the indigenous people they conquered. The first successful European colony in the territory that would become the United States dates from 1565, when the Spanish founded St. Augustine in northern Florida, forty-two years before Jamestown and fifty-five years before Plymouth. The Spanish settled in New Mexico in 1598, and Spanish Mexicans made the first settlements in Texas at the end of the 1600s and in California in 1769. Most Spaniards who came in the 1500s and 1600s were soldiers and priests. Florida (which included southern Alabama and Mississippi) remained under Spanish rule until 1819, and even though Louisiana was Spanish territory between 1762 and 1800, the population of Spaniards was minimal and consisted mostly of officials, many of whom returned to Spain.

Since 1820, however, more than 250,000 Spanish have come to the United States directly from Spain. Half of these came between 1900 and 1924, when there were great waves of southern and eastern European immigrants. Just as the Spanish wave began to increase, the United States began limiting immigration by imposing a quota system.

MEXICAN AMERICANS

People of Mexican heritage have been in this country since the 1600s. By 1821, the principal areas of settlement for people of Mexican heritage were Texas, California, New Mexico, and Arizona. The California gold rush attracted thousands of Mexican miners, mostly from the state of Sonora. Between 1880 and 1910, the Southwest continued to attract them with farming, ranching, and agriculture, as well as the railroad and mining industry. Large numbers came north after 1909, and immigration continued to be spurred by the need for cheap laborers.

Between 1910 and 1928, more than one million entered the United States either legally or illegally. They were able to come freely after the quota laws were established, since the quotas did not restrict immigrants coming from this continent. With the onset of the depression, however, immigration from Mexico declined. The U.S. government established a "voluntary" Repatriation Program between 1929 and 1935. More than 415,000 Mexican Americans (some U.S. citizens) were forced to return to Mexico, while another 85,000 left voluntarily.

\di'fin\ *vb*

Definitions

From 1942 through 1964, the *bracero* program (an agreement between the United States and Mexico) was set in place to import Mexican workers for periods of no longer than six months. It recruited more than four million seasonal workers.

Like Canadians, because of the proximity to their ancestral country, Mexican Americans have more continuous interaction with their homeland than other immigrant groups. They also have a low naturalization rate, since many expect to return to Mexico. Partly due to discrimination, Mexican Americans have also been slow to participate in education.

Mexican Americans are mostly of mixed Native American and Spanish ancestry, although many have a varied background: *peninsular* (those born in Spain); *criollo* (born in New Spain of pure Spanish ancestry); *mestizo* (Spanish and Indian ancestry); *mulato* (Spanish and African ancestry); and *zambo* (Indian and African ancestry). "Chicano" means an American born of Mexican heritage and reflects 1960s activism.

Mexican Americans are overwhelmingly Roman Catholic, but like the Italians, Mexicans were put off by American Catholic churches, which were dominated by Irish, so they had a low church attendance until they established their own parishes. To Mexican Americans, family means an extended, multigenerational group. They have had a low divorce rate until recent generations.

Before the United States owned the Southwest, many Spanish and Mexican individuals were landholders. After the U.S. conquest, however, many lost their lands or had to prove they owned it. The burden of proof was on the landowner, and many argued their cases before U.S. judges and land commissioners. Some of these hearings were delayed for up to forty years. If your ancestry dates back to the 1840s, you will want to check for these types of land cases (see Sources and Finding Aids, page 229).

PUERTO RICANS

A few Puerto Ricans immigrated before the Spanish-American War, but these were primarily political exiles. In the early 1900s, the first immigrants found work in cigar factories, and Puerto Rican women worked in the garment industry. Immigrants were largely unskilled and semiskilled workers. Puerto Ricans began arriving in great numbers in the late 1940s and 1950s, leaving an over-populated homeland and poverty, and being enticed by cheap air travel. These newer immigrants found work in the service trades, hotels, and restaurants, but many were also seasonal agricultural workers.

The largest settlements of Puerto Ricans can be found in the Northeast, particularly New York City (East Harlem and the Lower East Side), where they moved into the tenements as the Jews and Italians moved out. Others settled in Texas, Florida, and Illinois.

Puerto Ricans are a mixed race of people, representing native Tainos, African slaves, and white Europeans (mostly Spaniards). These immigrants do not need special papers to come to the United States, since U.S. citizenship was granted to them in 1917. Like Mexican Americans, because of the importance of family and the close proximity of their native homeland, they exhibit a pattern of migration that has been back and forth between their native land and the United States.

CUBANS

Cuban immigration dates back to the early 1830s, when a few came to Florida to work as cigar makers. In 1870, there were approximately five thousand Cubans in America, with concentrations in Florida, New York, and New Jersey. The majority settled in Miami's "Little Havana," but also in Key West and Tampa. These cities became centers for the Cuban cigar industry. After World War II, New York became their primary destination. Cuban immigrants began arriving in large numbers in the 1960s.

The number of resources listed below is a testimony to the numbers of people interested in researching these ethnic groups. Seek out ones specific to your group, and also join societies to network with others.

RESOURCES

Research Guides

Barton, Noel R. "Genealogical Research in the Records of the California Spanish Missions." *Genealogical Journal* 4 (March 1975): 13–33.

Byers, Paula K., ed. *Hispanic American Genealogical Sourcebook*. Detroit: Gale Research, 1995.

Carr, Peter E. *Guide to Cuban Genealogical Research: Records and Sources*. Chicago: Adams Press, 1991.

Platt, Lyman D. *Genealogical Research in Latin America and the Hispanic United States*. St. George, Utah: Teguayo Press, 1993.

———. *Hispanic Surnames and Family History*. Baltimore: Genealogical Publishing Co., 1996.

———. "Spanish and Mexican Immigration to the United States." *Genealogical Journal* 3 (1974): 23–24.

Prechtel-Kluskens, Claire. "Mexican Border Crossing Records." 3 parts. *NGS Newsletter* 25 (May–June 1999): 156–157, 159; (July–August 1999): 182–183; (September–October 1999): 278–281.

Ryskamp, George. *Finding Your Hispanic Roots*. Baltimore: Genealogical Publishing Co., 1997.

———. "Tracking Hispanic Family History." In *The Source: A Guidebook of American Genealogy*, rev. ed. Loretto Dennis Szucs and Sandra Hargreaves Luebking, eds. Salt Lake City: Ancestry, Inc., 1997.

Social Histories and Historical Sources

Alford, Harold J. *The Proud Peoples: The Heritage and Culture of Spanish-Speaking Peoples in the United States*. New York: New American Library, 1972.

Almaraz Jr., Felix D. *The San Antonio Missions and Their System of Land Tenure*. Austin: University of Texas Press, 1989.

Bannon, John F. *Spanish Borderlands Frontier, 1513–1821*. Albuquerque: University of New Mexico Press, 1974.

Campa, Arthur. *Hispanic Culture in the Southwest*. Norman: University of Oklahoma Press, 1993.

Chipman, Donald E. *Spanish Texas, 1519–1821*. Austin: University of Texas Press, 1992.

DeVarona, Frank. *Hispanic Presence in the United States: Historical Beginnings*. Miami: Mnemosyne Publishing Co., 1993.

Fernández-Shaw, Carlos M. *The Hispanic Presence in North America from 1492 to Today*. New York: Facts on File, 1991.

Gann, L.H. and Peter J. Duignan. *The Hispanics in the United States: A History*. Boulder: Westview Press, 1986.

Gerhard, Peter. *The Northern Frontier of New Spain*. Princeton, N.J.: Princeton University Press, 1982.

———. *The Southeast Frontier of New Spain*. Princeton, N.J.: Princeton University Press, 1979.

Kanellos, Nicolás with Christelia Pérez. *Chronology of Hispanic-American History: From Pre-Columbian Times to the Present*. New York: Gale Research, 1995.

McWilliams, Carey. *North From Mexico: The Spanish-Speaking People of the United States*. Westport, Conn.: Praeger Publishers, 1990.

Weber, David J. *Foreigners in Their Native Land: Historical Roots of the Mexican American.* Albuquerque: University of New Mexico Press, 1973.

———. *Myth and History of the Spanish Southwest.* Albuquerque: University of New Mexico Press, 1988.

———. *The Spanish Frontier in North America.* New Haven, Conn.: Yale University Press, 1992.

Sources and Finding Aids

Beers, Henry Putney. *Spanish and Mexican Records of the American Southwest.* Tucson: University of Arizona Press, 1979.

Chávez, Fray Angelico. *Origins of New Mexico Families: A Genealogy of the Spanish Colonial Period.* Santa Fe: Historical Society of New Mexico, 1992.

Cottler, Susan M. *Finding Aids to the Microfilmed Manuscript Collection of the Genealogical Society of Utah: Preliminary Survey of Mexican Collection.* Salt Lake City: University of Utah Press, 1978.

Diaz, Albert J. *A Guide to the Microfilm of Papers Relating to New Mexico Land Grants.* University of New Mexico Publications, Library Series, No. 1. Albuquerque: University of New Mexico Press, 1960.

Guide to Spanish and Mexican Land Grants in South Texas. Austin: Texas General Land Office, 1988.

Hinton, Rose Marie B. *Places of Mexico.* Salt Lake City: Instituto Genealógico e Histórico Latinoamericano, 1987.

Jenkins, Myra E. *Guide to the Microfilm of the Spanish Archives of New Mexico, 1621–1821, in the Archives Division of the State of New Mexico Records Center.* Santa Fe: State of New Mexico Records Center, 1967.

Mills, Donna Rachal. *Florida's First Families: Translated Abstracts of Pre-1821 Spanish Censuses.* Tuscaloosa, Ala.: Mills Historical Press, 1992.

Northrop, Marie E. *Spanish-American Families of Early California, 1769–1850.* Burbank: Southern California Genealogical Society, 1984.

———. *Spanish-Mexican Families of Early California, 1769–1850.* New Orleans: Polyanthos, 1976.

Olmsted, Virginia L. *New Mexico Spanish and Mexican Colonial Censuses, 1790, 1823, 1945.* Albuquerque: New Mexico Genealogical Society, 1975.

———. *Spanish and Mexican Censuses of New Mexico, 1750 to 1830.* Albuquerque: New Mexico Genealogical Society, 1981.

Platt, Lyman D. *Census Records for Latin America and the Hispanic United States.* Baltimore: Genealogical Publishing Co., 1998.

Robinson, David J. *Finding Aids to the Microfilmed Manuscript Collection of the Genealogical Society of Utah: Research Inventory of the Mexican Collection of Colonial Parish Records.* Salt Lake City: University of Utah Press, 1980.

Woods, Robert D. *Reference Materials on Mexican Americans: An Annotated Bibliography.* Metuchen, N.J.: Scarecrow Press, 1976.

Organizations, Periodicals, and Internet Sites

Caribbean Historical and Genealogical Journal

TCI Genealogical Resources, P.O. Box 15839, San Luis Obispo, CA 93406

Cuban Genealogical Resources
    Web site: http://www.cubagenweb.org
Cuban Genealogical Society
    P.O. Box 2650, Salt Lake City, UT 84110-2650   *Phone:* (801) 968-7312
    Publishes *Revista*
Genealogical Society of Hispanic America
    P.O. Box 9606, Denver, CO 80209   Publishes *Nuestras Raices Quarterly Journal* and *Nuestras Raices Newsletter*
Hispanic Genealogical Society
    P.O. Box 231271, Houston, TX 77223   Publishes *Hispanic Genealogical Journal*
Latino Web
    Web site: http://www.latinoweb.com/
Mexican American Research Guide
    Web site: http://www.usc.edu/Library/Ref/Ethnic/mex_main.html
Puerto Rican/Hispanic Genealogical Society
    P.O. Box 260118, Bellerose, NY 11426-0118   *Phone:* (516) 834-2511
    E-mail: latinoblu@aol.com *Web site:* http://www.rootsweb.com/~prhgs
Society for Hispanic Historical and Ancestral Research
    P.O. Box 5294, Fullerton, CA 92535
Spanish American Genealogical Association
    P.O. Box 794, Corpus Christi, TX 78403-0794   *Phone:* (512) 855-1183
    E-mail: SagaCorpus@aol.com *Web site:* http://members.aol.com/sagacorpus/saga.htm

Welsh and Cornish

Few Welsh came during the colonial period, and of those who came, most became fully absorbed by English society. An early group of Baptist Welsh came in 1677, and they founded Swansea, Massachusetts. Between 1683 and 1699, several Welsh Quakers came to Pennsylvania, acquiring a tract of land containing forty thousand acres. It was located west of Philadelphia, along what is now the main route of the Pennsylvania Railroad, and was known for several generations as the "Welsh Barony." In 1729, Welshmen founded the Welsh Society of Pennsylvania to assist fellow newcomers.

More Welsh came in the early nineteenth century. They gravitated toward farming, mining, and industry jobs. Few came as organized parties; they came rather as individual links in the chain migration, when early migrants wrote home and enticed friends and relatives to join them. Industrial towns and mining communities drew men from Wales because of higher wages. Welsh and Cornish skills were in high demand, for example, men from Cornwall emigrated and went to southwestern Wisconsin to work in the lead mines between 1830 and 1850. But economic depressions and mining strikes drove some back to Wales. As skilled laborers, Welsh iron workers came after 1815, coal miners after 1830, slate quarrymen after 1840, and tin-platers as late as the 1890s.

The ordinary Welshman considered himself successful if he acquired the position of foreman and was able to buy his own house or farm. Eventually, he would earn enough money to send for his family. The average number of children in a Welsh family was eight. A single Welsh girl was considered an old maid if she was not married by twenty-two. Rural Welsh families preserved the Old-Country routine of breakfast, midmorning lunch, dinner, midafternoon lunch, supper, and late evening meal.

Although there may not be as many resources for Welsh family history as there are for English or some of the other countries of the British Isles, there is certainly enough available to get you started on the right track.

RESOURCES

Research Guides

Hamilton-Edwards, Gerald. *In Search of Welsh Ancestry*. Baltimore: Genealogical Publishing Co., 1986.

Rowlands, John and Sheila Rowlands, eds. *Second Stages in Researching Welsh Ancestry*. Baltimore: Genealogical Publishing Co., 1999.

Rowlands, John, ed. *Welsh Family History: A Guide to Research*, 2nd ed. Baltimore: Genealogical Publishing Co., 1999.

Social Histories and Historical Sources

Ashton, Elwyn T. *The Welsh in the United States*. Hove, Sussex, England: Caldra House, 1984.

Davies, Phillips G. *The Welsh in Wisconsin*. Madison: The State Historical Society of Wisconsin, 1982.

Dodd, Arthur H. *The Character of Early Welsh Emigration to the United States*. Cardiff, Wales: 1957.

Hartmann, Edward George. *Americans From Wales*. Boston: Christopher Publishing House, 1967. Reprint, New York: Octagon Books, 1987.

Rowse, A.L. *The Cousin Jacks: The Cornish in America*. New York: Charles Scribner's Sons, 1969.

Sources and Finding Aids

Browning, Charles H. *Welsh Tract of Pennsylvania: The Early Settlers (Extracted From the Welsh Settlement of Pennsylvania)*. Philadelphia: William J. Campbell, 1912. Extract reprinted, Westminster, Md.: Family Line Publications, 1990.

Glenn, Thomas Allen. *Welsh Founders of Pennsylvania*. 2 vols. Reprint, Baltimore: Clearfield Co., 1970.

Guide to Sources at the Cornwall Record Office. Truro, Cornwall: Cornwall County Council, 1995.

Rowlands, John and Sheila Rowlands. *The Surnames of Wales: For Family Historians and Others*. Baltimore: Genealogical Publishing Co., 1996.

Sources for Cornish Family History, rev. ed. Truro, Cornwall: Cornwall County Council, 1996.

Organizations, Periodicals, and Internet Sites

Welsh-American Family History Association
4202 Clark St., Kansas City, MO 64111

Welsh-American Genealogical Society
13 Norton Ave., Poultney, VT 05764-1011   *E-mail:* wagsjan@sover.net
Publishes *Newsletter*

PART THREE

Leaving a Legacy

Writing Your Ethnic/ Immigrant Family History

S o now what? You've studied the social history of your ancestors' ethnic groups, you've researched records they've generated, and perhaps you have even made a trip to your ancestral homeland to do some research. That's all well and good and certainly commendable, but if you neglect to *record* your research and discoveries, it's all going to die when you do. I'm not talking about leaving a legacy of notes, pedigree charts, and file folders filled with photocopies. When you are involved in genealogy long enough, you, too, will hear the horror stories of how all this valued material becomes a lovely bonfire after the family historian dies. What can you do to prevent this from happening, aside from leaving a stipulation in your will to have the material donated to some repository? The best solution is to write about your immigrant and ethnic family history, turning your research findings it into a factual narrative account.

You don't have to actually publish your family history for it to be a legacy to your descendants; just write it, then put it in a binder and label it with the title of your story. You can include some pedigree charts if you want, but nongenealogists aren't interested in charts, which give just names and dates. People like to read about other people's lives; otherwise, they'd be content to read the phone book. Though a nongenealogist may toss the charts, a family history written as a narrative will be kept and passed on to others.

Writing about immigrant and ethnic ancestors, whether they came in the 1600s or the 1900s, is a lot of fun and a rewarding experience. Our immigrant and ethnic ancestors present some interesting topics to research and write about.

Technique

Reminder

TOPICS TO INCLUDE WHEN WRITING ABOUT IMMIGRANT ANCESTORS

- **Homeland.** Describe the lifestyle, geography, types of houses, climate, different occupations, predominant religion, and so forth.
- **Motivation to Leave.** What was pushing your ancestors to leave? Did the

husband come first and bring his wife and family later? Was he a bird of passage? Did the whole family come together? Was there someone already in America that likely enticed them to emigrate?

- **Shipboard Experience.** What kind of vessel did they travel on: sailing or steam? How long did the voyage take? What occupied their time during the voyage? How many people could the ship hold? How many actually traveled with your ancestors?

- **Arrival and Processing.** Where did your ancestors arrive? Did your ancestors come before or after federal immigrant processing was initiated? If after, what was it like to process through Ellis Island or another receiving station?

- **Settlement and Internal Migration.** Where did your immigrant ancestors initially settle and why? Where and with whom did they live when they got here? Did they live in an ethnic enclave or cluster around others from their homeland? How long did they stay in a given area? Where did they go after this place? How did they get there?

- **New Environment.** Describe the lifestyle in their new environment in America, the geography, types of houses, climate, and so forth. How similar or dissimilar was it to their homeland? What kind of work did they do? Was this the same type of work they did in their homeland?

- **Assimilation.** How were they treated once they got here? Were they eager to become naturalized? Did they join fraternal benefit societies? What church did they attend? What newspapers did they read? Did they Anglicize or change their names? Did they send their children to school? Did the immigrant's daughters or sons marry outside the ethnic group?

TOPICS TO INCLUDE WHEN WRITING ABOUT AFRICAN-AMERICAN SLAVE ANCESTORS

- **Enslavement Experience.** How did villagers become enslaved in Africa?
- **Shipboard Experience.** What were slave ships like? How long did the voyage take? How many slaves typically died enroute?
- **Arrival and Processing.** What were the typical ports of arrival? How were slaves auctioned?
- **Settlement.** Where did the slave owner live? Describe the climate, geography, types of houses, etc.
- **Assimilation.** How would a new slave be treated? Would the slave rebel and try to escape? What work was expected of the slave?

TOPICS TO INCLUDE WHEN WRITING ABOUT AMERICAN INDIAN ANCESTORS

- **Settlement.** Where was the tribe living when whites encroached upon the area? Describe the climate, geography, living conditions of the tribe, and its customs and culture. How did contact with European settlers affect these? Did whites expose the tribe to deadly diseases? Did whites devise the written form of the Indian language?

- **Relocation.** Was the tribe forced to relocate? If so, where? Did they go peacefully? Was there a treaty stipulating purchase of the land or promises in exchange for the land? Describe the new location in terms of climate, geography, living conditions, etc. Was the tribe moved a second time? Third time?

- **Assimilation.** Did the tribe eventually assimilate into white society? Is the tribe still in existence? How were they treated? Did members of the tribe marry into other tribes or with whites or blacks?

The answers to practically all of these questions will come from your genealogical research, oral history interviews, home sources, and learning what the typical experience was like for other members of the same ethnic group who lived during the same time period as your ancestors and who settled in the same areas. For example, I do not know the exact experience of my great-grandparents who came from Italy and were processed through Ellis Island in the early 1900s, but I can still write about it in factual detail. From reading social histories on the immigrant experience at Ellis Island, I can portray what it was probably like for my own ancestors and still keep it an authentic account.

Here I have paraphrased the general, typical experience, as written about in Thomas M. Pitkin's *Keepers of the Gate: A History of Ellis Island* (pp. 68–69):

> At the first station in the huge Registry Hall, a surgeon checked each arrival's health inspection card from aboard ship. After stamping it, he handed it back to the immigrant and watched. The unsuspecting person would look to see what the inspector had stamped on the card and inadvertently revealed any eye problems.

You could use material like this as it is, or you can weave your ancestor's story into it:

> At the first station in the huge Registry Hall, a surgeon checked each arrival's health inspection card from aboard ship, and *he no doubt checked* Salvatore Ebetino's, too. After stamping it, the surgeon *would have handed* it back to Salvatore and watched. The unsuspecting immigrant *probably looked* to see what the inspector had stamped on the card, and Salvatore *would have inadvertently revealed* any eye problems.

For More Info

For a more detailed narrative about the Ellis Island experience, see "The Immigrant Experience: From Steerage to Ellis Island," in Sharon DeBartolo Carmack's, *Italian-American Family History: A Guide to Researching and Writing About Your Heritage.*

Note the language in italics that clearly indicates that I'm speculating on Salvatore's experience.

Unless I have documented proof that this is what actually happened to Salvatore, I cannot word the paragraph as if it were fact.

You can write about your ancestors in historical context for any time period and for any group of people. Start with details you learn from genealogical sources, then augment that data with general information from social histories. On page 238 is a narrative example of the Fearn family, who came from England in 1838. In this example, I've used just three sources to write seven paragraphs.

The only source that revealed specific details on the Fearns was their passenger arrival list. All of the other information came from newspaper accounts of the ship's arrival and a social history on immigrants to America. I blended all the information together into one flowing narrative. You can do the same with your own ancestors.

For it to be a factual narrative, not only do you want to make it clear when you speculate about experiences that *probably* happened to your ancestors, but **you also want to include source citations** or, as we genealogists say, documentation. The rules are simple: For every fact, cite a source where that fact came from. If you say the Fearns came on the *Portsmouth* in the summer of 1838, that's a fact that requires documentation. Where did that information come from? The other rule is to cite as much information about the source as necessary for you or another researcher to find that source again. The citation for the Fearns' passenger arrival list is "Passenger Lists of Vessels arriving at New York, 1820–1897, *Portsmouth*, NARA (National Archives and Records Administration) (microfilm) M237, roll 37, manifest 543." With this information, anyone can go to a repository that has this National Archives microfilm and find the exact page where the Fearns are listed. Put your documentation in footnotes or endnotes grouped at the end of the story. (For the finer points of citing sources, see Elizabeth Shown Mills, *Evidence! Citation and Analysis for the Family Historian*.)

Citing Sources

Some people have excuses not to cite their sources: notes interfere with the reading of the narrative; the family won't care where the information came from; notes look intimidating to readers. These are just that: excuses. You've gone to a lot of trouble and work to research the family history. Aren't you proud of your efforts? Don't you want to show off your work and impress your family and friends with all those nifty historical records you found? You're the expert, after all. Citing sources simply is not an option in writing family history; it is required. Sad, but true, an undocumented family history is reduced to nothing more than a family tale or legend. Other researchers will use your work merely for clues, not as facts. Make it a true legacy by telling others your sources of information.

Writing your immigrant and ethnic ancestors' stories leaves a legacy. **You, the family historian, have the responsibility not only to learn about your ancestors through research, but to pass that information along to future generations.** On a chart, John and Margaret Fearn are just names. In a narrative, they become people. You've gone through all the time, expense, and trouble to get to know your ancestors, to appreciate what it took for them to leave behind loved ones and their country, to settle in a strange land, either willingly or unwillingly. What a terrible waste and injustice it would be to leave them as just names on a chart. Share the stories of your immigrant and ethnic ancestors. They deserve to be remembered. They are, after all, American history.

Important

AN EXAMPLE OF HOW TO WRITE ABOUT IMMIGRANT ANCESTORS
John and Margaret Fearn:
Nineteenth-Century Immigrants From England

John and Margaret Fearn probably sold almost all of their possessions before they left England. By the late 1830s, John Fearn, a tailor, had decided to uproot his family and start a new life in America. What encouraged them to come to America, and ultimately to Ohio, is uncertain; but they may have been following Thomas Fearn. Thomas was probably some relation to John—perhaps a brother—since he, too, was born in England a few years after John, and purchased land in the same township and county where John and Margaret settled upon arrival in the United States.

Leaving the port in Liverpool and traveling with John and Margaret were their eight children: George, age eighteen; William, fourteen; Frederick, thirteen; Albert, eleven; Charles, nine; Edmund, seven; Henry, five; and Emma, two.[1]

The 520-ton *Portsmouth,* which the Fearns boarded in the summer of 1838, was probably a small sailing ship, since steam passenger vessels were not in wide use until after the 1840s. There were only two first-class passengers traveling on this voyage; the Fearns were among the seventy steerage passengers. The voyage took forty days.[2]

Many of these small vessels, like the *Portsmouth,* were not designed to carry passengers, but cargo, such as iron, anvils, salt, and coal. Ships' masters installed temporary rough pine berths that were dismantled when it was necessary to carry cargo instead of humans. The passengers were berthed undivided, with men, women, and children in one steerage compartment. (Steerage was so named because it was where the steering mechanism was located.) Captains largely ignored a law forbidding the accommodation of men, women, and children together. Ventilation and inadequate lavatories were common problems in steerage. The only way passengers like the Fearns could get air was by opening the hatches, but if there was bad weather, these had to be kept shut. Unpleasant stenches from lavatories and cramped passengers were typical.[3]

Emigrants such as John and Margaret were expected to cook their own food during the voyage. Law required ships to carry a certain amount of provisions for the passengers, but many travelers also brought along their own food. According to the passengers' contract ticket:

In addition to any Provisions which the Passengers may themselves bring, the following quantities, at least, of Water and Provisions will be supplied to each Passenger by the Master of the Ship, as required by law, and also Fires and suitable places for cooking: 3 Quarts of Water daily. 2½ lbs. of Bread or Biscuit, not inferior in quality to Navy Biscuit, 1 lb. of Wheaten Flour; 5 lbs. of Oatmeal*; ½ lb. of Sugar, ½ lb. of Molasses; 2 oz. of Tea—per week.

*5 lbs. of good Potatoes may, at the option of the Master of the Ship, be substituted for 1 lb. of Oatmeal or Rice, and in Ships sailing from Liverpool, or from Irish or Scotch Ports, Oatmeal may be substituted in equal quantities for the whole or any part of the issues of Rice.[4]

Along with a concern for food during the voyage, passengers like the Fearns lived with the fear of fire, shipwreck, or plagues. Wooden sailing ships always held the possibility of fire or shipwreck that would end in significant loss of life. Sometimes passengers caused fires by cooking over flames on deck. Plagues were even more common. Typhus, also known as "ship fever," was carried aboard by emigrants and spread to other passengers. This disease was highly contagious and often fatal. Cholera epidemics were another possibility.[5] Apparently, however, there were no fires, shipwrecks, or plagues that created problems for the passengers of the *Portsmouth*. John, Margaret, and their children arrived safely at the Port of New York on 7 September 1838.[6]

---

[1] Passenger Lists of Vessels arriving at New York, 1820–1897, *Portsmouth*, NARA M237, roll 37, manifest 543. Frederick's name is written as Fredrich, Albert as Abert, Edmund as Edwin, Henry as Henery, and Emma as Anner.

[2] Passenger Lists of Vessels arriving at New York, 1820–1897, *Portsmouth*, NARA M237, roll 37, manifest 543; Maldwyn A. Jones, *Destination America* (New York: Holt, Rinehart, and Winston, 1976), 26; *The Evening Post*, New York, NY, 6 Sept. 1838, p. 3, col., 1; *Morning Herald*, New York, NY, 7 Sept. 1838, p. 3, col. 2.

[3] Jones, *Destination America*, 26–27.

[4] Jones, *Destination America*, 26–27.

[5] Jones, *Destination America*, 33–35.

[6] Passenger Lists of Vessels arriving at New York, 1820–1897, *Portsmouth*, NARA M237, roll 37, manifest 543. New York City newspapers reported the *Portsmouth* "Arrived this day" and that there were 70 steerage passengers, *The Evening Post*, New York, NY, 6 Sept. 1838, p. 3, col. 1; *Morning Herald*, New York, NY, 7 Sept. 1838, p. 3, col. 2.

Selected Historical Glossary

T he following definitions are taken from common usage in social history but are also compatible with most college dictionaries. Dictionaries will offer more comprehensive definitions of these terms, but these are designed for family history usage. This glossary was created by Katherine Scott Sturdevant with Sharon DeBartolo Carmack.

assimilate—to absorb new people into the culture of an established population by making them become, over time, more similar to its members; to take on the characteristics of a population, gradually, in order to become part of it

bird of passage—a person who leads an unsettled, transient life; in this context, particularly one who traveled back and forth, frequently or regularly, especially overseas on immigrant ships

chain migration—the pattern that develops when a series of members of the same family, group, neighborhood, or community immigrate or migrate to the same country or place, one or a few at a time, using group planning and communication

declaration of intention—the first step in becoming a citizen, where an immigrant renounced his allegiance to his homeland and declared his intention to become a U.S. citizen; also called the "first papers"

emigrant—a person who left his/her homeland to settle elsewhere permanently (this term emphasizes leaving *from* a place)

emigrate—to leave one's homeland with the intention of settling elsewhere permanently (this term emphasizes leaving *from* a place)

émigré—an emigrant, but especially one forced to emigrate for political reasons, such as during a revolution

ethnic—whatever may be characteristic of a particular cultural group of origin, especially a group from a common national background, including religious, cultural, social, ancestral linguistic, physical, behavioral, and attitudinal characteristics

ethnic enclave—a distinct cultural unit, such as a neighborhood or small community of one cultural group, which has formed within a larger, older, or more dominant cultural group's territory

ethnicity—the whole body of what makes a person or group ethnic; one's awareness of, and usually pride in, being ethnic

"final or second papers"—*see* petition for naturalization

"first papers"—*see* declaration of intention

geographic affinity—a person's or group's liking and attraction to a settling place because of territorial and climatic features that remind them, consciously or not, of their native homeland

immigrant—a person who comes to a new country, of which he/she was not native, in order to take up permanent residence there (this term emphasizes coming *to* a place)

immigrate—to move to a new country, having left one's homeland, with the intention of taking up permanent residence (this term emphasizes coming *to* a place)

indentured servant—a person, usually an English immigrant to colonial America, who contracted or "bound," before departure, to a property owner in order to work as a servant for a specified time (average seven years), usually in exchange for ship's passage from Europe and for minimal shelter, food, and clothing

migrant—a person who moves residence from one region or country to another, usually temporarily, repeatedly, or seasonally; a person who so moves to follow work opportunities (this term emphasizes the travel and refers to both the places *from* and *to* equally)

migrate—to move one's residence, especially as part of a group or pattern, from one region or country to another, usually temporarily, repeatedly, or seasonally (this term emphasizes the travel and refers to both the places *from* and *to* equally)

nativism—the prejudice, among a native population, toward immigrants; in American history, usually the prejudice and policies of early White Anglo-Saxon Protestant Americans (and their descendants) against later arrivals, particularly those of markedly different languages, cultures, and religions

nativist—a person, group, statement, or policy that is prejudiced against later immigrant groups and that favors the earlier, supposedly "native" groups

necronym—a name for a newborn child taken from a previously deceased child, usually in the same family, used as a tribute to the children and to the name

patronymic—a name or surname derived from the father or paternal male ancestor's name, meaning child of that ancestor, usually formed by adding a suffix, such as Jans*sen* and Peders*datter*, or a prefix, such as *Fitz*Hugh and *Mac*Donald

petition for naturalization—the final step to becoming a citizen, where an immigrant who had already filed the intention papers and had met the residency requirements made a formal application for citizenship; also known as the "second or final papers"

redemptioner—an indentured servant who had not contracted before departure, but whose servant contract was sold by the ship's captain if he/she could not repay passage within a designated period (such as two weeks) after arrival in colonial America (more common among German families than Englishmen)

repatriate—to return to one's country of birth for permanent residence, usually also to return to that original citizenship, after a period of residence (and citizenship) in another country

return migration—to return to one's original homeland after immigrating to another country, neither move having been necessarily permanent

"second or final papers"—*see* petition for naturalization

Ethnic Archives and Libraries in the United States

Balch Institute for Ethnic Studies

18 S. Seventh St., Philadelphia, PA 19106   *Phone:* (215) 925-8090

E-mail: balchlib@hslc.org   *Web site:* http://www.libertynet.org:80/~balch/

Publishes *New Dimensions*

The Balch Institute is a six-story library/museum with the mission of documenting and interpreting American ethnic and immigration history. Its purpose is to collect and preserve publications, archival and manuscript materials, photographs, and other sources that provide information on how and why immigrants came to North America and how they and their descendants adapted and lived after they arrived here. There is a published guide to the manuscript collections available from the Institute.

Center for Migration Studies

209 Flagg Pl., Staten Island, NY 10304-1148   *Phone:* (212) 351-8800

Publishes *International Migration Review* and *Migration Today*

The Center for Migration Studies (CMS) is an educational, nonprofit institute founded in 1964 to encourage the study of sociological, demographic, historical, economic, political, and legislative aspects of migration and ethnic-group relations. It publishes the *International Migration Review*, a quarterly journal devoted to immigration and ethnicity; and *Migration Today*, a bimonthly magazine on migrants that discusses books, monographs, bibliographies, documents, and occasional papers. CMS also publishes from five to seven books annually; write for a list of publications. The CMS library has more than 1,100 volumes in the field of migration and ethnicity. A three-volume *Guide to the Archives* outlines the holdings.

Ellis Island Immigration Museum and Research Library

Liberty Island, New York, NY 10004
Phone: Museum (212) 363-5804; Library (212) 363-6307
Fax: Museum (212) 363-8347; Library (212) 363-6302
Web site: http://www.ellisisland.org

See chapter four for information on Ellis Island computer databases, but in addition to these, the museum and research library offer a wealth of material on the immigrant experience. The library collects books, articles, and photographs about the history of Ellis Island and immigration in general. Call ahead and make an appointment to visit the research library. There are no original records, such as passenger lists, at this facility, however. See chapter six for accessing passenger lists.

Immigration History Research Center

University of Minnesota, 311 Elmer L. Andersen Library, 222 Twenty-first Ave. S, Minneapolis, MN 55455-0439
Phone: (612) 625-4800   *Fax:* (612) 626-0018
E-mail: ihrc@gold.tc.umn.edu   *Web site:* http://www.umn.edu/ihrc
Publishes *Journal of American Ethnic History* and *The Immigration History Newsletter*

The Immigration History Research Center (IHRC) in conjunction with the University of Minnesota has an extensive collection of manuscript and published materials, focusing on numerous ethnic groups. According to the IHRC's *A Guide to Collections*, the focus is "primarily on the experiences of immigrants and generally consists of documentation they themselves generated as opposed to information recorded by government officials or others involved in processing newcomers through American ports or assigning citizenship." Items found at the IHRC include ethnic newspapers and serials; fraternal society materials; church records and publications; manuscript collections; oral histories, memoirs, and family histories; and a reference collection. Advance notice of research visits is encouraged. The collection does not circulate, but some items are available on microfilm through interlibrary loan.

Other Collections

Other repositories may specialize in a particular ethnic group, such as the Italian American Heritage Center at Catholic University in Washington, DC. Some large, metropolitan public libraries and historical societies may also have a focus on immigration and certain ethnic groups, such as the New York Public Library, Fifth Avenue at Forty-second Street, New York, New York 10018, and the Western Reserve Historical Society Library, 10825 East Boulevard, Cleveland, Ohio 44106-1777.

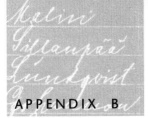

Addresses

National Genealogical Organizations

Federation of Genealogical Societies
P.O. Box 200940, Austin, TX 78720-0940   *Phone and Fax:* (512) 336-2731
E-mail: fgs-office@fgs.org   *Web site:* http://www.fgs.org

National Genealogical Society and National Genealogical Society
Computer Interest Group
4527 Seventeenth St., N., Arlington, VA 22207-2399   *Phone:* (800) 473-0060
Fax: (703) 525-0052   *Web site:* http://ngsgenealogy.org

The New England Historic Genealogical Society
101 Newbury St., Boston, MA 02116
Phone: (617) 536-5740   *Fax:* (617) 536-7307
E-mail: membership@nehgs.org
Web site: http://www.NewEnglandAncestors.org

Professional Genealogists

Accredited Genealogists
Family History Library, 35 N.W. Temple, Salt Lake City, UT 84150

Association of Professional Genealogists
P.O. Box 40393, Denver, CO 80204-0393   *E-mail:* apg-admin@apgen.org
Web site: http://www.apgen.org/

Board for Certification of Genealogists
P.O. Box 14291, Washington, DC 20044
Web site: http://www.bcgcertification.org/

Correspondence Courses in Genealogy

Brigham Young University's Independent Study
236 Harman Bldg., P.O. Box 21514, Provo, UT 84602-1514
Phone: (800) 298-8792   *E-mail:* indstudy@coned1.byu.edu
Web site: http://coned.byu.edu/is/indstudy.htm

National Genealogical Society's American Genealogy: A Basic Course
(see address under Genealogical Societies)
Offers traditional correspondence course and an online course
Writer's Digest School
1507 Dana Ave., Cincinnati, OH 45207   *Phone:* (800) 759-0963
E-mail: wds@fwpubs.com   *Web site:* http://www.wdwow.com
Web site: http://www.familytreemagazine.com
Offers traditional correspondence courses and online courses such as
"Writing Your Life Story," and "Focus on the Memoir/Family History"

Research Repositories

Family History Library of the Church of Jesus Christ of Latter-day Saints
35 N.W. Temple, Salt Lake City, UT 84150   *Phone:* (801) 240-2331
E-mail: fhl@ldschurch.org   *Web site:* http://www.familysearch.org
Immigration and Naturalization Service
425 I St., NW, Washington, DC 20536
Web site: http://www.ins.usdoj.gov
Library of Congress
Local History and Genealogy Reading Room,
10 First St., SE, Washington, DC 20540   *Phone:* (202) 707-5537
E-mail: lcweb@loc.gov   *Web site:* http://lcweb.loc.gov/rr/genealogy
National Archives and Records Administration I
Eighth and Pennsylvania avenues, NW, Washington, DC 20408
Phone: (202) 501-5400   *E-mail:* webmaster@nara.gov
Web site: http://www.nara.gov/genealogy
National Archives and Records Administration II
8601 Adelphi Rd., College Park, MD 20740   *Phone:* (301) 713-6800
Fax: (301) 713-6905   *E-mail:* inquire@arch2.nara.gov
Regional Records Service Facilities of the National Archives
For street, E-mail, and Web addresses, telephone and fax numbers, and
holdings and areas served, please visit the Web site at <http://www.nara.gov/
regional/nrmenu.html>.

Genealogical Books, Software, and Supplies

(Books, CD-ROMs, Forms, Charts, and Conference Tapes)
Ancestry Incorporated
P.O. Box 476, Salt Lake City, UT 84110   *Phone:* (800) 262-3787
Fax: (801) 531-1798   *E-mail:* info@ancestry.com
Web site: http://www.ancestry.com
Betterway Books
F&W Publications, 1507 Dana Ave., Cincinnati, OH 45207
Phone: (800) 289-0963 (to order books); (800) 289-0963, ext. 394
(for catalog)   *Web site:* http://www.familytreemagazine.com
Brøderbund Software
Banner Blue Division, 39500 Stevenson Pl., Ste. 204, Fremont, CA 94539
Phone: (800) 315-0672   *Fax:* (415) 382-4419

E-mail: sales@familytreemaker.com

Web site: http://www.familytreemaker.com/

Everton Publishers

P.O. Box 368, Logan, UT 84321   *Phone:* (800) 443-6325

Fax: (801) 752-0425   *E-mail:* order@everton.com

Web site: http://www.everton.com

Federation of Genealogical Societies' Forum

(see address listed under Federation of Genealogical Societies)

Frontier Press

P.O. Box 126, Cooperstown, NY 13326   *Phone:* (800) 772-7559

Fax: (607) 547-9415   *E-mail:* KGFrontier@aol.com

Web site: http://www.frontierpress.com

Genealogical Publishing Co., Inc.

1001 N. Calvert St., Baltimore, MD 21202   *Phone:* (800) 296-6687

Fax: (410) 752-8492   *Web site:* www.genealogybookshop.com

Hearthstone Bookshop

5736-A Telegraph Rd., Alexandria, VA 22303   *Phone:* (703) 960-0086

Web site: http://www.hearthstonebooks.com

Heritage Books

1540-E Pointer Ridge Pl., Bowie, MD 20716   *Phone:* (800) 398-7709

Fax: (800) 276-1760   *E-mail:* heritagebooks@pipeline.com

Web site: http://www.heritagebooks.com/

Heritage Quest

P.O. Box 329, Bountiful, UT 84011-0329   *Phone:* (800) 658-7755

Fax: (801) 298-5468   *E-mail:* sales@heritagequest.com

Web site: http://www.heritagequest.com/

National Archives Trust Fund

NEPS Dept. 735, P.O. Box 100793, Atlanta, GA 30384

E-mail: inquire@nara.gov   *Web site:* http://www.nara.gov

Repeat Performance

(national genealogical conference tapes)

2911 Crabapple Ln., Hobart, IN 46342   *Phone:* (219) 465-1234

Fax: (219) 477-5492   *Web site:* http://www.repeatperformance.com

Lending Libraries

Heritage Quest (formerly American Genealogical Lending Library)

P.O. Box 329, Bountiful, UT 84011-0329   *Phone:* (800) 760-AGLL

Fax: (801) 298-5468   *E-mail:* sales@heritagequest.com

Web site: http://www.heritagequest.com

National Archives Microfilm Rental Program

P.O. Box 30, Annapolis Junction, MD 20701-0030

National Genealogical Society

(see address listed under Genealogical Societies)

New England Historic and Genealogical Society

(see address listed under Genealogical Societies)

Genealogical Magazines

Ancestry
   (see address listed under Ancestry Incorporated)

Everton's Genealogical Helper
   (see address listed under Everton Publishers)

Family Chronicle and *History Magazine*
   505 Consumers Rd., Ste. 500, Toronto, Ontario, M2J 4V8 Canada
   Phone: (888) 326-2476   *E-mail:* magazine@familychronicle.com
   Web site: http://www.familychronicle.com

Family Tree Magazine
   (see address listed under Betterway Books)

Heritage Quest
   (see address listed under Heritage Quest)

Bibliography

Passenger Lists, Immigration, and Naturalization

Abbott, Edith. *Immigration: Select Documents and Case Records*. Chicago: University of Chicago Press, 1924.

Allan, Morton. *Morton Allan Directory of European Passenger Steamship Arrivals*. Reprint, Baltimore: Genealogical Publishing Co., 1980.

Anuta, Michael J. *Ships of Our Ancestors*. Menominee, Mich.: Ships of Our Ancestors, Inc., 1983.

Coldham, Peter Wilson. *American Migrations, 1765–1799*. Baltimore: Genealogical Publishing Co., 2000.

———. *Bonded Passengers to America*. 9 vols. Baltimore: Genealogical Publishing Co., 1983-1985.

———. *The Complete Book of Emigrants, 1607–1660*. Baltimore: Genealogical Publishing Co., 1987.

———. *The Complete Book of Emigrants, 1661–1699*. Baltimore: Genealogical Publishing Co., 1990.

———. *The Complete Book of Emigrants, 1700–1750*. Baltimore: Genealogical Publishing Co., 1992.

———. *The Complete Book of Emigrants in Bondage, 1614–1775*. Baltimore: Genealogical Publishing Co., 1988.

———. *Emigrants in Chains, 1607–1776*. Baltimore: Genealogical Publishing Co., 1992.

———. *Supplement to the Complete Book of Emigrants in Bondage, 1614–1775*. Baltimore: Genealogical Publishing Co., 1992.

Coleman, Terry. *Going to America*. Baltimore: Genealogical Publishing Co., 1972.

Colletta, John Philip. *They Came in Ships*, rev. ed. Salt Lake City: Ancestry Inc., 1993.

Filby, P. William. *Passenger and Immigration Lists Bibliography, 1538–1900: Being a Guide to Published Lists of Arrivals in the United States and Canada*.

Detroit: Gale Research Co., 1981; supplement, 1984; cumulative edition, 1988.

Filby, P. William and Mary K. Meyer. *Passenger and Immigration Lists Index: A Guide to Published Arrival Records of About 500,000 Passengers Who Came to the United States and Canada in the 17th, 18th, and 19th Centuries.* 3 vols. Detroit: Gale Research Co., 1981. Supplemental volumes.

Guide to Genealogical Research in the National Archives, rev. ed. Washington, D.C.: National Archives Trust Fund Board, 1985.

Guillet, Edwin C. *The Great Migration: The Atlantic Crossing by Sailing-Ship Since 1770.* Toronto: University of Toronto Press, 1963.

Hutchinson, E.P. *Legislative History of American Immigration Policy, 1798–1965.* Philadelphia: University of Pennsylvania Press, 1981.

Immigrant and Passenger Arrivals: A Select Catalog of the National Archives Microfilm Publications, 2nd ed. Washington, D.C.: National Archives Trust Fund Board, 1983.

Jones, Maldwyn. *Destination America.* New York: Holt, Rinehart and Winston, 1976.

Kansas, Sidney. *U.S. Immigration, Exclusion and Deportation and Citizenship of the United States of America*, 3rd ed. New York: Matthew Bender Co., 1948.

Kludas, Arnold. *Great Passenger Ships of the World.* 5 vols. Cambridge, Mass.: Stephens, 1975–1977.

Lind, Marilyn. *Immigration, Migration, and Settlement in the United States: A Genealogical Guidebook.* Cloquet, Minn.: Linden Tree, 1985.

Newman, John J. *American Naturalization Processes and Procedures, 1790–1985.* Indianapolis: Indiana Historical Society, 1985. Reprint, Bountiful, Utah: Heritage Quest, 1998.

Schaefer, Christina K. *Guide to Naturalization Records of the United States.* Baltimore: Genealogical Publishing Co., 1997.

Smith, Eugene W. *Passenger Ships of the World Past and Present.* Boston: George H. Dean Co., 1978.

Smith, Marian L. "The Creation and Destruction of Ellis Island Immigration Manifests." 2 parts. *Prologue* 28 (Fall 1996): 240–245; (Winter 1996): 314–318.

————. "Interpreting U.S. Immigration Manifest Annotations." *Avotaynu: The International Review of Jewish Genealogy* 12 (Spring 1996): 10–13.

————. "Women and Naturalization, ca. 1802–1940." *Prologue* 30 (Summer 1998): 146–153.

Szucs, Loretto Dennis. *They Became Americans: Finding Naturalization Records and Ethnic Origins.* Salt Lake City: Ancestry Inc. 1998.

Tepper, Michael H. *American Passenger Arrival Records: A Guide to the Records of Immigrants Arriving at American Ports by Sail and Steam*, rev. ed. Baltimore: Genealogical Publishing Co., 1993.

Ellis Island

Benton, Barbara. *Ellis Island: A Pictorial History.* New York: Facts on File, 1984.

Bolino, August C. *The Ellis Island Source Book*. Washington, D.C.: Kensington Historical Press, 1985.

Brownstone, David M., Irene M. Franck, and Douglass L. Brownstone. *Island of Hope, Island of Tears*. New York: Viking Press, 1979.

Chermayeff, Ivan, Fred Wasserman, and Mary J. Shapiro. *Ellis Island: An Illustrated History of the Immigrant Experience*. New York: Macmillan Publishing Co., 1991.

Coan, Peter Morton. *Ellis Island Interviews: In Their Own Words*. New York: Facts on File, 1997.

Pitkin, Thomas M. *Keepers of the Gate: A History of Ellis Island*. New York: New York University Press, 1975.

Shapiro, Mary J. *Gateway to Liberty: The Story of the Statue of Liberty and Ellis Island*. New York: Vintage Books, 1986.

Tifft, Wilton S. *Ellis Island*. Chicago: Contemporary Books, Inc., 1990.

Yans-McLaughlin, Virginia and Marjorie Lightman. *Ellis Island and the Peopling of America: The Official Guide*. New York: New Press, 1997.

Ethnic Research Guides and Social Histories: General

Archdeacon, Thomas J. *Becoming American: An Ethnic History*. New York: Free Press, 1983.

Bentley, Elizabeth Petty. "Part 3: Ethnic and Religious Organizations and Research Centers." *The Genealogist's Address Book*, 4th ed. Baltimore: Genealogical Publishing Co., 1998.

Berrol, Selma Cantor. *Growing Up American: Immigrant Children in America Then and Now*. New York: Twayne Publishers, 1995.

Bodnar, John. *The Transplanted: A History of Immigrants in Urban America*. Bloomington: Indiana University Press, 1985.

Bourque, Monique and R. Joseph Anderson. *A Guide to Manuscript and Microfilm Collections of the Research Library of the Balch Institute for Ethnic Studies*. Philadelphia: Balch Institute, 1992.

Brown, Linda Keller and Kay Mussell, eds. *Ethnic and Regional Foodways in the United States: The Performance of Group Identity*. Knoxville: University of Tennessee Press, 1984.

Buenker, John D. and L.A. Ratner. *Multiculturalism in the United States: A Comparative Guide to Acculturation and Ethnicity*. New York: Greenwood Press, 1992.

Buenker, John D, Nicholas C. Burckel, and Rudolph J. Vecoli. *Immigration and Ethnicity: A Guide to Information Sources*. Detroit: Gale Research Co., 1977.

Carmack, Sharon DeBartolo. "Immigrant Women and Family Planning: Historical Perspectives for Genealogical Research." *National Genealogical Society Quarterly* 84 (June 1996): 102–114.

———. "Panunzio's Deportation Cases of 1919–20: A Neglected Source and an Index." *National Genealogical Society Quarterly* 83 (December 1995): 293–300.

Caroli, Betty. *Immigrants Who Returned Home.* New York: Chelsea House, 1990.

Daniels, Roger. *Coming to America: A History of Immigration and Ethnicity in American Life.* New York: HarperCollins, 1990.

Dinnerstein, Leonard. *Natives and Strangers: Blacks, Indians, and Immigrants in America*, 2nd ed. New York: Oxford University Press, 1990.

Dinnerstein, Leonard and David M. Reimers. *Ethnic Americans: A History of Immigration and Assimilation.* New York: Dodd, Mead & Co., 1975.

Ewen, Elizabeth. *Immigrant Women in the Land of Dollars: Life and Culture on the Lower East Side, 1890-1925.* New York: Monthly Review Press, 1985.

Gabaccia, Donna. *From the Other Side: Women, Gender, and Immigrant Life in the U.S.* Bloomington: Indiana University Press, 1994.

Handlin, Oscar. *The Uprooted: The Epic Story of the Great Migrations That Made the American People*, 2nd ed. Boston: Little, Brown and Company, 1973.

Harwood, Alan, ed. *Ethnicity and Medical Care.* Cambridge, Mass.: Harvard University Press, 1981.

Higham, John. *Strangers in the Land: Patterns of American Nativism, 1860–1925.* New Brunswick, N.J.: Rutgers University Press, 1955.

Kraut, Alan M. *Silent Travelers: Germs, Genes, and the "Immigrant Menace."* New York: Basic Books, 1994.

Marinbach, Bernard. *Galveston: Ellis Island of the West.* Albany: State University of New York Press, 1993.

McGinty, Brian. "Angel Island: The Half-Closed Door." *American History Illustrated* (October 1990): 50-51, 71.

McGoldrick, Monica, Joe Giordano, and John K. Pearce, eds. *Ethnicity and Family Therapy.* 2nd ed. New York: Guildford Press, 1996.

Meyer, Richard E., ed. *Ethnicity and the American Cemetery.* Bowling Green, Ohio: Bowling Green State University Popular Press, 1993.

Meyerink, Kory L. and Loretto Dennis Szucs. "Immigration: Finding Immigrant Origins." In *The Source: A Guidebook of American Genealogy*, rev. ed. Loretto Dennis Szucs and Sandra Hargreaves Luebking, eds. Salt Lake City: Ancestry, Inc., 1997.

Mindel, Charles, Robert W. Habenstein, and Roosevelt Wright Jr., eds. *Ethnic Families in America: Patterns and Variations*, 4th ed. New York: Prentice-Hall, 1997.

Montalto, Nicholas, V. *The International Institute Movement: A Guide to Records of Immigrant Society Agencies in the United States.* St. Paul, Minn.: Immigration History Research Center, 1978.

Moody, Suzanne and Joel Wurl. *The Immigration History Research Center: A Guide to Collections.* New York: Greenwood Press, 1991.

Morrison, Joan and Charlotte Fox Zabusky. *American Mosaic: The Immigrant Experience in the Words of Those Who Lived It.* New York: E.P. Dutton, 1980.

Panunzio, Constantine M. *The Deportation Cases of 1919–1920.* New York: Commission on the Church and Social Service, 1921.

Parrillo, Vincent N. *Strangers to These Shores*, 4th ed. New York: Macmillan Publishing Co., 1994.

Riis, Jacob A. *How the Other Half Lives: Studies Among the Tenements of New York*. New York: Bedford Books, 1996.

Smith, Jessie Carney, ed. *Ethnic Genealogy: A Research Guide*. Westport, Conn.: Greenwood Press, 1983.

Sowell, Thomas. *Ethnic America: A History*. New York: HarperCollins, 1981.

———. *Migrations and Cultures: A World View*. New York: Basic Books, 1996.

Stolarik, M. Mark, ed. *Forgotten Doors: The Other Ports of Entry to the United States*. Philadelphia: Balch Institute Press, 1988.

Taylor, Phillip. *The Distant Magnet: European Emigration to the U.S.A.* London: Eyre & Spottiswoode, 1971.

Thernstrom, Stephan and Ann Orlov, eds. *Harvard Encyclopedia of American Ethnic Groups*. Cambridge, Mass.: Belknap Press, 1980.

Vecoli, Rudolph J. and Suzanne M. Sinke, eds. *A Century of European Migrations, 1830-1930*. Urbana, Ill.: University of Chicago Press, 1991.

Wasserman, P. and A. Kennington, eds. *Ethnic Information Sources of the United States*. Detroit: Gale Research Co., 1983.

Weatherford, Doris. *Foreign and Female: Immigrant Women in America, 1840–1930*. New York: Schocken Books, 1986.

Wittke, Carl. *We Who Built America: The Saga of the Immigrant*. New York: Prentice-Hall, 1939.

Wynar, Lubomyr. *Encyclopedic Directory of Ethnic Organizations in the United States*. Littleton, Colo.: Libraries Unlimited, 1975.

Wynar, Lubomyr and Anna T. Wynar. *Encyclopedic Directory of Ethnic Newspapers and Periodicals in the United States*. Littleton, Colo.: Libraries Unlimited, 1976.

General Genealogical Guides

Arends, Marthe. *Genealogy on CD-ROM*. Baltimore: Genealogical Publishing Co., 1999.

———. *Genealogy Software Guide*. Baltimore: Genealogical Publishing Co., 1998.

Barsi, James C. *The Basic Researcher's Guide to Homesteads and Other Federal Land Records*. Colorado Springs, Colo.: Nuthatch Grove Press, 1994.

Bentley, Elizabeth Petty. *The Genealogist's Address Book*, 4th ed. Baltimore: Genealogical Publishing Co., 1998.

Bockstruck, Lloyd D. *Revolutionary War Bounty Land Grants Awarded by State Governments*. Baltimore: Genealogical Publishing Co., 1996.

Carmack, Sharon DeBartolo. *A Genealogist's Guide to Discovering Your Female Ancestors*. Cincinnati: Betterway Books, 1998.

———. *The Genealogy Sourcebook*. Los Angeles: Lowell House, 1997.

Davies, Thomas L. *Shoots: A Guide to Your Family's Photographic Heritage*. Danbury, N.H.: Addison House, 1977.

Everton, George B., comp. *The Handy Book for Genealogists*, 8th ed. Logan, Utah: Everton Publishers, 1991.

Eichholz, Alice. *Ancestry's Red Book: American State, County, and Town Sources.* Salt Lake City: Ancestry, Inc., 1989.

Fletcher, William. *Recording Your Family History: A Guide to Preserving Oral History Using Audio and Video Tape.* Berkeley, Calif.: Ten Speed Press, 1989.

Greenwood, Val D. *The Researcher's Guide to American Genealogy*, 3rd ed. Baltimore: Genealogical Publishing Co., 2000.

Hinckley, Kathleen W. *Locating Lost Family Members and Friends.* Cincinnati: Betterway Books, 1999.

Hone, E. Wade. *Land and Property Research in the United States.* Salt Lake City: Ancestry, Inc., 1997.

Howells, Cyndi. *Cyndi's List: A Comprehensive List of 40,000 Genealogy Sites on the Internet.* Baltimore: Genealogical Publishing Co., 1999.

————. *Netting Your Ancestors: Genealogical Research on the Internet.* Baltimore: Genealogical Publishing Co., 1997.

Kaminkow, Marion J. ed. *A Complement to Genealogies in the Library of Congress: A Bibliography.* Baltimore: Magna Carta Book Co., 1981.

————. *Genealogies in the Library of Congress: A Bibliography.* 2 vols. Baltimore: Magna Carta Book Co., 1972. Suppl. for 1972–1976 publ. 1977; 2nd suppl. 1976–1986 publ. 1986.

Kemp, Thomas Jay. *Virtual Roots: A Guide to Genealogy and Local History on the World Wide Web.* Wilmington, Del.: Scholarly Resources, 1997.

Lainhart, Ann S. *State Census Records.* Baltimore: Genealogical Publishing Co., 1992.

McClure, Rhonda. "Fraternal Organizations: Can You Find Your Ancestors?" *Genealogical Helper* 53 (July-August 1999): 12–13.

Meyerink, Kory, ed. *Printed Sources: A Guide to Published Genealogical Records.* Salt Lake City: Ancestry, Inc., 1998.

Mills, Elizabeth Shown. *Evidence! Citation and Analysis for the Family Historian.* Baltimore: Genealogical Publishing Co., 1997.

Neagles, James C. *U.S. Military Records.* Salt Lake City: Ancestry Inc., 1994.

Nugent, Nell Marion. *Cavaliers and Pioneers: Abstracts of Virginia Land Patents and Grants.* Volume 1: 1623–1666, reprint, Baltimore: Genealogical Publishing Co., 1983. Volume 2: 1666–1695 and Volume 3: 1695–1732, Richmond: Virginia State Library, 1977 and 1979.

Redmonds, George. *Surnames and Genealogy: A New Approach.* Boston: New England Historic Genealogical Society, 1997.

Rose, Christine and Kay Germain Ingalls. *The Complete Idiot's Guide to Genealogy.* New York: Alpha Books, 1997.

Rubincam, Milton. *Pitfalls in Genealogical Research.* Salt Lake City: Ancestry, Inc., 1987.

Schaefer, Christina K. *The Hidden Half of the Family: A Sourcebook for Women's Genealogy.* Baltimore: Genealogical Publishing Co., 1999.

————. *Instant Information on the Internet! A Genealogist's No-Frills Guide to the Fifty States and the District of Columbia.* Baltimore: Genealogical Publishing Co., 1999.

Szucs, Loretto Dennis and Sandra Hargreaves Luebking, eds. *The Archives: A Guide to the National Archives Field Branches*. Salt Lake City: Ancestry, Inc., 1988.

———, eds. *The Source: A Guidebook of American Genealogy*, rev. ed. Salt Lake City: Ancestry, Inc., 1997.

Taylor, Maureen. *Uncovering Your Ancestry Through Family Photographs*. Cincinnati: Betterway Books, 1999.

White, Virgil D. *Genealogical Abstracts of Revolutionary War Pension Files*. 4 vols. Waynesboro, Tenn.: National Historical Publishing Co.; 1990–. There is also a cumulative index to this set.

———. *Index to War of 1812 Pension Files*, 1815–1926. 3 vols. Waynesboro, Tenn.: National Historical Publishing Co., 1989.

General Social Histories

Anderson, Margo J. *The American Census: A Social History*. New Haven, Conn.: Yale University Press, 1988.

Camp, Charles. *American Foodways: What, When, Why, and How We Eat in America*. Little Rock: August House, 1989.

Crosby, Alfred W. *America's Forgotten Pandemic: The Influenza of 1918*. Cambridge, Mass.: Cambridge University Press, 1989.

Hooker, Richard J. *A History of Food and Drink in America*. Indianapolis: Bobbs Merrill, 1981.

Holt, Marilyn Irvin. *The Orphan Trains: Placing Out in America*. Lincoln: University of Nebraska Press, 1992.

Jackson, Kenneth T. and Camilo Jose Vergara. *Silent Cities: The Evolution of the American Cemetery*. New York: Princeton Architectural Press, 1989.

Kolata, Gina. *Flu: The Story of the Great Influenza Pandemic of 1918 and the Search for the Virus That Caused It*. New York: Farrar, Straus & Giroux, 1999.

Mintz, Steven and Susan Kellogg. *Domestic Revolutions: A Social History of American Family Life*. New York: The Free Press, 1988.

Nasaw, David. *Children of the City: At Work and at Play*. New York: Oxford University Press, 1986.

Rothman, Sheila M. *Living in the Shadow of Death: Tuberculosis and the Social Experience of Illness in American History*. New York: Basic Books, 1994.

Shammas, Carole, Marylynn Salmon, and Michel Dahlin. *Inheritance in America: From Colonial Times to the Present*. New Brunswick, N.J.: Rutgers University Press, 1987.

Stewart, George R. *American Given Names: Their Origin and History in the Context of the English Language*. New York: Oxford University Press, 1979.

West, Elliot. *Growing Up With the Country: Childhood on the Far Western Frontier*. Albuquerque: University of New Mexico Press, 1997.

Index